Chambers
Card
Games

100 best-loved games

Peter Arnold

CHAMBERS
An imprint of Chambers Harrap Publishers Ltd
338 Euston Road, London, NW1 3BH

Chambers Harrap Publishers Ltd is an Hachette UK company

© Chambers Harrap Publishers Ltd 2011

Chambers® is a registered trademark of Chambers Harrap Publishers Ltd

This second edition published by Chambers Harrap Publishers Ltd 2011
First published in 2007, reprinted 2010

Database right Chambers Harrap Publishers Ltd (makers)

A CIP catalogue record for this book is available from the British Library.

10 9 8 7 6 5 4 3 2 1

ISBN 978 0550 10179 2

We have made every effort to mark as such all words which we believe to be
trademarks. We should also like to make it clear that the presence of a word in this
book, whether marked or unmarked, in no way affects its legal status as a trademark.

Every reasonable effort has been made by the author and the publishers to trace the
copyright holders of material quoted or illustrations used in this book. Any errors or
omissions should be notified in writing to the publishers, who will endeavour to rectify
the situation for any reprints and future editions.

www.chambers.co.uk

Designed by Chambers Harrap Publishers
Printed and bound in Spain

Contributors

Author
Peter Arnold

Chambers Editor
Hazel Norris

Editorial Assistance
Katie Brooks
Alison Pickering

Prepress
Andrew Butterworth
Becky Pickard

Illustrations
Andrew Butterworth
Andrew Laycock
Heather Macpherson

About the author

Peter Arnold is an author and editor, most of whose 50 or so books concern sports and games. He has written histories and encyclopedias of boxing, cricket, football and the Olympic Games, and wrote the official FIFA guide to the 1994 Football World Cup in the USA. He has also worked as editor and main contributor of part-works on boxing and football, and has ghost-written instruction books for a West Indian Test fast bowler and a Canadian world snooker champion.

Peter devised some of the mental games for the television series *The Crystal Maze*. Several of his books are on table games, including some on individual card games, and he has written three books on gambling, one of which was described by a New York author as 'the best history of gambling'. Many of his books have been published in the USA and in foreign-language editions.

Contents

More About Playing Cards

Index

Introduction by Peter Arnold

For hundreds of years the standard pack of 52 playing cards has brought pleasure to millions all over the world. However, it wasn't always so. As early as 1423 St Bernard of Siena, a Franciscan friar, in a sermon preached at Bologna described cards as 'the invention of the Devil'. Some Puritans still call the pack 'the Devil's picture book'. In the 15th century in England, playing at cards became fashionable at Christmas, this being the only season during which the working classes were allowed to play with them. And in 1526, a Proclamation attempted to ban them altogether, despite Henry VIII's well-known partiality for gambling at cards.

Nothing stopped the advance of card playing, however, and more and more games were devised. Some games described in this book have been played for centuries, while others are mere striplings of a few years' existence. Some games at times seem to swamp all others: Bridge, for instance, and Canasta in the 1950s, while Poker is currently all the rage, especially on the Internet. Of course, old games disappear over the years, but enough remain for this book to include descriptions of 100 games, and many of those have variants which might double that number.

When people sit down to play cards the most important consideration when deciding what to play is the number of players. Some games are specifically for a certain number, others are designed for a certain number but can be played by more or fewer, while yet others can be played by any reasonable number. The descriptions in this book are headed by a panel which indicates how many players the game is best for and which other numbers can be accommodated. There is also an index of games arranged by number of players at the back of the book.

The introductory panel also gives an indication of the type of game. Games fall into many categories. The games which involve winning tricks (there is an explanation of tricks in the section Card Games Basics on p382) are among the oldest of games. Whist and Bridge are among these, but there is also a whole family of trick-taking games in which the hands dealt are of five cards only. These include Écarté, Euchre and Napoleon. Another distinct family of trick-taking games, in which the object is to win tricks containing certain value cards, is based on the old game of All Fours. These games include Cinch and Pitch. The Hearts family, which includes Black Maria, is also a trick-taking family, but in this instance the object is mainly to avoid winning tricks carrying penalty cards.

Games which do not involve trick-taking often involve melding, in which the object is to acquire groups of cards, either cards of the same rank or cards of the same suit in sequence. These games are often called Rummy games, Rummy being the most popular, though certainly not the earliest. These games include Gin Rummy, Coon Can, Panguingue and the latest double-pack addition to the family, Canasta.

There are games which combine trick-taking with melding, and these are among the most interesting and rewarding of games. Bezique and Pinochle are two instances. Piquet is another game which combines trick-taking and melding, but it also has other features which make it unique and is, in the opinion of many, the best two-player card game of all.

Cribbage is another outstanding two-player game which combines melding, in the sense that points are scored for certain combinations of cards, with a counting system which makes it unique. The fact that it is said to have been given its final polish by an outstanding poet soldier who committed suicide at 33 adds some romance to playing it.

What is often called the Stops family is a collection of games in which players attempt to get rid of their cards while others try to stop them. Stops is another name for Newmarket, which is in this group, as are the Switch variations and the children's game of Fan Tan.

Betting games are in a distinct class of their own. In these players bet on the strength of their hands. The most famous is Poker, in its numerous guises. The latest form of Poker to cause excitement is Texas Hold 'Em, with its million-dollar televised tournaments and its availability for players to play each other in groups on the Internet. A particular branch of gambling games comprises those in which there is a banker. Pontoon is the leader in this field. Other games are usually played in a casino, including Blackjack, which is the casino version of Pontoon, and games of the Baccarat family.

Card games for one, called Patiences in Great Britain and Solitaires in the USA, are very popular, and a variety of the best are included in this book.

There still remain plenty of games which do not fit exactly into the categories mentioned, including Skat, the national card game of Germany, Klaberjass, Casino, Calypso, two games from the East which – like the children's games Old Maid and Pig – seek to find a loser to humiliate and which are called President and Shithead, not to mention others, all of which are excellent games which reward playing. All these are included in this book. The index at the back also lists games by alternative names, by type and by player type.

Despite the large number of card games worth playing, and the huge number of people who play card games, most players know probably fewer than a dozen, and even if they are regular players probably play no more than four or five. Most people learn games from friends, and it is no doubt difficult, even for regular players, to pick up the real essence of a game from a description in a book. With this in mind, this book attempts to describe games simply, with explanations of any technical terms used as it goes along. It also includes a large glossary at the end for quick reference if necessary. Where it is thought to be helpful, examples of games, or parts of games, are included which the reader can set up with a pack of cards and play out. To make this easier to follow, where there are four players, they are usually distinguished by the terms North, East, South and West, as is the custom in Bridge literature. Elsewhere, they are Players A, B, C and so on. Where the sequence of play is set out in trick-taking games, the card which wins the trick is underlined, and the player who wins the trick leads to the next.

In presenting a book which describes how to play card games, it should be pointed out that these games have evolved over time and that – except in a few instances where clubs or federations have drawn up rules to facilitate competitive play – there are no hard-and-fast rules. People might play the same game slightly differently in different parts of the street, let alone the world. This book explains what is thought to be best practice and often mentions the commonest variants from it at the end of each game, under the unimaginative heading of 'Variants'.

It is hoped that the reader will try some of the games described which are new to him, and will like them enough to add them to his repertoire, and to play them at all times, not just Christmas.

Peter Arnold

Card Games

Accordion

Accordion is the simplest of all patience games, so simple that it probably wasn't invented consciously but just evolved, or – more accurately – just happened. It has acquired the name Accordion because it takes place in one line of cards that during the game tends to get longer and shorter, rather like the way an accordion does when it is being played.

Type	Patience
Alternative names	None
Players	One
Special requirements	None

Aim
To end with all 52 cards in one face-up pile.

Cards
The standard pack of 52 cards is used.

Preparation
A single pack of cards is shuffled and held face down in the hand.

Play
Cards are turned over one at a time and played to the table. The first is dealt to the top left of the available playing space. The second card is played to its right and the third to the right of that and so on, so that the tableau, if it can be so called, is a single line of cards, or piles of cards.

A card that is played to the right of a card that it matches in either suit or rank can be packed upon it. Similarly, if a card matches in suit or rank a card third to its left, it can be packed upon it (ie the card will have to jump over two other cards). Those are the only two moves allowed. A move must always be made when possible. Sometimes a card can be packed in either of these two places, when the player must decide which of the two is preferable. Sometimes one move allows another, and the turn of one card might provoke several moves and shorten the 'accordion' accordingly.

When a card is the top card of a pile, then it governs the whole pile, and if it can be moved to the left it takes the whole pile with it – the pile should never be split. When a gap in the line is created by moving a card or pile forward along the line, then the card or cards to the right move to the left to close the gap. If the line gets so long that there is no space for further cards then a second line is started below the first, but the two lines must be considered as one continuous line.

The game ends when all the cards from the hand are dealt to the table. The game is won if there is only one pile on the table. If more, it is lost.

Accordion is a difficult game to win, and can be very frustrating, as you can approach the end with perhaps only three or four piles on the table and then deal seven or eight cards in a line, none of which can be moved.

Example game

Suppose there is a line of five piles, as illustrated.

Tableau

Next card

The next card turned up is the ♣9. The ♣9 is played to ♣7, and that pile played to ♦9. Then ♣K is played to ♣9 and then to ♠K. The accordion is then reduced to two piles, headed by ♣K and ♦3. If the next card is ♦K or ♣3, then the piles would be reduced to one. Notice, however, that if in the position shown, the ♣9 had been played to the ♣K instead of the ♣7, the only other move possible would have been ♣9 to ♦9, and the accordion would be left with four piles instead of two.

All Fours

All Fours is an ancient game from which others have been developed, such as California Jack, Cinch and Pitch. It is mentioned by Charles Cotton in *The Compleat Gamester*, published in 1674, as being popular in Kent and is referred to in *The Pickwick Papers* by Charles Dickens. It became popular in the USA in the 19th century, and was the favoured game of gamblers until displaced by Poker. All Fours is a simple game which nevertheless rewards careful play.

Type	Trick-taking
Alternative names	High-Low-Jack, Old Sledge, Seven-Up
Players	Two; three or four for variants
Special requirements	Pen and paper for scoring

Aim
To win the game by scoring seven points; points are scored for capturing certain cards during tricks.

Cards
The standard pack of 52 cards is used, the cards ranking from Ace (high) to 2 (low).

Preparation
Each player draws a card to determine the first dealer, the highest dealing. Thereafter each player deals in turn. The dealer shuffles the pack and the non-dealer cuts.

Each player is dealt six cards face down in two bundles of three, beginning with the non-dealer. The next card is turned up to indicate the trump suit. If it is a Jack, the dealer immediately scores one point.

Play
Begging When the deal has been made, the players look at their cards and the non-dealer has the option of either 'standing' or 'begging'. If he says 'I stand', the turn up is accepted as trumps and the trick-taking phase begins.

Alternatively, the trump card can be rejected, and the non-dealer instead says 'I beg'. This gives the dealer the option of accepting or rejecting the trump card. If the dealer accepts the trumps, he says 'Take one' and has to give the non-dealer one point for 'gift'. The trick-taking phase then begins.

However, if the dealer also does not like the trump card, he says 'I refuse the gift' or 'I run the cards', which mean the same. Remember that if the non-dealer has six points, needing one to win the game, the dealer must always refuse the gift; otherwise he would lose immediately.

Running the cards When the dealer runs the cards, the rejected turn up is discarded face down and each player is dealt another bundle of three cards face down, turning up the next card. If it is different from the rejected trump card it becomes trumps. If, however, it is the same suit as the rejected trump suit, it too is discarded face down as are the two bundles of three cards, without the players looking at them. A further three cards are dealt to each hand and a third face-up card is dealt to indicate trumps. If necessary, this exercise is repeated until a new trump suit is established (in the unlikely event of the pack being exhausted without the trump suit being established, the deal is abandoned). If the card establishing the new trump suit is a Jack, the dealer scores one point. (The dealer does not score a point if in running the cards the Jack of the rejected trump suit is turned up.)

The new trump suit cannot be rejected, and once it is established the players pick up the three new cards they have been dealt and add them to their hands. They now each hold nine cards and have to reduce their hands to six by discarding three face down.

Trick-taking The trick-taking phase now begins, with the non-dealer leading to the first of the six tricks; see p383 for an explanation of tricks and trick-taking. A trick is won, as usual, by the higher trump it contains or the higher card of the suit led. In a departure from most trick-taking games, the second player is allowed to trump even if able to follow suit. The player cannot discard, however, if a card of the suit led is held – the player must either follow suit or trump. If unable to follow suit, the player can trump or discard as desired. If trumps are led, the second player must follow suit, if able to. The winner of a trick leads to the next.

When all six tricks have been played the scores are calculated in the order below.

Scoring Four main points are at stake in each deal, hence the name All Fours. The four points are scored as follows:

High   for winning the highest trump in play;

Low   for winning the lowest trump in play;

Jack   for winning the Jack of trumps, if in play;

Game   for winning the highest value of scoring cards in tricks, the scoring scale being

Ace	4
King	3
Queen	2
Jack	1
10	10

If the players have an equal count the non-dealer scores the point.

Of course the player dealt the highest trump in play must win the point for High, since he must win a trick with it. If there is only one trump in play it wins the point for both High and Low. Similarly, if the Jack of trumps is highest or lowest trump, it wins the point for High or Low as well as for Jack, and could in fact win all three points. If the Jack is not in play, the point for Jack is not scored, meaning that only three main points are scored in that deal.

The winner is the first to seven points, the main points after each deal being taken in the order High, Low, Jack, Game, except when Jack is turned up as the trump indicator, in which case the dealer scores for it immediately. Another point can be scored immediately during the deal for gift, as explained above.

It sometimes happens that a player will 'count out' during a deal (for example, if a player on six points holds the Ace of trumps, he must win the point for High, which is counted first, and therefore must win). In that case, most players prefer not to play out the deal.

Example hand
The cards are dealt as shown in the illustration, with ♣4 turned up to indicate the trump suit.

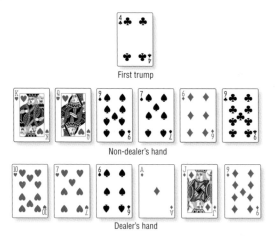

First trump

Non-dealer's hand

Dealer's hand

After the deal the non-dealer begs, as he holds only one middling club. The dealer, who holds no trumps, refuses the gift and runs the cards as illustrated below.

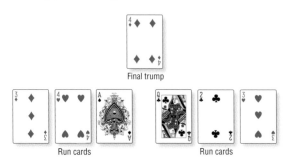

Final trump

Run cards   Run cards

Diamonds is the new trump suit, and the players pick up their extra three cards. Diamonds is excellent for the dealer, as he already holds ♦A, J, 9. With these he keeps ♥10, 7, 3. His policy is to lead hearts and hope to make at least ♦A, J and ♥10, which should ensure he gains at least three, and probably four, points. The non-dealer keeps ♦6, 3, ♠A, 9, ♥K, Q. The final hand of each player is shown below.

Non-dealer's final hand

Dealer's final hand

The non-dealer leads to the first trick and play proceeds as follows:

	Non-dealer	Dealer
1	♠9	♦J
2	♦3	♥3
3	♠A	♦9
4	♥K	♥7
5	♥Q	♦A
6	♦6	♥10

On the first lead, the dealer made sure of a point by playing the Jack of trumps, and followed his policy by leading ♥3. The non-dealer, instead of winning the trick with his ♥K, decided to trump with ♦3, which would be likely to gain him a point for Low. He then led ♠A, which the dealer took with ♦9, leading another heart, which this time drew ♥K. Now the non-dealer led his last heart, which the dealer trumped with Ace, and then led his ♥10, expecting it to win. Unfortunately, the non-dealer had a trump left and won the last trick.

So the deal ended at two points each, with the dealer scoring for High and Jack, and the non-dealer for Low and Game, his count for the game being 13 to 11.

Where the dealer, who had much the better hand, went wrong, was not so much in his play of the cards but in the choice of his hand. He would have done better to have discarded the ♥10, because no matter what other cards he held with his three trumps, he would have won the point for Game.

Variants

In the original game of All Fours, the point for Low was awarded to the player who held the lowest trump in the deal, rather than to the player who won it in the trick-taking phase, and in many books this is still how the game is described. However, the game is obviously better if the point is awarded to the player winning the card, rather than to the one fortuitously dealt it, and that is how modern players play it, and how the game is described above; some books might describe the above game as a descendant of the original game.

Three-handed All Fours In this variation there are three players, who play as individuals. Only the dealer and the eldest hand (the player on the dealer's left) look at their cards after the deal. The eldest hand has the option of standing or begging, as described, and the dealer of playing with the original trump or running the cards. Only when the trump is established does the third player pick up his cards. If the cards have been run, all players reduce their hands to six cards and play proceeds as above.

When there is a tie in the count for Game, if it is between the dealer and a non-dealer, the non-dealer gets the point; if between the two non-dealers the point for game is not scored.

Four-handed All Fours This variation for four players is played in two partnerships, partners sitting opposite each other. The dealer and the eldest hand only take part in the determination of the trump suit. The other players do not pick up their hands until the trick-taking phase begins when all players, if necessary, reduce their hands to six cards. The partners' tricks are combined for scoring purposes, so scoring is the same as in the two-handed game.

Baccarat

Baccarat is the ultimate gambling game, at which in the golden days of the casinos at Deauville and Monte Carlo in the 1920s fortunes were literally made and lost on the turn of a single card. It is a very simple game, of practically no skill, designed to redistribute vast sums of wealth quickly in casinos. Invented in France in the 19th century, it became popular in casinos and was played by the rich and aristocratic, thus gaining a glamorous image.

Baccarat is basically a two-handed game, between the banker (also the dealer) and the non-dealer. In the basic game described the casino provides the bank and the banker. The players, who bet against the bank, do not take an active part in the game, except for one who acts for them as a whole, usually the player who has made the biggest bet. The game is often called Baccarat-banque, because the casino is the bank and provides the dealer, or Baccarat à deux tableaux, because the dealer plays against two other hands simultaneously, represented by tableau one and tableau two.

Type	Gambling, played in casinos
Alternative names	Baccara, Chemin de Fer, Punto Banco
Players	Up to twelve
Special requirements	Played in a casino, which provides the venue, table, cards, chips and the croupier

Aim
To hold a hand of a higher point value than that of the banker.

Cards
Six standard packs of 52 cards are normally used.

Preparation
The players seat themselves around the table in the twelve numbered places. If more wish to play they stand behind those seated. The banker and a croupier (who deals with the disposal of stakes and cards) sit or stand as shown opposite.

After shuffling, the cards are placed in a *sabot*, or dealing shoe, with a marker placed before the tenth card from the back, these last cards not being used.

Players may bet that tableau 1, tableau 2 or both will beat the banker. Stakes are placed in the spaces marked 1 or 2 on the table respectively. The croupier will place stakes for players who cannot reach the appropriate space. A player may bet that both tableaux will beat the banker, and the stake for this is placed on the line between 1 and 2; the player wins if both tableaux beat the banker, loses if both lose and retains his stake if one wins and the other loses. This bet is called *à cheval*.

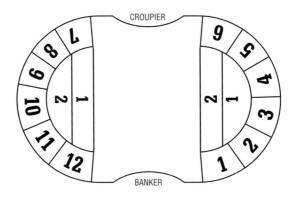

Play

When all bets are placed, the dealer deals one card at a time from the sabot, beginning with tableau 1 (to his right) then tableau 2 (to his left) and then to himself, until all three hands consist of two cards.

All cards count their pip value, with Ace counting one and court cards ten. The values of the two cards are added together to obtain a 'point', but if the value exceeds ten, the second digit only of the sum counts as the point. Thus a 7 and 6, which equal 13, count as a point of 3. A King and a 5 give a point of 5 ($10 + 5 = 15$), a 6 and a 4 a point of zero. The highest point possible is therefore 9.

A two-card hand with a point of 9 is known in French as *le grand*, and is the best hand possible. A two-card hand with a point of 8 is *le petit*, which beats everything except *le grand*. British and US players call these hands 'naturals' – natural 9 and natural 8.

In certain circumstances, described below, a player or banker will draw a third card, his point being calculated in the same way, by adding the values of the three cards and taking the second digit, if necessary.

Once the initial cards have been dealt, the players representing each tableau and the banker then look at their cards, and if any holds a natural 9 or 8 the hand is exposed, since these cannot be beaten, and wins immediately (except that, of course, a natural 8 loses to a natural 9). Otherwise the hands are replaced face down.

If the banker does not have a natural, he must deal in turn with the two hands against him, beginning with tableau 1. The player representing tableau 1 must state whether he wishes to stand with the point he has, or draw a third card. With all points except 5 he has no choice (he is, of course, only representative of all the players who have bet on tableau 1). He must choose to stand with a point of 6 or 7 and draw with a point of 0, 1, 2, 3 or 4. This has been worked out as the best strategy, anyway, and is called the Table of Play. Only with a point of 5 has he a choice; it has been estimated that it is slightly better in this situation to stand than to draw.

A player who draws a third card has this dealt face up, but leaves the two cards previously dealt to him face down on the table, so only he knows his final point.

Having dealt with tableau 1, the banker repeats the process with tableau 2, and then must consider his own hand. The banker also has a Table of Play which, like that for the player, sets out the optimum play, but in his case it can only be advisory, since the banker is playing against two opponents at once, and the Table of Play might indicate drawing against one and standing against the other. In practice, of course, the banker will estimate which tableau is carrying the higher stake, and follow the Table of Play as if playing against that hand only. The banker's Table of Play is set out here, and applies also to the Chemin de Fer variant which follows.

Banker's Table of Play for Baccarat and Chemin de Fer

Banker's point	Banker draws if player draws	Banker stands if player draws	Banker has option if player draws
3	0, 1, 2, 3, 4, 5, 6, 7	8	9
4	2, 3, 4, 5, 6, 7	0, 1, 8, 9	–
5	5, 6, 7	0, 1, 2, 3, 8, 9	4
6	6, 7	0, 1, 2, 3, 4, 5, 8, 9	–

Note: The banker always draws on 0, 1 and 2, stands on 7 and exposes a natural on 8 or 9. If the player does not draw, the banker is advised to stand on 6 and draw on 3, 4 and 5.

When all hands are complete, with either two or three cards, they are exposed, and the players win or lose according to whether their point is higher or lower than the banker's. The side, banker or player, with the higher point is the winner, with the proviso that a natural 9 or 8 beats any three-card point. If they win, they win the amount of their stake, and if they lose, they lose their stake. Where the banker's and player's hands are equal, the player retains his stake.

Variants
Chemin de Fer Chemin de Fer is played in casinos on a table with a different layout. The main difference from the parent game is that the players themselves hold the bank in turn, with the casino charging a commission. This is the version of the game most suitable for play at home, as it can be managed without the refinements of the casino table and the croupier to manage the settlement of the bets. In a casino the sabot is passed round the table, stopping at each player as a train might at each station, hence the name Chemin de Fer, the French for 'railway'. The sabot will usually contain at least six packs with a marker placed towards the back so that not all are used. For games among friends at home, of course, a single pack shuffled after each deal might be regarded as acceptable.

The first banker can be chosen in two ways. Either the player willing to put up the biggest bank becomes the banker, or the banker can be chosen by lot, whichever the players prefer. The banker places the amount of the bank before him.

The game is a straight two-handed contest between banker and players. The players place their stakes in front of them, beginning with the player to the banker's right. That player may bet any amount, up to the amount of the bank. The next

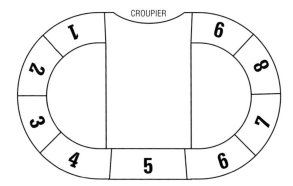

player does likewise and so on until the total of the players' stakes is equal to the bank. It follows that some players may not get the chance to bet on every hand. If when all players have made their bets the amount in the bank is not covered, the surplus is removed by the banker.

There are, however, three 'preferential' bets allowed. Before the deal any player may call '*banco*', which allows that player to bet the whole of the amount in the bank himself. If two or more players wish to call banco, the precedence goes to the player nearest to the banker's right. The second preferential call, which has precedence over all others, operates only after a call of banco. If the caller loses his bet and the banker collects the stake, which thereby doubles the size of the bank, the loser is entitled to call '*banco suivi*', which allows him to bet the whole amount of the bank again. After this he may call banco again, but his status is only that of the other players.

The third preferential call, and the third in rank, is '*avec la table*'. This allows the caller to bet half the value of the bank, the other players being at liberty to bet the remainder as normal.

When all bets are made the banker deals the two hands face down, one card at a time, to players and himself alternately, so that both hands are of two cards. The player placing the highest stake holds the cards for players.

As described in Baccarat, above, the aim is to have the highest point, ie that closest to 9. Banker and player look at their hands and expose them if a natural 8 or 9 is held, which settles bets immediately. Otherwise, the rules for standing or drawing apply as for Baccarat, ie the player drawing with 0, 1, 2, 3 or 4, standing with 6 or 7 and having the option with 5, while the banker must then stand or draw according to the Table of Play set out above. However, there is one exception, which occurs when 'banco' or 'banco suivi' has been called. It arises from the fact that the player in these cases is playing only for himself and not for all the players as a group. In this case, some casinos allow both player and banker to ignore the rules and draw or stand at their discretion, a practice known as '*faux tirages*', or 'false draws'. Players in private games must decide in advance whether to allow them.

As in Baccarat, when the hands are complete they are compared, and if the players win they are paid from the bank, which eliminates it, or they pay the bank, which doubles it. When the bank is eliminated the player to the right of the banker becomes the new banker, if he wishes, and places an amount on the table to form the bank. If that player declines to be the banker, the bank passes to the player to the right and so on.

A banker who wins can either withdraw the bank with his winnings and pass the opportunity to be banker to the right, or retain the bank, in which case the whole of it remains for the next deal. The player is not allowed to withdraw part of it and carry on with the rest, unless in a casino and the bank exceeds the casino's limit.

Punto Banco Punto Banco is a simplified version of Chemin de Fer that is popular in casinos. It is an automatic game of chance with no options at all. Up to twelve players sit at spaces marked, and there are two spaces for croupiers. One croupier deals and the other plays the players' hand. Each player in turn is given the opportunity to play the banker's hand. Thus the names 'players' and 'bank' have no significance other than to give a name to the two hands. Nobody is required to put up a bank and players make the simple choice of which side will win; they will either lose their stake to the casino or be paid out by the casino accordingly.

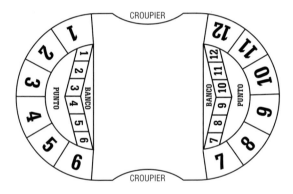

A player makes bets by placing a stake of any amount between the casino's limits in the spaces provided. A bet on *punto*, or players (in some casinos the table is marked 'players' instead of 'punto'), is placed in the big numbered box before him, while a bet on banco, or bank, is placed in the smaller box corresponding to his number.

A croupier deals from a sabot the two hands of two cards, one at a time. The players' hand is dealt to the croupier opposite and the bank's hand to the player whose turn it is to play it. As in the two versions described above, the aim is to obtain the closest point value to 9. However, neither side has any options, and both must obey the Table of Play:

Player's Table of Play for Punto Banco

Point

0, 1, 2, 3, 4, 5	Draws
6, 7	Stands
8, 9	Exposes cards

Banker's Table of Play for Punto Banco

Point	Draws if player draws	Stands if player draws
0, 1, 2	0, 1, 2, 3, 4, 5, 6, 7, 8, 9	
3	0, 1, 2, 3, 4, 5, 6, 7, 9	8
4	2, 3, 4, 5, 6, 7	0, 1, 8, 9
5	4, 5, 6, 7	0, 1, 2, 3, 8, 9
6	6, 7	0, 1, 2, 3, 4, 5, 8, 9
7	Stands	
8, 9	Exposes cards	

Note: If the player does not draw, banker draws on 0, 1, 2, 3, 4 and 5, stands on 6 and 7, and exposes his cards on 8 and 9.

Bets are settled when both hands are completed. Bets on punto, or players, are settled at a straightforward even money, or 1–1, but on banco, or bank, at odds of 19–20 ie at 5% less than 1–1. It has been estimated that the bank hand has a 1.34% advantage over the players' hand when the likelihood of it winning is calculated, which means that players betting on the players' hand are conceding the casino a 1.34% edge, while those betting on the bank hand are conceding 1.20%. The bank hand is therefore the slightly better bet.

Beggar My Neighbour

Beggar My Neighbour is a very simple children's game – often the first game that children learn – and probably arises from an early gambling game. There is no skill involved and the outcome depends entirely on luck.

Type	Children's
Alternative names	Beat Your Neighbour Out of Doors, Strip Jack Naked
Players	Any reasonable number
Special requirements	None

Aim
To capture all the cards in the pack.

Cards
The standard pack of 52 cards is used.

Preparation
A dealer is chosen by any method. The cards are shuffled and dealt clockwise face down, beginning with the player to the dealer's left, one at a time to all players including the dealer until all the cards are exhausted. It does not matter if some players have more cards than others.

Play
The players take their cards into their hands, holding them in a face-down pile. Beginning with the player to the dealer's left, each player plays the top card of his hand face up to the table one on top of the other to form a central pile. There are 16 honour cards: the Ace, King, Queen and Jack of each suit. When an honour is played, the following player has to cover it with a specific number of other cards:

Ace	four cards	Queen	two cards
King	three cards	Jack	one card

If while doing this he deals an honour, then the following player has to cover the new honour at the same rate: four for an Ace and so on. If an honour is played and the required number of cards are played to it without another honour appearing then the player of the honour takes the whole of the pile from the table and adds them face down to the bottom of the stack of cards in his hand. The player nearest his left then begins a new round of play.

A player who has played all his cards to the table retires from the game. If he runs out of cards while fulfilling the obligations in playing to an honour, then the player of the honour takes the pile as usual.

Gradually the players are knocked out of the game one by one, until only one is left and is declared the winner.

Belvedere

Belvedere is a very simple patience game with an attractive layout, which takes only about five minutes to play. It is annoying in that it rarely comes out, but satisfying in that progress is maintained until only a few cards are left.

Type	Patience
Alternative names	None
Players	One
Special requirements	None

Aim
To end with four piles of cards, irrespective of suit, in sequence from Ace up to King.

Cards
The standard pack of 52 cards is used.

Preparation
Any Ace is picked from the pack and played to the centre of the table to become the first foundation card. Twenty-four cards are then dealt to the table face-up in bundles of three and arranged in eight fans. If a King appears in any fan, it is moved to the bottom (ie the left) of the fan. This forms the tableau. The next three cards are then dealt face up in a row below the tableau. These form the first three cards of the reserve. The remaining cards form the stock, which is taken into the hand face down.

Play
The other three Aces must be released and played to the centre as foundation cards, and then all four Aces built on in ascending sequence, regardless of suit and colour, to the four Kings. The cards available to be built to the foundations are the top cards (ie the right-hand cards) of each fan and the three cards which top the reserve piles.

In addition, the top card of any fan may be packed on the top card of another fan in descending order of rank, irrespective of suit or colour. The top cards of the reserve piles may also be packed onto fans in the same manner. Only one card may be played at a time.

When all the cards in a fan have been played to a foundation or another fan, the space in the tableau is not filled.

After the initial layout, when all the moves initially possible have been made, three cards are dealt face up to the reserve, to cover each card or to fill any vacancies. All moves that now become possible are made, and another three cards are then dealt to the reserve. When all the cards in the stock have been dealt (there will be nine deals), the player builds any exposed cards he can to the foundations and wins if he can end with four piles headed by the Kings.

Example game
The cards are dealt as in the illustration.

Foundations

Tableau

Reserve

The ♦A is played to a place in the foundation row. The ♣J is packed on the ♥Q, followed by the ♦10, and the ♥9. The ♣2 is built to the foundation followed by the ♦3 and ♣4. The ♣7 is packed on the ♦8, followed by the ♠6. The ♦5 is played to the foundation from the reserve and the ♠6, ♣7 and ♦8 are built on it. The ♥9, ♦10, ♣J and ♥Q follow. The ♠Q is packed on the ♥K, followed by the ♦J. The ♥2 can be built to a foundation, followed by the ♥3 and ♥4. The ♥10 is packed on the ♦J, followed by the ♣9. The ♣8 is packed on the ♠9 and the ♦7 from the reserve is played to it. The ♣5 is built on the foundation.

This exhausts the moves possible, leaving only three fans in the tableau and one card in the reserve. The next three cards from the stock are now played to the reserve, two to the empty spaces and one to cover the ♠J which remains there.

Let us suppose these cards are the ♦9, ♠5 and ♣6. Several more cards could now be built to foundations, including a King. However, it is best not to play Kings to the foundation immediately, but to leave them in the tableau. This allows the next King to appear when dealt to the reserve from the stock to be played immediately to a foundation rather than blocking a reserve pile, which will make the game almost impossible to get out.

Bezique

Bezique originated in 19th-century France, and attracted little notice when first mentioned in the UK in 1861, but it became the fashion when discovered by Queen Victoria's son Alfred, Duke of Edinburgh, soon afterwards. Pinochle, which developed from it, became extremely popular in the USA but both games faded somewhat with the craze for Bridge in the 20th century. It remains, however, an entertaining game.

Type	Trick-taking and melding
Alternative names	None
Players	Two; three or four for variants
Special requirements	Two packs of cards; a large playing surface, as the game needs more than average space; pen and paper for scoring, although special Bezique markers are available

Aim
To score the most points.

Cards
Two standard packs of cards, preferably identical, are used, from which are removed the 6s, 5s, 4s, 3s and 2s, leaving a pack of 64 cards. The cards rank Ace (high), 10, King, Queen, Jack, 9, 8, 7 (low).

Preparation
Players cut the cards to determine the first dealer, and the player with the lowest card deals. The dealer shuffles and the non-dealer cuts the pack.

The dealer deals eight cards to each player, in bundles of three, two and three, beginning with the non-dealer. The next card is turned over to denote trumps, and placed in the centre of the table. The rest of the pack is placed face down beside it to form the stock. If the trump indicator is a seven, the dealer scores ten points for it.

Play
The non-dealer leads to the first trick, and subsequently the winner of the trick leads to the next; see p383 for an explanation of tricks and trick-taking. There is no requirement until the end-game (see End-game, below) to follow suit to the card led; any card may be played. If two identical cards are played, then the card led takes the trick.

The winner of the trick can 'declare' (see Scoring, below) any of the point-scoring combinations in the table on p22. He then places the two cards forming the trick to one side for later examination for brisques, and takes the top card of the stock into his hand. The loser of the trick takes the next card from the stock and the winner of the trick leads to the next. In this way each player's hand continues to be of eight cards, although any number of these might be laid on the table in declarations.

Cards laid on the table in declarations remain part of the hand and any of them can be played at any time in the trick-taking phase. The winning of a trick does not score, except in so far as it might contain a brisque (to be scored for later), but the winning of tricks is necessary to declare combinations.

Scoring Points are scored in various ways, mainly by declarations. Upon winning a trick a player may declare a point-scoring combination of cards by placing them on the table in front of him. These combinations are in three categories: beziques, sequences and quartets. Only one declaration can be made at a time – a player holding two or three must declare them one by one separately by winning two or three tricks.

Either player, on winning a trick, may exchange the trump 7 (known as *dix*, pronounced 'deece') for the upturned trump card and score ten points, or may declare the trump 7 and score ten points.

A final way to win points is to take an Ace or a 10 in a trick. These are known as brisques, and each Ace and 10 scores ten points, which are added to the score at the end of the deal.

The scores for these are also set out in the table overleaf.

A card may be used in two or more different declarations. For example, a player who declares the ♠K, Q as a marriage and, while they are still declared on the table, acquires the ♦J, may add this to the ♠Q and declare bezique. Similarly, a card declared in a marriage, while still on the table, can be used in the declaration of a quartet or sequence. However, once a card declared has been played, it cannot be retrieved or replaced. For example, if ♦K, Q is declared as a marriage, and the player subsequently plays ♦K, leaving ♦Q temporarily on the table, the player cannot, if he should then acquire the second ♦K, add it to the ♦Q to score a second marriage. No card can be used twice for the same declaration.

A double bezique scores 500 only if all four cards are declared at one time. However, if a single bezique is declared for 40, and while the cards are still on the table the player of it plays a second bezique for 40, that player can, on the next trick he wins, add the two together and score 500 for double bezique.

The sequence of A, 10, K, Q, J of trumps scores 250. Note that this includes a royal marriage, but the player of it does not score an extra 40 for royal marriage. However, if he declares a royal marriage (K, Q of trumps) for 40, and subsequently on winning a later trick adds A, 10, J, the whole 250 is then scored for the sequence.

Bezique

Table of combinations and scores for Bezique

Beziques

Bezique (single)	♠Q, ♦J	40
Double bezique	♠Q, ♦J, ♠Q, ♦J	500

Sequences

Sequence	A, 10, K, Q, J of trumps	250
Royal marriage	K, Q of trumps	40
Common marriage	K, Q of plain suit	20

Quartets

Hundred Aces	Any four Aces	100
Eighty Kings	Any four Kings	80
Sixty Queens	Any four Queens	60
Forty Jacks	Any four Jacks	40

Other scores

Dix	7 of trumps	10
Brisques	Each Ace and 10 won in tricks	10

End-game After 23 tricks have been played, there will be two cards left in the centre of the table – the last card of the stock, face down, and the face-up trump indicator, which will usually be the 7, it having been exchanged for the original trump indicator. The winner of the last trick of this phase now takes the last of the stock into his hand (with which he can make a last declaration) and the loser the last trump.

No further declarations can now be made, so players take any of their cards on the table in declarations into their hands, which will still consist of eight cards each. They now play off the last eight tricks but the rules are very different.

Now it is not only obligatory to follow suit to the card led, but if possible to win the trick by playing a higher card in the suit. If no cards in the led suit are held, the player must trump. Only if it is impossible to follow suit or trump may he discard. Discarding or playing a lower card in the suit led (because he doesn't have a higher one) are the only ways to concede the trick to the leader.

Tricks taken are added to each player's pile of tricks won, and the winner of the last trick scores ten points.

Each player then checks his tricks won, adds up his points for brisques (the two players share 160 points for brisques) and adds his score to the points already scored for combinations, etc. If only one hand is played, the player with the higher score wins, otherwise the non-dealer for the first hand deals for the second.

The winner is the player with the most points, or, in a series of games, who is the first to reach a certain number of points agreed beforehand; 1,000 or 2,000 are suggested as totals for a shorter or longer game.

Example hand

Hands are dealt as in the illustration.

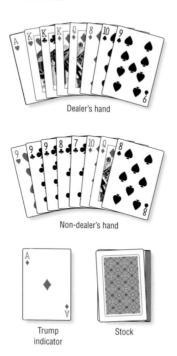

Dealer's hand

Non-dealer's hand

Trump
indicator

Stock

The ♦A is turned up as trump indicator. The dealer starts with much the more powerful hand, including a royal marriage. Play proceeds as follows:

	Cards played		Cards drawn	
	Dealer	*Non-dealer*	*Dealer*	*Non-dealer*
1	♠9	♠8		

Before drawing the cards the dealer declares royal marriage by placing ♦K, Q on the table and scoring 40 points.

	Cards played		Cards drawn	
1			♥J	♣10
2	♦8	♣7	♥8	♣A
3	♥8	♣8	♠A	♦7
4	♠10	♣9	♥10	♣10
5	♥J	♣9	♥A	♠J

Things are going very well for the dealer, who has three Aces and three Kings, and no cards he really wishes to lead. The non-dealer needs to win a trick to exchange his ♦7 for ♦A, and score 10 points.

6	♥10	♥9	♠K	♥7

The dealer now has four Kings.

7	♦Q	♥7		

The dealer declares his four Kings and scores 80.

7			♠10	♣J
8	♠10	♣10	♣K	♦K
9	♣K	♣10		

The non-dealer at last wins a trick and exchanges ♦7 for ♦A.

9			♠A	♣A

The non-dealer is now holding three Aces, a royal marriage, and needs ♦J for sequence.

10	♠K	♠J		

The dealer declares four Aces for 100 points.

10			♠8	♦A
11	♠8	♣J	♠9	♠Q
12	♠9	♠Q		

The non-dealer sacrifices ♠Q (and chance of bezique) in order to declare four Aces. The non-dealer scores 100.

12			♠Q	♦7
13	♠A	♣A		

The non-dealer declares royal marriage for 40 points.

13			♣J	♦8
14	♣J	♦7		

The non-dealer scores 10 points for playing ♦7.

14			♥7	♥10
15	♥7	♥10	♣8	♣Q
16	♣8	♦8	♦J	♥Q

The dealer now has bezique, the non-dealer three Queens.

| 17 | ♣K | ♣A | ♦9 | ♠J |
| 18 | ♦9 | ♠J | | |

The dealer declares bezique and scores 40 points.

18			♠K	♦10
19	♥K	♦10	♠7	♥8
20	♥A	♥8		

The dealer declares common marriage ♠K, Q for 20 points.

20			♣Q	♥J
21	♠7	♥J	♥K	♦9
22	♥K	♦9	♥9	♦J

The non-dealer now has sequence and is anxious to declare it. Holding both Aces of trumps, he is certain to win the next trick.

| 23 | ♥9 | ♦A | | |

The non-dealer declares sequence and scores 250 points.

| 23 | | | ♣7 | ♥Q |

The non-dealer now has four Queens, but to declare them must win the last trick of this phase.

| 24 | ♣7 | ♦A | | |

The non-dealer declares four Queens for 60 points, and takes the last card, ♠7, into his hand, while the dealer takes the upturned trump indicator, ♦7.

The end-game now takes place, with the non-dealer, having won the last trick, leading first. Knowing both Aces of trumps have been played, he knows ♦10, K will win the first two tricks and reduce the dealer's trumps.

Dealer	Non-dealer
♦7	♦10
♦J	♦K
♠Q	♠7
♥A	♥Q
♠A	♦J
♣Q	♣Q
♦K	♥Q
♠K	♦Q

The non-dealer scores 10 points for making the last trick. The scores so far are the dealer 280 and the non-dealer 480. When the brisques are counted, the dealer scores 60 points to the non-dealer's 100, the final scores for the hand being the dealer 340 and the non-dealer 580. The non-dealer's achieving sequence near the end made all the difference.

Variants

Some players prefer to change the suits of the bezique cards if spades or diamonds are trumps. If spades are trumps, bezique is ♣Q, ♦J, if diamonds are trumps bezique is ♠Q, ♥J. Others prefer ♣Q, ♥J to form bezique if either spades or diamonds are trumps.

Some players do not turn up a card to denote trumps at the beginning of play. The game is played without trumps until a marriage or sequence is declared, whereupon its suit automatically becomes the trump suit, and the marriage or sequence is scored accordingly. The seven of trumps has no special properties and dix is not scored.

Bezique for three players Three packs shorn of 6s, 5s, 4s, 3s and 2s are used, ie 96 cards. Players play as individuals. The winner of a trick draws first from the stock, the player on his left second, and the remaining player third. A new, albeit rare, combination, triple bezique, becomes possible and scores 1,500 points. After each hand, the deal passes to the left. Game is usually first to 2,000 points.

Bezique for four players Four shortened packs are used, ie 128 cards. Players play as individuals in the same way as for three-player Bezique. The new (very rare) combination available, quadruple bezique, scores 1,500, as for triple bezique, but of course a player can score single, double, triple and quadruple beziques in separate declarations.

Rubicon Bezique Rubicon Bezique is for two players, using cards from four shortened packs (ie 128 cards). Differences from the standard game are that each player is dealt nine cards instead of eight, in three bundles of three. There is no turn-up for trumps, and play is without trumps until the first marriage (or very rarely a sequence, which of course includes a marriage) is declared, upon which its suit becomes trumps. There are additional scores: 1,500 for triple bezique, 4,500 for quadruple bezique and 150 for a sequence (A, 10, K, Q, J) in a plain suit. There is also a new score for *carte blanche*. A player with a hand without a court card (K, Q, J) scores 50 points by showing it to his opponent. Thereafter he may score another 50 points after each draw in which he fails to draw a court card by showing the drawn card (A, 10, 9, 8, 7). Once he draws a court card, he cannot score again for carte blanche. Brisques are not scored, except to break a tie at the end of the game, or to assist the loser to reach the rubicon (see below).

There are also differences in the play. If a player declares a combination, and later plays one of the cards from it, he may later, having won a trick, play a replacement card to the same combination, and score for it again. Similarly, if a player has two identical marriages on the table, and plays, say, one of the Queens, he may on a subsequent declaration switch the other Queen to the lonely King and score for another marriage. Should there be three identical marriages declared, after playing one of the cards the player may make on subsequent declarations four other marriages if he pairs the remaining monarchs in all the possible marriages. The winner of the last trick scores 50 instead of 10.

The game is of one deal only, and at the end, each player works out his points total and rounds down to the nearest 100 (for example 1,440 rounds down to 1,400). If the rounded down totals are equal, each player counts his brisques (Aces and 10s won in tricks) and adds the total to his original scores, which is again rounded down to the nearest 100. If the totals are still level, the player with the higher original score rounds up instead of down to give a difference between the two players of 100.

The winner of the game scores the difference between the two totals plus 500 for winning. However, if the loser fails to reach the rubicon of 1,000, he is penalized twice, and loses by an extra 500 points, that is by the difference in totals plus 1,000. This applies even if the winner, also, fails to pass the rubicon. However, if the loser fails to reach the rubicon with his original score, he is entitled to add on his brisques, in which case the winner does, too. If the loser's rounded down total now reaches 1,000 or more, he is not rubiconed and does not have the extra 500 points added to his losses.

The actual margin of victory will not be important to non-gamblers, who might be satisfied by just winning without needing to work out the exact margin of victory.

Rubicon Bezique for four players Six packs, without 6s, 5s, 4s, 3s, and 2s are used, ie 192 cards. Two pairs play in partnership. After the cards are shuffled and cut, the dealer plays 24 cards face down to the table to begin the stock, and places a marker on the top card, the purpose being to warn players when the stock is near exhaustion. Four hands of nine cards are then dealt to all players in bundles of three, the remainder of the cards being placed face down on top of the marker to complete the stock.

The differences with the game for two players lie in scoring and declaring. The points score differences are:

Carte blanche	100
Double carte blanche (neither partner being dealt a court card)	500
Quintuple bezique	13,500
Sextuple bezique	40,500
Any four Aces	1,000
Any four 10s	900
Any four Kings	800
Any four Queens	600
Any four Jacks	400

The game bonus to be added to the difference in scores is 1,000 points, to be doubled if the rubicon of 2,500 is not reached.

Differences in the play arise from the partnership principle. A player winning a trick may declare a combination which uses cards already declared by his partner, for example if the partner has declared a bezique of ♠Q, ♦J, he can declare ♠K for a marriage or even another ♠Q, ♦J for double bezique. Indeed, since a player has only nine cards, quintuple or sextuple bezique can be scored only in partnership. Also a player winning a trick may offer the chance it gives him to declare to his partner (but cannot claim it back if his partner declines). Needless to say, partners must not make signals to each other in this respect.

Each deal is a complete game and the deal, and the order of playing to the tricks, passes to the left.

Chinese Bezique Chinese Bezique is a variation developed in the early 20th century and is possibly the most popular version of the game. It was a favourite of Sir Winston Churchill, who was said to be very good at it.

Chinese Bezique is for two players using six of the shortened packs, ie 192 cards. Players cut for choice of deal and higher has choice (in this and this only, the 10 takes its normal place between Jack and 9). The non-dealer has a slight advantage, so the winner usually passes the deal to his opponent. The dealer shuffles (a difficult task with 192 cards). The non-dealer cuts. The dealer then takes up a batch of cards from the top of the pack, trying to pick up 24, because if he succeeds he will score 250 points. When he has picked them up, the non-dealer guesses how many he has picked up. The dealer then deals 12 cards to each hand, one at a time. If he deals exactly the cards he picked up, he scores 250; if he falls short or has some over, he must either take more from the stock or return some. In both cases the number of cards he picked up is calculated, and if the non-dealer guessed right, he gets 150 points.

There is no turn-up for the trump suit, which is determined by the first marriage or sequence declared. Usually the declaration bezique requires the Queen of the trump suit with a Jack as follows: ♠Q with ♦J, ♦Q with ♠J, ♣Q with ♥J, and ♥Q with ♣J. Bezique, naturally, cannot be declared before the trump suit is established. Some players prefer to have ♠Q and ♦J as bezique no matter the trump suit.

There are additional declarations:

Carte blanche (for each time it is declared)	250	Any four Jacks	40
Four Aces of trumps	1,000	Sequence of trumps	250
Four 10s of trumps	900	Sequence of plain suit	150
Four Kings of trumps	800	Royal marriage	40
Four Queens of trumps	600	Common marriage	20
Four Jacks of trumps	400	Bezique	40
Any four Aces	100	Double bezique	500
Any four Kings	80	Triple bezique	1,500
Any four Queens	60	Quadruple bezique	4,500

There are no special scores for quintuple or sextuple bezique. An extra score is 250 for taking the final trick. Brisques are not scored, making it unnecessary for players to keep their tricks, which are left in the centre of the table.

As described in Rubicon Bezique (which differs from the basic game), declarations can be repeated with replacement cards when a card has been played from the table.

The play is as in Bezique, with players being able to play any card they wish and drawing from the stock as usual. When the last two cards have been taken, players take their declared cards into their hands and play out the final twelve tricks as the rules for the Bezique end-game, players having to follow suit if possible, to trump if possible if unable to follow suit, and having to win the trick if they can.

A game is of one deal, and the player with most points wins. Both scores are rounded down to the nearest hundred, and the winner wins the difference in scores plus 1,000. If the loser does not reach 3,000 points he is rubiconed and the winner adds the loser's points to his as well as the 1,000 bonus.

Fildinski Fildinski is also known as Polish Bezique. It is a game many prefer to Bezique, claiming it as being more skilful. It is different from other games in this section in that declarations are made not from hand, but from cards won in tricks.

The game is for two players, using two of the shortened packs, ie 64 cards. The deal, with the turn-up for determining trumps, and the value of the combinations are the same as for Bezique. Dix is scored in the same way, the first to obtain a 7 of the trump suit scoring ten points and having the option of exchanging it for the trump indicator, the holder of the second 7 of trumps also scoring ten points. Brisques also have the same value but are scored immediately as won in tricks, rather than totalled up at the end of the first trick-taking phase. Players have eight cards in each hand, as in Bezique, and the rules governing the two phases of the trick-taking are the same.

The big difference comes in the trick-taking phases. A player winning a trick does not lay the two cards aside for examination later, but lays down on the table any cards from that trick which might prove of value in declaring combinations. Other cards (ie 9s, 8s and plain suits 7s) are put to one side face down. A winner of a trick may use either or both of the cards in the trick to combine with any of his cards on the table to make a declaration and score for it immediately. The cards remain on the table throughout, and are not part of the players' hands as they are in Bezique. After each trick players replenish their hands from stock, winner first, as in Bezique, so that their hands remain at eight cards. Cards in hand are not used in declarations. The winner of the last trick which exhausts the stock scores ten points (a departure from Bezique, where the points go to the winner of the last trick of all). The player who picks up dix as the upturned trump indicator does not score ten points for it.

The play of the last eight tricks is as in Bezique: players must follow suit or trump if possible, and win the trick if they can. However, in another departure from Bezique, the player who wins a trick can continue to use the cards to make declarations right up to the end. The deal changes with each hand, and the winner is the first to 2,000 points. Points are scored more quickly than in Bezique, as the cards suitable for combinations always remain available to one or other player and are not put to one side when played to a trick, as in Bezique.

Bisley

Bisley lends itself to some skill, as choosing whether to pack up or down in the tableau can influence the outcome. It will often be successful.

Type	Patience
Alternative names	None
Players	One
Special requirements	Playing surface large enough for five rows of twelve cards

Aim
To end with all the cards stacked in ascending suit sequences from the Aces upwards, or in descending suit sequences from the Kings downwards; it does not matter where the two sequences divide.

Cards
The standard pack of 52 cards is used.

Preparation
The four Aces are placed in a row to the top left of the space for the tableau, leaving space for a row of cards above them. The remaining cards are shuffled and dealt face up, the first nine to the right of the Aces, and the rest in three rows of 13 beneath.

Play
All cards at the foot of a column are available for play or to be played on.

The Kings and Aces are foundations, and when Kings become available they are played to the space above their respective Aces. Cards available are played to their foundations, in ascending suit sequence on the Aces and descending suit sequence on the Kings.

In addition any available card can be played in ascending or descending suit sequence, according to choice, to cards at the foot of the columns. When a card is played from the foot of a column the card above it becomes available. A column which is cleared is not replaced.

Example game
In the layout illustrated opposite, the ♥2 and ♣2 can immediately be played to their respective Ace foundations, and the ♠K can be played to its foundation space above the ♠A. The ♥8 can be packed on ♥9, followed by ♥7 and ♥6, releasing the ♦K to be played to its foundation spot. The ♦7 can be played to the ♦8, the ♠6 to the ♠5 and the ♣10 to the ♣9. This releases the ♣K to its foundation. The ♠10 can be packed on ♠9 and the ♣Q can be played to its King foundation. The ♥6, 7, 8, 9 can be packed on the ♥5, releasing ♠Q to its King foundation, and so on.

This example game can be got out if played carefully.

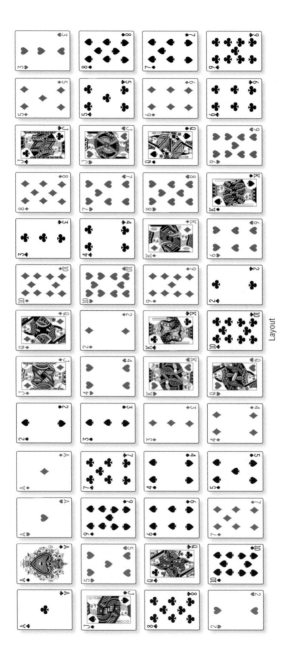

Layout

Blackjack

Blackjack got its name when a US casino, in order to advertise the game known as Twenty-One, offered a bonus to any player holding a winning hand consisting of an Ace of spades with either of the black Jacks. This hand became known as a 'blackjack', which quickly became the name for the game itself. It is the streamlined version of the game known originally (and in France, still) as Vingt-et-Un and in the UK as Pontoon. Pontoon is better for private play, the casino version being much more mechanical.

Type	Gambling, played in casinos
Alternative names	None; Vingt-et-Un, Pontoon and Twenty-One are alternative names of the domestic games of which Blackjack is a version
Players	Any number against the bank; a casino table often has space for seven players
Special requirements	Played in a casino, which provides the venue, table, cards, chips and the croupier (banker)

Aim
To hold a hand of higher point value than that of the banker.

Cards
Four standard packs of 52 cards are used. Plain cards have their pip value, and court cards each count as ten. Aces, when held by a player, have a value of one or eleven, according to the player's discretion. An Ace has the same dual value when held by the banker, but with limits, as described below.

Preparation
Players sit round the roughly semi-circular table as illustrated, facing the banker. If space is available at the tables a player may occupy two adjacent spaces and

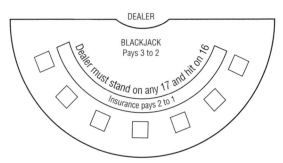

operate two hands against the banker. The two hands are entirely separate, and a player plays out one before he plays out the other.

The cards are shuffled together by the banker. Any player may cut by inserting an indicator card into the face-down pack. The cut is completed by the banker who reverses the positions of the cards below and above the indicator, removing the indicator card. The pack is placed face down in a *sabot*, or dealing shoe, and the indicator card is inserted some 50 cards from the end of the pack. When this is reached during play, the deal in which it occurs will be completed, but no further deals will be made with this pack, the cards remaining in the sabot not being used.

Players first of all place a stake, which can be of any amount within the minimum and maximum limits of the casino (or, indeed, the table, since casinos may have tables with differing limits). The stake is placed in the rectangle marked on the table in front of each player.

Play

The banker deals and 'burns' the first card dealt from the sabot, ie discards it without its value being shown.

Then, beginning with the player sitting to his extreme left, the banker deals a card in turn face up to all players, including himself. He then deals a second card to each, face up in the players' cases, and face down in his.

The player's object is to obtain a hand, with two or more cards, with a point count higher than that of the banker, without exceeding a maximum of 21. Should his count exceed 21 he has 'busted', and loses his stake.

A count of 21 with two cards, ie an Ace and a ten-point card, is known as a 'blackjack' or 'natural', and beats all other hands. (Note that a blackjack is now any two-card count of 21, and a Jack, either black or red, is not an essential part of it.) When a player wins with a blackjack, the bank pays him at odds of 3–2, which is usually stated on the table layout. Otherwise, bets are settled at odds of 1–1. If the player's and banker's hands are tied, neither wins, and the player retains his stake.

If the banker has a blackjack, he wins all the stakes immediately, except those from a player who also has a blackjack, in which case there is a tie. If the banker's face-up card is an Ace or a ten-count card, he looks at his face-down card and, if it gives him a blackjack, he reveals it and collects the players' stakes without further ado. If not, he replaces the card face-down and play continues. If the banker's face-up card is an Ace, however, he offers the players the opportunity to insure against his holding a blackjack. A player who wishes to insure places a premium of half his stake in the betting space before him. The banker then looks at his face-down card, and if it gives him a blackjack he declares it. Players who insured are paid at odds of 2–1 (this will be stated on the blackjack table itself) on their premium, so receive on the insurance the stake they lost on the play. In practice, they retain their stake and their premium and neither lose nor win on the deal. Players who did not insure, of course, lose their stakes. Should the banker not have a blackjack, he returns his card face-down to his hand, and play proceeds as usual, with players who insured losing their premium but remaining in the game. The banker now deals with all the players in turn, beginning with the player on his extreme left.

Each player has three options (plus a fourth should his two cards be of equal rank). They are to:

Stand   This means that he is satisfied with his hand as it is, and does not wish to try to improve it. He will usually be satisfied with a total of 19, 20 or 21.

Draw   A player not happy with his count may ask the banker to deal him additional cards until he is. This is often done by tapping his cards and saying 'Hit me'. Thus 'to hit' has become a term meaning to draw a card. Should the player receive a card when drawing which takes his count over 21, he busts and loses his stake. The banker will collect his stake immediately and dispose of his cards.

Split   A player dealt two cards of the same rank (in this respect all cards which count ten are regarded as being of the same rank) may split them. He separates the two cards, which become the first cards of two separate hands. The player puts a second stake, equal to his original stake, on the second hand. The banker then deals him a second card to each hand, and each hand is then dealt with in turn, beginning with the one to the player's right. The player has the same choices with split hands as with any other hand (including the opportunity to split either hand further, should the second card dealt to it be of the same rank as the first) with one exception. Should he split a pair of Aces, the second card dealt to each hand completes it (unless it is another Ace, when he may split again). If splitting Aces, he cannot draw a third card to the hand. This means, in practice, that Aces in split hands count as eleven and not one. The count of a hand which does not contain an Ace, or which counts an Ace as one, is known as a 'hard' count, whereas a count in which an Ace is counted as eleven is a 'soft' count. A blackjack occurring in a split hand wins, of course, but is paid at the usual odds of 1–1 instead of the special blackjack odds of 3–2.

Double down   A player may double his stake and receive a third card face down. This completes the hand, and the card remains face down until the banker faces it when settling.

The optimum strategies for players are detailed in the table opposite.

When the banker has dealt with each player and, in the case of those who busted, collected their stakes and disposed of their cards, he exposes his face-down card. He has no options in playing his hand. If his total count is 17, 18, 19 or 20 he must stand, if it is 16 or fewer he must draw and continue to draw until it reaches 17 to 21, when he must stand. If while drawing his count exceeds 21, he busts and pays out to all players still in the game.

An Ace can still count as one or eleven for the banker but he has no control over it. For example, if his hand is A, 4 and if his third card is a 9, he then has a hard 14, counting Ace as one, and must draw again. On the other hand, if his third card was a 2, he would have a soft 17 and he must therefore stand on 17. He cannot regard his hand as a hard 7 and draw again, as he would do if he had the choice and all the players had counts of 18 or more.

When the banker stands, he pays all players with a higher count than him and collects the stakes of those with a lower count. Players who tie retain their stakes and neither win nor lose.

Strategy This book is not meant for professional gamblers who might spend their lives trying to beat the casino at Blackjack by sophisticated methods of card counting – logging the ranks of the cards played to assess which remain and betting accordingly – but as mathematicians have worked out the optimum play for all situations, it would be useful to include the methods here.

With best play, the casino edge (the percentage of the stakes it would expect to win over the long run) is low – less than 1%. The casino has the advantage, despite the player having all the options in the game, and a tie being a stand-off, with neither side winning. The casino's advantage cancels out all others: the banker plays second. When a player busts, he loses. When the banker busts, he loses only to those players who haven't already bust. In this respect a tie isn't a stand-off – if player and banker both bust, banker wins.

A player's main choice is whether to stand, be hit or double down. The accompanying table sets out what most accept as the best options.

Player's optimum play at Blackjack

	Player holds	*Dealer's face-up card*									
		2	**3**	**4**	**5**	**6**	**7**	**8**	**9**	**10**	**A**
	17	S	S	S	S	S	S	S	S	S	S
Hard	**16**	S	S	S	S	S	H	H	H	S	S
2-card	**15**	S	S	S	S	S	H	H	H	H	H
Total	**14**	S	S	S	S	S	H	H	H	H	H
	13	S	S	S	S	S	H	H	H	H	H
	12	H	H	S	S	S	H	H	H	H	H
	11	D	D	D	D	D	D	D	D	D	D
	10	D	D	D	D	D	D	D	D	H	H
	9	D	D	D	D	D	H	H	H	H	H
	19	S	S	S	S	S	S	S	S	S	S
Soft	**18**	S	S	S	S	S	S	H	H	H	H
2-card	**17**	D	D	D	D	D	H	H	H	H	H
total	**16**	H	H	H	H	D	H	H	H	H	H
	15	H	H	H	H	D	H	H	H	H	H
	14	H	H	H	H	D	H	H	H	H	H
	13	H	H	H	H	D	H	H	H	H	H

S = stand, H = hit, D = double down.

Note: always stand on hard hands of 17 or more and soft hands of 19 and 20.

A further choice confronts a player who holds a pair of cards of equal rank. The accompanying table is a consensus of expert opinion on whether he should split his pair:

Advisability of splitting pairs

Player's pair	Dealer's face-up card									
	2	3	4	5	6	7	8	9	10	A
A	S	S	S	S	S	S	S	S	S	S
10	X	X	X	X	X	X	X	X	X	X
9	S	S	S	S	S	X	X	X	X	X
8	S	S	S	S	S	S	S	X	X	S
7	S	S	S	S	S	S	X	X	X	X
6	S	S	S	S	S	X	X	X	X	X
5	X	X	X	X	X	X	X	X	X	X
4	X	X	X	X	X	X	X	X	X	X
3	S	S	S	S	S	S	X	X	X	X
2	S	S	S	S	S	S	X	X	X	X

S = split, X = do not split.

When it comes to the choice of whether or not to take insurance, the advice is incontestably 'no'. Insurance is really a bet. It is a bet that when the banker's face-up card is an Ace, his face-down card will be of a ten-count. Card-counting aside, the proportion of ten-counts in the pack is 16 to 36. The actual odds against a blackjack, therefore, are 9–4, while the odds offered by the casino are 2–1, a casino edge of over 7%. To be fair to casinos, however, the edge is possibly modest compared to that of real insurance companies charging premiums on policies for more everyday risks.

Variants
Casinos around the world might not operate the game exactly as described above. Variants which might be encountered include:

i)   Bankers will draw on soft 17. This will be a rule, and will be stated. Bankers should never have options, since they are playing against several players, and what might favour them against one player might disfavour them against another.

ii) Players' initial cards will be dealt face down. This does not affect the game.

iii) Doubling down might be restricted, say, to hands of a count of eleven only, or to ten and eleven, or nine, ten and eleven.

iv) Insurance will not be offered, or will be offered only to a player holding blackjack.

v)   Splitting pairs of 4, 5, or 10 will be barred.

vi) The banker will not deal a second card to himself until he has dealt with all the other hands and betting is completed.

All these variants except the last are harmless and tend to follow the optimum play for players. The last, like some of the others, was introduced by the Gaming Board of Great Britain to prevent collusion between the banker and a player or players. It means that players might double down when the banker's hand turns out to be a blackjack, and thereby lose stakes which otherwise would be saved. It gives the banker an extra advantage, and it also skews the tables of optimum play, making it inadvisable when the banker's first card is an Ace or ten-count to double down at all, or to split any pairs but Aces.

Black Maria

Black Maria is probably the most popular form of the Hearts family of games, and is played widely in the UK and the USA, while relations of it are also played in European countries.

Type	Trick-taking
Alternative names	Black Lady, Black Widow, Scabby Queen, Slippery Anne, Slippery Bitch
Players	Three; up to seven for variants
Special requirements	Pen and paper for scoring

Aim
To hold the lowest number of points at the end of the game, by avoiding winning tricks containing penalty cards (the ♠Q and all the hearts).

Cards
The standard pack of 52 cards is used, from which the ♣2 is removed, leaving 51 cards. The cards rank from the Ace (high) to 2 (low), and there is no trump suit.

Preparation
Any method may be used to determine the first dealer, the deal subsequently passing in rotation to the left. The dealer deals 17 cards face down to each player, one at a time, beginning with the player on his left.

Play
After looking at his cards, each player passes three cards, face down, to the player on his right. A player must not look at the cards received from the player to his left until his own cards have been passed on.

The game is a trick-taking game in which players must follow suit to the card led and may discard any card they like when unable to; see p383 for an explanation of tricks and trick-taking. The player to the dealer's left leads to the first trick and players play to the trick clockwise. The highest card played in the suit led wins the trick.

The object is to avoid taking in a trick any of the 14 penalty cards, which are the ♠Q (the Black Maria) which carries a penalty of 13 points, and any heart, each of which carries a penalty of one point. The tricks themselves are of no value. A winner of a trick takes the cards won, places them face down before him, and leads to the next trick. At the end of the deal players look at their cards won and total up their penalties, which are entered on a score-sheet. As a check, penalties should total 26 for each hand. Play continues to the point where at the end of a deal one player has passed 50 penalty points, when the player with the fewer points of the other two wins.

Example hand

The three players are dealt hands as follows:

Player A	♠ K, Q, 9, 2 ♥ Q, 10, 7, 2 ♣ 7, 6 ♦ Q, 10, 7, 5, 4, 3, 2
Player B	♠ A, 10, 8, 6, 5, 4 ♥ J, 9, 8, 6, 4 ♣ J, 9, 8, 3 ♦ 9, 8
Player C	♠ J, 7, 3 ♥ A, K, 5, 3 ♣ A, K, Q, 10, 5, 4 ♦ A, K, J, 6

Player A is the dealer, and Player B will lead to the first trick, after each player has passed on three cards to the player on his right.

Player A has an excellent hand. His diamonds look safe, his clubs relatively so. He passes on to Player C the ♠Q, but keeps ♠K on the grounds that as he plays after Player C he can play ♠K on any spade, provided Player C doesn't play the Queen. He also passes on ♥Q, 10 since these could be troublesome if hearts are led.

Player B also has quite a good hand. His spades look reasonably safe, but all his 9s and 8s look tricky. He passes to Player A the ♥J, 9 and the ♣J.

Player C has a bad hand and looks sure to collect many points. He passes on to Player B ♥A and ♦A, K.

The players' new hands are as illustrated opposite, and play proceeds as follows, with Player B leading:

Player A	Player B	Player C
♣ J	♣ 9	♣ 10
♦ 5	♦ A	♦ J
♣ 7	♣ 8	♣ A
♦ 4	♦ K	♦ 6
♠ K	♠ 4	♠ J
♣ 6	♣ 3	♣ 5
♦ 7	♦ 8	♠ Q

An unexpected and very welcome turn of events for Player C. Player B now has problems. His spades are suddenly very vulnerable, as he knows ♠3 and ♠2 can still be led against him, in which case he would win the tricks, and if they and ♠9 are in the same hand, he will pick up at least two hearts from the third players, who will not be able to follow suit with spades, so will be free to discard the hearts which he must hold. But if the ♠3 and ♠2 are split, his best lead could be ♠5,

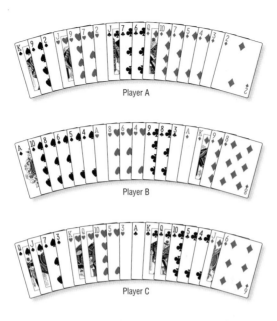

Player A

Player B

Player C

either to make an opponent win the trick with ♠7 or ♠9, or to himself win a trick comprising only spades, which he tries.

♠9	♠5	♠7
♠2	♠6	♠3

Player B's spades are now safe, but he can only lose the lead with hearts now – his opponents hold no more spades, and there is no point in leading ♦9 as he knows Player A has lower diamonds and Player C has none, and will play a heart. He must hope to lose the lead with ♥4 or ♥6. He therefore leads ♥4.

♥2	♥4	♥3
♥J	♥6	♥5
♥7	♥A	♥K
♥9	♥8	♥Q

Player C will now win the remaining tricks, which include his own ♥10. So at the end of the first deal, Player B has 19 points, Player C has 4 points and Player A has 3 points. Player C is delighted.

Player B's strategy should have been to lead spades at the beginning and continue at every opportunity. The likeliest outcome then is that Player B would have kept his score to four, and Player C would have collected 19.

Variants

More than three people can play (always playing for themselves and not as partners). Each must have the same number of cards, so for four players use the full pack of 52, for five remove the ♣2 and ♦2, and so on. More than seven players are not recommended, since this reduces the hands to six cards or fewer.

When passing on cards after the deal, some players prefer to pass on cards to the left rather than to the right. This allows each player to lead through his left-hand opponent's weakness, but is regarded as less skilful. Some players prefer to make it illegal to pass on penalty cards, but there seems little merit to this.

Some players like to prohibit the lead of hearts early in the game, since this is a simple option for players holding low hearts to get some of the penalty cards out of the way early. The preferred method is to ban the lead of a heart before one has been played as a penalty card to a lead of another suit. Another method is to disallow the lead of a heart until the fourth round of play.

Some players insist that when a player cannot follow suit he must play a penalty card (the ♠Q if he holds it) rather than a harmless card. This is to prevent favouritism, ie players penalizing one opponent rather than another. However, this sometimes forces a player who cannot follow suit to lose the game. For example, Player B has the second-highest number of points, holds the ♠Q and cannot follow suit. He is forced to play ♠Q. The trick is won by Player A, who already had the highest number of points and now has more than 50, so the game ends. Player C, who held fewer points than either Player A or Player B at the start, wins the game. Player B has been forced to play ♠Q to his own disadvantage, and hence this variant is not recommended.

Many variations in the values and identities of penalty cards are used by players, mainly to compensate for the wide disparity between the penalties for ♠Q (13 points) and the hearts (1 point each). Thus penalty values are sometimes given to the ♠A and ♠K (usually 7 and 10 points respectively). Sometimes the ♥Q is given a penalty value of 13 points to equal the ♠Q (in this instance, the ♥Q is known as the Pink Lady). Other players like to give the top hearts more value than the others, for example Ace 5, King 4, Queen 3 and Jack 2 points. Some players give a plus value for capturing the ♦10.

For players who like more action than the simple 13 points for ♠Q and one point each for hearts, the game Omnibus Hearts, which incorporates a sensible selection of these scoring variations, is recommended.

Hitting the Moon This is a variation to the scoring which is widely played and can be recommended. A player who takes all the penalty cards, instead of earning a huge penalty, reduces his total score to zero. This gives a player who is given a very bad hand the chance to turn his bad luck to advantage. If a player decides to try hitting the moon, he must do it as surreptitiously as possible so that when his opponents realize his aim it might be too late to prevent it. A player might decide to try hitting the moon before he passes three cards on after the deal. A good holding of hearts, headed perhaps by A, K, Q, the possession of ♠A, K, Q, to be certain of the ♠Q, and a long suit headed by A, K, Q with which to keep the lead are all useful.

Brag

Brag is one of the oldest card games, although the way it is played has changed radically over the centuries. Games of cards on which players bet on the value of the hands they hold have been played everywhere in the world, with the 16th-century Italian game of Primiera often cited as the root from which grew both Brag and Poker. Primero, as it was known in England, is mentioned by Shakespeare as having been played by Henry VIII, and was a favourite of Elizabeth I. It is related to Poker, which in the past few years has overtaken it completely.

The game described, known as Modern Brag, is a version that is played popularly today. The classical game, now practically extinct, is described here as a variant.

Type	Gambling
Alternative names	None
Players	Any reasonable number; four to eight is best
Special requirements	Chips or coins for staking

Aim
To hold a better hand than that of the other players.

Cards
The standard pack of 52 cards is used, the cards ranking from Ace (high) to 2 (low). Ace can also rank low in the sequence A, 2, 3, although the sequence itself ranks high.

Preparation
Minimum and maximum stakes must be agreed beforehand. The maximum should be for each raise, and also for the total to be staked by a player on any one hand. It is recommended that all players begin with an equal bank, and that a game ends when one player loses his entire bank (another game can be started between those who wish to carry on). Otherwise a time should be agreed for stopping, to prevent bad feeling when losers want to carry on to recoup their losses while winners want to get to bed.

All players should deal an equal number of times. It should also be agreed as to whether the cards should be shuffled between deals and, if so, whether it should be a light shuffle or a thorough shuffle. Some prefer to shuffle only when a 'prial' appears. A light shuffle is recommended.

The first dealer can be determined by any acceptable method, and the deal passes to the left after each hand.

Play

The dealer places an 'ante' to the table before him. This is a compulsory bet, usually of the minimum stake. He then deals three cards face down to each player. The remainder of the cards are placed face up to the centre of the table.

Players look at their cards. The object is to hold the best hand after the 'showdown', when the hands are exposed at the end of the deal (see Scoring, below).

The eldest hand (the player to the dealer's left) now has three options: to drop out, by stacking his cards face up on the pile; to 'stay', by putting on the table in front of him a stake equal to the ante; or to 'raise', which is done by putting in a stake equal to the ante, plus another. Thus, if the ante is one unit, he could announce 'stay for one and raise by three', putting in four units in all.

Subsequently all players in their turn must either drop out, stay, in which case they put in a stake equal to the current level of the stake, or raise, as described.

When the turn to bet comes round again to a player who has already bet, that player again has the same options: to drop out; to stay, by adding to his stake enough to bring it to the new level if it has risen since the last bet; or to raise.

A deal can end in one of four ways:

i) all players can drop out except one, who wins and collects the total stake

ii) if two players remain in, either can 'call' the other, by equalizing the stake and announcing 'I'll see you', upon which the player called exposes his hand and wins or loses accordingly (the caller, if the loser, can concede without exposing his own hand if he wishes)

iii) if all players remaining in have equal stakes and have declined the opportunity to raise, in which case they expose their hands

iv) if the total staked by each player has reached the maximum agreed beforehand, when all hands are exposed

When the winner has collected all the stakes on the table, and the final hands have been returned face up to the stack, the next deal takes place.

If no players bet, ie all drop out on the first round, the dealer retrieves his ante and an amount equivalent to the ante from all the other players.

Scoring The classes of hand, in ranking order, and the probability of their being dealt, are shown in the table that follows.

Among the classes of hand, a prial of 3s ranks highest, then Aces down to 2s.

Among running flushes and runs, A, 2, 3 ranks highest, then A, K, Q, followed by K, Q, J down to 4, 3, 2.

Among equal pairs, the unmatched card decides the ranking.

Among high cards, if the highest card of two or more hands is equal, the next highest decides, if equal the third highest.

There can be ties in all classes except prials.

Classes of hands in Modern Brag, in ranking order

Name	Description	Possible hands	Probability of being dealt
Prial	Three of the same rank (for example 6, 6, 6)	52	0.24%
Running flush	Three in sequence of the same suit (for example ♦ 7, 8, 9)	48	0.22%
Run	Three in sequence (for example 4, 5, 6)	720	3.27%
Flush	Three of the same suit (for example ♥ A, 4, 2)	1,096	4.96%
Pair	Two of the same rank plus another (for example J, J, 3)	3,744	16.94%
High card	None of the above	16,440	74.39%

There is an anomaly in the rankings, since a running flush is slightly less likely to be dealt than the higher ranking prial. That a run ranks higher than a flush, the opposite to the case in Poker, is not an anomaly; the probability of its occurring is different due to the hands being of a different number of cards.

Variants

Blind betting Much interest is added to the version described above when blind betting is allowed. Any player may bet without looking at his cards (which should not even be touched), which entitles him to stake only half of the stake contributed by 'open' players (ie those who look at their hands). If the first player to bet bets blind, then subsequent blind betters must equal the stake in order to stay; an open better must double it to stay. If the first better bets open, then a subsequent blind better cannot bet more than half the stake of the open better. Subsequently, an open better must increase his stake to that of the previous open better to stay, or can raise or drop out by stacking his cards. A blind better who on his turn wishes to continue betting blind must increase his stake to that of the previous blind better, or half that of the previous open better, to stay, or may raise by no more than half the maximum stake agreed before the game. He has another option, however: he may look at his cards. He can then either drop out, or remain in as an open better, in which case he must raise his stake to that of other open betters in order to stay.

There is a showdown when all open betters have equalized their stakes with each other, and all blind betters have done likewise, and all betters have declined in turn the opportunity to raise. Alternatively, the rule described above – that when only two players remain, one can see the other – applies only if both are open players. If one is open and the other blind, there is a rule that 'you cannot see a blind man', so if the blind player is so inclined, he can continue raising and forcing the open player to double his raises until the maximum stake is reached. The rule about not being able to see a blind man can be relaxed if the last two betters are both blind, when it can be permitted that one can see the other.

In all cases, of course, the winner collects all stakes on the table, including those of players who drop out. If all players drop out except a blind player, who thus wins without the need to expose his hand, he is allowed to keep the same hand unexposed, for the next deal, provided his first bet is a blind bet. He is still dealt a hand for the next deal, which is immediately stacked, because superstitious players do not like the sequence of hands to be disturbed.

While Brag players can claim the game allows a modicum of skill insofar as the value of a hand, and its likelihood of winning, must be judged, blind betters eliminate even that, and the game for them becomes a gamble pure and simple.

Wild cards In all forms of Modern Brag, wild cards (ie cards which can represent any card the holder wishes) can be used. Usually, the black 2s are chosen, but some players like all 2s to be wild. The object is to obtain more higher-value hands, but purists would say they cheapen the hands and find them unappealing.

Seven-card Brag Seven-card Brag lacks the progressive betting of Modern Brag, but uses the same classes of hands. Up to seven may play with the standard pack. Each player, including the dealer, antes an agreed stake to the centre of the table. Seven cards are dealt to each player, from which the player makes the two best Brag hands possible, discarding the seventh card face down. When all have completed their hands, each player exposes his better hand, and the holder of the best hand is decided. All players then expose their second hands, and if the best hand is held by the same player, he wins all the stakes. If, however, the two hands are won by different players, nobody wins, the pool of stakes remains on the table, and each player adds a further stake to it. The cards are then shuffled and re-dealt by the player to the left of the dealer. The adding to the pool increases with each round in which it isn't won, until finally a player wins both hands and scoops the lot.

It is not compulsory to make your best hand from the seven cards, and often advisable not to. Suppose a player is dealt the seven cards in the illustration above. The best possible hand is a prial of Jacks, with an excellent chance of winning, but the second hand, a pair of 10s, is unlikely to win. If, on the other hand, the first hand was chosen as ♣Q, J, 10, it would have a reasonable chance of winning, and if it did the second hand of ♥J, 10, 9 is practically certain to win, too, so the second choice of hands would be the more sound.

Nine-card Brag In Nine-card Brag (for which five players is the maximum), each player is dealt nine cards from which he makes three Brag hands. The mechanics of the game are the same as for Seven-card Brag above, ie to win a player must win all three hands, otherwise all players add another stake to the pool and the cards are re-dealt.

Simple Brag A version of Brag played in the UK but hardly noticed in the text books does not involve raising or the convention of a showdown when stakes are equalized. It is a 'freeze-out' game, in the respect that it cannot end until only two players are left in or a limit reached. Before play begins it is best to agree a limit beyond which a single player's stakes on a hand cannot rise. If the limit is reached and all players stakes are equalized, there is a showdown. There is a uniform stake, which is agreed beforehand, and a maximum number of times which a player may stake on one hand – say 20, 40, 100, or whatever.

Each player deals in turn, the deal rotating to the left, with any acceptable method used to decide the first dealer. Three cards are dealt face down to each player, and the remaining cards placed face down to the dealer's left. As players drop out, their cards are added face down to the pile.

Each player puts the standard stake into a pool as an ante, and the eldest hand has the first opportunity to bet. The hands are valued as for the game of Modern Brag above. Each player in turn must either drop out or add the standard stake to the pool, and this continues round the table for as many rounds as is necessary. There is no raising. Every time a player's turn to bet comes round, the player either adds the uniform stake to the pool or drops out. Only when just two players are left in the game may either bring the game to an end by putting in his stake and announcing 'I'll see you', whereupon his opponent shows his hand. If the hand exposed is the better hand, the first player can concede without the need to show his own hand, if he wishes. If the exposed hand is the weaker, then the winning hand must also be exposed to prove it is the better. If the game ends because the staking limit has been reached, all players still playing equalize their stakes and all show their hands, the winner taking the whole pool. If there is a tie the pool is shared among the winners.

Classical Brag Because this is the version of the game played in Great Britain in the 18th century it often takes precedence in books, but it would be hard to find it played nowadays.

The main differences from the game described above lie in the classes of hands and the fact that three wild cards, called 'braggers', are used. The braggers, of equal status, are ♦A, ♣J, ♦9, and they can be used as whatever card the holder wishes. If used as a card of their own rank they cease to be regarded as braggers.

Runs and flushes are not considered as classes of hand, so suits have no significance. There are only three recognized classes, as follows, in ranking order:

Pair-royal   Three cards of the same rank

Pair   Two cards of the same rank with an unmatched card

High card   None of the above

The highest pair-royal (from which derives the word 'prial', used in Modern Brag) is A, A, A and the lowest 2, 2, 2. The highest pair is A, A, the lowest 2, 2.

A natural pair-royal (one without a bragger) beats a pair-royal with one bragger, which beats a pair-royal with two, and a natural pair beats a pair with a bragger.

With equal pairs, the rank of the unmatched card determines precedence. If the high card in high-card hands is equal, the rank of the second card, or if also equal the third, decides precedence.

Between two hands exactly equal, that held by the player nearest the dealer's left wins. The betting and raising are as for Modern Brag.

Three-stake Brag In this variant of Classical Brag, each player places three stakes, of an agreed amount, before him on the table. These stakes are, in effect, the stakes for three separate games to be played with the same hands.

The dealer deals three cards to each player, as usual, but this time the third card is dealt face up. The rank of this card determines the winner of the first stake, the highest face-up card being the winner. For this round, the braggers ($\blacklozenge$A, $\clubsuit$J, $\blacklozenge$9) represent their actual ranks. If two or more players tie with turned-up cards of equal rank, the one nearest the dealer's left wins the stakes (the dealer being regarded as farthest from his left).

The second stake is decided by the game of Brag as described, with the three braggers counting as wild cards. The initial stake put in by each player is regarded as a bet, and beginning with the eldest hand, each player in turn drops out, stays or raises, and so on as usual, the eventual winner taking all the stakes bet for this round.

Players then place their hands face up before them to decide the winner of the third stake. Braggers once again take their natural value. The object is to achieve a total nearest to 31 with the cards, with or without a draw, with Aces counting eleven, court cards ten and other cards their pip value. Each player can see, with all the cards exposed, the total to beat.

Beginning with the eldest hand, each player can draw one or more cards, passed by the dealer, to get his total nearer to 31. If his total goes over 31, he 'busts' and loses. He can stop when he likes. If two or more hands are equal, the player nearest to the dealer's left wins (it follows that if a player reaches 31 exactly he must win). Note that if a player holds an original hand of three Aces, or two Aces with a court card or a 10, he will have a count of 32 or 33. This is not counted as having 'bust', but of being one or two away from 31, and in the final reckoning will equal a hand of 30 or 29 respectively.

American Brag American Brag was very popular in the USA in the 19th century and is a variant of Classical Brag, except that instead of the braggers being $\blacklozenge$A, $\clubsuit$J and $\blacklozenge$9, all Jacks and all Nines are braggers. All braggers are considered equal. A peculiarity is that a hand which includes braggers is considered better than a hand of the same class with fewer or no braggers. The best hand is therefore a hand of three braggers. The use of eight braggers rather than three makes the appearance of pairs-royal and pairs much more frequent, of course.

Bridge

Bridge developed from what was once regarded as the English national card game, Whist. It is often suggested, though it is far from certain, that the name came from a Russian game called Biritch, after a pamphlet was published in London in 1886 entitled *Biritch, or Russian Whist*. The main difference from Whist was that the dealer was entitled to name the trump suit, rather than it being decided by turning a card. Auction Bridge, in which all players could bid to name the trump suit, began to be played about 1904.

The development which made the game what it is today was the complex scoring system, which introduced bonus scores and the concept of vulnerability. Harold S Vanderbilt, a New York millionaire, and some friends perfected this on a famous cruise in 1925–6 and by the end of the decade their game was widely played in New York and London clubs. Largely through the writings in the 1930s of a prominent player, Ely Culbertson, the game took off and became the best-known and most-played card game in the world, although it has been overtaken lately by Poker.

When Bridge is discussed these days the game referred to is almost always Contract Bridge, which is the game described here (in particular, Rubber Bridge).

Type	Trick-taking
Alternative names	None
Players	Four, playing in partnerships of two
Special requirements	Usually two packs of cards, although one will suffice; pen and paper for scoring, although printed score-sheets are sold in pads at some games shops and in some stationers

Aim

The object of each partnership in Rubber Bridge is to score more points than their opponents in the course of a 'rubber'. To win a rubber a side must win two 'games', so a rubber might consist of three games (and be won 2–1) or two games (2–0). A game might consist of one deal or several (rarely more than four or five) according to how the scoring develops.

(Note: Rubber Bridge is the game played casually at home by four players. In organized clubs, Duplicate Bridge might be played. The principles are the same, but the same hands are played by each competing team, and there are refinements in the scoring. Most newspaper and magazine articles refer to Duplicate Bridge, as this facilitates easy comparisons in the way hands are played.)

Cards

The standard pack of 52 cards is used, but it is usual to play with two packs, which need not be of the same design, as they are used separately. While one pack is being dealt, the other is being shuffled. The cards rank from Ace (high) to 2 (low). The suits are also ranked in the order spades (highest), hearts, diamonds, clubs (lowest). Spades and hearts are 'major' suits, and diamonds and clubs 'minor' suits.

Preparation

Unless partnerships are agreed beforehand (for example one couple challenges another) partners are decided by spreading the pack face down on the table and each player drawing a card. The players with the two highest cards (Ace high, 2 low) become partners, and the higher of the two is the first dealer. If two or more players draw cards of the same rank, then the suit decides precedence between them, in the order spades, hearts, diamonds, clubs. Partners sit opposite each other. It should be decided which player is to keep the score.

There are two distinct parts to Bridge. The first is an 'auction' in which each player in turn may make a 'bid'; a bid is an offer for that player's partnership to make a certain number of tricks, which must be seven or more, with the trump suit of their choice. The auction continues until a bid is made which the opposition does not wish to exceed, whereupon that bid becomes the 'contract'.

The play of the cards then takes place, in which the contracting side attempts to make the number of tricks promised, and their opponents, called the 'defenders', attempt to prevent them. Points are scored according to the extent of the success or failure of the contracting side to make its contract. There is also a number of bonus points to be made (see Scoring, below).

Dealing The player to the dealer's left shuffles the pack, which is then cut by the player on the dealer's right. The dealer then deals the cards one at a time to each player, beginning with the player to his left, so that each has 13 cards. While he is dealing, his partner shuffles the second pack ready for the next deal, and this arrangement continues for each deal.

Auction During the auction, each player in turn to the left, beginning with the dealer, makes a 'call'. There are four options: to pass, to bid, to double or to redouble. A player who passes is not prevented from making any of the other calls if his turn comes round again.

Pass   A player who does not wish to bid, ie to contract to make a certain number of tricks, may pass. This is usually indicated by the player saying 'no bid', but 'no' or 'pass' are acceptable.

Bid   By making a bid a player undertakes to make the majority of the tricks with a named trump suit, or with no trumps. To make a bid he states the number of tricks in excess of six he intends to make and the trump suit. The suits rank in the order given above, with a contract in no-trumps ranking above spades. The lowest bid available is therefore 'one club' (an offer to make seven tricks with clubs as trumps). This is followed by 'one diamond', 'one heart', 'one spade', 'one no-trump', 'two clubs' and so on up to 'seven no-trumps'. Once a bid has been made, any subsequent bid must be in a higher-ranking suit or for a greater number of tricks.

Double   Rather than bid himself, a player on his turn may double the preceding bid, if it were made by an opponent. This does not change the contract, which will still be played by the opponents, but will increase the points at stake. It does not bring the bidding to a halt, and successive players of either side may bid on provided the new bid is higher than the previous bid, whether it were doubled or not. A double applies only to the opponents' last bid, and not to any subsequent bids which might be made, although they can be doubled in their turn. A player cannot double a bid made by his partner.

Redouble When a bid is doubled, a player on the side making the bid may redouble, which has the effect of increasing still further the points at stake. As with a double, a redouble does not affect the level required for a subsequent bid, nor does it apply to any such bid.

The auction ends when three players have passed consecutively, the last bid becoming the contract. The player on the contracting side who first named the trump suit becomes the 'declarer'. (Note: he is not necessarily the player who made the final bid.)

It is possible that no player will wish to bid, and all will pass, in which case the hand is abandoned and the deal passes to the left.

Hundreds of books have been written about bidding at Bridge, and the subject is dealt with more fully under the heading Bidding strategy, later.

Play

When the bidding is completed, the playing of the tricks begins and the declarer tries to make his contract. The 'opening lead' is made by the player to the declarer's left. At this stage the declarer's partner lays his hand face up on the table with the cards arranged in columns by suit, with the trump suit to his right (which is the dealer's left), as illustrated below. This hand is known as the 'dummy'. Declarer's partner takes no part in the play of the hand, although he may warn the declarer should he be about to lead from the wrong hand. The declarer plays both his hand and the dummy. To avoid the need to continually stretch across the table he may call a card from dummy, ie instruct his partner to play a specified card, but he must name the card – the partner has no part to play in its choice.

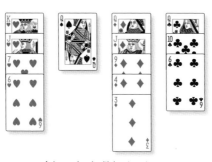

A dummy hand, with hearts as trumps

The usual rules of trick-taking games apply; see p383 for an explanation of tricks and trick-taking. Players must follow suit to the card led when able, and if unable they may play a trump or discard. The trick is won by the highest trump it contains, or if there is none, the highest card of the suit led.

The winner of a trick leads to the next trick, and if the winning card came from dummy the next lead must too.

One member of each side keeps the tricks won by his side. Tricks won should be squared up and kept face down overlapping each other so that it is clear at a glance how many there are. With the exception that a player may look at the last trick won provided his side has not yet played to the next trick, tricks may not be looked at during play. When all 13 tricks have been played, the score is calculated and entered on the score-sheet.

Scoring A blank score-sheet from a pad is shown below. There is room on this sheet for a whole rubber to be scored. Players drawing their own score-sheets need only two columns, headed 'we/they' or 'us/them', with a line dividing the columns across the middle. The most important thing is the line which divides each column in two. This is because certain scores are entered 'below the line', and others 'above the line'.

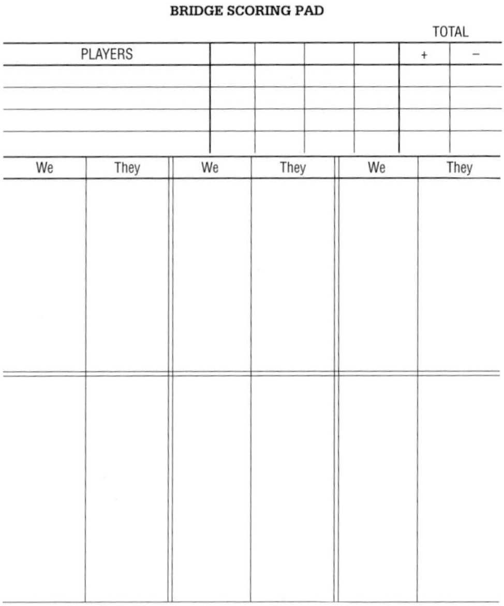

BRIDGE SCORING PAD

When a declarer makes his contract, the score for it is entered below the line. All other scores, including those made by the opponents when the declarer fails to make his contract, are entered above the line.

The significance is that only the scores entered below the line count towards the winning of a game. Other scores count in the final reckoning, of course, but the importance of winning games is that the first to win two games wins the rubber, which earns a large bonus.

To win a game, a partnership must score 100 points below the line. This can be done in one hand, but some contracts are worth less than 100 points (for example a contract of two hearts, written 2♥, is worth only 60 points). A score less than 100 is entered below the line, and is known as a 'part-score'. A partnership with a part-score must obviously land another contract to win the game.

When a partnership wins a game a fresh line is drawn below the scores on the score-sheet, so that each side begins the next game with nothing below the line.

As stated, the object is to win two games to win the rubber. A side which wins a game is said to be 'vulnerable' (a term suggested to Vanderbilt on his cruise by another passenger, and thought to be from another game). A vulnerable side is subject to higher penalties and bonus scores on subsequent contracts. If a rubber goes to a third and deciding game, both sides are vulnerable, of course.

Scores in Bridge

When a side makes its contract exactly it scores (below the line):

in no-trumps	40 points for the first trick and 30 points for each subsequent trick
in spades and hearts	30 points for each trick
in diamonds and clubs	20 points for each trick

Doubling and redoubling
The above points are doubled if the contract has been doubled, and quadrupled if it has been redoubled.

When a side makes its contract with more tricks than is contracted for (called 'overtricks') it scores for each overtrick (above the line):

if undoubled	the basic value for each trick as listed above
if doubled	100 points for each overtrick if not vulnerable; 200 points for each overtrick if vulnerable
if redoubled	200 points for each overtrick if not vulnerable; 400 points for each overtrick if vulnerable

When a side fails to make its contract, the opponents score (above the line):

if undoubled	for each trick short of the contract (called an 'undertrick'), 50 points if the contracting side is not vulnerable; 100 points if the contracting side is vulnerable
if doubled	100 points for the first trick and 200 points for each subsequent trick if the contracting side is not vulnerable; 200 points for the first trick and 300 points for each subsequent trick if the contracting side is vulnerable
if redoubled	200 points for the first trick and 400 points for each subsequent trick if the contracting side is not vulnerable; 400 points for the first trick and 600 points for each subsequent trick if the contracting side is vulnerable

There are bonus scores as follows (all entered above the line):

for bidding and making a contract of seven (ie making all 13 tricks, called a 'grand slam')	1,000 points if not vulnerable; 1,500 points if vulnerable
for bidding and making a contract of six (ie making twelve tricks, called a 'small slam')	500 points if not vulnerable; 750 points if vulnerable
if either partner holds all four Aces in a no-trump contract, or all five honours (A, K, Q, J, 10 of trumps) in a suit contract	150 points
if either partner holds four of the five honours (A, K, Q, J, 10 of trumps) in a suit contract	100 points
for making a doubled contract	50 points
and for making a redoubled contract	100 points (for the 'insult', some players say)

The side which wins a rubber scores (above the line):

if it wins in two straight games	700 points
if it wins in three games	500 points

Modern players often ignore the bonus for holding all four Aces in a no-trump contract or all five honours in a suit contract, and for holding four of the five honours in a suit contract, considering them somewhat archaic, since a side lucky enough to have been dealt such good cards hardly deserves an additional bonus. When these bonuses are allowed, it is best to claim them at the end of the hand, since it is pointless to reveal your hand before the play. (In the unlikely event that one of the defenders can claim these bonuses, they can only claim them at the end of the hand, as to do so before would give unfair information to their partner.)

General view and notation Bridge is a game in which a statement of the mechanics of the game is not quite sufficient to allow new players to get started, so further description is required. It is usual in articles and books for the four players to be known by the points of the compass, ie South, East, North and West. A hand of Bridge, with its bidding, is set out opposite.

The illustrated hand that follows states that neither side is vulnerable, and that East is the dealer (this could be deduced anyway by the fact that the bidding table shows East has called first, and declined to bid). South 'opened the bidding' with a bid of 1♠, which West 'overcalled' with a bid of 2♥. North, who has a poor hand, and cannot support his partner's bid, passes. East, who has good hearts to support his partner's suit, 'raises' his partner's bid to 4♥. He did this, rather than bid 3♥, since if his side can make 4♥ (ie take ten tricks with hearts as trumps, which they should), he and his partner will score 120 points (30 per trick above six) which will be entered below the line. This is sufficient to give his side the first game of the rubber. Had he bid 3♥, a contract worth 90 points and therefore not enough for game, he would be forcing his partner, West, to decide whether or not to bid 4♥, without giving West any indication of the strength of his own hand.

Dealer East, no side vulnerable

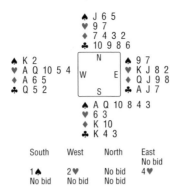

```
              ♠ J 6 5
              ♥ 9 7
              ♦ 7 4 3 2
              ♣ 10 9 8 6
                    N
♠ K 2                        ♠ 9 7
♥ A Q 10 5 4   W      E      ♥ K J 8 2
♦ A 6 5                      ♦ Q J 9 8
♣ Q 5 2              S       ♣ A J 7
              ♠ A Q 10 8 4 3
              ♥ 6 3
              ♦ K 10
              ♣ K 4 3
```

South	West	North	East
			No bid
1♠	2♥	No bid	4♥
No bid	No bid	No bid	

This is a simple hand, but newcomers to the game will wonder how the East–West partnership so readily found themselves in the correct contract. The majority of books about Bridge concentrate on bidding and bidding methods and over the years complicated systems of bidding have been developed. All modern players use a system, and the hardest task for a learner is to grasp the niceties of bidding.

Bidding strategy The aim of bidding is for a partnership to reach the best contract. There are no restrictions to what a player may bid, except that each bid must be superior to the previous one. Bidding can be looked upon as a conversation between partners in which they pass each other information about their hands. At the same time they listen to the opponents' bids and gather information from that. The difficult part is that this must be done with the use of around 16 words only: the numbers one to seven, the names of all the four suits, and the phrases 'no trumps', 'no bid', 'double' and redouble'. No other way of passing information, by demeanour, gesture, signals, sighs, inflections in the voice or phrases like 'I'll try a dodgy one no-trump', are allowed. That is cheating.

However, systems have been devised over the years to enlarge this vocabulary by giving certain bids specific meanings. There are many systems of bidding, and they get refined all the time. Players can invent their own systems. They are not meant to be secret systems and players can ask opponents what system they use and what is meant by certain bids. In practice, most players in the UK use versions of the 'Acol' system, which was named after a road in London where the system was developed in a Bridge club in 1934. The recommendations in this section are based upon it, as being suitable for a beginner. They concentrate particularly on the initial stages of an auction to give the beginner the idea of what the players are trying to achieve in the bidding, without attempting to cover every eventuality that might arise as the bidding progresses.

The special bids mentioned are called 'artificial' or 'conventional' bids, as opposed to 'natural' bids. If a player's hand includes a lot of spades, and he makes a bid in spades, he is making a natural bid. However, if he bids 2♣, he may not hold a single club in his hand (as will be explained later); this bid is a conventional one and conveys a special meaning.

The obvious drawback to bidding artificially is that each partner must be sure what each bid means. Even expert players occasionally misunderstand bids. The result can be spectacularly bad. The first requirement in bidding is not to mislead your partner.

The first thing to do when picking up your hand is to evaluate it, and a basic universal method for this is known as the 'Work count', after Milton Work, a player who publicized it. Also known as the 'point count', it gives each Ace in the hand a value of four, each King three, each Queen two and each Jack one. It is very crude but has stood the test of time. Thus there are 40 'high-card points' in a pack of cards and a hand containing more than ten is above average.

Apart from high cards, the shape of a hand, ie the number of cards in each suit, is also important. This is called the 'distribution'. The most common distribution is to have the suits split 4–4–3–2, which occurs just over 20% of the time. This is called an 'even', 'flat' or 'balanced' hand. A hand of 4–3–3–3 is even more balanced, but slightly less common. An 'unbalanced' hand is one with at least six cards in one suit or two suits of five or more cards. A long suit of trumps, of course, guarantees a good haul of tricks. And conversely a 'void' (no cards in a suit) and a 'singleton' (one card only) are also valuable as they may provide the opportunity to win tricks by trumping when cards from that suit are led. Some players add points to their hand for unbalanced distribution, but for simplicity we will stick to the point count only for evaluating hands, with the proviso that we know that not all twelve-point hands, say, are of equal value. The distribution, and how the points are made up, will distinguish between a 'good' twelve-pointer, and a bad one.

Evaluating the hand is most crucial when it comes to deciding whether to 'open the bidding', ie to be the first player to make a bid. Thirteen points is considered the requirement to open, although with good distribution this can be shaded down to twelve, or exceptionally eleven. Remember that if you open the bidding and your partner becomes declarer, he will expect the dummy you reveal to contain at least 13 high-card points. If it has only eleven, there must be compensation elsewhere, such as an unusually long suit, which might yield a few tricks.

It is as well to bear in mind that to get a game in one hand, you need to score 100 points, which represents making a contract of 3NT (100 points), 4♠ or 4♥ (120 points) or 5♦ or 5♣ (100 points), or a contract of a lesser amount which has been doubled. A rough guide of the high-card points needed in the combined hands to make these contracts (nothing is guaranteed, of course) is 25 for a contract in no-trumps, 25 with eight or more trumps for a major-suit contract, and 28 with eight or more trumps for a minor-suit contract. So if you open with a bid of, say, 1♥, your partner will assume you have at least 13 points and four, perhaps five hearts. Should he hold 12 points or more and four hearts (or three high ones), he will consider that you probably have the values for a game and might bid 4♥.

Opening bids of one in a suit The four hands in the following illustration are all good examples of hands on which to open with a bid of one.

Hand A is a 13-pointer with a good spade suit and useful hearts. Open 1♠.

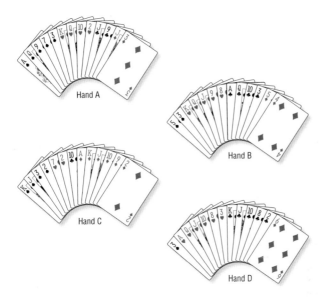

Hand B is a 12-pointer with five good hearts and tricks in clubs which just justifies an opening of 1♥.

Hand C is another 12-pointer with six good diamonds and support for anything your partner might have in spades, and is worth a bid of 1♦.

Hand D is only an 11-pointer but is such a good two-suiter that you should open with 1♥.

Generally speaking, you should open one of a suit with a point count of around 13–19, although distribution might encourage opening with 11 or 12 points. You should name your longest suit irrespective of whether or not it is richest in high cards.

Opening bids of two in a suit An opening bid of two in a suit (excluding 2♣, which is a special case) shows a very strong hand with at least six cards in the suit named, including high cards, and 20–22 points or the ability to take eight tricks. It tells your partner that provided he has five or six points, with a little support in your suit, you should be able to make the game. You need your partner to tell you his strongest suit, which should allow you to judge whether to bid game or not. Many players regard an opening of two in a suit to be 'forcing', which means that the partner must bid, even with no high-card points, to ensure that you get another chance to bid yourself. This is a point you and partner must agree to beforehand.

A bid of 2♣, as mentioned before, is a conventional bid, and indicates a very powerful hand of 23 points or more, or at the minimum 20 points with a strong suit and excellent distribution. It says nothing of your strongest suit (one might be very weak in clubs) so your partner must respond, to give you the chance to bid in your strongest suit.

Hand A

Hand B

Hand C

Hand D

The hands in the illustration above are suitable for an opening bid of two of a suit.

Hand A has 19 high-card points and a very powerful seven-card spade suit. You can almost guarantee nine tricks yourself with spades as trumps so you need your partner to contribute only one for you to make a game. You should open 2♠.

Hand B has a mere 16 points, but with eight tricks in hearts virtually guaranteed you should open 2♥.

Hand C has 21 points and is worth of bid of 2♦ even though a game in diamonds, a minor suit, requires making 11 tricks and there are two heart losers. Your partner's responses to the bid and your following bid will decide whether you can proceed to game.

Hand D is a typical 2♣ opening; with 23 points and two good suits it needs little from your partner to guarantee game.

Opening bids of three in a suit Contrary to what one might expect, an opening bid of three in a suit is an indication of weakness not strength. It is called a 'pre-emptive' bid, and is designed to restrict the opponents by taking the bidding high before they have the chance to bid themselves. It is used when you assume the opponents have the stronger hands, but you are strong enough in one suit to bid it without too much risk to your side.

Bridge

An example of a good hand for a pre-emptive bid is shown above. You are the dealer and have a mere six points, and unless your partner has a good hand it is likely that your opponents have enough for a game in hearts or spades. You would do well to open 3♦. It means the opposition has to start bidding at the level of 3♥ or more. They might go wrong or they might miss out altogether. If you end up as declarer in 3♦, you should make six tricks yourself, so cannot go down by more than three tricks. And if your partner cannot make a trick or two it suggests that the opposition have missed out on an easy game which will make the 'sacrifice' worthwhile. However, beware making a pre-emptive bid when vulnerable, as of course failing to make a contract when vulnerable and doubled can be expensive. Also, realize that there is limited value in a pre-emptive bid when the opponents have already bid, and that it is pointless to pre-empt in fourth position after three passes. You might as well pass and hope for a better hand next time.

Opening bids of four or five in a suit Opening bids of four and five are also pre-emptive, and are made with the same sort of hand as a pre-empt of three, but with a stronger suit. If you are not vulnerable and can make seven or eight tricks, you can bid at the four level, making things very difficult for your opponents. A good example is shown below.

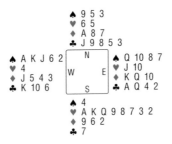

South, the dealer, pre-empts with 4♥. West has 12 points, but will he be brave enough to bid 4♠? Probably not, and nor will East after his partner has passed. South will go one down in his contract, which, even if he were doubled, will cost only 100 points, while East–West have missed out on a game in spades. Had South pre-empted with 3♥, West might well have bid 3♠ and East might have raised him to 4♠.

No-trump openings To open the bidding with a bid of one no-trump (conventionally written 1NT), you need a strong balanced hand, ie a hand where the suits are divided 4–3–3–3, 4–4–3–2 or 5–3–3–2, containing 16–18 points. You need a 'guard', or near-guard, in each suit. A guard is a card that prevents an opponent picking up several tricks with a long suit. An Ace is the best guard, and a King, Queen holding is the next best, since an opponent can make only the Ace before giving you the lead. A King with another card, or preferably two, is a near-guard, as it will win the second trick if the Ace is played first. If the hand contains a doubleton (a suit of two cards only) then one card must be an Ace or King.

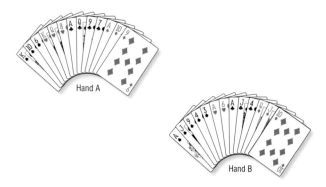

The illustration above shows two hands on which a 1NT bid is best.

Hand A is a perfectly balanced hand of 18 points, while Hand B, although less balanced and of 17 points, has guards or near-guards in all suits.

This illustration shows a hand which doesn't quite qualify, although reasonably balanced and of 17 points, because the spades are too weak. Unless your partner holds a guard or two in spades, the opposition could quickly make the first four tricks or so.

An opening bid of 2NT indicates a hand with the same balanced properties as that of a 1NT hand, but with roughly four more points, ie 20–22. The illustration that follows shows a good hand to open 2NT. Your partner needs only four or five high-card points to be able to raise the bid to game (3NT). Opening bids of 3NT are not generally advisable; a hand that is too strong to be opened with 2NT can be opened with a conventional bid of 2♣.

Responses to opening bids An opening bid, as has been shown, conveys some information to a partner, and now he must 'respond'.

Suppose the opening bid is one of a suit. The responder knows his partner probably has twelve or more points, with four or more cards in his named suit. There are a variety of responses he can make, as follows:

Denial pass If the hand is so poor that it could not conceivably help your partner to make a game it is best to pass. Five points or fewer with no significant support for his suit would qualify for a pass. Even if your partner opened with 17 or 18 high-card points, your five will not raise the value of the combined hands to sufficient for game, so why bid on and risk going down? Holding the hand shown below and responding to a partner's opening 1♠, you should pass. Five points and two small spades will not help him.

Limit bid A limit bid gives your partner some encouragement, but not too much, and would be appropriate if your hand held six to nine high-card points. If it holds support for your partner's suit (say four cards), raise his bid to two. This is called a 'single raise'. Responding to 1♥ with the hand in the illustration below, raise to 2♥. Your partner can judge what to bid next according to his hand – had he opened with 18 points he might now raise to 4♥. With six to nine points but without support in your partner's suit, bid 1NT.

The illustration below shows a hand with the same eight points as that in the previous illustration, but without the heart support for your partner's opening 1♥. In this case bid 1NT.

Change of suit If your partner has opened the bidding in one suit, and you are weak in that suit but strong in another, it helps to let your partner know this, as it might be better to play in your suit rather than his when it comes to the final contract. There isn't really a limit to the number of points required for this bid. It is basically to give information. If your partner is also strong in your suit, he can confirm it by bidding it on his turn, if not, he might 'rebid' his suit. The point to remember with a change of suit bid is that both partners have offered a suit as the trump suit, but there has been no agreement yet as to what the trump suit should be. So if the responder changes suit, it is up to the opening bidder to bid again. This makes a change of suit response a 'forcing' bid, not allowing your partner to pass. (It might be worth emphasizing here that it is only the bidding system agreed by the partners that forces the opening bidder to bid again, not the laws of the game, which allow him to do what he likes.) The illustration below shows a hand worthy of a change of suit bid. Suppose the opening bid is of 1♠ or 1♥. In neither case could the holder of this hand offer much support, but even with only eight points he would be justified in responding 2♦. If the opening bidder has support for diamonds this could well be the suit to play the contract in.

Invitation to game If facing an opening bid of one in a suit in which the responder's hand is strong enough to hope that he and his partner have between them the values for a game, there are two ways he can suggest this. Neither way suggests a game is certain, so the bid is limited. One is to bid 2NT and the other involves a 'double raise'.

A bid of 2NT is made on a balanced hand of 11–13 points. The point range is important. If the opener has opened with, say, 15 points, he knows with a response of 2NT that the points value of the combined hand is 26–28 points, usually considered adequate for a game in 3NT, and he will probably make this the final bid of the auction. The illustration below shows a hand suitable for a response of 2NT over an opening bid of 1♥, a suit in which the hand is weak.

A double raise, also called a 'jump' raise, is made with a good hand which also contains support for the opener's suit. It is a raise which misses out one level by raising the opening bid of one to three, for example 1♥ to 3♥, and promises the opening bidder around ten to twelve points with at least four cards in his suit. Distributional values are important here. A hand with good five-card support for the opener's suit, plus a void or singleton say, would justify a jump raise with as few as eight points. In response to an opening bid of 1♥, both the hands illustrated below are worth a jump to 3♥. The first hand has ten points and good support for hearts, including a doubleton. The second hand has eight points only but excellent hearts and a void in diamonds.

Bids direct to game   If you have a very strong hand with a good fit with your partner, you can respond to an opening bid of one by bidding direct to game.

There are two routes: bidding 3NT or four in your partner's suit if it is a major suit or, more rarely, five if it is a minor.

To raise to 3NT you need a good balanced hand (including some cards in your partner's suit) and 14–17 points. This should ensure you have between you the necessary points to make a game in 3NT a good proposition. The hand illustrated below is suitable for bidding 3NT over an opening bid of 1♠. You have 16 points, high cards in all suits except your partner's spades, with a certain four tricks in your own hand.

To bid four in your partner's major suit (a 'triple raise') you will need at least four cards in your partner's suit, including at least one honour, and a good distribution. The points requirement is variable and depends on distribution. Two suitable hands are shown below. In both cases partner has opened with 1♥. Hand A has only eight points but these include the Ace of trumps. Raise to 4♥. You and your partner should hold at least nine trumps, and with the ♦A and a singleton and doubleton in your hand you would expect the partnership to make ten tricks. Hand B has 13 points, meaning you and your partner should hold at least 26 points and be very strong in trumps.

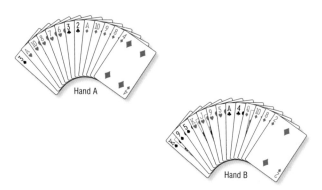

Hand A

Hand B

It is rare for a raise to five if the opening bid is one in a minor suit. If the responder had such a good hand to warrant thinking about it, it would probably be better to bid more slowly and investigate the possibility of bidding a small slam.

Jump in a new suit
The strongest response to an opening of one in a suit is to jump in a new suit, thus combining two of the options mentioned previously, a change of suit and double raise. The requirement to jump in a new suit is 16 or more high-card points. This could be cut to 15 with a solid long suit such as six cards headed by Ace, King, Queen or a slightly less solid suit with such good support for your partner's suit that it is bound to make that suit solid, such as Ace, Queen, 10. In the second instance you bid your own suit first and let your partner know the fit with his suit on your next bid.

The illustration below shows two such hands. In both cases the opener has opened 1♥. Hand A has 17 high-card points, including a solid spade suit and ability to win the first two rounds of diamonds. It is probable that this hand is stronger than the opener's hand. You should bid 2♠. Hand B has only 15 points but the ♥A, K, 10 almost certainly make the opener's suit solid, and the very strong spades and singleton and doubleton (in suits in which the opener must have high cards to justify his opening bid) make this a very good hand for a jump raise to 2♠.

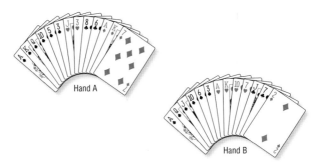

Hand A

Hand B

Responses to bids of two in a suit If your partner opens with two in a suit you must respond for at least one round. To pass is not an option. Except for the artificial bid of 2♣, the negative response to an opening bid of two is 2NT. This tells the opener that you have five points or fewer. This will probably tell the opener that, between you, you do not have enough for game, and he will repeat his suit at the three level whereupon you pass. However, should your partner introduce a new suit, it is again forcing for one round, so you must respond. If the responder has four or five cards in this second suit he can raise the bid to the level of four. Otherwise he repeats the opener's suit at the lowest level he can, whereupon the bidding will stop. The hands in the illustration overleaf show an example. If West opens 2♠, East responds with 2NT (negative). West bids 3♦. East cannot respond in diamonds either so bids 3♠ at which the bidding should end.

```
♠ A Q 10 7 5    N      ♠ 4 3
♥ —                    ♥ Q 6 5 2
♦ A Q J 5 2   W   E    ♦ 10 9 7
♣ K J 2          S     ♣ Q 6 4 3
```

An opening bid of 2♣ is a forcing bid to which the negative response is 2♦, which shows you have six points or fewer. Any other response shows seven or more points, and you should bid your longest suit, or with a balanced hand 2NT.

Responses to pre-emptive bids A bid of three in a suit means your partner is weak, holding a long suit and almost nothing else. The chances are you might have a strongish hand yourself, but beware of bidding over him. With your longest suit as trumps he is unlikely to be able to support you at all, and even if your long suit is as strong as his, it might still be better to play in his.

However, if your partner's pre-empt is in a major suit, it might be that you hold vital cards in his suit, plus a trick or two in outside suits. On the assumption that he should be able to make six tricks himself (not vulnerable) or seven (vulnerable), it might be possible to raise his suit to game, or to bid 3NT.

The hand illustrated below is one such hand. If your partner has pre-empted with 3♥ (not vulnerable), and can make six tricks from his hand, then your King of trumps could provide another, and your ♠A, ♦A, K and a small trump on the second round of clubs up to four more. It is worth a raise to 4♥.

A response of 3NT to a pre-emptive bid of three in a suit entails having guards in all the three suits not bid by your partner, plus at least three cards in his suit to be used as entries to his hand. If he has pre-empted with 3♦, it is no use playing in 3NT unless you can enter his hand (which will be dummy) to make his diamond tricks. You need a hand like that below to bid 3NT over your partner's pre-emptive 3♦. You can probably resist the lead of spades, hearts or clubs twice (long enough to force out the opponents' high diamonds and 'establish' dummy's diamonds as winners) and 3NT is a better bet than 5♦. In this case 3NT is regarded as a 'signing-off' bid. In other words, the responder has decided 3NT is the contract to play in, and any attempts to change it by his partner is more likely than not to end in disaster.

Responses to an opening bid in no-trumps Responses to a no-trump opening are relatively straightforward as the responder knows to within three points or so the point count of his partner, and that his partner has a balanced hand.

Opening of 1NT Since the responder knows his partner has 16–18 points he can assess reasonably well the prospect of a game, as a combined count of 25 points is regarded as necessary. If the responder has a balanced hand himself, he knows that if he has seven points or more, there is a chance, and therefore he should bid. If his hand is balanced with no more than six points, game is doubtful, and there is no point in bidding further. He should pass.

With seven or eight points, the combined count could be 23–26. His response should be 2NT. This tells his partner that if his opening bid was made at the top end of the scale, he can bid 3NT. If not, 2NT will be the contract. With nine points or more, the responder can bid 3NT himself, which his partner will regard as a sign-off.

Responding to a bid of 1NT with an unbalanced hand is less straightforward. With four points or fewer, pass. With five to seven points, and a suit of five cards or more, respond with a bid of two in the long suit, unless it is clubs. A 2♣ response is another conventional bid, as will be seen. If the suit bid is the opener's weakest, he should let the bidding end there, otherwise he will sign off with a bid of 2NT.

An unbalanced hand of eight points or more, and a five-card major suit, offers a chance of a game, and the response to 1NT should be a jump in the major suit, ie to 3♠ or 3♥. The opener can then decide whether to convert to 3NT or raise to four of the suit bid.

A responder holding an unbalanced hand of nine points or more with a long minor suit is best advised to sign off in 3NT, rather than naming his minor suit, since a game in a minor suit requires eleven tricks. Such a hand is shown below. Nine tricks in no-trumps is likely to be easier to make with this hand than eleven in diamonds. Your partner is likely to have the King or Jack of diamonds, so five or six tricks are possible from the suit even if they aren't trumps.

If the responder holds nine or more points with a weakness in one suit to discourage a contract in no-trumps, but holds a strong four-card major, he can use the conventional bid of 2♣. This is not to be confused with an opening bid of 2♣, which as we have seen indicates a very strong hand. The response of 2♣ to a bid of 1NT is known as a 'Stayman bid', after its inventor. It asks the opening bidder to bid 2♠ if he holds four or more spades and 2♥ if he holds four or more hearts. If he holds four of both suits, he bids the stronger suit. If he does not hold four cards in either major suit, he bids 2♦. If the opening bidder now bids a major of which the responder himself holds four cards, the responder raises the bid to four, knowing that the partnership has at least eight cards in the trump suit and a minimum of 25 points between them, which should be enough for game. If he bids the major suit of which the responder does not hold four cards, or if he bids 2♦, the responder signs off with 2NT or 3NT. The ten-point hand illustrated below is held by the responder to a bid of 1NT. He actually holds four cards in both major suits, with weaknesses in the minor suits. He is ideally placed to bid a Stayman 2♣. If his partner bids a major suit, he raises it to four, confident of making the contract. If not, he will bid 3NT, confident that the partnership has a combined minimum of 26 points.

Opening of 2NT The responder with a balanced hand can raise his partner to 3NT with as few as five points, since he knows the combined count will be at least 25 points. With four points and four or five intermediate cards (10s and 9s) he could still try 3NT. But without them or with fewer than four points, he should pass.

If the responder has five or more points and a major suit of at least five cards, he can bid three in the major. The bid is forcing, although it does not necessarily indicate a strong hand. The opening bidder knows the least number of points the partnership holds (by adding five to his count). If he holds good cards to support the responder's major, he can bid four in the suit; if not, he can convert to 3NT.

If the responder has twelve or more points facing a bid of 2NT, there is the possibility of slam, dealt with below.

Bidding to slam To bid a slam you will usually need more points than you would to bid a game. As a rule of thumb, a combined 33 points are required for a small slam and 37 for a grand slam. How do you know when this is a possibility? It helps, of course, if your partner has opened 2♣, showing 23 or more points, and you are holding, say, a dozen points. The combined total of 35 puts you in the slam zone. If you have 15 points and your partner opens two of anything, you can think about a slam. When you open with, say, 19 points, and your partner makes a jump response, implying 16 points or so, you are in slam territory.

Two conventions are useful when approaching the bidding for a slam. One is the 'cue' bid. Once the partnership has decided on the trump suit, a bid of a new suit at a new level indicates that you have a first-round control of that suit, which could mean that you hold the Ace, or that you are void and can trump.

The second method is the 'Blackwood convention', named after its inventor Easley Blackwood, and widely used since 1933. It is a way of enquiring how many Aces your partner holds, and it is done by bidding 4NT. Your partner responds as follows:

>   5♣ with no Aces or four
>
>   5♦ with one Ace
>
>   5♥ with two Aces
>
>   5♠ with three Aces

If you need to know how many Kings he holds, you can then bid 5NT, which is answered in the same manner, with a bid of 6♣ showing no or four Kings, and so on. However, if you bid 5NT you are already committing yourself to a slam, as the response must be at small slam level. The 5NT bid therefore is used only if you are undecided about bidding a small slam or a grand slam.

```
        ♠ A J 10 7        N      ♠ K Q 9 8 3
        ♥ A 4 3                  ♥ K 8
        ♦ 8 7       W        E   ♦ A J 6
        ♣ A K Q 9        S      ♣ J 5 4
```

South	West	North	East
	1♣	No bid	1♠
No bid	3♠	No bid	4♦
No bid	4♥	No bid	4NT
No bid	5♠	No bid	6♠
No bid	No bid	No bid	

The East–West hands illustrated above with the accompanying bidding shows how a cue bid and Blackwood can help in the bidding of a slam. West, the dealer, with 18 points, opens 1♣ (he could have opened 1♠ but 1♣ gives more bidding room). East shows his longest suit by bidding 1♠. With his strong spades, West agrees spades as the trump suit, and at the same time informs his partner that his opening bid was near the top of the range for a bid of one in a suit, by jumping to 3♠. This alerts East to the possibilities of a slam, as he realizes that the partnership probably has over 30 points and a fit in spades. He bids 4♦, a cue bid, to show his partner that he has first round control of diamonds and has a slam in mind. West responds with a cue bid of his own, 4♥, showing control of that suit. East can reckon from his partner's bidding that he must hold one of the black Aces, and that if he holds both a slam is on so bids 4NT (Blackwood). West's response of 5♠, showing three Aces, confirms East's small slam bid of 6♠. The small slam should be made.

Defensive bidding We have looked at bidding from the point of view of arriving at the correct contract, but what can the 'defenders' do? So far as the auction is concerned, the defenders are the side which does not open the bidding. They have two ways to enter the auction themselves, the 'overcall' and the 'take-out double'.

Overcall   An overcall is the bid of a suit, or no trumps, over the opponents' bid. It is usually made in second position, and can serve two or three purposes. The points requirement of an overcall at the level of one is anything from eight to 16, with the essential being a good five-card suit. A good hand for an overcall is that in the illustration below. If the dealer to your right has opened 1♣, one can overcall with 1♠. It forces the player to your left to respond to his partner at the two level, cutting down the opposition bidding space. If your partner has a good hand, especially with a spade fit, your own side might even win the contract. And if the other side wins the contract, you have at least provided your partner with the news that a spade lead might be profitable.

To overcall at the level of two, you need about twelve points and a good suit. You have to remember that if you win the contract you have to make eight tricks. Your opponent has already shown he has about 13 points. Your partner might have practically nothing at all, and to go down by three or four tricks doubled is expensive.

If you have 12–16 points, meaning that your side could hold the balance of power, and also hold the strong suit, one can make a jump overcall. The illustration below shows such a hand. Suppose the dealer has opened 1♦. With this hand you would be justified to bid 2♠. This forces the opener's partner to enter the bidding, if he wishes to name a suit, at the three level.

Suppose you have such a good hand that you wish to bid over your opponents' bid but you do not have a long suit. You can bid 1NT provided you hold 16–18 points and guards in your opponents' suit. For example, you hold the hand illustrated below and the dealer to your right has bid 1♦. You have 18 points (which means your opponents cannot hold more than 22 between them) and you have honours in the suit bid. You can safely bid 1NT.

However, the last hand suggests another ploy. If a couple of your clubs were diamonds, giving you five good cards in the bid suit, you might pass, hoping that your opponents will bid themselves into a contract they cannot make. This is called a 'trap pass'.

Responses to an overcall
If you are in fourth position, and your partner has overcalled the dealer in a suit, and the second opponent has passed, you can support your partner even with a weak hand. Provided you have three cards in your partner's suit you can raise him by one even with as few as three points. There is every chance that the opponents have the balance of power, and even if you go down, you will probably have prevented them making a contract, even perhaps game.

A response to an overcall of 1NT is easy to make, since you know your partner has 16–18 points, and can respond as if he had made an opening bid of 1NT.

In fourth position you can make an overcall yourself, but you must bear in mind that your partner has already passed, and is therefore weak.

Take-out double
A convention that has been in the game since about 1912 is the take-out double, which is a call not meant to double the points at stake (which was the original purpose of the double), but to send a message to your partner. Suppose the opposition has made a bid and you hold a hand with which you would have opened the bidding yourself, and contains values in all three suits not bid. You double. Your double asks your partner to bid his strongest suit in the knowledge that you can support it to some extent. An ideal distribution would be 5–4–4–0, but a three-card suit is not a bar to this call. The hand in the illustration overleaf is excellent for a take-out double. The opponent to your left has bid 1♦. Unless your partner holds a lot of diamonds, he will have at least a four-card suit to bid, giving one a trump suit of eight, and the prospect of a good contract. A take-out double can be used only when

a partner has not bid. Any double made after one partner of the team has bid is for penalties.

Sacrifice bids Occasionally it is clear that one side has the balance of power and can make game. In this situation it might pay the other side to bid to make a contract they know they cannot make, as the penalty may be less damaging than letting the opposition make game. This would particularly apply if the game would give the opposition the rubber. A bid in this situation, to gain a contract which you know you will lose, is called a 'sacrifice bid'. The bidding in the illustration below shows a sacrifice. It was certain that North–South, vulnerable, could make 4♥, which would give them the rubber. East decides to sacrifice in 5♣, and although North–South, on the cards, could have made 5♥, South decided to double. East–West cannot make more than seven tricks so went four down doubled, for a penalty of 700 points. Later events would prove if it was worth it.

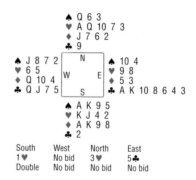

	♠ Q 6 3	
	♥ A Q 10 7 3	
	♦ J 7 6 2	
	♣ 9	

♠ J 8 7 2	N	♠ 10 4
♥ 6 5		♥ 9 8
♦ Q 10 4	W E	♦ 5 3
♣ Q J 7 5	S	♣ A K 10 8 6 4 3

	♠ A K 9 5	
	♥ K J 4 2	
	♦ A K 9 8	
	♣ 2	

South	West	North	East
1♥	No bid	3♥	5♣
Double	No bid	No bid	No bid

Bidding summary The description of bidding here cannot cover everything that might happen in an auction as there are thousands of possible permutations of bids. Even the brief outline here will probably daunt a newcomer, who will think he never could remember the requirements needed to bid this or respond to that. These things come with practice. It is important to grasp the point-count system of evaluating the hand, as it is used in most books, articles and discussions of the game. It is also important to appreciate that a bidding system is an agreement between two partners, and any unilateral deviation from it will assuredly backfire, as the offender's partner will be the player most deceived.

On the other hand, it would be a mistake to think that Bridge is a mechanical game played solely by formula. Experts often disagree about what the correct bid should be in any given situation.

Playing strategy Bridge is unlike other popular trick-taking games in that it is played with a dummy. All three players (ie excluding dummy) know the contents of two hands. The declarer knows all 26 cards held by his side and all 26 held by the opposition. This means that Bridge sets new problems in the play.

```
♠ 10 6 2        N        ♠ A 8 5
♥ A K J 4   W       E    ♥ 9 6 3
♦ K Q 2                  ♦ J 9 8 3
♣ A J 3         S        ♣ K 6 4
```

The first thing to do when dummy goes down is for all players to study it. The declarer can seek to plan his play. For example, the illustration above shows two hands. West is declarer in 3NT, North leads ♣5, and East's hand becomes dummy. The declarer can see that he has five tricks 'on top', in ♠A, ♥A, K, ♣A, K. Because of the club lead, he is certain to make ♣J (if South plays ♣Q, West wins with ♣A, making ♣K, J 'masters', while if South does not play ♣Q, West wins with ♣J. The master card in a suit is the highest card in the suit not yet played, and therefore the card that controls that suit, and a sure winner – unless trumped, of course, which it cannot be in the present instance, as the contract is in no-trumps. Thus, when ♣A and ♣Q have been played, ♣K and ♣J, unless played in the same trick, will both win.) This is six tricks, and West is certain to win two of ♦K, Q, J as only ♦A can beat them. That makes eight tricks, and his ninth could come from ♥J, by 'finessing' (see below) or by a 'long' heart or diamond (having the only heart or diamond left when three rounds are played). His danger, however, is the spade suit, as he can win only one round of spades and, once his Ace has gone, the defenders might make three or more spade tricks.

So he forms his strategy. After taking the opening lead with the ♣A or ♣J, he must lead the ♦2 toward dummy's ♦J. If the defenders take the ♦A, then he has established his ♦K, Q (ie made them the master cards in the suit) and can take them before the defenders can take their hearts. If the defenders 'duck' (ie hold back the ♦A), then the ♦J makes the trick and the declarer repeats the process by leading ♦3 from dummy towards the ♦K. No matter when the defence take their ♦A, West is sure of his two diamond tricks. Of course, if on the lead of ♦2 North plays the Ace, then East merely plays his ♦3 and has established three tricks in diamonds and his contract is safe.

Maximizing tricks Because the declarer plays two hands, his and dummy's, there are techniques to conjure up 'extra' tricks to those which are certain. The 'finesse' gives you an even-money chance of winning an extra trick in a suit if you hold certain cards. If, as South, you have ♥ A, Q, 5 in dummy, and a heart in hand, you can convert your one certain trick in hearts to two provided West holds the ♥K, which is a 50 per cent chance. You lead a heart to dummy and, if West plays the King, you win with the Ace, which leaves the ♥Q as the master for a second heart trick. If West does not play the King, you play the Queen, which will win the trick (East having no higher card), with the Ace still available for a second heart trick. This manoeuvre is called 'finessing the Queen'.

♥ A J 9

♥ 4 3 2

An extension of this technique is to assume 'split honours' in opposing hands, in other words if there are two or three of the honour cards (A, K, Q, J, 10) against you, you can maximize the chances of winning two tricks by assuming the missing honours are shared in a certain way by your opponents. The illustration above shows the principle. The ♥K, Q, 10 are against your ♥A, J, 9. You lead a small heart from South, hoping that East holds the King or Queen, and West the other two honours. If West plays low, you finesse the 9. To beat it East must play his King or Queen. You will then be able to make both Ace and Jack by leading towards them and beating whichever card West plays. Notice that if West had played his 10 on the first lead, then you cover it with the Jack, leaving East again to win with his honour, but creating the same result for you. You must win the two tricks with Ace or 9. Any pair of cards, such as A, Q, held over an opposing pair held by the right-hand opponent such as K, J, is known as a 'tenace'. Provided the opponent has to play first, the tenace cards must win both tricks.

Playing towards honours Playing towards honours is another way of conjuring up a trick. With the situation illustrated below, there is apparently only one certain trick, but by leading twice towards North you can make a second if West holds the ♥A. If West plays his Ace you merely play ♥3 from dummy, the Ace being wasted on two small cards. Whether West plays his Ace or holds it back, he cannot stop you making both King and Queen eventually.

♥ K Q 3

♥ 5 4 2

Percentage plays The above techniques can be called 'playing the percentages', or making the most of your chances. There are many opportunities to do this in Bridge, and the more expert you become the more they will be recognized. An example, illustrated below, gives the flavour. West, declarer in no-trumps, needs four tricks in hearts with ♥Q, J against him. First he leads the Ace. If both opponents follow, when next in dummy he leads ♥7, and 'covers' in hand (ie beats) whatever card South plays. If South plays ♥8, he plays ♥10. If North can win the trick with ♥Q or ♥J, it will leave only one heart outstanding which the declarer must win.

♥ A K 10 5 3 [W E] ♥ 9 7 4

Squeeze plays A phrase often used in Bridge literature is the 'squeeze'. It is the device by which a declarer forces a defender to discard a guard in a suit which otherwise would prevent the declarer making the contract. The illustration below shows an example of what is meant. South, with Spades as trumps, needs all four tricks. At present, he can make a trump, a heart and a club only. But when he leads his last trump, the ♠8, West is squeezed. He cannot retain his guards in both hearts and clubs. If he discards ♥9, the declarer will discard ♣10, and make the two hearts in dummy and the ♣A. If West instead discards the ♣Q, declarer will discard ♥8 in dummy, and make two clubs in hand and ♥A.

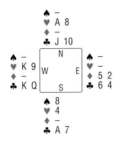

Defenders' play While the declarer has most of the initiative in the play, controlling two hands, there are conventions which help defenders.

The first decision a defender has to make is the opening lead, made before the dummy is laid down. As the best chance of beating a no-trump contract is the establishment of a long suit, the usual lead against it is the fourth highest card of the leader's longest suit, or if your partner has bid, a card of his suit, on the assumption that this might help him establish a suit. The idea of leading the fourth highest card of your suit, means that your partner can estimate the strength of the declarer's hand in that suit. This is done by 'the rule of eleven'. By subtracting the value of the card led from eleven, your partner knows how many cards higher than that are held by himself, dummy and declarer, and since he can see how many he holds and how many there are in dummy, he can work out how many the declarer holds too. The hands illustrated below show the principle. Declarer in 3NT is South, and West leads the ♦5. Five from eleven is six. Dummy contains three diamonds higher than ♦5, and East holds two, so he knows the declarer holds only one. He also knows that declarer cannot hold more than three cards in the suit. By beating whatever card North plays, ie by beating Jack with King, or 7 with 9, he will win the trick or force out declarer's high card. With this knowledge East–West should win three tricks in diamonds.

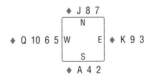

Another technique is the 'peter', or high-low play. If a player holds two cards in a suit, the playing of the higher one first tells his partner that after the second card he is void. This is particularly useful in situations like that illustrated below. South is declarer in a suit contract and West leads Ace of a side suit. East plays 8, and when West follows with the lead of the King, East plays 5, completing the peter. West knows that his partner is now void so he can lead the suit again allowing his partner to trump.

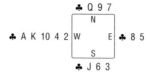

The peter can be used with a three-card suit, as it carries the same message: 'lead the suit again'. In the illustration below, when West leads the Ace and East plays the 4, South will play the 8. An alert West could spot the 4 as the beginning of a peter. Assuming South has played his lowest card, 8, where is the 2? West can see dummy hasn't got it, so East must have it, and be petering. He leads King, East plays the 2, and West leads the suit again. This time East wins with the Queen.

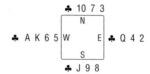

These terms are mentioned since they will frequently be found in Bridge columns in newspapers, the reading of which is recommended for the aspiring Bridge player.

Example hand
South deals the cards as shown below, and with 17 points decides to open 1NT (although his hand is not very well balanced, as his clubs are weak). With nobody else bidding, North, with nine points, raises to 3NT. West leads the fourth highest

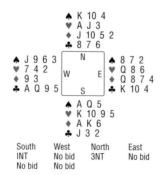

of the stronger of his long suits, ♣5. When the dummy goes down, South reviews his position. He is dismayed to see dummy's clubs, and hopes to lose no more than four tricks in the suit, which still means he has to win all the other tricks. He can make three spades, and two diamonds, and must make either four hearts (with a successful finesse or long card) or three hearts and an extra diamond.

When the ♣5 is led, East can see by the rule of eleven that the declarer has only one card above the 5 of the suit and decides to play his King which cannot lose anything even if the declarer has the Ace. In fact the declarer hasn't and the defenders take the first four tricks. The declarer has an awkward choice of discards on the fourth, and discards ♠4 and ♦6. East discards ♦4. West then plays the fourth card of his other four-suiter the ♠3, which dummy takes with the King. The declarer now tackles the hearts by leading the Ace then the 3 from dummy, finessing the 10, which holds. He now plays King and with great relief drops both 7 and Queen. He is home, playing off ♠A, Q, ♥9 and ♦A, K for his contract.

The play has gone:

West	North	East	South
♣5	♣6	♣K	♣2
♣9	♣7	♣4	♣3
♣A	♣8	♣10	♣J
♣Q	♠4	♦4	♦6
♠3	♠K	♠2	♠5
♥2	♥A	♥6	♥5
♥4	♥J	♥8	♥9
♥7	♥3	♥Q	♥K
♠6	♠10	♠7	♠A
♠9	♦2	♠8	♠Q
♠J	♦5	♦7	♥10
♦3	♦10	♦8	♦A
♦9	♦J	♦Q	♦K

So South lands his contract of 3NT and scores 100 points below the line.

General

The easiest way to learn Bridge is to play with friends, or to join a club, or both, and to read Bridge books and the columns in newspapers and magazines.

When learning, of course, the atmosphere is informal and you can discuss the play fully. However, there is plenty of etiquette when it comes to playing properly. Do not discuss play when it is in progress, nor touch dummy's cards (even if it was your hand) or the tricks already played. After the hand, you may ask for comments on your play, but do not comment on other people's play, even your partner's, unless asked. Bridge players can be touchy!

Calabresella

Calabresella is an Italian game that possibly takes its name from Calabria, in the south of Italy. It is related to Tressette, a partnership game dating back to the early 17th century, which is still popular in Italy. Calabresella was introduced to the UK in 1870, and the game is described here in the form in which it was adapted from the Italian game.

Type	Trick-taking
Alternative names	Terziglio
Players	Three
Special requirements	Pen and paper for scoring

Aim
To make more points than the other players.

Cards
The standard pack of 52 cards is used, from which are removed the 10s, 9s and 8s, leaving a short pack of 40 cards equivalent to the traditional Italian or Spanish pack. The cards rank in an unusual order: 3 (high), 2, A, K, Q, J, 7, 6, 5, 4 (low). Points are awarded for winning certain of these cards in tricks: the Ace has a value of three points, and the 3, 2, K, Q, J one point each. These are called 'counting cards'.

Preparation
Players cut for deal, the lowest (with the cards ranking as above) being the first dealer. Thereafter the deal passes to the left.

The dealer deals twelve cards face down to each player, and four to the centre of the table as a 'widow'. Cards are dealt in batches of four, in the following manner: four to each player, four as a widow, then two more batches of four to each player.

Play
The players study their hands and the eldest hand (the player to the dealer's left) may choose to be the solo player, known just as the Player, by declaring 'I play', or he may pass. The next player clockwise then has the choice. If he passes it is the dealer's choice. If all pass the bidding goes round again, when any player on his turn may choose to be the Player. One who becomes Player on the second round of bidding has an advantage. He can call for any 3 not in his hand, asking for it by specific suit, and whoever has the 3 must give it to him, receiving in exchange a card face down (ie it is not shown to the third player). If the Player already has all the 3s in his hand, he may ask for any 2 to be given him, but must show that he does in fact hold all the 3s. Should neither opponent hold the card called for (it might be one of the four in the widow) the Player does not get the chance to call for another.

Since there is a big advantage in becoming the Player on the second round of bidding in comparison to the first round, a player would need to hold a very strong hand to declare himself Player on the first round. His only reason for doing so would be to make sure an opponent doesn't declare himself Player first.

After the exchange of cards has taken place (or not, if the asked for card is in the widow) the Player discards a minimum of one and a maximum of four cards from his hand face down. He then exposes the four cards in the widow and chooses a card or cards from it to bring his hand back to twelve cards. Any remaining cards in the widow are then turned face down and discarded if no counting cards remain, or put to one side for later scoring if there are counting cards left.

The trick-taking phase of the game now takes place, with the Player playing against the other two in partnership; see p383 for an explanation of tricks and trick-taking. The opening lead is made by the eldest hand, irrespective of who is the Player, and play is clockwise. There are no trumps, and normal trick-taking rules apply, ie one must follow suit to the card led if possible and discard if not. The winner of a trick leads to the next.

Scoring As well as the 32 points in the pack for counting cards (the A, 3, 2, K, Q, J of each suit) a bonus of three points goes to the winner of the last trick, making 35 available in all, so the aim of each side is to win 18 points or more.

Each side counts the value of the cards won in tricks. The taker of the last trick wins a bonus of three points, and also scores the points for any counting cards left in the widow. One side must win in each hand since there are an odd number of points (35) available. The winning side wins by the difference between the two totals.

If the game is being played for stakes, settlement can be made after each hand, for example if the Player wins 20–15, each opponent gives him five units. If he loses 20–15, he pays each opponent five units.

Otherwise a score can be kept for settlement later. If the Player wins 20–15, he scores five points, if he loses 20–15 both opponents score five points. At settlement each player pays the difference to a player with more points than him and receives the difference from a player with fewer.

If the game is being played for interest only, the score is kept in the same way, with the winner being the leader after an agreed number of deals, or the first to reach an agreed number of points, for example 25.

Example hand
Suppose the hands are dealt as follows, with Player C as the dealer, and Player A as the eldest hand:

Player A	♠ A, Q ♥ 4 ♣ K, Q, 7 ♦ 2, A, 7, 6, 5, 4
Player B	♠ 3, 2, 4 ♥ 3, 2, A, K, J, 5 ♣ 2, A ♦ J
Player C	♠ K, 6, 5 ♥ Q, 7, 6 ♣ 3, J, 6 ♦ 3, K, Q

Only Player B has much chance of winning 18 points on his own. He has a superb hand, which would be even better when he has called up, or taken from the widow, the ♦ 3. He could make at least eight tricks with 15 points practically certain. But without the lead he has a weakness in the diamond suit which could prove fatal.

Nevertheless, after passing on the first round of bidding, he declares himself Player on the second and calls up the ♦3, passing Player C the ♠4 in return.

Player B has to discard at least one card, although he'd rather not, and decides to discard his ♥5, although it is an almost certain winner once he has the lead. He hopes that the ♦2 or ♦A is in the widow to strengthen his hand further. However, the widow is ♠J, 7, ♣5, 4.

Player B takes the ♠J into his hand, leaving the three hands as shown below.

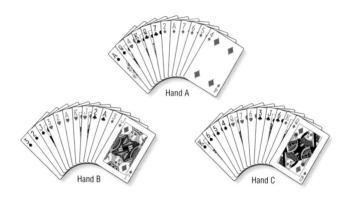

Hand A

Hand B

Hand C

Player A, knowing he holds all the diamonds except four, leads the ♦7, hoping that Player B's ♦3 is bare (ie that Player B holds no other diamonds) and that the lead of ♦7 will force it out. Player C could then make lots of diamond tricks if he could regain the lead. The play proceeds as follows, with Player A leading:

	Player A	Player B	Player C
1	♦7	♦J	<u>♦K</u>
2	♦6	<u>♦3</u>	♦Q
3	♥4	<u>♥3</u>	♥6
4	♣7	<u>♥2</u>	♥7
5	♦5	<u>♥A</u>	♥Q
6	♦4	♥K	♣6
7	♣Q	<u>♥J</u>	♠4
8	♠Q	<u>♠3</u>	♠5

Player B has a crucial decision to make here. He has 13 points and needs five more. If he sacrifices his ♣2 now, and Player A happened to hold the ♣3 and ♦A, 2, as is possible, Player A will win the next three tricks, and Player B would have to choose whether to keep his ♠2 or ♣A to win the last trick, which would decide whether he won or lost. The same choice would be forced on him should he lead his ♠J now (in fact, as the cards lie, if he played ♠J now, he would lose all of the last four tricks, a disaster). He decides to play ♠2 and see what happens.

	Player A	Player B	Player C
9	♠A	♠2	♠6
10	♣K	♣2	♣J
11	♦A	♠J	♠K
12	♦2	♣A	♣3

Player C wins 3 extra points as the winner of the last trick, and Player B wins the hand by 20 points to 15.

Player B did well not to win with his ♦3 on the first trick, as his ♦J would have remained a problem right to the end. On the other hand, had Player A led his ♦A on the first trick, would Player B have declined to take it? On trick 10, Player C did well not to win with ♣3, instead saving it for the last trick and the bonus three points.

Variants
Some players prefer that the solo player can call for a card no matter whether he declares on the first round of bidding or second.

Calculation

Calculation is a single-pack patience game with a simple layout which nevertheless rewards careful play. It is a difficult game to get out, but sometimes unpromising situations suddenly come to life.

Type	Patience
Alternative names	Broken Intervals
Players	One
Special requirements	None

Aim

To build all the cards into four piles upon foundations, each of which will be headed by a King.

Cards

The standard pack of 52 cards is used, the cards ranking from Ace (low) to King (high).

Preparation

Any Ace, 2, 3 and 4 are placed in a row on the table. They are the foundations. Below each foundation should be space for a waste heap.

Play

The pack is taken in hand face down and is dealt to the table one card at a time face up. A card may be played to a foundation, or to any waste heap. Cards should be played to the foundations to build sequences as follows.

The first pile begins with an Ace, and is built on in the order, irrespective of suits:
A, 2, 3, 4, 5, 6, 7, 8, 9, 10, J, Q, K

The second pile begins with a 2, and is built on in intervals of two:
2, 4, 6, 8, 10, Q, A, 3, 5, 7, 9, J, K

The third pile begins with a 3, and is built on in intervals of three:
3, 6, 9, Q, 2, 5, 8, J, A, 4, 7, 10, K

The fourth pile begins with a 4, and is built on in intervals of four:
4, 8, Q, 3, 7, J, 2, 6, 10, A, 5, 9, K

The top card of a waste heap is always available to play to a foundation, but it may not be played to another waste heap. The cards on the waste heaps can be slightly overlapping, so that the ranks of the cards below the top one can be seen.

The pack is dealt once only, although play may continue to be made from waste heaps so long as there is a card to be played to a foundation. If the pack is exhausted and none of the cards on the top of the waste heaps may be played to a foundation the game is lost.

The skill lies in deciding on which waste heap to lay a card which cannot be played to a foundation. An attempt should be made to build up runs in the waste heaps of cards at intervals of one, two, three or four to each other, so that when a card will eventually fit on a foundation, others will follow.

Example game

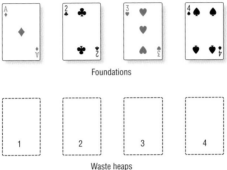

Foundations

Waste heaps

Suppose the first card turned up from the pack is a 9. Place this on the space for the first waste heap. The next card is a Queen. Place this on the second waste heap space. The next card is a 2. This is played to the Ace foundation. The next card is a 3, which also goes on the Ace foundation. Next another 3. This will not be needed for some time, so can go on waste heap 3. The next card is a 5, which can be played to waste heap 3. The next card is a King. As Kings end at the top of all the foundation piles, they will be among the last to be played, and it is as well to reserve a waste heap for these, so place it on waste heap 4. The next card is a Queen, which can go onto the waste heap 2 above the other Queen. The next card is 8, which goes to the 4 foundation, followed by the Queen from waste heap 2. The next card dealt is a 6. This is played to the 3 foundation, followed by the 9 from waste heap 1 and the other Queen from waste heap 2. The next card dealt, a Jack, is played to waste heap 1, where it might remain for a little while.

The next card is a 4. This will fit onto either the Ace or 2 foundations. The best play would be to play it to the Ace foundation, since this will allow the 5 on waste heap 3 to follow onto the Ace foundation, uncovering the 3 to go on the 4 foundation. The next card is 7 which also goes onto the 4 foundation, allowing the Jack from waste heap 1 to follow it. The next card is 2, which fits onto the 3 foundation. As the game progresses, 9 goes to waste heap 1, a 10 to waste heap 2, a Queen to waste heap 3, a King to waste heap 4, an Ace to waste heap 1, a 5 to the 3 foundation, a Jack to waste heap 3, a 4 to the 2 foundation, an 8 to the 3 foundation, followed by the Jack from waste heap 3 and the Ace from waste heap 1, and so on.

As the game stands, a 6 is needed for the Ace and 2 foundations, a 4 for the 3 foundation and a 2 for the 4 foundation. This is a very good start and very few games will go as smoothly as this. Any reader who has followed with a pack of cards can shuffle the remaining cards and, dealing them one by one, see how much further the game can progress.

California Jack

California Jack is a game of the All Fours family, but all the cards in the pack come into play instead of only those which are dealt out. This and other changes in the rules of play mean the element of luck is reduced, and California Jack is regarded as a more complete and skilful game than its parent.

Type	Trick-taking
Alternative names	French Fours
Players	Two
Special requirements	Pen and paper for scoring

Aim
To win the game by scoring ten points; points are scored for capturing certain cards during tricks.

Cards
The standard pack of 52 cards is used, the cards ranking from Ace (high) to 2 (low).

Preparation
Each player draws a card from a face-down spread out pack, and the player with the higher ranking card deals.

The dealer shuffles and the non-dealer cuts the pack and shows the bottom card of the packet in his hand. The suit of this card becomes the trump suit for the deal. The dealer shuffles the cards again and the non-dealer cuts. The dealer then deals six cards to each player, one at a time, starting with the non-dealer. The remaining 40 cards are placed in a squared-up pack face up in the centre of the table to form the stock. The deal alternates with each hand.

Play
The non-dealer leads to the first trick. Unlike the game All Fours, the normal rules of trick-taking apply, ie a player must follow suit if possible and, if unable, may trump or discard; see p383 for an explanation of tricks and trick-taking. The trick is won by the higher trump played, or the higher card in the suit led.

The winner of a trick puts it to one side and takes into his hand the top card of the stock while the loser takes the next card, being careful to leave the stock squared up so that only the top card is exposed. Before each lead, therefore, both hands are restored to six cards. The winner of the trick leads to the next. When the stock is exhausted, the players play out the last six tricks, and then claim the points won as detailed under Scoring, below.

Players must decide at each trick whether it is worth winning the top card of the stock or not. If the card is the Ace, 2 or Jack of the trump suit, each player will be anxious to win it, and his chances of winning it would be best if he were leading. On the other hand, if the card were a useless one, he might prefer to lose the trick and hope for a better one, even though this would mean losing the lead. It follows that having a losing card in the hand can, at times, be useful. A good player is one who can memorize the cards played and thus as the game progresses form a good idea of the cards in his opponent's hand and those remaining in the stock. He can then make a judgement on whether to try to win or lose each trick.

Scoring   Four points are at stake on each deal, as follows:

High   for winning the Ace of trumps;

Low   for winning the 2 of trumps;

Jack   for winning the Jack of trumps;

Game   for winning the highest value of scoring cards in tricks, as follows

Ace	4
King	3
Queen	2
Jack	1
10	10

The point for game is not scored if the players tie.

The winner is the first to reach ten points (although some players prefer to play to seven points). The points are taken in the order above, so that a player may reach the target of ten while the deal is in progress. For example, if a player leads 9–8, and during the play wins the Ace of trumps, he must win, since the score for high is counted first, and the fact that his opponent could win, or might already have won, all three of the other points available in the deal will not affect the outcome. In these cases it is customary not to play out the rest of the deal.

Example hand
The hands are dealt as in the illustration. The trump suit is clubs.

Non-dealer's hand   Dealer's hand   Stock

The card exposed at the top of the stock is ♠7, a card which is quite worthless. The non-dealer decides to lead ♠3 in an attempt to lose it, with the hope that the second card is better. Play proceeds as follows:

	Non-dealer	Dealer	Card exposed	Second card
1	<u>♠3</u>	♠2	♠7	♥3
2	♦K	<u>♦A</u>	♣A	♠Q

The non-dealer was unexpectedly forced to win the first trick with ♠3, taking ♠7 from stock. The second card, which the dealer took, was ♥3, another worthless card. The non-dealer was pleased he won the first trick when the next card exposed on the stock was the Ace of trumps, and led ♦K, expecting to win it. Again he was surprised, as the dealer held ♦A and won the trick.

3	<u>♦10</u>	♦8	♦J	♣J

Another slice of luck for the dealer. The non-dealer won the ♦J with ♦10, which will give him ten points towards Game, but the card below it was ♣J, making it likely that the dealer will score points for both High and Jack.

4	♠7	<u>♠K</u>	♥Q	♣7
5	<u>♥4</u>	♥3	♠8	♥2
6	<u>♠8</u>	♦4	♣4	♥J
7	<u>♠Q</u>	♥2	♣9	♥6
8	<u>♠4</u>	♥6	♠J	♥10
9	<u>♠J</u>	♦5	♥K	♠6
10	♣4	<u>♣J</u>	♥5	♥9

The non-dealer forces the dealer to play his ♣J and take the useless ♥5, but only gets ♥9 himself.

11	<u>♥K</u>	♥Q	♣8	♣K

Another disappointment for the non-dealer who, having used ♥K to win the 8 of trumps, finds the dealer gets the King of trumps.

12	♣6	<u>♣K</u>	♥A	♣5
13	♥9	<u>♥J</u>	♣3	♦3
14	<u>♣5</u>	♥A	♣2	♦7

The dealer uses his ♥A in an attempt to win ♣2 and a likely point for Low, as he knows it leaves his ♥10 the master heart, but the non-dealer trumps to take ♣2.

15	♦3	<u>♦7</u>	♥8	♥7
16	♥7	<u>♥10</u>	♣Q	♠10

The dealer wanted ♣Q and knew his ♥10 would win the trick, as it was the master heart (the A, K, Q, J having been played) and the non-dealer had just picked the ♥7, so would be unable to trump. By winning with ♥10 he also makes sure of ten points towards Game.

17	♠10	♠6	♠9	♦9
18	♠9	♦9	♦2	♦6
19	♦J	♣3	♠A	♣10

The dealer trumps in order to win ♠A, but the non-dealer gets ♣10, an excellent card.

| 20 | ♦2 | ♦6 | ♠5 | ♦Q |

The stock is now exhausted. Each player should know how many trumps the other has, and in fact should know that the dealer has the two highest and the non-dealer the five lowest. The remaining tricks are something of a formality:

21	♣2	♥8
22	♣7	♣Q
23	♣8	♥5
24	♣9	♣A
25	♣10	♠A
26	♦Q	♠5

So the dealer scores the points for High and Jack and the non-dealer for Low. A count of points for Game shows the dealer with 32 and the non-dealer with 48, so the non-dealer wins the point for Game. After the first hand the score is therefore 2–2.

Variants

All Fives Although descending ultimately from the parent game of All Fours, All Fives is more a variant of California Jack, because it is played in exactly the same way, the only difference being in the scoring.

There are six cards which automatically bring points to the winner of them in a trick, as follows:

Ace of trumps	4
King of trumps	3
Queen of trumps	2
Jack of trumps	1
10 of trumps	10
5 of trumps	5

In a departure from California Jack, these points are counted as they are won, rather than at the end of the deal. There is also one point for game, which is scored at the end of the deal, with the value of the cards won in tricks being as follows:

all Aces	4
all Kings	3
all Queens	2
all Jacks	1
all 10s	10
5 of trumps	5

There are therefore 85 points counting towards game, and the player with 43 or more scores the one point for game. Each deal therefore has 26 points at stake.

The winner of the game is first to 61, which makes it very convenient to score on a Cribbage board (see the illustration at Cribbage), once up and down the board being 61 points.

Shasta Sam This game is played in exactly the same way as California Jack except that the stock is face down rather than face up. Since this removes the principal element of skill in the game, it seems somewhat pointless.

Calypso

Calypso was invented in 1953 by an Englishman, R Willis, who was living in Trinidad. He was possibly inspired by the success of Canasta, which swept the world in the early 1950s. It is an ingenious and unique game which was energetically promoted in the UK and the USA in 1954 by card companies hoping to repeat the Canasta craze, but it was too soon and failed to shift Canasta from its perch.

Calypso is nevertheless an interesting game which combines elements of trick-taking from Whist or Bridge with melding from the Rummy family, and is well worth trying. Perhaps with the enthusiasm for Canasta diminishing, it deserves a re-launch.

Type	Trick-taking and melding
Alternative names	None
Players	Four, in partnerships of two; three for variants
Special requirements	Four identical packs of cards; pen and paper for scoring

Aim
To score more points than the opposition; points are scored by winning tricks and forming 'calypsos' – a complete set, from Ace to 2, of a player's own trump suit.

Cards
Four identical standard packs of 52 cards are used, shuffled together, making a pack of 208 cards. The cards rank from Ace (high) to 2 (low).

Preparation
The four players each draw a card from the joint pack, and the two who draw the highest cards become partners. If two or more players draw cards of the same rank, they redraw to decide precedence between them. The player who draws the highest card of all chooses his seat (and also becomes the first dealer), and his partner sits opposite him, with the other players taking the other seats.

In this game each player has his own trump suit, and the drawer of the highest card also has the privilege of choosing which suit will be his trumps. His choice also determines his partner's trump suit, since hearts and spades always form one partnership, with diamonds and clubs the other. Thus if the chooser takes hearts as his trump suit, his partner's trump suit will be spades. It also follows that the opponent to his left will have clubs as his trump suit and the opponent to his right diamonds, since the trump suits always follow the pattern of spades, diamonds, hearts, clubs in a clockwise direction. The arrangement is shown in the illustration overleaf, using the Bridge convention of calling the players North, South, East and West.

No suit has precedence over another – all are equal. Once each player's trump suit is established, he keeps it for the whole game.

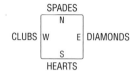

The cards are shuffled (all players may help, but the dealer has the final shuffle). The dealer places the pack before the opponent to his right, who cuts it. The dealer then takes sufficient cards into his hand to deal 13 cards to each player, one at a time, beginning with the player to his left and proceeding clockwise round the table. All remaining cards are then put to one side, as they are not needed until the next deal. A game consists of four deals, so each player will deal once (the deal passing to the left) and all the cards will be used once only.

Play

The player to the dealer's left leads to the first trick, and thereafter the winner of a trick leads to the next; see p383 for an explanation of tricks and trick-taking. Each player must follow suit to the card led if possible. If unable to, he may trump (with his personal trump suit) or discard, by playing a card of one of the other two suits.

A lead can be of a player's personal trump suit, or it can be of a plain suit. If he leads his trump suit, and all other players follow suit, he must win the trick, since the card he played was a trump. However, he is not certain to win the trick, because a player who does not hold a card of that suit may trump with his own personal trump suit. In this case, the player who trumps in wins the trick whether or not the rank of his trump is higher than the card led.

If the lead is of a side suit (ie not the leader's personal trump suit) and all follow suit, the highest ranked card in the suit wins. This is true even though one of the other players must have used a card from his personal trump suit. In this case he is considered to be following suit, and only wins the trick if his card is the highest ranked in the trick.

A lead, whether of a personal trump suit or a side suit, may be trumped by one, two or three of the other players, each using his personal trump suit. The first player to trump in will win the trick, unless a second player trumps in. In that case the second player must overtrump the first trumper by playing a card of a higher rank. If a third player trumps in, he must also trump higher to win. Thus when two or more players trump, the highest trump wins. If two or three players should trump with equally ranked trumps, the trick is won by the player whose card was played first.

The following separate examples show eight possibilities, using the Bridge convention of calling the players North, South, East and West. In each example South leads. Each player's trump suit is indicated in brackets, and the card which wins the trick is underlined – the reason why it wins is explained below the table.

	South (♥)	West (♣)	North (♠)	East (♦)
1	♥<u>7</u>	♥3	♥A	♥5
2	♦7	<u>♣</u>2	♦8	♦7
3	♦7	♦5	♦J	<u>♦A</u>
4	♦7	♦5	<u>♦J</u>	♦9
5	♥7	<u>♣</u>4	♥8	♥5
6	♥7	♣4	<u>♠</u>9	♥6
7	♥7	<u>♣</u>4	♠4	♥6
8	♥7	<u>♣</u>4	♣10	♥6

In trick 1, South wins the trick, not North, because the card South led was his own personal trump.

In trick 2, West trumped and won the trick.

In trick 3, East won the trick because he played the highest card in the suit led, not because diamonds are his personal trump suit.

In trick 4, North won because he played the highest card in the suit led, East's 9 not being regarded as a trump because it was the suit led.

In trick 5, West won because he trumped. Although South led his personal trump suit, East can win with a trump of his own suit, even though his trump is smaller than the trump led by South. South's card is regarded as the card led rather than a trump as soon as West trumps.

In trick 6, North won because, although West trumped with the ♣4, North overtrumped with the ♠9.

In trick 7, West won because, although both East and North trumped with the 4 of their personal trump suit, he was first to play.

In trick 8, West won because his ♣4 was a personal trump and North's ♣10 was a discard.

Making calypsos When a player makes a trick, he leaves face up on the table any cards which may contribute to a calypso for himself, ie cards of his own trump suit. He should arrange them clearly in sequence from Ace to 2 so that all players can see which cards he has towards a calypso and which he needs. Any cards in the trick in his partner's suit he passes to his partner, who does likewise. Cards in the opponents' suits are turned face down as rejects and kept to one side. They cannot be looked at until the end of the game. It is best if one player on each side keeps the reject pile for the side.

Calypsos can only be built one at a time. Once a calypso has been completed, it is stacked in a pile in sequence face up, with Ace at the top. A player who completes a calypso can then begin building another. In the meantime any cards won in tricks in the player's or his partner's suit which duplicate cards already on the table in a partly formed calypso must be added to the reject pile. For example, if a player has

♥A, K, 10, 9, 7, 5, 4 on the table towards a calypso, and wins a trick containing ♥J, 6, 5, he can leave the ♥J, 6 on the table and place them in sequence towards his calypso, but must discard the ♥5 in the reject pile (there are, of course, four ♥5s in the combined pack, so this doesn't necessarily scupper the chance of a second calypso, but the first must be completed before the second is begun).

A player can begin building a second calypso with cards picked up in the same trick as a card or cards which complete the first. For example, if he needs only ♥8 to complete his calypso and wins a trick containing ♥8, 6, 6, 3, he can complete his calypso with ♥8 and begin a new one with ♥6, 3. However, the other ♥6 in the trick must be rejected.

The same applies to any cards he might pass to his partner, of course. Cards which duplicate cards that the partner already has on the table in a part-calypso must be consigned to the reject pile.

Subsequent deals After the first deal, any complete and incomplete calypsos are left on the table. The original dealer cuts the cards in the unused portion of the pack (156 cards) and passes them to the player on his left, who deals 13 cards to each player in the manner described above, placing the unused 104 cards to one side for the next dealer. The player to the left of the new dealer makes the initial lead to the first trick of the second hand. In the same way, the deal passes to the next two players in turn until all four players have dealt and all cards are used. The scores are then calculated as follows. Each player scores:

For the first calypso	500 points
For the second calypso	750 points
For any subsequent calypso	1,000 points
For each card in an incomplete calypso	20 points

The above scores are scored individually; for example, if each player scores one calypso, the partnership scores 1,000 points. It is only if one player scores a second or third calypso (a fourth is highly unlikely) that the increased bonuses operate. When a partnership has added together the two players' scores, they add 10 points for each card in their joint reject pile. The partnership with the higher points total wins.

Example hand

The hands are dealt as shown below.

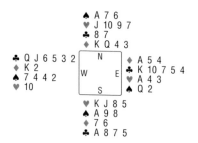

The personal trump suit of each player is shown at the top of his hand: South's suit is hearts, West's is clubs, North's is spades and East's is diamonds. South is the dealer and West makes the opening lead. West, who is rich in his own trump suit, decides to lead small trumps to pick up as many cards as possible towards a calypso as quickly as he can. The play begins:

	West (♣)	North (♠)	East (♦)	South (♥)
1	♣2	♣8	♣4	♣5
2	♣3	♣7	♣10	♣7
3	♣6	♠6	♣5	♣8

West loses his clubs as North trumps in. East plays ♣5 since he knows his partner already has ♣5 towards his calypso, so can afford to lose it to North. North now proceeds to try to win some spades by leading his own trump suit.

	West (♣)	North (♠)	East (♦)	South (♥)
4	♠2	♠7	♠2	♠8
5	♠7	♠A	♠Q	♠9
6	♦K	♦3	♦A	♦6

Having run out of spades, North led East's trump suit, hoping his partner might hold the highest diamond in play and rob East of some diamonds, but East holds the Ace and wins four diamonds towards a calypso. He leads his suit again.

	West (♣)	North (♠)	East (♦)	South (♥)
7	♦2	♦K	♦4	♦7
8	♣J	♦4	♦5	♥5

When East led diamonds again, South trumped with ♥5, but West came to the rescue by overtrumping with ♣J, thus winning back ♦5 for his partner.

	West (♣)	North (♠)	East (♦)	South (♥)
9	♠4	♦Q	♥3	♠A
10	♥10	♥J	♥4	♥K
11	♣Q	♥10	♥A	♥8
12	♣5	♥7	♣K	♣A
13	♠4	♥9	♣7	♥J

So West has eleven clubs towards a calypso, North and East eight and South six. However, the fact that ♣5 and ♣7 each appeared three times in the first hand of the game means it will be difficult for West to achieve a second calypso. In fact there were 17 clubs dealt in the first hand.

The deal showed examples of players ensuring that cards contributed to their partner's tricks were useful ones, and playing unwanted duplicate cards to their opponents' tricks. East and South both missed chances of good play. East on trick 7 might have led his ♥A, which would have removed four of South's suit from the game immediately, and South would have done well to lead ♣A at trick 10 to reduce West's trumps. Readers can construct the hands and see how these plays would have worked out. Nobody made the mistake of leading their partner's suit, since their partner would be the only player not able to trump it.

Variants

Calypso for three players This can be played by using three packs and removing one suit from it, making a combined pack of 117 cards. Each player plays for himself, and the game ends when each has dealt once. All other details of play are the same as above.

Solo calypso Solo calypso can be played by four players in the same manner as the game described, with the exception that each player scores for himself. It is less interesting and less skilful than the partnership game.

Canasta

Canasta is a Spanish word for a form of basket, but why the game is so called is a mystery. The game was invented by bored women in a club in Montevideo, Uruguay, around 1940 and swept the world with unprecedented speed. By 1950 it had conquered Uruguay, Argentina, the USA and had reached the UK, and for a while during 1950 and 1951 it ousted Bridge as the most popular game in North America.

Canasta was the game which led card manufacturers to include a second Joker in each pack – these packs were originally called Canasta packs. While the passion for the game subsided gradually, it is still a popular and interesting game.

Type	Melding
Alternative names	None
Players	Four, in partnerships of two; two, three or six players, or four playing individually, for variants
Special requirements	Two packs of cards; pen and paper for scoring

Aim
To win by scoring a total of 5,000 points.

Cards
Two standard packs of 52 cards are required, each including two Jokers, making a pack of 108 cards. All 'deuces' (2s) and Jokers are wild cards and can represent any rank of card their holders wish. 'Treys' (3s) have special qualities which will become apparent.

Preparation
The shuffled pack is spread and each player draws a card to determine first player and the partnerships. For the purpose of this draw only, the cards rank first by suit: spades (high), hearts, diamonds, clubs (low), and within suits from Ace (high) to 2 (low). If a Joker is drawn it is void, and another card drawn. The highest ranking card drawn indicates the first player (not the first dealer), and drawers of the top two cards play the lower two. Partners sit opposite each other.

The player sitting to the right of the first player deals. Thereafter the deal passes to the left with each hand. The dealer shuffles and the player to his right cuts. The dealer deals eleven cards, one at a time to each player clockwise. The undealt cards are placed face down in the centre of the table to form the stock. The top card is then turned over and placed face up beside the stock as the 'upcard'. It is the beginning of the 'discard' pile. If the upcard is a red trey (♥3 or ♦3) or a wild card, another card must be turned from the stock and placed over it, and if that is a red trey or wild card then another, until the discard pile is topped by a natural card. At all times during the game only the top card of the discard pile is to be visible: care must be taken to keep the pile squared up.

If there is a red trey or a wild card in the discard pile, the pile is said to be 'frozen', and this will be explained below.

Red trey Red treys are bonus cards that can count for or against the side which holds them, but they are not part of a player's hand. If a player is dealt one, he must place it face up on the table before him and draw the top card from the stock to replenish his hand. Similarly, a player who draws a red trey from the stock during play must lay it on the table and draw another card. If a player takes a discard pile containing a red trey, he must lay it on the table but in this case he does not draw another card from the stock.

Points Points are made by forming 'melds' (sets). A meld is a collection of three or more cards of the same rank (sequences are of no value in Canasta). The meld must contain at least two natural (ie not wild) cards, and no more than three wild cards (with the exception that wild cards can be added without restriction to an already completed 'canasta', which is a meld of seven cards of the same rank, with or without wild cards). Examples of melds are shown opposite. There are bonuses available, including one for 'going out' (playing all your cards to the table) but forming melds is the main object of play. A game consists of as many deals as it takes for a side to reach 5,000 points.

Play

The first player (ie the player who drew the highest card in the draw, sitting to the left of the dealer) is the first to take his turn, and thereafter the turn passes to the left, clockwise. A turn comprises a draw, a meld (which is optional) and a discard.

Each player in turn may first of all take the upcard, ie the top card of the discard pile. To do this he must add the card to a meld his side already has on the table, or make a new meld. For example, let us assume the upcard is a Queen. If the side already has a meld of Queens on the table, he may merely add the Queen to the meld. If the side does not have a meld of Queens on the table he must make a new meld by laying the upcard on the table and adding to it from his hand either two or more Queens (if the discard pile is frozen) or a single Queen with a wild card (if the discard pile is not frozen). The explanation of whether the pile is frozen or not follows.

However, a player who makes his side's initial meld in a deal has a further restriction: he must satisfy certain scoring requirements, which are also set out below.

A player who takes the top card of the discard pile, and melds satisfactorily, then takes the remainder of the discard pile into his hand. This might give him an opportunity to make more melds, or add to the initial ones, or both. Once he has made all the melds he wishes, he discards, ie begins a new discard pile by laying a card from his hand face up next to the stock pile.

A player who does not wish to, or cannot, take the top card of the discard pile, draws the top card from the stock and takes it into his hand. He can then meld, if he wishes, provided he can satisfy the minimum count required should it be his side's initial meld in the deal (see below). Whether he melds or not, he ends his turn by discarding a card from his hand face up to the top of the discard pile.

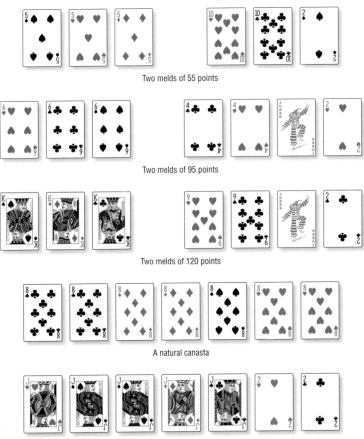

Two melds of 55 points

Two melds of 95 points

Two melds of 120 points

A natural canasta

A mixed canasta

Initial melds The first meld a side makes in each deal is subject to a 'minimum count' which depends upon that side's total number of points at the beginning of the deal. The count of a meld depends upon the cards it contains, which are valued as follows:

Each Joker counts	50
Each Deuce counts	20
Each Ace counts	20
Each K, Q, J, 10, 9, 8 counts	10
Each 7, 6, 5, 4, black 3 counts	5

The minimum count demanded of a side for its initial meld depends on its score at the beginning of the deal, as follows:

Side's score	Minimum count
Any minus score	0
0 to 1,495	50
1,500 to 2,995	90
3,000 or more	120

To achieve the minimum count to enable his side to meld, a player may make more than one meld; indeed, it is often necessary. Once the initial meld has been made, further melds can be made without satisfying a count.

The illustration on the previous page shows, from top to bottom, melds in pairs counting the minimum 50, 90 and 120 points, a natural canasta and a mixed canasta.

Frozen discard pile At times the discard pile is said to be frozen to one side or both. The restriction which a frozen discard pile brings is that a player may draw the top card from it (and subsequently take the whole pile) only if he can make a new meld by adding the top card to two natural cards from his hand. When it is not frozen, he can take the top card to meld it with only one natural card plus a wild card, or he can take it to add to a meld his side already has on the table.

There are three circumstances in which the discard pile is frozen:

i)   It is frozen to a side which has not yet melded in the deal.

ii) It is frozen to both sides if it contains a wild card or a red trey.

iii) It is frozen for one turn only if the upcard is a black trey.

The effect of a player discarding a black trey to the discard pile means that the next player must draw from the stock. When he has drawn and discarded, his discard automatically unfreezes the discard pile, unless that discard is itself a black trey or a wild card. When a player discards a wild card to freeze the pack it is customary to lay it at right angles to the pack, so that it protrudes, indicating the pack is frozen. The pack remains frozen (and indeed may have other wild cards added to it) until it is taken.

Black treys Black treys (of which there are four) are used, as described above, to freeze the discard pile for one turn. They cannot be melded during play except as a final meld. A player who wishes to go out while holding black treys can, if he holds one, do so by making it his final discard, or if he holds three or four by making them his final meld (he cannot add wild cards to them). However, he cannot go out if he holds two black treys, and must play on a little longer.

End of stock If nobody has gone out when the last card of the stock has been drawn, play continues so long as each player in turn takes and melds the card discarded by the previous player, making his own discard in turn. When the stock is exhausted, it is compulsory for a player to take the discard if it can be added to his side's melds. However, if the discard pile consists of a single card, a player with only one card in hand is not allowed to take it (if he were allowed to, he would 'go out', explained below). To make a discard deliberately so that the following player must take it, thereby keeping the deal going, is called 'forcing'. A player may, if he wishes, take the discard to form a new meld, but he is not obliged to. The play ceases when a player fails to take the discard, either because he cannot do so, or because he does not choose to use it to make a new meld. Should the last card of the stock be a red trey, the drawer cannot meld or discard, and play ends.

Going out A player goes out when he empties his hand by playing all his cards to the table in melds. He may not do so unless his side has melded at least one canasta. However, he is allowed to make that initial canasta in the process of going out. It is customary, but not obligatory, for a player who can go out, and wishes to, to ask permission of his partner. If he does so, his partner may answer only 'Yes' or 'No' (no discussion is allowed) and he is bound by the reply. If he gets permission and then finds he is unable to go out, he is penalized 100 points. When going out a player may make a final discard or not, as he wishes. Play ends when a player goes out.

Going out concealed A player may go out with a 'concealed hand' (for which there is a bonus score) if he melds all his cards at once, not having previously melded, or having laid cards on melds made by his partner. In doing so he must meld a canasta himself and cannot add to his partner's melds in the process of going out. However, he is not obliged to meet the minimum requirement for an initial meld. He may make a final discard or not, as he wishes.

Scoring When play ends, either because one player has gone out or the stock has become exhausted, a side's score is calculated by adding the total face values of all the cards melded (given above under the heading 'Initial melds') and deducting the total face values of all the cards left in the hands. It is possible, of course, that this might give a minus score. To this sum is added bonus scores as follows:

Going out (unconcealed)	100
Going out (concealed)	200
Each natural canasta	500
Each mixed canasta	300
If all four red treys are held	800
Otherwise, each red trey held	100

A side which has not melded, deducts from its score the value of any red treys it holds.

Game is to 5,000 points, and all deals are played out, even if it is clear that one side has passed 5,000 during a deal. If both sides pass 5,000 during a deal, the higher total wins. Settlement is based on the difference between the two totals.

It is important that the score of each deal is kept together with a running total after each deal. It is a side's cumulative total which determines the minimum count required for it to make an initial meld in each deal.

Strategy The chief aim is to make melds, in particular canastas. To make plenty of melds it is necessary to take a large discard pile as early as possible – the side which gets the first discard pile is on the offensive and often remains so throughout the hand. A side which has melded will seek to get down as many melds as possible, but should beware of reducing too much the cards held in hand, as the side with the most ranks, and particularly pairs, in hand is the more likely to be able to take discard piles. It follows that the initial meld should be made as economically as possible.

A side with a huge advantage of melds on the table might find it convenient to go out if the opportunity arises, particularly if it has canastas on the table and the other side looks as if it might complete one soon. On the other hand, going out can be seen as a defensive measure, as a side seeing their opponents with a huge number of cards in their hands and an advantage on the table might see going out as a damage limitation exercise.

One should try to keep safe discards, such as black treys, for when they are vital, and beware of freezing the pack unnecessarily.

Variants

Canasta for two players Canasta can be played by two individuals rather than two pairs in exactly the same way with the following exceptions: the hands are of 15 cards each; at each draw from the stock two cards are drawn and one discarded; two canastas are required to go out.

Canasta for three players Three players can play, each playing for himself, in the same manner as the parent game, with the following exceptions: the hands are of 13 cards each; at each draw from the stock two cards are drawn and one discarded.

Canasta for four individual players Four players can play, each playing for himself rather than in partnership, in the same manner as the parent game.

Canasta for six players The commonest version of the game for six players involves playing in two partnerships of three against three. Players sit alternately round the table, so that each player has an opponent each side of him. It is best played with three packs, including six jokers, making a combined pack of 162 cards. It is played as the parent game with the following exceptions: the hands are of 13 cards each; two canastas are required to go out. There are also necessary alterations to the scoring. Red treys (there are now six of them) count 100 points each up to three, and 200 points each if four or more are held. A game is to 10,000 points. The minimum counts required for an initial meld are as follows:

Side's score	Minimum count
Any minus score	0
0 to 1,495	50
1,500 to 2,995	90
3,000 to 6,995	120
7,000 or more	150

A player wishing to go out may ask permission from his left-hand partner, who may answer 'Yes', 'No' or 'Pass'. If the last the request must be answered by the other partner 'Yes' or 'No'. The player who asks is bound by the answer.

Samba Samba is an extension of Canasta in that it incorporates melding by sequence in addition to melding by rank. A sequence is of three cards or more of the same suit in ranking sequence, with the Ace ranking high. The red and black treys have the same function as in Canasta, as do deuces and Jokers, and cannot be melded in sequences. Wild cards may not be used in melds by sequence. A sequence of seven is called a 'samba'.

The differences from Canasta are:

Players	Two or three playing as individuals, four or six as two partnerships.
Cards	Three packs, each with two jokers, are used, making a combined pack of 162 cards.
Deal	Each player receives 15 cards.
Draw	Each player when drawing from the stock draws two cards and discards one.
Melds	Cards can be melded by rank or sequence. In a departure from Canasta, a meld by rank cannot include more than two wild cards, nor can it include more than seven cards (ie a canasta cannot have extra cards added to it). Three or more cards of the same suit and in sequence can be melded. This is sometimes called an *escalera* (staircase). The highest sequence of three is A, K, Q, the lowest 4, 5, 6. A sequence may not include any wild cards, and it is limited to seven cards, when it is called a 'samba'. A samba carries a bonus score of 1,500 (ie it is worth three natural canastas).
Taking the discard pile	The discard pile, if frozen, may be taken only by melding its top card with a natural pair from the hand, or, if not frozen, by adding the top card to a meld on the table. It cannot be taken by using the top card to form a sequence meld. A sequence meld must come wholly from the hand.
Going out	A side requires two canastas or two sambas or one of each to go out.
Initial meld	The requirements for an initial meld are the same as for Canasta for six players given above.
Red treys	In order to count its red treys as a plus, a side requires two canastas and/or sambas. If it holds all six red treys, they are worth 1,000 points, otherwise they count 100 points each.
Game	Game is to 10,000 points.

Casino

Nobody knows how Casino acquired its name. The assumption is that it was simply named after a casino, where it might have been found as a gambling game. Whether this is true or not, many people also spell it Cassino, with a double 's', and it appeared as Cassino in its first description in English in 1797. Ever since there have been writers who wish to correct the 'printer's error', and others (the majority) who prefer Cassino, on the grounds that even if it were a misprint it is a fortuitous one, distinguishing the game from the building. Here Casino has been chosen as it was preferred by the late George F Hervey, an expert on card games.

Casino is believed to have originated in Italy, where it would be played with the 40-card Italian pack, ie one lacking the 8s, 9s and 10s. It is often thought of as a children's game, and indeed children enjoy it, but it is just as often pointed out that it is a game of skill, where a player who can memorize the cards played has an advantage.

Type	Fishing
Alternative names	None
Players	Two; three or four for variants
Special requirements	Pen and paper for scoring

Aim
To score the most points; points are won by capturing the majority of cards from the layout, with particular attention to certain cards which carry bonuses.

Cards
The standard pack of 52 cards is used. The numeral cards count their pip values. Aces count as one. Court cards have no numerical value and are used only to make pairs.

Preparation
The players cut a spread pack, and the player who cuts the higher card (King high, Ace low) is the first dealer.

The dealer deals two cards face down to his opponent, two face up to the table layout, then two face down to himself. He repeats this so that both hands, and the table layout, contain four cards. The table layout is four cards in a line. The remaining cards are placed face down on the table.

Play
Each player, beginning with the non-dealer, plays a card in turn until their hands are exhausted. The same dealer (who deals throughout) then takes the pack and deals another four cards to each player, two at a time as before, but none to the layout (which is replenished during play, as will be seen below). The process is

repeated each time the hands are exhausted until, after six deals, the pack itself is exhausted. Before the last deal the dealer must announce 'Last'.

During the play, players capture cards from the layout. These cards, together with the cards that capture them, the player keeps face down beside him until the end of the hand.

Occasionally during play, the layout is temporarily denuded of cards. This is called a 'sweep'. The player who captures the card or cards which causes the sweep, turns one of the cards face up when adding them to his captured pile. This enables him at the end of the hand to count his total of sweeps, each of which earns a point.

A player has four choices of play, as follows:

Pairing   A player may pair a card from his hand with a card or cards from the layout and thus capture them. For example, if the layout contains one or more 3s, and the player has a 3 in his hand, he may use his 3 to capture them. He shows his 3, picks up the 3s from the layout and places the cards before him face down. This is the only way in which court cards can be captured.

Combining   A player may capture two or more cards from the table with a card the pip total of which equals the sum of the pip totals of the cards. For example, an 8 can capture a 6 and a 2, or a 4, 3 and Ace. As with pairing, a player can capture more than one combination with the same card, and may capture cards by both pairing and combining at the same time; for example, an 8 could capture an 8 (pairing) plus two 4s (combining). Note, however, that a card in the layout cannot be counted twice, ie as part of two combinations. For example, if the layout contained 6,3,3,3, a player holding a 9 could use it to capture the three 3s, or the 6 and a 3, but cannot capture all the cards, as that would involve counting one of the threes twice.

Building   A player, instead of capturing, may play a card to the layout which will allow him to capture on a future turn. For example, if there is a 3 in the layout, and the player holds a 5 and an 8, he may play the 5 to the 3 on the layout, overlapping the cards and saying 'building 8s', intending to take the two cards on a future turn. He must hold the card which will allow him to capture – he cannot build 8s without holding an 8 in his hand. This is called a 'simple build'.

           He is not obliged to capture the build on his next turn, and may prefer to make another capture first, particularly if his opponent makes a build which he himself can capture. A build is not the property only of the player making it.

           A player can make a 'multiple build' by adding other cards to the layout. For example, in the instance above, where a player adds a 5 to a 3 in the layout to build 8s, he could also play a 7 to an Ace to the layout on his next turn, with the intention of capturing all four cards with his 8 on a future turn.

           A player can also make a multiple build on a single card. Suppose there is a 6 in the layout, and the player holds two 6s. Instead of using one 6 to capture that in the layout, thus capturing two cards, he could play one of his 6s to the 6 in the layout and announce 'building 6s'. On his next turn he could then capture both 6s in the layout with his remaining 6, thus capturing three cards rather than two. In the same way, if he holds two 6s and the layout includes a 4 and a 2, he can combine the 4 and 2 and play one 6 to them announcing 'building 6s', enabling him to capture all three cards next turn with his remaining 6.

A build can also be increased. Suppose there is a 3 in the layout, and the player holds a 6 and a 9, he can play the 6 to the 3 and build 9s. If he also has an Ace and a 10, he can on his next turn add the Ace to the build and announce 'building 10s', using his 10 on his next turn to capture all three cards. As 10 is the highest card in the pack, it follows that a build cannot exceed ten.

As stated, a build is not the property of the player making it, and as well as capturing his opponent's build, a player may add to it. Suppose the opponent is building 7s, and a player holds a 9 and a 2. He can add the 2 to the build and announce 'building 9s'. Building on an opponent's build is a good move, since it not only provides three cards in the layout which can be captured, but leaves the opponent holding a card (in the example a 7) which he now cannot use.

It is not permitted, however, to increase a multiple build. For example, if a player building 6s has a 4 and a 2, and also a 5 and an Ace, in the layout, it is not permitted to add a card to one of the builds to increase it further. Note the difference between a multiple build and a simple build. If, for example, a player builds a 3 to another 3, and announces 'building 3s', in order to take both 3s with a third 3, that is a multiple build which therefore cannot be built on. However, had he announced 'building 6s', with the intention of taking both 3s with a 6, that is a simple build, and can be built on, for example by playing a 2 to it and announcing 'building 8s'.

Once a card is part of a build, it cannot be captured individually. For example, if a 2 in the layout has had a 3 added to it by a player building 5s, neither the 2 not the 3 can be captured by a player holding another 2 or 3.

It is worth emphasizing that to make a build, the player must hold in his hand a card to take it. If, for example, there is a 5 in the layout, and a player holds A, 2, 8, Q, he cannot add the Ace to the 5 and announce 'building 6s', and next turn add the 2 and announce 'building 8s', with the intention of taking all three cards with his 8, because he does not hold a 6 which would have permitted him to build 6s in the first place. A player who builds without holding the requisite card in his hand automatically loses the game.

Trailing If a player on his turn cannot pair, combine or build, he must trail, which is to add a card from his hand face up to the layout. This is how the layout is replenished, and may become larger than the original four cards. A player may trail even if he is able to pair, combine or build, unless he has a build in the layout, when he is obliged to capture it before he can trail.

When a sweep occurs, and the layout is cleared of cards, the next player has no option but to trail.

Scoring Points are scored as follows:

Cards The player who captures the majority of the cards (ie 27 or more) scores three points.

Spades The player who captures the majority of the spades (ie seven or more) scores one point.

Big casino The player who captures the ♦10 scores two points.

Little casino The player who captures the ♠2 scores one point.

Aces A player scores one point for each Ace captured.

There are therefore eleven points at stake to be won in this manner, though the points for cards is not scored if each player captures 26 cards.

A further point is scored for each sweep recorded by each player, ie for each time a player clears the layout. As mentioned earlier, this is best recorded by turning a card in the captured pile face up – each face-up card represents a point.

If there are cards in the layout when all play has finished, then the player who made the last capture takes them. This does not count as a sweep, but the cards count in all the categories.

Game Games can be played as one deal (ie until the pack is exhausted), in which case the player with the most points wins. Otherwise the game is to 21 points. In this case it is best to play every deal to the end, then count each player's points in the order set out above, from cards down to sweeps, and then add them to the previous total. When players approach 21 the points should still be taken in this order, and hence someone might win with 21 having scored three points for cards first, even if the opponent would score the next five points and finish with a higher total overall.

Example hand
The layout and hands are dealt as shown.

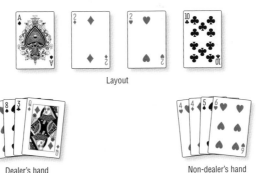

Layout

Dealer's hand

Non-dealer's hand

The non-dealer has a number of options on his first turn. He can capture the A, 2, 2, with his 5. Or he could add the two 2s together and play a 4 to them announcing 'building 4s', with the intention of taking all three cards with his other 4. He could play his 5 to the Ace and announce 'building 6s', and take them with his 6 next time, leaving the 2s and 4s to be taken later.

He decides on the first course, since he wants to make sure of the Ace for a point, and by doing this he captures four cards, including the Ace and two spades. Notice that had he left the Ace untouched, the dealer would have played his 7 to it, building 8s, and would have captured it himself.

The non-dealer therefore captures ♠A, ♦2, ♥2 with ♠5. The dealer trails his Queen. The non-dealer trails ♦4, intending to capture this 4 with his other 4 next turn. The dealer builds ♣3 onto ♦4, announcing 'building 7s', thus thwarting the non-dealer's plan; instead the non-dealer now trails ♥4. The dealer captures ♦4, ♣3 with ♥7. The non-dealer trails ♥6. The dealer trails ♠8.

So after the first hand, the non-dealer has captured four cards, including an Ace and two spades, and the dealer three. There are five cards in the layout. The dealer now picks up the non-used part of the pack and deals four cards to each two at a time, and play begins again.

Variants

Some players prefer not to count scores for sweep on the grounds that sweeps are gained more by luck than judgement, and the points for sweep unbalance the scores.

Casino for three players Casino is played by three players in exactly the same manner as for two, with each player playing for himself. There are only four hands each per deal, ie before the pack is exhausted. The eldest hand (the player to the dealer's left) plays first and the dealer last. It is considered that the eldest hand and the dealer have an advantage over the other player, so it is fairer not to play to a set total of points, but to total the scores after each player has dealt once. If there is a tie on the count for cards or spades, no points are scored.

Casino for four players Casino can be played by four players in partnerships of two, with partners sitting opposite each other. While partners combine the points made in captures, the rules are exactly the same as in the basic game. For example, a player seeing his partner build 7s, say, cannot himself build a 7 for his partner to take, without himself holding a 7. There will be only three hands per deal. Players can agree on the length of a game. It could be of 21 points, or a number of deals: one per side, or one per player.

Royal Casino Royal Casino is often thought to be a better game than the parent game in that more skill and concentration are required. There are two differences. Court cards are given values and treated like the other cards: Jack counts as 11, Queen as 12 and King as 13. In addition Ace can count as 1 or 14 at the discretion of the player. Thus 6, 4, 3 might be captured with a King, or it might have an Ace added to it, building 14s, which could be captured by another Ace. Scoring is as for the parent game, and two to four people can play.

Spade Casino Spade Casino is played the same way as the basic game, but with a change to the scoring. Instead of the category spades, in which a player or side scores a point for the majority of spades, one point is awarded for each spade captured, with an extra point for the Jack. As the ♠A and ♠2 also earn an extra point for being an Ace and little casino respectively, this means that ♠A, J and 2 are worth two points each, the other spades one. The total points available, excluding sweeps, is thus 24 (as opposed to eleven in the parent game). If not played to an agreed number of deals, the game is played to 61 points, which makes a Cribbage board (see the illustration at Cribbage) a convenient means of scoring.

Draw Casino Draw Casino introduces a different method of dealing which can be applied to any of the variants above. After the first deal of the hands and layout, the remaining cards are placed in the centre face down to form a stock. Each time a player plays a card he draws the top card of the stock to replace it. By this means each player's hand remains at four cards, and no further deals are necessary. When the stock is exhausted, each player plays his last four cards in the usual way.

Cheat

Cheat is a very simple children's game.

Type	Children's
Alternative names	I Doubt It
Players	Three to eight; five to eight is best
Special requirements	None

Aim
To get rid of all the cards in your hand.

Cards
The standard pack of 52 cards is used.

Preparation
From a pack scattered face down on the table, each player draws a card to determine the first dealer. The drawer of the highest card deals. Cards for this purpose rank from Ace (high) to 2 (low). If two or more players tie for highest card they draw again.

The dealer deals one card at a time face down to all players until the pack is exhausted. It does not matter if some players receive one card more than others.

Play
The players take their cards into their hands. The player to the dealer's left then plays up to four cards, of any rank or suit, face down in a fan to the centre of the table. At the same time he announces how many cards are being played and that

they are of the same rank, for example calling 'four 2s', 'one King' or 'two 9s'. The player can either announce correctly what he has played, or can choose to lie. Thus three cards played and announced as 'three Aces', for example, may indeed be three Aces; but they may instead comprise A, 2, 6, or 3, Q, K, or any other combination of cards from the player's hand.

The next player clockwise must then play up to four cards face down to the first card, and announces them as the next higher value. For example, if the first player had announced 'one 6', the next player must announce between one and four '7s'. The following player must then play a card or cards and announce a number of '8s', and so on. The sequence is endless, with Ace following King. These cards might be played as announced or they might not, as each player can lay whatever cards he likes. Indeed, he may not even hold a card of the denomination required, and is therefore forced to lie.

At any time a player who thinks that an opponent has lied in announcing the value of the card or cards played may call out 'cheat'. The card or cards are then turned over for all to see. If the player did indeed cheat, and the card or cards are not what he announced, then the one who cheated must pick up all the cards on the table and add them to his hand. The player who successfully called him then leads a card or cards to start a new round, announcing the rank (either truly or falsely, as desired).

If the player called did not cheat and the card or cards are what was announced, then the player who wrongly called 'cheat' must pick up all the cards and add them to his hand, while the virtuous player who was falsely accused leads to a new round.

If more than one player calls 'cheat' and there is an argument as to who was first, the one sitting nearest to the left of the accused is regarded as first.

If a player has lied about the cards played, but no one calls 'cheat' and the next person plays his cards to the table, he has cheated successfully and cannot be called a 'cheat' retrospectively. He is the only one to know of his deception, and smugly continues to play in the usual way.

As soon as a player realizes that to call 'cheat' risks having to pick up all the cards, and that it is best to allow somebody else to shout 'cheat', then he is getting too old for the game. But young children get fun out of accusing others of cheating. Parents should appreciate that if a player laying down his last card is accused of 'cheating', as he always should be, it is extremely likely that he is cheating, and will have to pick up the cards. So the game continues … and continues …

Variants
Some people play that only one card can be put down at a time, making for an even lengthier game.

Alternatively, some people play that any number of cards can be put on the table at one go, but, as they must be announced as the same rank, four remains the maximum that can be announced. This necessitates some skill on the part of players placing cards on the table to ensure that a carefully arranged fan of 'four' cards isn't nudged as it is put down to reveal other cards hidden beneath. This kind of audacious cheating often causes great hilarity when discovered, but can lead to ever more outrageous attempts to cheat, leaving the game to descend into outright silliness.

Cinch

Cinch is a version of All Fours with bidding added. It became very popular in Denver, Colorado, about 1885 and quickly spread through the USA until the success of Auction Bridge began to take over. The name is believed to come from a verb meaning to fix a strong restraining saddle-girth on a horse, which came to describe the way a player can make sure of not losing a trick to a valuable card by cinching it. Cinch is a skilful game, best played in partnerships, which might intrigue Bridge players.

Type	Trick-taking
Alternative names	Double Pedro, High Five
Players	Four, in partnerships of two; two to six for variants
Special requirements	Pen and paper for scoring

Aim
To score more points than your opponents.

Cards
The standard pack of 52 cards is used. The cards rank from Ace (high) to 2 (low), but there is one peculiarity. There is a trump suit which contains an extra card: the 5 of the suit of the same colour as the nominated trump suit. This card ranks between the 5 and 4 of the trump suit, and is a trump itself. Thus if spades are trumps, the ♣5 is also a trump, and the trump suit ranks ♠A, K, Q, J, 10, 9, 8, 7, 6, 5, ♣5, ♠4, 3, 2.

The 5 of the trump suit is called the 'right pedro', while the 5 of the same colour is called the 'left pedro'.

Preparation
From a spread pack, players each draw a card, those drawing the two highest playing against the two lowest, with players drawing cards of equal rank (unless they are equal lowest) drawing again to determine precedence. The highest drawer becomes the first dealer. Partners sit opposite each other.

The dealer has the right to shuffle last, and the player to his right cuts the pack before the deal. The dealer deals nine cards to each player, in bundles of three, beginning with the player to his left, and proceeding clockwise.

Bidding On examining their hands, each player, beginning with the eldest hand (the player to the dealer's left) and proceeding clockwise, makes a bid or passes. A bid is made by indicating the number of points a player promises to make, together with his partner, with the trump suit of his choice. He does not, at this stage, name the trump suit. Each bid must be higher than a previous bid, or a player can pass without bidding. The minimum bid is one, and the maximum 14, which promises to take all the points. There is only one round of bidding, each player having only one opportunity to bid. Partners must not collude in any way in the bidding.

When all players have either bid or passed, the highest bidder names the trump suit. If the first three players pass, then the dealer may name the trump suit without the need to contract to make a certain number of tricks.

Discarding The next stage is to reduce all hands to six cards. To begin, each player in clockwise order may discard as many cards as he wishes, with a minimum of three. No player may discard a trump, unless he is forced to by holding more than six originally, in which case he shows the trump to the others as he discards it. A player who discards more than three cards will have his hand replenished by the dealer. In practice most players will discard all cards that aren't trumps, although some players sometimes keep one or more plain cards.

The eldest hand is first to discard, and have his hand made up to six. When it is the dealer's turn, the procedure is different. He is allowed to 'rob the pack'. This entitles him to look through the remaining cards and take any cards he wishes into his hand. He will naturally take all the trumps that remain. If his hand plus the remainder of the pack contains more than six trumps he cannot take them all into his hand, and must show to the other players any trumps which are outstanding.

Of course, if there are no trumps outstanding, and no player has been forced to discard any by being dealt seven or more, in the trick-taking phase of the game 14 of the 24 cards in play will be trumps.

Play
The player who named the trump suit (the 'maker') leads to the first trick, and subsequently the winner of a trick leads to the next; see p383 for an explanation of tricks and trick-taking.

If a trump is led, a player must follow suit if he can. If a plain suit is led, a player who can follow suit has the choice to follow suit or trump as he wishes, but he may not discard. If unable to follow suit, he may trump or discard. A trick is won by the highest trump it contains, or, failing a trump, the highest card of the suit led.

Scoring When the trick-taking phase has ended, each side counts the number of points it has won. Points are made by winning tricks containing certain cards in the trump suit. These are:

Right pedro (5 of trumps)	5	2 (known as 'low')	1
Left pedro (5 of same colour)	5	Jack (known as 'jack')	1
Ace (known as 'high')	1	10 (known as 'game')	1

There are thus 14 points available in each deal.

If the making side has made its contract, by winning the amount of points or more that it bid, the side with the higher number of points wins the difference between the two sides, for example if the making side makes nine points, it makes the difference between nine and the opposition's five, ie four. However, it does not follow that the making side, even if it makes its contract, scores the points. If the contract had been six, and six points were made, the opposition side would have eight and thus score the difference between the two sides themselves, ie two.

If the making side fails to make its contract it scores nothing. The opposing side scores all the points they took in tricks, plus the amount of the bid. Thus, if the bid were nine, and the bidding side made only eight, their opponents would score six for the points they made plus nine for the value of the failed bid, ie 15.

If all players passed, and the dealer made trumps without a contract, then each side scores the points it makes in the play.

If settlement is not per deal, and a running score is kept, the winning side by tradition is the first to 51 points, but the convenience of the Cribbage board (see the illustration at Cribbage) has led to many players taking 61 as the requirement, this being once up and down the board.

Strategy A side making its contract and taking all 14 points will add 14 points to its running total towards winning the game. This is the maximum it can make. On the other hand, the minimum it can lose if it fails to make its contract is 15 points (if it makes one fewer point than it bid; it loses 14 points plus the number it was short of its bid). It follows that a side should be careful not to overbid.

Since all the cards which contribute towards the points total at the end of a deal are trumps, it follows that it is impossible to win any points with cards from plain suits. This is why in discarding most players keep only their trumps and discard all the rest. The lead is not an advantage, unless a player has enough master trumps to capture all the scoring cards straight away. The player in fourth position has the advantage of knowing what he has to beat. The capture of the pedros plays a major part in the play, and it is dangerous to allow a player playing last to a trick to be in a position to win it with a pedro, thus ensuring five points for his side. A player in third position will prevent this if he can by playing a higher trump than the 5. This is known as 'cinching'.

A simple bidding system has gained some currency to help players convey information to their partners legitimately (as in Bridge). It is as follows (with x meaning a small trump):

With a 5	bid five
With A, x, x or A, x, x, x	bid six
With A, K	bid seven
With A, K, J, x, x or better	bid eleven
With A, K, Q, x	bid eleven

Example hand
The Bridge convention of calling the players North, South, East and West is used in the following example. South bid eight and, as the highest bidder, named clubs as trumps. He had been dealt ♣A, Q, 10, 8, and drew ♠5 (left pedro) and ♦8. His partner drew four and unluckily failed to get another trump. East drew four and picked up a trump and West robbed the pack of four trumps, including right pedro, leaving the hands as illustrated overleaf.

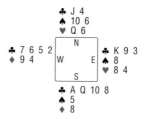

```
              ♣ J 4
              ♠ 10 6
              ♥ Q 6
              ┌───N───┐
♣ 7 6 5 2     │       │    ♣ K 9 3
♦ 9 4       W │       │ E  ♠ 8
              │       │    ♥ 8 4
              └───S───┘
              ♣ A Q 10 8
              ♠ 5
              ♦ 8
```

South has to win his Ace, left pedro, 10 (game) and another point to make his contract.

The play went as follows:

	South	West	North	East
1	♣A	♣6	♣J	♣3
2	♣8	♣7	♣4	♣9
3	♣Q	♣2	♠6	♣K
4	♦8	♦4	♥6	♥4
5	♠5	♣5	♥Q	♥8
6	♣10	♦9	♠10	♠8

South had mixed feelings after the first lead. He picked up the points for Ace and Jack, but because his partner had not played left pedro, he knew that the opponents held it.

The clever play of West at trick 3 scuppered South's hopes of his contract. Under his partner's King, West could have played left pedro, assuring five points for his side, but he realized that ten trumps had been played, leaving four, and that he held two of them. If he played his pedro, leaving himself with only the ♣2, and South, as was likely, held both the other two trumps, his side might not make another point and South would probably make nine points and his contract. Whereas if he kept his right pedro, and South held ♣10, ♠5, he would still be sure to make it. So he played ♣2, contributing the point for low to his side. He could have played right pedro on trick 4, knowing North did not possess a trump, but cleverly held it back again.

On trick 5, South needed to make both his trumps for his contract, and after East had followed to the heart lead, had to assume East held right pedro, as it was the only way to make his contract. He therefore played left pedro on trick 5, hoping to win right pedro with his ♣10 on the last trick, to land his contract by 13 points to one, a contribution of twelve points towards the overall game. But West took the trick, and although South won the last trick he failed miserably to make his contract, scoring just three points (for Jack, Ace and 10). East–West therefore scored the sum of their points won (11) plus the value of the failed contract (8), a total of 19.

Variants

Some players insist that when discarding, all players must discard all cards which are not trumps. By this means each player knows the minimum number of trumps each other player holds.

Cut-throat Cinch Two to six players can play, with each player playing for himself in all cases. The dealer does not rob the pack, instead discarding and drawing in the same way as the other players. With five or six players, each player is dealt six cards only, and therefore receives the same number of cards as he discards.

With two players, the scoring is as described for the partnership game above. With three to six players when a contract is made, the maker scores the difference between the two totals if he makes the majority of points. If the maker fails to make the majority of points, even though he makes his contract, each of the other players scores the difference. If the maker fails to make his contract, each of the other players scores the amount of the bid, plus the number of points he himself made as an individual.

Auction Cinch Auction Cinch is for five or six players and is also known as Razzle Dazzle. It is the most popular version of the game when five or six play. Each player plays for himself.

Six cards are dealt to each player in bundles of three, and players bid and discard as in the parent game, so that all hands remain at six cards. At the discard stage players must keep all trumps and discard all non-trumps.

The maker then names a card of the trump suit which is not in his own hand (usually, of course, the highest trump he is missing). The holder of that trump acknowledges it, and he and the maker become partners against the other three or four players. All players remain seated where they are, so the two playing as partners might find themselves next to each other.

Scoring is as in the parent game; if the contract is made each player on the side with most points scores the difference. If the contract fails, each player of the non-contracting side scores the number of the contract plus the number of points he made as an individual.

Cinch with a widow This is an interesting variation of the parent game, for two partnerships of two. Thirteen cards are dealt to each player, the usual nine in bundles of three, and an extra bundle of four which is dealt between the first and second bundles of three and is dealt apart from the remainder, so that when each player picks up his nine-card hand, the extra four cards remain face down before him. These cards form a 'widow'. After the bidding, instead of the drawing, each player takes the cards from his widow into his hand and the maker announces the trump suit. Players then each discard seven cards to bring their hands to six cards. If a player is forced to discard a trump he must show it to all players. Scoring is as in the parent game.

Clock

There are at least two patience games with a clock layout for the tableau: one is usually called Clock, and the other Grandfather's Clock. This is the first, and the simplest. It is a good game to teach a child learning to tell the time, but its attractive layout means it can be diverting for all ages.

Type	Patience
Alternative names	Sundial, Travellers
Players	One
Special requirements	Playing surface large enough for a clock face layout

Aim
To end with every card turned face up in piles by rank, laid out in the form of a clock face.

Cards
The standard pack of 52 cards is used.

Preparation
The cards are shuffled and dealt to a tableau in the form of a clock face: twelve packets of four cards are dealt face down to positions representing the twelve numbers on the dial. It does not matter whether the cards are dealt one at a time to each position in turn, or in batches of four. A final packet of four is placed in the centre of the clock face.

Play
Play begins with the top card of the centre packet being turned over and placed face up on the outside of the packet on the clock face which represents the number of the rank of the card. For example, a 3 of any suit would be placed face up outside the packet at the three o'clock position on the dial. An Ace represents 1 o'clock, a Jack 11 o'clock and a Queen 12 o'clock. A King which is turned up is placed face up next to the packet in the centre.

When a card has been played to its spot on the dial or the centre, the top card is taken from the face-down packet in that position and played in turn to its appropriate position, with a card being taken from there and played to its spot, and so on. The illustration opposite shows a game in progress.

The game ends in failure if the fourth King appears before all the numbers on the clock face are filled with face-up cards, because when the fourth King appears and is played to the middle there are no more face-down cards there with which to carry on the game. The game is won if every card gets turned face up (ie, if the final card to be turned face up is the fourth King).

113

Comet

Comet is one of the earliest known games of the stops family. It was described in 1768 as a 'new game', but is believed to have got its name in 1758 with the reappearance, as predicted, of Halley's Comet. 'Comet' became popular as a brand name for all sorts of products for many years.

Type	Stops
Alternative names	Commit
Players	Two; three to five for variants
Special requirements	Two identical packs of cards; pen and paper for scoring if a series of deals is desired

Aim
To get rid of all the cards in your hand by playing them to the table.

Cards
Two identical standard packs of 52 cards are required, from which are removed the Aces. The red cards are then separated from the black cards. A ♦9 is taken from the red pack and swapped with a ♣9 in the black pack. Two 48-card packs are thus formed, a black pack containing a ♦9 and a red pack containing a ♣9. The two packs are used alternately. The odd card in each pack is called the 'comet', and it is used as a wild card. The other cards are ranked from King (high) to 2 (low), and suits are of no significance.

Preparation
Players cut the pack which is to be first used, and the player cutting the lower card becomes the dealer.

The dealer shuffles, the non-dealer cuts and the dealer deals 18 cards to each player in bundles of three. The remaining twelve cards are set aside face down and take no further part in the game.

Play
The non-dealer plays any card to the centre of the table, and continues to play cards to it in ascending sequence irrespective of suit, announcing the rank of the cards as he plays them and announcing the number at which he is forced to stop, for example he may say '5, 6, 7, 8, without 9'; instead of 'without 9' he might say 'no 9'. The turn then passes to the dealer who, if he can, continues the sequence. To follow the example he may announce and play, '9, 10, Jack, without Queen'. The turn to play passes back and forth until one player plays all his cards to the table.

If a player on his turn cannot continue the sequence, he says 'Pass', and the turn passes back to his opponent, who then begins a new sequence by playing any card or cards he wishes. A King is always a stop, and the player playing it begins a new sequence with another card or cards.

All cards played by both players are played to one face-up pile in the centre of the table. Neither player during the play may look back to check which cards have already been played.

Players must play if they can, and cannot pass or stop if able to play a card. There is one exception: a player may reserve the comet if that is the only card he can play.

Only one card can be played at a time, except when a player holds all four cards of the same rank, or three 9s, with or without the comet. He can then play them simultaneously if he wishes. For example, he may play and announce '7, four 8s, three 9s, 10, without Jack'.

The comet can be played at any time in a player's turn, and can represent any card the player wishes. It always acts as a stop. The player who plays the comet then begins a new sequence, with any card he chooses.

Scoring When a player goes out, ie gets rid of all his cards, he scores the total number of pips of the cards remaining in his opponent's hand, with court cards counting as ten points each. If a player is caught with the comet in his hand when his opponent goes out, his count for all unplayed cards is doubled.

When a player goes out by playing the comet as his last card (not as a 9) he scores double the count of the cards left in his opponent's hand, and if he goes out by playing the comet as his last card, representing a 9, he scores quadruple his opponent's count.

If the non-dealer goes out on his first turn, he scores double the pip count of his opponent's cards (quadruple if his opponent holds comet). However, if the dealer can also go out in one turn, the deal is a tie.

If the deal is not to be regarded as a game in itself, but that play should continue for an agreed number of deals, or to an agreed number of points, then the score can be kept by pencil and paper, or on a Cribbage board (see the illustration at Cribbage), when 121 would be a reasonable total for game.

Strategy In the early play, one should try to get rid of duplicated ranks first. As play progresses it is important to remember which ranks constitute stops for the opponent and to try to play up to them. If the opponent looks close to going out, it is wise to try to play high-ranking cards and to beware of being caught with the comet when the opponent goes out.

Variants

Comet for three to five players Comet can be played by up to five players by reducing the number of cards dealt. With three players each receives twelve cards in bundles of three, leaving twelve cards inactive; with four players, each receives ten cards in bundles of two, with eight inactive; with five players, each receives nine cards in bundles of three, with three inactive.

The turn of play passes to the left, and if all pass on a stop round to the player who caused the stop, then that player begins a new sequence.

Scoring is as before, but if the game is to be over a series of deals a plus and minus score must be kept for each player.

Commit Commit is really the same as Comet, the alternative name coming about, it is thought, merely because of a misspelling as long ago as the early 19th century. The game described above is sometimes called Commit in books, but some use the name Commit to describe this variation, for from three to seven players.

Only one pack is required, from which the ♦8 is removed and not used, leaving a 51-card pack. The ♦9 is the comet. The game is usually played as a gambling game. Cards rank from King (high) to Ace (low).

Each player puts a stake of one unit into a pool before the deal. Cards are dealt one at a time. With three players, each receives 15 cards, six remaining face down to one side. With four players each receives twelve cards, with five each receives ten cards, with six each receives eight cards and with seven each receives seven cards, thereby leaving between one and three cards dead on each deal.

A difference from Comet is that sequences have to be of the same suit. The eldest hand (the player to the dealer's left) plays first and can play to the centre any card or sequence of cards he wishes, bearing in mind sequences are in suits, so he may say '3, 4 of hearts, missing 5'. Play circulates to the left, so the player to the eldest hand's left either plays the ♥5 or says 'pass', whereupon the next player has the opportunity. If all pass, the player who last played a card begins a new sequence.

The comet also has a different function to that in Comet. The player who holds it may play it at any time on his turn. The player on his left then has the choice of continuing the sequence where it was, or using the comet (♦9) as the beginning of a new sequence and continuing with ♦10. If he can do neither, the opportunity passes to his left. As soon as a player plays a card to follow the comet the sequence is determined and play continues as normal. From then on, it is unnecessary for play to proceed clockwise. As soon as a card is played, the holder of the next in sequence may announce it and play it. It will be quickly clear when a stop is reached, and the player of the last card begins a new one.

The player of the comet wins two units of the stake from each player. The player of a King wins one unit from each player. The first player to get rid of his cards wins the pool, and also wins an extra unit for each King any player is holding at the end, and two from a player careless enough to be holding comet.

Coon Can

Coon Can is the oldest-known type of Rummy game. Its name is derived from *con quien*, the Spanish for 'with whom', although nobody can explain how or why. It was first noted as a widely played game in Mexico and Texas in the 1880s and described in 1898 as Conquian. 'Coon Can' is also used in the USA as an alternative name for Double Rummy, although it is quite a different game.

Type	Melding
Alternative names	Conquian
Players	Two
Special requirements	None

Aim

To get rid of your cards by melding them into sets, either by rank or sequence; you must finish with eleven cards melded, so the last play must be to draw a card, which you need not discard.

Cards

As this is a Mexican game, the Spanish pack of 40 cards is used. The usual practice in reducing the standard 52-card pack to a 40-card pack is to remove the 8s, 9s and 10s, but since this is a game in which sequences feature, it seems logical to remove the court cards from a standard pack. This prevents the awkwardness of a sequence of 6, 7, J, Q. The cards rank in each suit from 10 (high) down to Ace (low).

Preparation

Each player draws a card, and the lowest deals first. The dealer deals ten cards to each player in bundles of two at a time. The remaining pack is placed face down in the centre to form the stock.

Play

The non-dealer takes the top card from the stock and exposes it face up beside the stock. If he can meld it, by laying on the table two or three cards of the same rank from hand, or two or more cards of the same suit in sequence with the turned up card added to them, he may do so, if he wishes. A meld must be of at least three cards. If not, he pushes it towards the dealer, who may take it in the same manner. If he cannot use it, he passes it, by turning it face down and moving it to one side to begin a pile of discards. Once a card has been discarded in this manner, it is out of the game altogether.

When a player passes a card, he turns over the next card of the stock, placing it by the stock face up. He has the first opportunity to meld this card, and if he cannot, or does not wish to, he pushes it towards his opponent, who may take it or pass.

When a player takes a card and melds, he must discard from hand, by pushing his discard towards his opponent, who has the same choices, either to meld with it or to pass. A player who has already melded, may take an available card to add to an existing meld, and discard.

Unlike many games of the Rummy family, a player cannot take a card into his hand for possible later use.

It will be noted that each player each turn has the choice of two cards – the card offered to him, and if he doesn't want it, the top card of the stock.

Going out A player does not discard when going out. To go out a player must have eleven cards melded. Since his hand is of ten cards only, it follows that his last meld, or addition to a meld, must be made without a discard. If a player has ten cards melded, and therefore none in hand, he must continue drawing until he draws a card which he can add to an existing meld, and thus go out.

Hitting A player may, on his turn, hit a meld of his own to create a new meld. For example, if he has a meld of four 8s on the table and holds ♦6, 9 in hand, and ♦7 is available, he may 'switch' the melded cards, by taking ♦8 from his existing meld and melding ♦6, 7, 8, 9. It is possible to hit only a four-card meld, since the meld left on the table must be a legitimate one, ie of at least three cards. Similarly, it is possible to hit a sequence meld, but only by taking a card from either end, ie of ♦2, 3, 4, 5, it is only allowed to take the 2 or 5, since a legitimate meld would remain, but not the 3 or 4, since the sequence would be spoiled.

Forcing A player may 'force' his opponent to take a card which he doesn't want. There are two ways to do this. Suppose Player A has two four-card sequences on the table as melds, with two cards in hand, and he draws from the stock a card which he could add to his melds, but refuses it and pushes it towards his opponent. Player B will reason that he would only do this if he held in his hand a pair or two cards in sequence and is waiting for a matching card to enable him to go out. So Player B may force Player A to take the card by picking it up and adding to his meld, saying 'discard'. Player A will then have to discard, having one card in his hand, and the necessity, because of the need to meld 11 cards, to draw two more meldable cards instead of one.

The other way of forcing is when Player A holds in his hand a card which could be added to one of Player B's melds, Player B holding two cards in his hand. When Player A melds, and thus has to discard from hand, he may 'play off' this card to Player B's meld, thus forcing his opponent to discard, which ends his turn, leaving him with one card only in his hand, and the need to meld twice more.

Scoring The game ends when one player has melded eleven cards. It can (and often does) happen that a player has melded ten cards and therefore has none in his hand. Play continues until he can take an available card and add it to one of his melds, or until his opponent goes out.

If neither player goes out before the stock is exhausted, the game is a tie, called a 'tableau', or 'tab'.

Each deal is a game in itself. If the game is played for stakes, settlement is made after each game, and when a tableau occurs, each player puts a stake into a pool, and the winner of the next game takes the pool, as well as the stake for winning. A stake is added to the pool for each tie.

Strategy It will be noticed that the biggest single meld possible is of ten cards, a complete sequence. So to win a player needs at least two melds. The first task is therefore to sort the hand and identify all pairs of cards which might be melded by the addition of another, and take care not to discard any card which might be useful.

The illustration above shows a hand in which there are three pairs, of Aces, 6s and 7s, and two possible sequences containing ♣8, 10 and ♦6, 7. There is no chance at the moment of melding a sequence of hearts, since one cannot pick up the ♥2, 3 or ♥5, 6. The ♠2 and ♥4 are the only unusable cards at the moment. However, if one could meld 6s, the ♥4 and ♥7 become a possible meld, because if the four 6s could be obtained, the availability of the ♥5 would allow the 6s to be hit, and the ♥6 used in a meld of ♥4, 5, 6, 7. Therefore, the ♠2 should be discarded at the first meld. If the ♥5 is passed before the 6s can be melded, then of course the ♥4 is useless.

As play progresses, good players will get an idea of their opponent's hand by noticing the discards, and will discard accordingly when they meld.

Crazy Eights

Crazy Eights is a simple gambling game. The name 'Crazy Eights' is also sometimes used for a version of the game included in this book under the name Switch. Switch is a game in which the wild cards are variable and when the wild cards are, for instance, Aces or Jacks, the game is often called Crazy Aces or Crazy Jacks. A popular version with 8s as the wild cards has become known as Eights, but some people like to call it Crazy Eights. The name is reserved in this book for the following game, quite unrelated to Switch.

Type	Gambling
Alternative names	None
Players	Two to eight; four to eight is best
Special requirements	Chips or coins for staking

Aim
To play all your cards to the centre.

Cards
The standard pack of 52 cards is used. The ranking of the cards is immaterial, but for settlement purposes cards have the following points values: Aces 15, court cards 10, other cards their pip value.

Preparation
Any player may pick up the cards, shuffle and begin to deal cards one at a time to each player round the table until a Jack appears. The player dealt the Jack becomes the first dealer. The deal then rotates clockwise.

Each player puts a stake of two units into the centre to form a pool. The dealer shuffles, the player to his right cuts, and the dealer deals five cards face down to each player, including himself, one at a time. He then lays out the next eight cards face up to the centre in two rows of four, and puts the rest to one side. It doesn't matter if ranks are duplicated.

Play
Beginning with the eldest hand (the player to the dealer's left), each player in turn may lay one card only from his hand face up to a card in the centre matching it in rank. As play progresses, more than one player may play a card to the same card in the centre. A player who cannot match a card in his hand with one in the centre passes.

Should a player get rid of all his cards, he shouts 'Crazy Eights' and collects the whole pool.

Should the game end without any player being able to get rid of his cards, each player counts the total value of the cards in his hand, based on the scale already given. Half the pool goes to the player with the highest count, and half to the player with the lowest. If two or more share for highest or lowest, their half of the pool is divided between them, with any units over being left in the pool for the next game.

Example game

| Player A | Player B | Player C |

Table

| Player D | Player E | Player F |

In the illustration, no player managed to scoop the pool of twelve units. The scores were as follows:

Player A	15 (two cards left)
Player B	12 (two cards left)
Player C	23 (four cards left)
Player D	2 (one card left)
Player E	21 (three cards left)
Player F	2 (one card left)

Thus Player C took six units for highest, and Player D and Player F took three units each for joint lowest.

Cribbage

According to John Aubrey's *Brief Lives*, Cribbage was invented by Sir John Suckling (1609–42), and this is widely accepted, with the proviso that he developed it from an earlier game called Noddy. Although elements of it are found elsewhere, as a whole it is quite unlike other modern games.

Cribbage has changed little since its invention nearly 400 years ago, the main change being that in the 19th century the number of cards in each hand when dealt changed from the original five to six. Although five-card Cribbage is still played, the six-card version is so predominant that it is described here, with the five-card version outlined under variants.

Cribbage was originally for two players and, although it has been adapted for three or four, the two-handed version is described as the parent game, as it is one of the best card games for two players. It is nowadays often called Crib.

Type	Matching
Alternative names	Crib
Players	Two; three and four for variants
Special requirements	A Cribbage or Noddy board for scoring, or pen and paper

Aim
To be the first to reach a score of 121.

Cards
The standard pack of 52 cards is used, the cards ranking from King (high) to Ace (low).

Preparation
Cards are cut, and the player cutting the lower card deals. He shuffles and the non-dealer cuts.

The dealer deals six cards to each player, beginning with the non-dealer, one at a time, face down. The remainder of the pack is put to one side, face down, for the moment. The deal alternates with each hand.

Play
Each player examines his cards and each 'lays off' two cards face down to form a central pile of four called the 'crib' or, more commonly, the 'box'. The box is a third hand which in the second part of play, called the 'show', belongs to the dealer.

After laying off, the non-dealer cuts the pack and the dealer turns over the top card of the lower half and places it face up on the top of the reunited pack. This card is known as the 'start'. If it is a Jack, the dealer immediately scores two points (announced as 'two for his heels').

Pegging In the first part of the game cards have a value: court cards count ten, and other cards their pip value, with Ace counting as one. The score is usually kept on a Cribbage board, also called a Noddy board, which contains two groups of 60 holes, one on each side, with a central hole at each end, as illustrated below. Each player keeps his score with the use of two pegs. The first time he scores he puts a peg in the relevant hole, the second time he takes the second peg and advances it the required number of holes ahead of the first, and so on, with at each score the second peg leap-frogging the first. The game is to 121 points, ie twice round the board and into the end hole. Scoring is thus called 'pegging'.

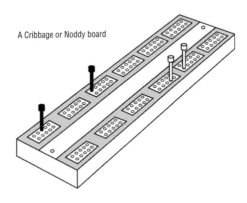

A Cribbage or Noddy board

The hands are now played out. The non-dealer lays his first card and announces its value (as given above). Players do not combine their cards as they will need them later. The dealer then plays a card announcing the cumulative score (the combined value of the cards played) and so on. The cumulative score cannot exceed 31. If a player cannot lay a card which will keep the score at 31 or below, he says 'Go' or 'No'. The other player then continues on his own, until he has played all his cards or he, too, cannot play a card which will not bring the cumulative score to 31 or below. A player cannot say 'No' if he can play a card legitimately, ie a card which will not take the total past 31. The last player to play a card pegs one (announced as 'last for one'), or if he brings the total to exactly 31 he pegs two (announced as '31 for two'). If either player has cards left they play a second round of pegging, beginning with the player who did not play the final card in the first round.

During the pegging, certain combinations also allow a player to peg as follows:

Fifteen   A player who brings the cumulative score to 15 pegs two (announced as 'fifteen two').

Pair   A player who plays a card of a rank his opponent has played pegs two (announced as 'Two for a pair', and also announcing the cumulative total; for example, if the cards laid had been 3, 6, 6 he would announce 'Fifteen two and two for a pair').

Pair-royal   If a player can play a third consecutive card of the same rank, he pegs six. To follow on with the example, if he played another six after the 3, 6, 6 he would announce 'Pair-royal for six, total 21'. Of course, in most games he might not be so formal as this, and might say 'And another for six, making 21'.

Double
pair-royal   If a player laid a fourth card of the same rank as the previous three (rare, but not unheard of) he pegs twelve, announcing, to follow the same example 'Double pair-royal for twelve, making 27', but would more likely say, with a touch of triumph 'And another 6 for twelve, total now 27'.

It should be noted that, although all court cards have a value of ten, only cards of the same rank, such as two Jacks or two Kings, count as a pair. It is impossible to score a double pair-royal with cards of a rank above 7 as the cumulative score would exceed 31.

Run or
sequence   During the pegging a player who plays a card which, with the two or more played before it, makes a run pegs one for each card it contains. Suits are irrelevant, as is the order of the cards played. Thus if the first three cards played are 2, 4, 3, the player who played the 3 pegs (and announces) 'three for a run'. If the next person plays 2, he, too, will peg three for a run (now comprising 4, 3, 2) and if the next player plays 5 he will peg four for a run (comprising 4, 3, 2, 5). A run cannot, of course, have two cards of the same rank within it, so while 6, 5, 7 is a run, adding another 5 to make 6, 5, 7, 5 does not achieve a run.

It is possible to score for a run or any other combination, and two points for bringing the cumulative total to 15 or 31, at the same time. For example, if the first three cards played are 4, 6, 5 the layer of the 5 pegs five – three for the run and two for 'fifteen'.

Show After the pegging, the players pick up their cards and score again for the show.

The non-dealer pegs first, and then the dealer pegs for his hand and then for his crib. For the show, the start is combined with the hand, making in effect a hand of five cards, although there is no need to move the start from its position on top of the pack. Points are scored for combinations as follows:

Fifteen   For each combination of two or more cards which total fifteen a player pegs two.

Pair   For each pair a player pegs two (note that this covers pairs-royal and double pairs-royal, since, for example, if a player holds three cards of the same rank three different pairs can be made from them).

Run   For each run of three or more cards a player pegs the number of cards in the run.

Flush   For four cards of the same suit a player pegs four. If the start is also of the same suit he pegs five. However, a flush in the crib is not scored unless the start is also of the same suit, when the dealer scores five.

His nob   If a player holds the Jack of the same suit as the start, he scores 'one for his nob'.

Cards can be used more than once in one or more combinations. Every possible combination is scored. The illustration shows two hands, A and B, with the start.

Hand A   Start   Hand B

Cribbage players lay their hands on the table and count their hands out loud.

For Hand A, the player would say 'Fifteen two, fifteen four, fifteen six, fifteen eight, two for the pair is ten and one for his nob eleven' (formed from ♦J, ♥2, ♠3, then ♣K, ♥2, ♠3, then ♦J, ♦2, ♠3, then ♣K, ♦2, ♠3, then ♥2, ♦2 and finally ♦J of the same suit as the start).

For Hand B, he would say 'Fifteen two, fifteen four, fifteen six, fifteen eight, two for the pair is ten and six for runs is 16' (formed from ♥7, ♥8, then ♣7, ♥8, then ♦2, ♠6, ♥7, then ♦2, ♠6, ♣7, then ♥7, ♣7, then ♠6, ♥7, ♥8 and finally ♠6, ♣7, ♥8).

Counting the hands aloud allows the opponent to count as well and check the score. If the scorer misses a combination and claims too few points, there is a convention by which his opponent can say 'Muggins' and count the overlooked points for himself, but friendly players need not play this rule and can allow the overlooked points to be scored. When meeting a new opponent, however, one should check if the 'Muggins' rule is in operation.

The highest score which can be achieved with one hand at the show is 29. The hand is J, 5, 5, 5, with the start the fourth 5, of the same suit as the Jack in the hand. This scores 16 for fifteens and 12 for the double pair-royal, plus one for his nob. All other scores up to 29 can be achieved except 19, 25, 26 and 27; sometimes players who score nothing claim a score of 19 as a joke.

Scoring As explained above, a game is to 121 points. On each deal the scores are taken in this order: his heels, the pegging, the non-dealer's hand in the show, the dealer's hand, the crib hand. Once a player has reached 121, it is customary not to finish the hand.

If a player fails to reach 61 before his opponent pegs 121, he is said to be 'lurched' and has lost the equivalent of two games, but this is only relevant if playing for money.

Example hand
Suppose dealer deals to the non-dealer the following first hand: ♣K ♥Q ♠J ♣6 ♠6 ♣5. To himself he deals ♠10 ♣9 ♥4 ♣3 ♠3 ♥2.

The non-dealer will put his pair of 6s into the crib. These are dangerous cards to give to the dealer in his crib, but it leaves him with an excellent hand himself, with plenty of opportunities for it to be improved by the start: any court card or 5 would be excellent.

The dealer will put ♠10 and ♣9 into his crib. They might form a run for him and keeping his small cards gives him six for runs which another 2, 3, or 4 would more than double. The start is turned up and is the ♦J. The dealer immediately pegs two for his heels.

The hands are shown below.

Dealer

Non-dealer

Crib

Start

The non-dealer leads ♣K (announcing 'ten'), the dealer plays ♣3 (13). The dealer knows that if the non-dealer plays a 2 for 'fifteen two', he can make a run with ♥4 and even if then the non-dealer makes a run also, he himself can make another. However, the non-dealer plays ♥Q (23). The dealer plays ♥4 (27), the non-dealer says 'Go' and the dealer plays ♠3 for 30 and pegs one for last.

The non-dealer now leads ♠J to begin another round, the dealer plays ♥2 (12) and the non-dealer plays ♣5 (17) to peg one for last.

So far the dealer has pegged three and the non-dealer one.

The non-dealer now scores his hand in the show. He has eight for fifteens, two for a pair and six for runs, pegging 16. The dealer has four for fifteens, two for a pair and six for runs, pegging twelve. The dealer now takes his crib, which is surprisingly good. He has four for fifteens, two for a pair and three for a run, pegging nine. So the dealer has so far pegged 24 and the non-dealer 17. The non-dealer now takes the cards and shuffles in preparation for the next hand.

Variants

Five-card Cribbage Many players think the traditional game, in which the two hands are of five cards only, is a more skilful game. The differences from the above are as follows.

Each hand is dealt five cards only. Each player lays away two cards to the crib, which thus consists of four cards, while the players' hands are reduced to three.

In the pegging stage, when 31 is reached, or when neither player can play a card, the pegging ends, irrespective of whether either or both players still have cards in their hands or not. A second round of pegging is not started, as it is in six-card Cribbage.

The game is to 61 points (once round the Cribbage board). Because of the smaller hands, scoring is slower than in six-card Cribbage.

The advantage of having the crib first is greater in five-card Cribbage than in six-card Cribbage, and to compensate the non-dealer pegs three points at the beginning of the game for 'last'. When six-card Cribbage became more popular, this convention was dropped.

In the show, a flush, of course, counts as only three, since the hand is of only three cards, but it counts four with the start. A flush in the crib counts only if it includes the start, when it counts five.

The strategy of five-card Cribbage is different. Because the hands are smaller in the show, they cannot score as many points, so the pegging gains in importance, as does laying away to the crib. The crib, with its extra card, often scores more than the hands. The dealer, therefore, in laying away, might favour putting his more promising cards into the crib, while the non-dealer, in laying away, will concentrate on 'baulking' the crib for the dealer, ie laying away cards from which it is difficult to make runs or fifteens, and trying to keep cards which would be useful in pegging. Five-card Cribbage, because of the way a high-scoring crib can affect the score, is a game in which fortunes can fluctuate quickly.

Seven-card Cribbage Some players like seven-card Cribbage, although it is far less popular than the other variants. It is played in the same manner as the six-card game with the following differences: seven cards are dealt to each hand, of which two are laid off to the crib. The hands thus consist of five cards and the crib four. It is possible to have four rounds of pegging. In the show a flush scores five, or six with the start (one point per card). A flush in the crib scores five, since it must match the start. Game is to 181 points.

Three-handed Cribbage Three players each play for themselves. The deal passes to the left, as does the turn to play. Players are dealt five cards each, and the dealer deals one card face down to the table to begin the crib. Each player lays off one card to the crib, which thereby consists of four cards. Play is as in the six-card game. In the pegging, when 31 is reached, or when no player can go further, the player to the left of the player who played the last card leads to the next round. At the show, the hands are scored in the order of the eldest hand (the player to the dealer's left), the player to his left, the dealer, crib. Game is to 61.

There are Cribbage boards for three players; they are either triangular, or the usual board contains an arm which folds away when two play, but swings out for three. They are also rare, so scoring is usually by pen and paper.

Four-handed Cribbage Four people play, in two partnerships of two. Partners are determined by all drawing from a spread pack, the two highest playing the two lowest. Partners sit opposite each other. The drawer of the lowest card is first to be the dealer.

The eldest hand cuts for the start, and leads. Play passes to the left, and proceeds as in six-card Cribbage described above. A Cribbage board is adequate for scoring, as partners' scores are combined. At the show, scores are taken in turn, from the eldest hand round to the dealer, who last of all pegs for his crib.

Demon

Demon and Klondike are the best-known games of patience. Both are often called Canfield in the UK, although the name is properly attached only to Demon. This is because it was said to have been invented by a famous US gambler and casino owner of the 19th and early 20th centuries, William A Canfield, who would 'sell' the pack to a punter for $52 ($1 per card) and pay out $5 for each card in the foundation row at the end of the game. However, the game may have been modified, since experience suggests that this is not so much in favour of Canfield as one would expect – while the game is difficult to get out entirely (about one in 30 succeeds), one can frequently obtain the eleven cards necessary in the foundation row to make a profit.

Type	Patience
Alternative names	Canfield, Fascination, Thirteen
Players	One
Special requirements	None

Aim
To end with four piles of cards, one for each suit, in sequence.

Cards
The standard pack of 52 cards is used.

Preparation
Thirteen cards are dealt face down in a pile, and the top card of the pile is turned face up. This pile is known as the 'heel'. The next four cards are dealt face up in a row to the right of the heel to form the tableau. The next card is dealt face up above the first card of the tableau. This is the first foundation card, and decides the rank of all the other foundation cards. The remaining cards form the stock.

Play
The other three cards of the foundation rank should be played in a row next to the right of the first foundation card as they become available. On these cards will be built up in suit and ascending sequence until all the cards are built on the foundations. The sequence is 'round-the-corner', ie Queen, King, Ace, 2, 3 and so on.

The exposed cards on the heel and the bottoms of the columns of the tableau are all available to play. Once all available moves have been made, the stock is taken face down in hand and turned over in bundles of three, without disturbing their order, to a waste pile, or 'talon'. The top card of the talon is now also available to play to the foundations or tableau. Cards are played to the tableau in columns in descending order of rank and in opposite colours, for example ♥4 or ♦4 may be played on ♠5 or ♣5. These sequences are also round-the-corner, so if an Ace is at the foot of a column, a King of the opposite colour can be played to it.

A whole column in the tableau may be transferred to another provided the sequence is maintained, for example a column headed by ♥8 or ♦8 can be transferred to a column ending with a ♠9 or ♣9. An emptied tableau column is filled immediately by the top card of the heel, the next card in the heel then being turned face up. If the heel becomes exhausted, an empty column is filled by an exposed card from the talon, but this need not be done immediately – one may wait until a more useful card is exposed.

When the whole stock has been played to the talon (the last bundle may be of only one or two cards), and all possible moves have been completed, the talon is picked up and turned over without rearrangement and is again played to the table as before in bundles of three. The game ends in success when all cards are built to the foundations; in failure when the whole stock has been played to the talon without it being possible to play a card to tableau or foundation.

Example game
The heel, foundation card and tableau are dealt as illustrated.

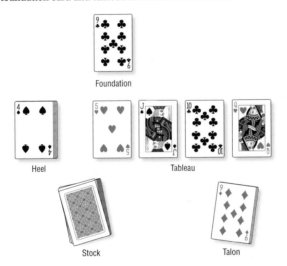

Foundation

Heel

Tableau

Stock

Talon

The play then begins with the ♠4 being built from the heel onto the ♥5, and the next card of the heel being faced. The ♣10 is then built on to the ♣9 in the foundation row and is replaced by the second card of the heel, the third card then being faced. The ♠J is built onto the ♥Q and its place in the tableau filled by the next card from the heel. The cards played from the heel may themselves offer chances to build further.

When all activity is over, the stock is taken in hand and the first bundle of three cards played to the table to begin the talon, as shown. The first card exposed is the ♦9, which being a foundation card is played to the foundation row to the right of the ♣9, and the ♦10 and then later diamonds are played to it as they become available. If the card in the talon exposed by the moving of the ♦9 will fit into the tableau or foundation row, it is moved there. If not, the next bundle of three cards are turned from the stock onto the talon, and any possible moves made, and so on.

Variants

A popular variant to this game is that instead of dealing a card to the foundation row to determine the rank of the foundations, the foundations are always the Aces (as they are in many patience games). Only eleven cards are dealt to the heel, and the top card is not faced. The heel is used only to supply a card to a column in the tableau which becomes empty, and only then is the card turned face up. Aces are played to the foundation row as they are exposed (either in the original four cards to the tableau, or as the top card in the waste pile, or as the card turned up from the heel to fill a gap in the tableau).

Easy Go

Easy Go is a gambling game of no skill whatever. It is a rapid method of redistributing wealth on the basis of luck.

Type	Gambling
Alternative names	None
Players	Any number to a maximum of eight
Special requirements	None

Aim
To win as much money as possible. Secondary aim: to lose it gracefully.

Cards
The standard pack of 52 cards is used.

Preparation
One player volunteers to be both banker and dealer. The bank passes round the table clockwise with each deal, the dealer always being also the banker. There is no advantage to being the banker.

The banker shuffles, the player to his right cuts, and the banker deals five cards, one at a time, to each player, except himself. Players display their hands face up on the table before them.

Play
The banker places a card face up before him on the table. A player whose hand includes the card of the same rank and colour places two units of the stake into a pool in the centre of the table, and a player whose hand includes a card of the same rank but opposite colour puts one unit into the pool. A player who holds two or three cards of the same rank has to put units into the pool for each.

The banker then places a second card face up before him. This time a player with the card of the same rank and colour puts in three units and a player with a card of the same rank and opposite colour two units.

The banker turns up in the same manner three more cards. On the third card the rates for putting into the pool are five units for the same colour, four for the opposite. On the fourth card the rates are nine units and eight units, and on the last 17 units and 16 units.

When all players have finished putting into the pool the opposite process begins.

The five cards used by the banker are put to one side and the banker deals himself the first of a second batch of five cards face up. This time a player with a card of the same rank and colour takes two units from the pool and a player with a card of the same rank but opposite colour takes one unit. The same procedure is followed for four more deals, the players taking from the pool the numbers of units corresponding to the numbers they were required to put in on the first five of the banker's cards.

If during the taking-out stage the pool is exhausted, the banker is obliged to put more units in to enable all the players to be paid. On the other hand if, after the taking-out stage, some stakes remain, the banker takes them.

The cards are collected together and handed to the player on the banker's left, who becomes both banker and dealer for the next hand.

Example hand

Five cards each are dealt to five players, Players A to E, as in the illustration opposite.

The banker's five cards for the putting-in stage are shown underneath.

On the first card, Player A and Player D both have a 6 of the opposite colour and put one unit into the pool. On the second card Player B puts in three units and Player E two. At the end of the putting-in phase, Player A has put in one unit, Player B eleven, Player C none, Player D 18 and Player E eleven, a total of 41 units in the pool.

The banker's five cards for the taking-out stage are also shown.

The players took out as follows: Player A eight units, Player B six, Player C 16, Player D two and Player E 18, a total of 50 units.

Overall, Player C won 16 units, and Player A and Player E seven each. Player B lost five units and Player D 16. The banker lost 9 units, having been 24 in profit before his last card, which forced him to add to the pool.

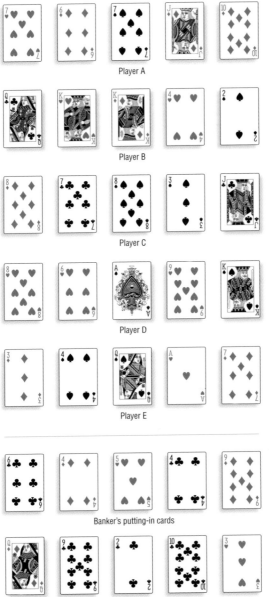

Player A

Player B

Player C

Player D

Player E

Banker's putting-in cards

Banker's taking-out cards

Écarté

Écarté evolved from Triomphe, a trick-taking game dating back to the 15th century, from which the word 'trump' derives. Triomphe was the basis of most of today's trick-taking games of five-card hands. Écarté reached its peak in France in the 19th century, when it became the main gambling game with cards in French casinos and remained so until superseded by Baccarat and Blackjack in the 20th century. It is a game of skill, insofar as winning depends on knowing the probabilities relating to various decisions in play.

Type	Trick-taking
Alternative names	None
Players	Two
Special requirements	A set of ten counters, or ten coins, provides a convenient way to score, or otherwise pen and paper

Aim

To be the first to score five points, by making the majority of the tricks.

Cards

The standard pack of 52 cards is used, from which are removed the 6s, 5s, 4s, 3s and 2s, making a pack of 32 cards. The cards rank King (high), Queen, Jack, Ace, 10, 9, 8, 7 (low).

Preparation

From the spread pack each player draws a card, the higher being the dealer. The dealer shuffles and the non-dealer cuts. If counters are used to score, the stack of ten is placed where both players can reach it.

The dealer deals five cards to each player either in bundles of three and two or in bundles of two and three according to his choice. His choice remains the order for succeeding deals. The dealer deals the eleventh card face up to the table to denote the trump suit. If it is a King the dealer immediately scores one point, and takes a counter from the stack. This is called 'marking' the King. The remainder of the pack is placed face down by the upcard to form the stock.

Playing or proposing The players pick up and examine their hands. The non-dealer begins, stating either 'I play' or 'I propose'. If he says 'I play', play begins immediately with the hands as dealt. The proposal is to exchange some cards from the hand with some from the stock. If he proposes, the dealer has the option of refusing or accepting the proposal. To refuse, he says 'I refuse' or 'I play', in which case the hands are played out. If he accepts the proposal, by saying 'I accept', each player may change any number of cards in his hand. The non-dealer begins, and must change at least one card. He discards a card or cards into a waste pile, and draws from the stock the same number to return his hand to five cards.

The dealer, while having the option to change, is not compelled to. The reason the dealer might accept the proposal to exchange cards without actually wishing to exchange any is that if, instead of accepting the proposal, he had decided to play, he would have faced a bigger penalty for failing to win (see Scoring, below).

When both players have exchanged (or not, in the dealer's case) the non-dealer again has the choice of playing or proposing, and if he proposes, the dealer again has the choice of refusing (and thus playing with the hands as they now are) or accepting.

If he accepts, the ritual of each player being able to exchange a card or cards (and the non-dealer being forced to change at least one) is repeated. When the stock is exhausted, however, whether a player has been able to exchange as many cards as he wishes or not, play must start, with the non-dealer leading to the first trick. Each player, of course, holds five cards.

Play

Trick-taking then begins; see p383 for an explanation of tricks and trick-taking. The non-dealer makes the opening lead. If either player has the King of trumps in his hand, he may announce it before he plays to the first trick and mark it, ie score a point for it. He is not compelled to announce it, and once he has laid a card he is not allowed to.

It is conventional and used to be a rule for the leader to each trick to announce the suit of the card led, but some modern players do not conform to this.

The usual rules of trick-taking do not apply. The second player to a trick must not only follow suit, but must win the trick if he can. If he cannot follow suit, he must trump if he can. Only if he cannot follow suit or trump, is he allowed to discard. The trick is won by the higher trump it contains, or, in the absence of a trump, by the higher card in the suit led.

Scoring The main object is to make the majority of tricks, called the 'trick'. If a player makes all five tricks, this is called the 'vole'.

If the hands as originally dealt are played, then the player who decided to play scores one point if he achieves trick, and two if he achieves vole. He takes the appropriate number of counters from the stack. If he fails to make trick, his opponent scores two points (there is no extra point for vole).

If any cards have been drawn (ie the hands played are not the original ones dealt) then it doesn't matter who finally decided to play; the winner of trick scores one point, and if he achieved vole, two points.

The points won during a deal can therefore vary from one (trick without the King of trumps) to three (vole plus the King of trumps).

The deal alternates. Game is to five points, and a player on four points who holds the King of trumps will expose it as he must win.

Example hand

The hands are dealt, and the ♦9 is turned up to denote the trump suit. The non-dealer is dealt ♦Q, ♣8, ♠8, ♥8, 7. The dealer is dealt ♥10, ♣10, 9, ♠J, 7.

The non-dealer has one trump, not enough to play, as he is almost certain to lose and forfeit two points if he does. He proposes. The dealer decides he also is unable to play, as he holds no trumps at all. He accepts.

The non-dealer discards all but his ♦ Q, and draws four cards. The dealer discards all five cards and receives a completely new hand. The two hands are now as shown.

Non-dealer

Dealer

The non-dealer notes that the dealer was not originally dealt a trump, so might not have any after the draw, and is unlikely to hold more than his own two. As he has the master club, together with a second, and the advantage of the lead, he decides to play. The play now goes as follows:

	Non-dealer	Dealer
1	♣K	♣J
2	♣7	♦10
3	♦7	♥K
4	♠10	♦A
5	♦Q	♥Q

The non-dealer, despite the dealer drawing two trumps and the two master hearts, therefore won trick for one point. The advantage of the lead is considerable. The non-dealer, as the cards lay, was almost certain to win the trick provided he did not make the mistake of leading one of his two 7s.

Jeux de règles Écarté might not seem a game to lend itself to the exercise of much skill, but knowledge of the probabilities of a hand's chances of winning to decide when to play, propose or accept is a big advantage. To play on the first deal risks losing two or winning one, so to choose to play requires a hand which stands a better than a 2–1 on chance of winning.

Because of the amount of betting in casinos and elsewhere on Écarté in the late 19th century, experts worked out what was required for such winning hands, based on the exact holdings in the side suits for each number of trumps held. The list of such hands is called the *jeu de règle*. To memorize such an extensive list would be a bore, and, as it would also detract from the pleasure of playing the game, it is not given here.

Euchre

Euchre is the US version of the five-card trick-taking games which derive from Triomphe, a trick-taking game from the 15th century which was the basis of most of today's trick-taking games of five-card hands.

Euchre is related to a German game called Jucker and might have been introduced to the USA by German immigrants in the 19th century. In the second half of that century it was considered to be the national game of the USA, and is also thought to have the distinction of being the game for which the Joker was invented, around the 1850s. The Joker is used in the version called Railroad Euchre, described below under Variants.

Type	Trick-taking
Alternative names	None
Players	Four, in two partnerships of two; two to six for variants
Special requirements	None

Aim
To score five points, by making the majority of the tricks.

Cards
The standard pack of 52 cards is used, from which are removed the 6s, 5s, 4s, 3s, and 2s, making a pack of 32 cards. Cards, except in the trump suit, rank from Ace (high) to 7 (low). In the trump suit, the Jack (called the 'right bower') is the highest trump, while the Jack of the same colour as the trump suit (called the 'left bower') is the second highest trump. If hearts were trumps, the trump suit would rank ♥J, ♦J, ♥A, K, Q, 10, 9, 8, 7.

The trump suit, therefore, has nine cards, the suit of the same colour (the 'next' suit) has seven, and the other two suits (the 'cross' suits) have eight cards each.

The usual practice is to use two packs, alternately deal by deal.

Preparation
From a spread pack, each player draws a card. The drawer of the lowest card is the first dealer (and chooses his seat), the second lowest is his partner and sits opposite. The dealer shuffles last, and the player to his right cuts the cards.

The dealer deals five cards to each player, clockwise, beginning with the eldest hand (the player to the dealer's left), in two bundles, either of three and two or of two and three, as he prefers. The remainder of the pack is placed face down on the table, and the top card turned over to propose the trump suit (which might or might not be accepted). The deal passes to the left on successive hands.

Making The turned-up card indicates a proposed trump suit, which each player in turn may accept or reject. If the proposed trump suit is accepted, no matter by which player, the turn-up is taken into the dealer's hand. To make room for it, the dealer discards one card by placing it face down crossways at the bottom of the pack. Traditionally, he does not take the turn-up into his hand but leaves it where it is until he actually plays it.

The eldest hand has the first chance to accept the suit of the turn-up as the trump suit. To do so he says 'I order it up' (ie he orders the dealer to take it). To reject the proposed trump suit he says 'I pass'. The remaining players in turn then have the same choice. Traditionally, the dealer's partner, if wishing to accept the trump suit, says 'I assist', rather than 'I order it up', and the dealer, if he wishes to accept it, merely places his discard under the pack.

If all pass, the dealer places the turn-up crossways at the foot of the pack face up, to denote that it is rejected.

If the proposed trump suit is rejected, the eldest hand now has the choice of naming one of the other three suits as trumps, or passing. If he passes, the other players in turn have the same choice. If a player makes trumps the same colour as the rejected turn-up, he is said to be 'making it next'. If he chooses one of the other suits he is said to be 'crossing it'.

If all the players pass on this round the deal is abandoned, and the deal passes to the left as usual.

Playing alone The player who makes trumps, either by accepting the turn-up on the first round, or naming a suit on the second, is known as the 'maker', and he has the right to play alone (for which he might make extra points). To play alone he must declare his intention before a card is led.

The partner of a player playing alone lays his cards face down on the table and takes no part in the play of the hand.

Play

If the maker plays alone, the opening lead is made by the player on his left. Otherwise the eldest hand makes the opening lead.

The normal rules of trick-taking apply, ie a player must follow suit to the card led, if able, otherwise he may trump or discard as he wishes; see p383 for an explanation of tricks and trick-taking. There is no obligation to attempt to win the trick as there is in some similar games.

The winner of a trick leads to the next.

Scoring Players attempt to win the majority of the tricks. If the making side (ie the side which chose the trump suit) fails to win at least three tricks it is 'euchred'. A side which wins all five tricks wins the 'march'.

If the maker plays with his partner, the side scores one point for making three or four tricks and two points for march. If the maker plays alone, the side still scores one point for three or four tricks, but four points for march.

If the making side is euchred, the opposing side scores two points.

Game is usually to five points, and it is usual for each side to keep its score by means of a 3 and 4 from the unused part of the pack, recording scores of one to four as shown.

One point   Two points   Three points   Four points

Some players prefer a longer game of seven or ten points, when perhaps pen and paper, or taking counters from a stack of 20, is easier.

Strategy The main chance to exercise judgement is in making the decisions regarding the trump suit. It is as well to remember that there are nine trumps, and that nearly two-thirds of the cards are dealt to the four hands. The average number of trumps in a hand is between 1.25 and 1.5. If one opponent is the dealer, he will get an extra trump if trumps are made on the first round. Also, by virtue of being able to discard, he will no doubt start play with a bare suit as well (to have a bare suit means to have no cards in one suit at all, and therefore to be able to trump that suit on the first round it is led).

It is generally reckoned that the eldest hand needs at least three probable tricks to order it up. An exception to this is when his side is 'at the bridge', meaning his side has four points and the opponents are lagging two or three behind. By ordering it up, the worst that can happen is that his side is euchred and loses two points, leaving them still in the game. And this prevents the dealer or his partner playing alone and getting four for the march, thus winning the game. The eldest hand might also decide to order it up if the score is four points each, and he has average trumps and an Ace or two in the cross suits.

The dealer's partner might assist on a hand strong in the cross suits, on the assumption that his partner will hold at least one trump and possibly two or three. He will be anxious to assist if his side is at the bridge, thus depriving the player in third position of the chance to play alone and snatch the game with march.

The player in third position must bear in mind that his partner has passed. He therefore needs a strong hand himself to order it up, with prospects of three tricks himself.

The dealer knows that if he makes trumps he will add the upcard to his hand. If this gives him three or more trumps he should take it up, irrespective of the rest of his hand.

If all pass on the first round, the eldest hand should make the next suit (as opposed to the cross suits) trumps if he can, on the assumption that if both the dealer and his partner turned down the proposed trump suit, they probably lack a bower, and are stronger in the suits of the opposite colour. If the eldest hand cannot make trumps, his partner would need a hand strong enough to play alone to do so, since the two passes from his partner indicate weakness. The dealer and his partner will make one of the cross suits trumps with two or more cards in the suit and a little strength elsewhere.

In the play for tricks, players should realize that it is extremely unlikely for a suit to go round twice, so there is no point in trying to establish a suit, and tricks should be taken when they can. For example, it is better to lead a King in a cross suit, hoping the Ace is not in play, rather than a small card hoping to make the King later.

Variants

Euchre for two players With two players, the 8s and 7s are also removed from the standard pack, leaving a pack of 24 cards. It is played exactly as above, except that there are, of course, no bonuses for playing alone, as each plays alone anyway.

Euchre for three players Each player plays for himself, but the maker of the trump suit is opposed by the other two players in temporary partnership. Since the maker therefore always plays alone, there is no bonus for playing alone. The maker scores one point for three or four tricks, and three for march. If he is euchred, each opponent scores two points.

Railroad Euchre This name is given to any partnership game which incorporates any of the following:

Joker	The Joker is added to the pack and is the top trump, above right bower, making the trump suit one of ten cards. If the Joker is the turn-up, the card below it can be exposed to denote the trump suit, or to avoid this, the trump suit can be decided in advance. In either case, it is the Joker which the dealer takes into his hand.
Call for best	If the maker plays alone, he is entitled to ask his partner for his best card, for which he exchanges a card from his hand. The partner decides his best card and neither card is exposed. If the dealer is the maker, he makes this exchange before he takes up the turn-up, so that if he wishes he can exchange his partner's card for the turn-up. If it is the dealer's partner that plays alone, the dealer takes the turn-up first, so that if it is his best card he may pass it to his partner in exchange for his partner's discard.
Opposing alone	If the maker is playing alone, either opponent may announce that he will oppose alone. He is thereby also entitled to exchange a card for his partner's best card. A lone player who euchres a lone player scores four points.
Jambone	The lone maker may expose his hand by laying it on the table. Neither opponent is allowed to defend alone. When the maker leads to a trick, his left-hand opponent instructs him which card to play, otherwise his right-hand opponent does so. The plays must be legal, of course, and the opponent may not consult. If a player calls jambone and achieves march, he scores eight points for it.
Jamboree	If the maker has the top five trumps he may expose them and score 16 points. There is no need to play out the hand. The dealer can score jamboree with or without the turn-up.

Laps	If a game is won by more than five points, the excess points are carried forward to the next game. The object of this is to encourage players to play alone even when it is not necessary to do so to win the game.
Slam	A game counts double if the opponents do not score a point.

Call-Ace Euchre This game can be played by any number from four to six. It is a cut-throat game (ie each player plays for himself), but temporary partnerships are formed with each hand.

The number of cards varies with the number of players. When six play, the usual 32-card Euchre pack is used. When five play, the 7s are stripped out, making a 28-card pack, and when four play the 8s are also stripped out, leaving a 24-card pack. It follows that there are only one, two or three cards sleeping (not in play) on each deal.

Before a card is dealt, the player who orders up the trump, or takes it up, or who makes it after it is turned down, names another suit. The holder of the best card in play in that suit becomes his partner, but he must not declare it. If a player holds the Ace of the suit named, then he knows he is the partner of the maker. But if the Ace is sleeping, the holder of the King (or even the Queen if both Ace and King are sleeping) becomes the maker's partner, and he will not know it. It may happen that the maker himself holds the highest card in the suit, in which case he is deemed to be playing alone. In most instances, a player holds the Ace and knows immediately that he is the maker's partner, but nobody else knows it until he plays the Ace in the normal course of play.

If the maker wishes, he may choose to play alone, or he may name a suit of which he knows he has the top card, in which case none of his opponents knows he is playing alone until he himself plays the Ace of the named suit.

If the maker and his partner win three or four tricks they score one point each. If they win all the tricks (march) they score two points if four players and three points if five or six players. If the maker plays alone, however, he scores one point for making three or four tricks and one point for each player, including himself, if he makes march.

If partners, or a lone player, are euchred, all other players score two points each.

Fan Tan

Fan Tan is this game's usual name, despite the fact it is popular with children and Fan Tan is also the name of a notorious Chinese gambling game in which punters bet on how many beans will remain in a pile from which they are being removed four at a time, and usually lose, often suspiciously.

Type	Stops
Alternative names	Card Dominoes, Parliament, Sevens
Players	Three to eight
Special requirements	None

Aim
To get rid of all your cards by playing them to the table.

Cards
The standard pack of 52 cards is used, the cards ranking from King (high) to Ace (low).

Preparation
Any player may shuffle the pack and deal the cards clockwise, beginning with the player to his left, one at a time face up, until a Jack appears. The player dealt the Jack becomes the dealer for the game. He shuffles and the player to his right cuts. If the game is played for stakes, each player puts one unit into the pool. Since the whole pack is dealt, some players might get one more card than others. In this case some prefer that those players with one card short put an extra unit into the pool. Others ignore it, as the deal rotates to the left anyway.

The dealer deals the cards clockwise to his left, one at a time face down until the whole pack is exhausted.

Play
The eldest hand (the player to the dealer's left) plays first, and must lay a 7 to the table. If he cannot, he passes and the next player must play a 7 if he can, and so on until a 7 is laid. When a 7 is laid a player on his turn can lay the 6 or the 8 of the same suit to one side of it. From then on a player on his turn can add to the sequence at either end, down to the Ace or up to the King, or lay another 7.

In this way the four suits get built up in rows from Ace to King. Only one card may be played at a time, and a player must go on his turn if he can. It is not permitted to hold up the development of a row by passing when one could play a card. A player who can play more than one card can choose which to play.

A player who cannot play a card passes, and if the game is being played for stakes he adds a unit to the pool. The first player to get rid of all his cards wins the pool. The other players, if the game is being played for stakes, add a unit to the pool for each card left in their hands.

The game is one enjoyed by children, and can of course be played without stakes, the winner being the player who plays all his cards to the table first.

Example hand

Fan Tan is a game which repays good judgement in the playing of the cards. At the beginning a player will usually have a choice of cards to play. His danger cards are Kings and Aces, and to a lesser extent Queens and 2s, because he cannot play these until other players have played the intermediate cards from the 7 towards the end of the sequence. So the player should try to play cards which get the sequences moving towards the ends where he holds the danger cards.

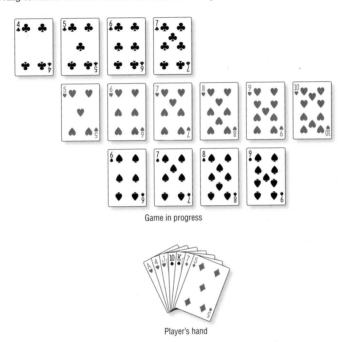

Game in progress

Player's hand

The illustration shows a layout soon after the start of a game, when 14 cards have been played, plus the hand of the player whose turn it is. He is in a strong position, because he holds four of the seven cards which can be played to the layout. He has the heart suit blocked, one end of the spade suit and also has the ♦7, so nobody can play a diamond until he lays it. He should hold back the ♦7 for as long as he can. The threats to his winning are the ♥A and the ♠K. He should play either the ♥4 or the ♠10, followed by the other on his next turn. By the turn after that, he might be able to get rid of the ♠K or ♥A, while everybody else still holds diamonds. In fact, he has an excellent chance of winning, if, as they say, he plays his cards right.

Five Hundred

Five Hundred has a strange history. It was devised in the 1890s and copyrighted by the United States Playing Card Company in 1904. It was based on Euchre, then the most popular game in the USA, and was invented to satisfy a perceived demand for a more skilful game than Euchre, but one without the complications of the up-and-coming Bridge, from which it borrowed the idea of the auction. It rapidly became hugely successful, and was the most fashionable social game in the USA for a while. Bridge eventually conquered as the major game, but Five Hundred remains popular in many parts of the world, and in Australia (at least) one can buy special packs containing the 11s, 12s and 13s of certain suits for six-handed play. It is sometimes called Bid Euchre, but cannot be considered a game of the Euchre family.

Type	Trick-taking
Alternative names	Bid Euchre
Players	Three is best; two to six for variants
Special requirements	Pen and paper for scoring

Aim

To be the first to score 500 points.

Cards

The number of cards used varies according to the number of players. For the three-player game outlined here, the standard pack of 52 cards is used, from which are removed the 6s, 5s, 4s, 3s and 2s and the Joker added, making a pack of 33 cards.

In plain suits, cards rank from Ace (high) to 7 (low). In the trump suit, the Jack of the suit of the same colour as the trump suit itself becomes a trump, thus reducing that suit to seven cards. The trump suit is headed by the Joker, and has ten cards, ranked as follows: Joker (high), Jack (known as 'right bower'), Jack of the same colour (known as 'left bower'), A, K, Q, 10, 9, 8, 7 (low). The suits rank in the order hearts, diamonds, clubs, spades.

Preparation

Players draw from a spread pack, and the lowest deals; for this the cards have a normal ranking, from King (high) to Ace (low), with the Joker lowest of all. The dealer shuffles and the player on his right cuts.

The dealer deals a bundle of three cards clockwise to each hand, beginning with the eldest hand (the player to the dealer's left), then three to the centre of the table to form a widow. He then deals a bundle of four to each hand, followed by a bundle of three so that each player holds a hand of ten cards, with three in the widow.

Bidding Players study their cards and the eldest hand begins the auction. Each player has one opportunity to bid or pass, each bid having to be higher than the previous bid. The highest bidder wins the contract and plays against the other two players in partnership.

To make a bid, a player must specify the number of tricks he will make, either naming the trump suit, or specifying that he will play in no trumps. In a no-trump contract, the Joker is the only trump. The values of the bids are:

	Six	Seven	Eight	Nine	Ten
Spades	40	140	240	340	440
Clubs	60	160	260	360	460
Diamonds	80	180	280	380	480
Hearts	100	200	300	400	500
No-trumps	120	220	320	420	520

If each player passes without making a bid, the deal is abandoned and the deal passes to the left.

Play

The player who wins the contract takes the widow into his hand, and discards three cards face down, keeping his hand to ten cards. He then leads to the first trick. The usual rules of trick-taking games apply, ie players must follow suit if able, and may trump or discard if unable to follow suit; see p383 for an explanation of tricks and trick-taking. The trick is won by the highest trump, or if there are none, by the highest card in the suit led.

In a no-trump contract, if the Joker is led, the leader specifies the suit to which the players must follow if able. The Joker wins the trick, of course.

The object of the declarer is to make his contract, and of the two opponents to defeat it. The two opponents keep the tricks they make individually.

Scoring When the bidder makes his contract, he scores its value in the table set out above. He does not score for any overtricks he makes, with one exception: if he makes all ten tricks he scores a minimum of 250, so if his bid was for less than this he will score more than his bid.

If the bidder is 'set back', ie he fails to make his contract, the value of his bid is deducted from his score. It follows that a player may have a minus score, when he is said to be 'in the hole'. A minus score is traditionally written down with a circle round it.

Each opponent of the bidder makes ten points for each trick he makes, whether the bidder was successful in his contract or not, which is why they keep their tricks separately.

As suggested by its name, game is to 500 points. Should two or more players pass 500 on the same deal, the bidder wins. Should the two non-bidders both pass 500 on the same deal, the player whose trick takes his score past 500 first wins. The game is usually discontinued at that point, unless the bidder will pass 500 if he makes his contract, in which case play must continue.

145

Strategy A simple strategy for evaluating the hand when bidding is to count any trump of Ace and above as one point, all trumps in excess of three as one point, and masters in other suits as one point, for example 'Ace counts one, A, K counts two'. A guarded King (for example King and another in the suit) could be counted as one point at a pinch. With six points, one can bid six of a suit, with seven one can bid seven, and so on.

Example hand

Player A deals the hands as follows:

Player A	♣A, K, J, 10 ♦10, 9 ♠8, 7 ♥10, 7
Player B	♥A, K, Q, 9, 8 ♠K, 9 ♦ A, J ♣7
Player C	Joker ♠A, Q, J, 10 ♦Q, 8 ♣Q, 8, ♥J

Player B has the first chance to bid. His strongest suit is hearts. With hearts as trumps, his ♦J becomes left bower. Even though he loses two trumps to Joker and right bower, he will make four trump tricks and the ♦A, with a possible ♠K making six tricks. The widow might give him a seventh. On the valuation mentioned under Strategy, above, he has six, maybe seven, points. He fears if he bids 6♥ he might get overbid in clubs or spades, and being an adventurous player makes a risky bid of 7♥.

Player C is indeed very strong in spades with a possible five tricks in trumps but to make a higher bid he has to bid 8♠ and decides his side suits are much too weak.

Player A has a poor hand and cannot compete, so Player B becomes declarer in 7♥ and picks up the widow.

The widow is ♦K, 7 and ♣9.

Player B decides immediately to discard ♣9, 7 but must rely for his seventh trick on ♠K or ♦7. He decides that rather than keep his ♠K guarded, he will discard ♠9, keeping three diamonds which, with hearts as trumps, is a seven-card only suit.

The final hands are as shown below.

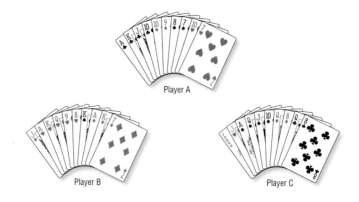

Player A

Player B

Player C

Player B decides on his strategy. He will lead his trumps, hoping that Joker and right bower might fall on the same round.

	Player A	Player B	Player C
1	♥7	♥Q	<u>♥J</u>

Player B's ploy was unsuccessful. Player C has a difficult choice of lead, and decides to lead ♠A. This would have been fatal if Player B had kept his ♠9, but as it happens it works well. Player B now needs to make ♦7 to land his contract.

2	♠7	♠K	<u>♠A</u>
3	♠8	♥9	♠Q

Player B continues with trumps.

4	♥10	♦J	Joker

Player C gives nothing away by leading spades again.

5	♣10	♥8	♠J

Player A tells Player C that he has clubs covered, so Player C should try to guard diamonds.

6	♦9	♥A	♣8
7	♦10	<u>♥K</u>	♣Q

Player B knows he is safe, as there are only two diamonds left.

8	♣J	♦A	♦8
9	♣K	♦K	♦Q
10	♣A	<u>♦7</u>	♠10

So Player B has made his contract, thanks to a favourable distribution of the cards and picking up ♦K in his widow. He scores 200 points and Player C scores 30 points for winning three tricks.

Player B, as the previous eldest hand, now deals.

Variants
In the bidding, some players allow the bidding to be progressive, ie that players continue bidding as long as each bid is higher than the previous bid, the bidding stopping as soon as two consecutive passes have occurred. Others allow continuous bidding, but a player who passes cannot re-enter the bidding later.

Some players also allow one or two further bids. A bid of *misère,* or *nullo,* is a bid to lose all the tricks, with no trumps (except the Joker). A player holding the Joker can play it only when void of the suit led, and if he leads it, must specify the suit it represents. The Joker always wins a trick in which it is included. The value of misère is 250, so it ranks between 8♠ and 8♣, and the bidder loses if he makes a single trick. In this contract the non-bidders score if the bidder fails. They each score ten points for each trick the bidder is forced to make.

Some players who allow the bid of misère will also allow 'open misère', which is played as misère except that the hand is exposed on the table. The two non-bidders must not collude in their play. The bid is worth 520 and is the highest bid which can be made.

Five Hundred for two players There are two ways to play with two players. First, deal as if for three players as described above, but put one hand aside face down. This method leaves ten cards unknown, which reduces the skill factor when it comes to bidding. The second method is to strip the 8s and 7s from the pack and not use the Joker, leaving 24 cards. Hands are of ten cards as usual, but the widow is of four cards.

Five Hundred for four players With four players the pack is increased to 43 cards by including the 6s and 5s and the red 4s, thus preserving the ten-card hands and three-card widows. It is played in partnerships, each player sitting opposite his partner. It is played as the three-handed game. Some players in the four-handed version prefer not to use the Joker, which reduces the widow to two cards.

Five Hundred for five players The full pack of 52 cards is used, plus the Joker. Each player gets ten cards and the widow three. Each player plays for himself, but in the play the successful bidder can call upon a partner or partners to join him against the rest. There are two ways in which the partner can be chosen. They are not interchangeable so the method must be agreed at the outset.

i) A player who bids six or seven may name his partner, who will probably be a player who made a bid himself, and is therefore strong in a suit. If he bids eight or more he is entitled to pick two partners, who join him against the other two players.

ii) Whatever his bid, a player may name the holder of a specific card to be his partner. This will probably be his highest missing trump or an Ace in a side suit. The holder of the card does not announce it, so the partner of the bidder is unknown to all but himself until he actually plays the card asked for.

Each partner scores the value of the contract if it is successful, and is debited with it if it fails. The opponents score ten points for each trick taken individually.

Five Hundred for six players To play with six players requires a special pack of 62 cards plus Joker. To the standard pack are added ranks of 11s and 12s, plus the 13s of hearts and diamonds. These cards rank between the Jack and 10. The game can be played in partnerships of two, where it is played as in the parent three-handed game described, with partners sitting opposite each other with two opponents between on each side, or in partnerships of three, as in the variant for two players, with each player sitting between two opponents.

Flower Garden

This one-pack patience game requires some skill, and is a difficult one to get out.

Type	Patience
Alternative names	Bouquet, The Garden
Players	One
Special requirements	Playing surface large enough for a crescent of 16 cards

Aim
To end with four piles of cards, one for each suit, in sequence from Ace up to King.

Cards
The standard pack of 52 cards is used.

Preparation
Six rows of six cards are dealt face up. These rows are known as the 'beds'. The remaining 16 cards are arranged in a crescent above them. This is the 'bouquet'. The four blank spaces are the foundations where the Aces will go when they become available.

Play
Aces should be released from the bouquet and, as they become available for play, from the beds. They should be placed in a row above the bouquet as foundations, and built upon in ascending suit sequences to the Kings.

All the cards at the base of the beds and all the cards in the bouquet are exposed and are available for play. They may be built on the foundations as they become available, or may be packed on the exposed card at the base of a bed in descending sequence, irrespective of suit or colour. A sequence may be moved from the base of one bed to another provided the sequence is retained. If a bed is cleared, the vacant space may be filled either with an exposed card or sequence from another bed, or with a card from the bouquet.

Strategy
The game can be difficult to get out if there are Aces and other low cards buried at the top of the beds and court cards, particularly Kings, at the base of the beds. The main aim is to release the Aces, 2s and 3s and to try to clear beds in order to fill the space with any Kings which are blocking cards in the beds they occupy. Packing a card from the bouquet on to a bed should be avoided if possible as it reduces the number of cards that can be played at any time, but it is sometimes necessary.

Example game

The bouquet and beds are as shown in the illustration opposite. It looks quite promising. The first tasks are to try to release the ♥3 from the head of the sixth bed and to transfer the ♥K, ♥Q, ♥J from the fourth bed to the head of the sixth.

The ♠A and ♥A can be moved from the bouquet to a row above as the first two foundations. Play might then proceed: ♥2 to foundation; ♠5 packed on ♥6; ♠2 to foundation; ♦3 packed on ♦4; ♣8 packed on ♦9; ♣A to foundation; ♦4, ♦3 packed on ♠5; ♥8 packed on ♠9; ♥3 to foundation; ♠7 packed on ♥8; ♦9, ♣8 packed on ♥10; ♥K to head of the empty sixth bed; ♥4 to foundation; ♦A to foundation; ♣2 to foundation; ♦2 from bouquet to foundation; ♦3 followed by ♦4 to foundation; ♥Q, ♥J packed on ♥K; ♠3 to foundation; and so on.

This game is progressing well. Readers who have set it up to follow it can play on. They will find that it comes out quite easily. The original layout is rarely as favourable as it was here, with two Kings nicely tucked away at the head of a bed where they were unable to block the play.

Variations

The bouquet cards may be held in the player's hand, rather than laid out. The beds may also be arranged on the table in fans, rather than in rows, with the exposed card on the right-hand of each fan available for play.

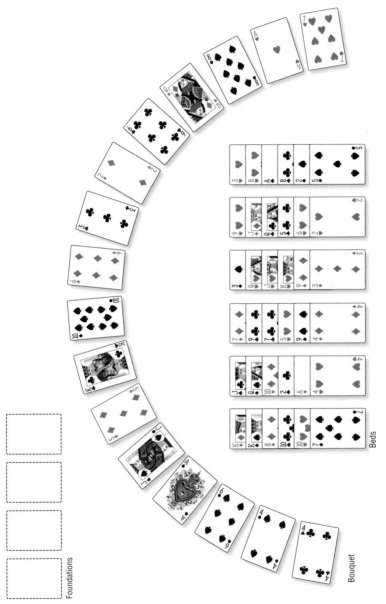

Flower Garden

Foundations

Beds

Bouquet

151

German Whist

There may not be any connection between German Whist and Germany, but it is nevertheless a good game, designed as a version of Whist suitable for two players, and using a similar take-or-draw principle to Bezique or Rummy.

Type	Trick-taking
Alternative names	None
Players	Two
Special requirements	Pen and paper for scoring if a series of hands is desired

Aim

To win the majority of 13 tricks.

Cards

The standard pack of 52 cards is used, the cards ranking from Ace (high) to 2 (low).

Preparation

The players cut for deal, highest dealing. The dealer shuffles and the non-dealer cuts. The dealer deals 13 cards one at a time alternately to each player, beginning with the non-dealer. He places the remainder, the 'stock', face down in the centre, turns over the top card and places it face up beside the pile. This card denotes trumps for the deal.

Play

The non-dealer leads to the first trick, and subsequently the winner of a trick leads to the next. The usual trick-taking rules apply: players must follow suit if able, and if not they may trump or discard. The trick is won by the higher trump, or if it does not contain a trump by the higher card in the suit led; see p383 for an explanation of tricks and trick-taking.

The winner of a trick takes the upcard into his hand, while the loser takes the top card of the stock, without showing it to his opponent. The next card of the stock is then turned over face up beside the pile and this is played for in the same manner.

The first 13 tricks (ie those played before the stock is exhausted) do not count towards the game, and are discarded face down by whoever wins them. The purpose of these tricks is to build your hand for the final 13 tricks, which do count. Obviously the turn-up in many cases will not be a card a player will want in his hand, so he will try to lose the trick, hoping that the top card of the stock will be a better one.

When the stock is exhausted, each player will still have 13 cards in his hand. If he has a good memory, he will know many of the cards his opponent holds, but not all. Each player should try to remember which trumps (or at least how many) have been used in the first stage of the game, because then he will know which trumps his opponent holds for the playing of the final 13 tricks. It is these tricks which count.

The winner of the majority of the last 13 tricks wins the game. If a series of deals is to be played, the winner scores the difference between his number of tricks and his opponent's. The target for game can be fixed according to how long one wants to play, but 11 points is reasonable.

Strategy Suppose in the early stages of the game a player holds the hand as illustrated and the upcard is the ♦K. Spades are trumps.

The ♦K is a good card to have, and the holder of the hand has to lead. It would be a mistake for him to play ♦A to win it, on the grounds that he will still hold the master diamond. This would leave his hand exactly as it was with nothing gained. It would be a better bet, if the ♣A has not yet appeared in play, to lead the ♣K. If it wins, so much to the good. If it loses, the player still holds the master club, as Ace and King will be discarded. And although his opponent has taken ♦K, the player still holds his Ace, as well as the master club.

Had the upcard been, say the ♥2, which the player does not want, he could lead ♥4. His opponent can get under it only with ♥3, and if by chance he has it and plays it, then taking the ♥2 in hand need not be a tragedy as it is an excellent card with which to lose the lead next time.

The trickiest judgements arise when the upcard is a middling to good one. The answer is to lead a middling card oneself. If it wins, fine, if not, it is no hardship. Suppose one is not the leader, but must decide whether to take a middling to good card by beating the lead. The answer depends on what card would have to be played to beat it. Obviously it is not good to win a plain-suit Queen by having to play a King in another suit to do so. The final judgement depends on what cards are held and how one is building up the hand.

Gin Rummy

Gin Rummy is a form of Knock Rummy (described in this book as a variant of Rummy), but is entitled to its own entry as it has taken on a distinct aura of its own. Popular myth says it was invented by E T Baker in 1909, and that he (or his son) called it Gin in alcoholic comparison to Rum, which is what Rummy was called in the USA. He introduced it to the Knickerbocker Whist Club of New York, to which he belonged, and it was played there and elsewhere desultorily until the 1940s. Respected historians, however, while acknowledging a contribution from Mr Baker, believe the evolution of the game was less clear cut. Whatever the truth, the game was taken up in a big way in 1941 by Hollywood film stars, and as their habits were publicized round the world Gin Rummy became extremely popular. It has retained its appeal.

Type	Melding
Alternative names	None
Players	Two; three or four for variants
Special requirements	Pen and paper for scoring

Aim
To play all your cards to the table first, by making melds of cards of the same rank or in suit sequence.

Cards
The standard pack of 52 cards is used, the cards ranking from King (high) to Ace (low).

Preparation
Each player draws a card and the drawer of the higher card has the choice of whether to deal first or not. The dealer shuffles and the non-dealer cuts. On subsequent deals, the winner of the previous hand deals.

The dealer deals ten cards, one at a time alternately to each player, beginning with his opponent. He places the remainder of the pack face down between the players to form the stock. The top card is turned over and placed face up beside the stock, to become the first upcard.

Play
The non-dealer has the option of taking the first upcard into his hand or refusing it, whereupon the dealer has the same right. If either player takes the upcard, he replaces it with a discard from his hand, retaining a ten-card hand.

If both players refuse the first upcard, the non-dealer takes the top card of the stock into his hand and discards by adding a card face up to the original upcard, this card now being the upcard. The card discarded may be the one taken from stock.

From now on, each player in turn has the opportunity of taking either the upcard or the top card of the stock into his hand, discarding onto what becomes a discard pile. Players may not look back through the discard pile to check which cards are now unavailable.

The object of each player is to form his hand into 'melds'. A meld is a set of at least three cards of the same rank or at least three cards of the same suit in sequence. Ace is low and is therefore in sequence with 2, 3 and not K, Q. Melds are not laid upon the table as they are formed but are kept in the hand.

Cards which do not belong to a meld are known as 'unmatched' cards. After drawing a card (and only then) a player whose unmatched cards, not counting the card he will discard, count ten points or fewer may go out (called 'knocking') by laying his cards on the table in melds with the unmatched cards to one side. Finally he discards. For the purposes of counting the unmatched cards, court cards count as ten, and other cards at their pip value, with Ace counting one.

The count of the unmatched cards is the score against the player. If he goes out with all his ten cards melded, and no unmatched cards, he is said to 'go gin' and the score against him is nought.

If the fiftieth card is drawn from stock, leaving only two cards in the stock, and the player who drew it discards without knocking, his opponent may take the discard (and if he can may knock) but he may not take a card from stock. The last two cards remain unplayed, and the deal is abandoned, the last dealer dealing again.

Laying off When a player knocks, his opponent lays down his own melds, and unless the knocker has gone gin he may also 'lay off' any unmatched cards in his hand to the knocker's sets. He thereby reduces the count against himself, and may even win the hand (see Scoring, below). An example of laying off is shown under Example hand, overleaf.

Scoring If the knocker has the lower count in unmatched cards, he scores the difference. If the opponent's count is equal to, or lower, however, then he has 'undercut' the knocker, and scores not only the difference, if any, but a bonus of 25 points. If the scores are equal, the opponent scores the bonus of 25 points for the undercut, but obviously nothing for the difference. An example of an undercut is shown under Example hand, overleaf.

When a player goes gin, his opponent is not allowed to lay off, and so is unable to undercut him. The knocker gets a bonus of 25 points for going gin to add to the points scored for the difference in the count.

A running score is kept of the result of each hand, and the first player to reach 100 points is the winner. Bonuses are then added to each player's scores. The winner gets 100 for game, and each player scores 25 for each hand (called a 'box' or 'line') won. The difference between the two totals is the margin of victory, unless the loser did not score a point, in which case the game is a 'shutout' and the loser is 'schneidered', 'skunked' or 'blitzed'; the winner's total is doubled.

Strategy At the beginning a player should keep all combinations likely to form a meld, especially those which offer multiple chances, for example ♥3, 4, ♠4, 5,

Gin Rummy

♦5 offers the possibility of four melds, of sets of 4s and 5s or sequences in hearts and spades. In fact any one of seven cards could allow a meld. However, as the game progresses, a player should consider how long to keep high-scoring cards. For example, being caught with a pair of Kings when the opponent knocks will cost 20 points. Many Gin hands are won after about five or six draws, especially when a player chances to knock with two or three small cards unmelded.

A player who is considering knocking after more than six or so draws, especially if his opponent has been taking cards into his hand, should beware being undercut. Rather than knock with a count of 9, say, it could pay to wait for a lower card to knock with.

On the other hand, it is usually a mistake to hold on for the chance of going gin when it is possible to knock, especially early in the hand.

Example hand

An example of laying off is shown in the illustration below. The knocker has gone out with the ♦4 as his unmatched card. His opponent then lays his two melds on the table, with three unmatched cards. One of those unmatched cards, ♠2, he can lay off on to the knocker's sequence, so the count against him is 6. Note that the knocker cannot lay off his unmatched card or cards onto his opponent's melds, so in this case the knocker is not allowed to put his ♦4 on to his opponent's sequence. It remains a count against him.

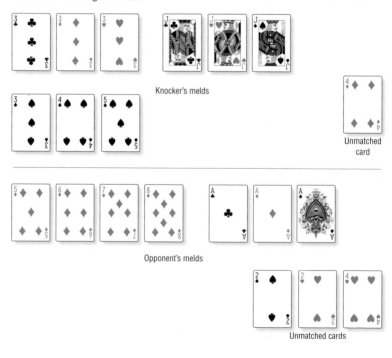

Knocker's melds

Unmatched card

Opponent's melds

Unmatched cards

The second example, below, shows an undercut. The knocker goes out for nine, but his opponent can lay off his ♥2, 3 on to the knocker's sequence for a count of three, thereby undercutting the knocker's count of six and scoring 31 points (the difference plus 25).

Knocker's melds

Unmatched cards

Opponent's melds

Unmatched cards

Variants

A system of scoring known as Hollywood Scoring helped the game to gain a surge of popularity in the 1940s. It is a system whereby three games can be played simultaneously. A scorecard is ruled up as shown below.

	GAME 1		GAME 2		GAME 3	
	Tom	Jerry	Tom	Jerry	Tom	Jerry
Box 1	5	12	16	38	7	
Box 2	21	50	23		12	
Box 3	28		28		29	
Box 4	33		45			
Box 5	50					
Box 6						

When a player wins his first hand, or box, his score is entered in Game 1 against Box 1. When he wins his second hand the score is added to his previous score and the running total entered against Box 2 in Game 1, but it also begins his score in Game 2, where it is entered as his first score, opposite Box 1. His third score is added to his running totals in Game 1 and Game 2 and begins his scoring in Game 3. Thus three games are progressing together. In the illustration on the previous page, Tom has won five hands, with counts of 5, 16, 7, 5 and 17, all of which are entered in Game 1, the last four in Game 2 and the last three in Game 3. Jerry has won two hands only, with counts of 12 and 38, so has failed to score yet in Game 3.

When a player's score reaches 100 in any Game, that Game is closed, and a line drawn across the column. No further scores are entered into it for either player. The play continues until all three Games are completed.

The winner of a Game scores a bonus of 100 points, plus 20 points for each box scored in excess of his opponent in that Game (or minus 20 points for each if his opponent has won more boxes). If a player fails to score in any Game, he is 'blitzed', and the total score of the winner of the Game is doubled. The points for each player in the three Games are totalled to discover the winner and winning margin in the three Games overall.

Oklahoma Gin In this variant, also known as Cedarhurst Gin, the upcard for each deal fixes the number of points at which a player can knock. For example, if the upcard is a 5, a player can knock only with unmatched cards counting five or fewer. Court cards count as ten. Some players rule that, if the upcard is an Ace, then a player must go gin to knock. Oklahoma Gin players also usually prefer to double all scores for any hand in which the upcard is a spade. Game is usually to 150 points.

Round-the-Corner Gin In this variant, the Ace can rank high or low in sequences, which can also go 'round the corner', ie ranking the Ace between King and 2. Thus A, 2, 3 and A, K, Q and K, A, 2 are all valid sequences. An unmatched Ace counts as 15 points. If the knocker goes gin, his opponent is allowed to lay off provided that by doing so he can reduce his own count to zero, in which case neither player scores for that hand.

At all times, players are allowed to look at the discards – a departure from most forms of Rummy. Game is to 125 points.

Go Fish

Go Fish is practically the same game as Authors, a proprietary card game of Victorian times, in which special cards contained quotations from famous authors, the object of the players being to collect sets of quotations. It was thought to be educational. Go Fish and the modern game Authors are slightly different versions of the game, both played with the normal pack of cards. The games are so alike that often one of them will appear in books under the name of the other, and if both appear in the same book the headings seem to be interchangeable. It is therefore best to look on them as the same game. The version here is the one best suited to younger children, with a variant for slightly older players.

Type	Children's
Alternative names	Authors, Fish
Players	Two to six, ideally aged from six to ten years
Special requirements	None

Aim
To collect sets of four cards of the same rank.

Cards
The standard pack of 52 cards is used. The rank of the cards is immaterial.

Preparation
The pack is spread face down and each player takes a card. The player with the highest card (Ace high, 2 low) is the first dealer. Thereafter the deal passes to the left.

If there are two players, the dealer deals each seven cards, one at a time alternately. With three or more players, each player is dealt five cards. The remainder of the pack is placed face down in the centre to form the stock.

Play
Beginning with the player at the dealer's left, each player in turn may ask any other player to hand over all the cards he holds of a certain rank; for example, he might say to a specific player 'give me your Kings' or 'have you any Kings?'. A player must hold a card in the rank that he is asking for; he cannot, for example, ask another player for Kings unless he himself holds a King. A player asked for cards must hand over all the cards he holds of that rank, even if it be three. If the asking player is successful, and is handed a card or cards, he has another turn, and may continue to ask whichever player he likes for cards (remembering that he has to hold at least one card of that rank himself), provided he continues to be successful.

Should the player asked not hold any cards in the rank specified, he says 'Go fish' or 'Fish'. The asking player must then take the top card of the stock into his hand.

If he is lucky enough to draw a card of the rank he asked for, he can show it and his turn continues. Otherwise his turn ends and the next player (to his left) takes a turn to ask.

If a player succeeds in getting four cards of the same rank he lays them face up in front of him on the table.

If during the course of play a player runs out of cards, through laying a set on the table or by being forced to hand them to another player, he may draw the top card of the stock when his turn comes round, but he may not use it to ask another player for a card until the following turn (by when, such is the cruelty of the game, he may have had to relinquish it, and be out of cards again).

When the stock is exhausted, play continues with each player asking for cards in turn, but of course being unable to draw if unsuccessful. A player who runs out of cards when the stock is exhausted must remain idle until the game ends.

The game will end when all 13 sets of cards are on the table, and the winner is the player who has most.

Variants

Some players allow a player to ask for a card he already holds. It adds deception and more skill to a game. For example, if Player A holds ♥3 and ♣3, and asks and gets from another player ♠3, he has another turn, and must try to find the ♦3. If he fails, the player holding the ♦3 can, on his turn, ask Player A for ♠3, knowing he has it. He knows Player A has at least one other 3 too, so having been passed ♠3, he might ask him for ♣3. Having acquired this, he must now try Player A or another player for ♥3. If he goes for Player A again he will have the set.

On the other hand, supposing on getting the ♠3, Player A had asked for the ♥3, a card which he holds. He will obviously fail to get it. The player holding ♦3, on his turn, will assume that Player A holds ♠3 (because he saw him take it) and ♣3 (since he must hold another 3 to ask for ♠3) but will assume that Player A doesn't hold ♥3, since he asked for it. So he might ask Player A for ♠3 and ♣3, but then try another for ♥3. He will fail of course and, on his turn, Player A will be able to pick up all the missing 3s to complete his set.

This variant adds another element to the game and is recommended.

Authors This version of the game is here called Authors, though not all card games writers would agree. It is more skilful, and the minimum age is more like nine or ten years. Even then it is best when played by children of much the same age, who therefore have similar skill in remembering which players hold which cards. Some adults play this game for stakes.

There are two main differences to Go Fish as described above. First, all the cards are dealt, meaning that some will get one more than others. It follows that there is not a stock from which to draw, and if a player does not get the card he asked for, his turn ends.

The second difference is that on his turn a player asks for a single specific card, naming suit and rank; for example he may ask a specific player 'have you the Queen of clubs?' He must hold in his hand a card of the rank of the card he asked for but of a different suit – in other words he cannot ask for a card he already holds.

A player gaining four of a kind must lay them on the table immediately.

It will be seen that a set has to be built gradually, and one cannot gain one by getting three cards all at once (unless he separately asks for three cards, naming the suit each time). Thus a player who can remember where the cards are has a big advantage.

Hasenpfeffer

Hasenpfeffer is a game of the Euchre family said to have been invented by the Pennsylvania Dutch, immigrants from Germany to Pennsylvania in the 18th century. Its name is popularly believed to come from their traditional dish of jugged hare with pepper, although there are alternative theories. It is an interesting game, played with a very short pack.

Type	Trick-taking
Alternative names	None
Players	Four; six for variants
Special requirements	Pen and paper for scoring

Aim
To make the number of tricks contracted for if you are the contracting side, or to prevent the contracting side from doing so if you are the opposing side.

Cards
The standard pack of 52 cards is used, from which are removed all the cards from the 8s to the 2s and a Joker added, making a pack of 25 cards.

The Joker is the highest trump card, and in the trump suit the cards rank: Joker, Jack ('right bower'), Jack of the same colour as the trump suit ('left bower'), A, K, Q, 10, 9.

In the plain suits the rank is normal: A, K, Q, J, 10, 9 (except that there is not a Jack in the suit of the same colour as the trump suit).

The trump suit therefore has eight cards, the suit of the same colour only five, with the other two suits having six cards.

Preparation
From a spread pack each player draws a card. The two who draw the lowest cards are partners, with the lower as the dealer. For the purposes of the draw Joker is high and other cards at their normal values. Players who tie draw again if necessary.

After the first deal, the deal passes clockwise with each hand.

The dealer deals six cards in two bundles of three to each player clockwise from his left. The final card is placed face down in the centre and is a widow.

Bidding Beginning with the eldest hand (the player to the dealer's left), each player has one opportunity (and one only) to bid. A bid is a promise by a player that his side will make a specified number of tricks or more with the trump suit of their choice. The trump suit is not mentioned in the bid, which consists of a number only, from one to six. Each bid must be higher than the previous one. A player may pass rather than bid. When all players have bid or passed, the highest bidder names the trump suit. If all players pass, the holder of the Joker must acknowledge it, and bid 'Three'. Only if the Joker happens to be the widow is the hand abandoned and the deal passes to the next player.

Play

The high bidder takes the widow into his hand and discards one card face down (it might be the widow, if he wishes). The high bidder makes the opening lead. The normal rules of trick-taking apply: players must follow suit to the card led if able, and otherwise may trump or discard. The trick is won by the highest trump it contains, or the highest card in the suit led. The winner of a trick leads to the next. See p383 for an explanation of tricks and trick-taking.

Scoring If the contracting side makes its contract it scores one point for each trick taken, including overtricks. If it fails, the amount of the bid is deducted from its score, which might result in a minus score. The opposing side scores one point for each trick it makes, whether the contract is made or not. Game is to ten points.

Strategy Bids can be at the level of one, but it is likely that the highest bidder will bid at least three. As the trump suit is of eight cards, there will be an average of two per hand. Three trumps and a side Ace is therefore considered the minimum holding for a bid of three. It assumes that the widow and partner might contribute a trick. Although failure to make a contract has a big effect on the score, it must be realized that naming the trump suit is a big advantage, and timid bidding might allow the opponents to win a contract and make four or five tricks which could have been your own. The big decision in play is whether or not to lead trumps. It is usually best, but sometimes it is necessary to establish a side suit first. Also, if one is depending upon your partner to make a trick, giving him an opportunity to trump a side suit early might be necessary.

Example hand

The hands are dealt as in the following illustration, using the Bridge convention of calling the players North, South, East and West. East was the dealer and South, who was dealt the ♦9 instead of the ♥10, bids four. With clubs as trumps he was sure to make the Joker and one of ♠J and ♣A. He expected to make ♥A, and hoped to get a fourth trick with the help of the widow or his partner, or with ♣J (right bower) falling under the Joker. The other hands passed.

The widow unhelpfully provided ♥10, which South took into his hand, discarding ♦9. Reviewing his hand, he wondered if his bid was somewhat ambitious. Unless his partner could provide a trick, he might have to rely upon making ♥10. Knowing

North

West

East

South

that there were only five diamonds in play, he decided to lead his ♦Q to see if his partner could play ♦A or trump. Luckily his partner trumped, and the play went as follows:

South	West	North	East
♦Q	♦10	♣Q	♦K
♥10	♥9	♥K	♥Q
♥A	♣10	♥J	♠K
♣A	♠A	♠9	♦A
Joker	♣K	♠10	♣9
♠J	♦J	♠Q	♣J

South made his contract, scoring four points for his side to his opponent's two. Note that had South led his trumps, losing the second round to East's ♣J (right bower), East could make his ♦A, but whatever he led next South could make the last three tricks with ♣A, ♥A and partner's ♥K, so would have made his contract.

Variants

Double Hasenpfeffer can be played with four or six players in two partnerships, either of two or three. Partners sit opposite each other. From two standard packs are taken all cards below 9, leaving a united pack of 48 cards. The Joker is not used. The whole pack is dealt, there being no widow. One bid per player is allowed, the minimum bid being one half of the available tricks. If all players pass, the dealer must bid the minimum bid. The high bidder may play alone, in which case he discards any two cards and receives any two his partner wishes to give him. A side making its contract scores one point per trick taken; if it fails it loses the amount of the bid. The opponents make a point for each trick made. However, if the dealer is forced to bid and loses, he loses only half the amount of his bid. If a lone player makes his contract he scores for his side twice the amount of cards per hand. If he fails he loses half this. Game is to 62 points.

Hearts

Hearts is the name of a family of trick-taking games in which the object is to lose tricks rather than win them. A game of similar principles, Reversis, dates back to around 1600 in France, but Hearts does not appear in English until the 1880s.

The plain game, described here, is rarely played nowadays. Over the years different methods of scoring have been used and additional penalty cards have been introduced, including the Queen of spades, which gives the name to Black Maria, the most popular version. Also included separately in this book is Omnibus Hearts, in which most of the 'extras' are included.

Type	Trick-taking
Alternative names	None
Players	Three to six; four is best
Special requirements	Pen and paper for scoring

Aim
To have the lowest score at the end of the game; to do so, avoid taking any tricks containing penalty cards (any hearts).

Cards
The standard pack of 52 cards is used for four players. For three players, the ♣2 is omitted; for five players, the ♣2 and ♦2 are omitted; for six players, the ♣3, 2, ♦2 and ♠2 are omitted (it is preferred to keep the ♥2 as a penalty card).

Cards rank from Ace (high) to 2 (low). There are no trumps.

Preparation
Players draw a card from a spread pack, the lowest card drawn indicating the first dealer. Thereafter the deal passes to the left. The dealer shuffles and the player to his right cuts.

The dealer deals one card at a time to all players clockwise until the pack is exhausted. All players must have the same number of cards.

Play
Trick-taking begins, and the eldest hand (the player to the dealer's left) makes the opening lead; see p383 for an explanation of tricks and trick-taking. Players must follow suit to the card led, and may discard when unable to. The trick is won by the player who played the highest card in the suit led, and the winner of the trick leads to the next.

Play continues until all the cards have been played.

Scoring Each heart taken by a player scores as a penalty point against him. There are thus 13 penalty points in each deal.

Cumulative scores are kept, the winner being the player with the lowest score at the end of the game. It is best to agree a number of deals as the duration of the game (for example four deals per player). Otherwise the player with the lowest total when another player reaches a set total is the winner (it could be say, 100 for three players, 80 for four, 60 for five and 50 for six).

If the game is played for stakes, then the average score is estimated by adding all the scores together and dividing by the number of players. Those with scores above the average pay the difference into a pool and those with scores below take the difference out (if there is anything over or short, the sums were wrong!).

A method of settling after every hand, which therefore dispenses with the need to keep a score, is known as the Howell settlement. For each heart he takes, each player puts into a pot as many chips as there are other players (for example, if he takes three hearts and there are three other players, he puts in nine chips). Each player then takes out of the pot one chip for every heart he didn't take (to continue the example, the player who took three hearts will take out 13–3, or ten chips).

The principle can be shown in the following table, assuming four players, North, East, South and West:

	North	East	South	West
Hearts taken	5	4	3	1
Put in pot	15	12	9	3
Take from pot	8	9	10	12
Win or loss	−7	−3	+1	+19

Strategy A long suit with low cards is valuable in that it is usually possible to get below the card led. However, a player should be aware that a long 'safe' suit can quickly become a liability if he becomes the only player holding that suit. If he is given the lead and doesn't hold a low card in another suit with which to lose it, the cards in his long suit become winners. A suit is distributed 4-3-3-3 (when four are playing) in only 10% of deals, so it is rare for it to be led three times without a player discarding a heart on it. Therefore a player holding, say, ♦A, 7, 2, might do well to play the Ace when diamonds are first led, risking taking a heart. If he gets under the lead of two rounds of diamonds with his 7 and 2, on the third round his Ace is quite likely to pick up a heart or two.

With only one or two good 'exit' cards, a player should preserve them for as long as possible, risking taking a heart or two by playing, say, 10s or 9s rather then playing his safe low cards on the first round of a suit.

Example hand

There are four players, and hands are dealt as in the illustration that follows. West deals, and North leads.

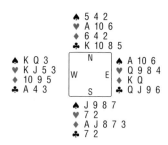

North has excellent spades and diamonds, but is vulnerable on hearts and clubs. He decides to lead ♦4.

East welcomes the lead, as diamonds is a dangerous suit (although all his suits are). South thinks spades is his most dangerous suit, and West realizes spades could be dangerous for him if he is forced to play his ♠3 early. The play proceeds as follows:

	North	East	South	West
1	♦ 4	♦ Q	♠ A	♦ 10
2	♣ K	♣ Q	♣ 7	♣ A
3	♣ 10	♣ 9	♣ 2	♣ 3
4	♠ 5	♠ A	♠ J	♠ K
5	♦ 6	♦ K	♦ 7	♦ 9
6	♠ 4	♠ 6	♠ 9	♠ Q

West took a chance with ♦Q and leads a third round of clubs with his safe ♣4.

7	♣ 5	♣ J	♠ 8	♣ 4

South is more worried about his middling spades and ditches one rather than saddling East with his ♥7. East is very pleased as he knows there is one more club left, and that it is bigger than his 6. Therefore he leads it.

8	♣ 8	♣ 6	♠ 7	♦ 5

South and East are comfortable with their hearts, and discard what they regard as their danger cards, to the relief of North, who could have been saddled with two hearts. He was not only let off but has got rid of his master club. Problems now face South and his diamonds could be his nemesis.

9	♦ 2	♠ 10	♦ 3	♥ K

South picks up the first heart. He now has a tricky choice. If he leads his ♥7, he could pick up four more hearts, but that would be his lot, as he could exit with ♥2. If he leads ♥2 first, he could conceivably be put back in the next round with his ♥7, when he would take all the rest of the tricks, and with them the hearts. He decides to risk ♥2.

10	♥6	♥4	♥2	♥3
11	♠2	♥Q	♥7	♠3
12	♥10	♥8	♦J	♥5
13	♥A	♥9	♦8	♥J

Unlucky North! He had assumed that East or South was more likely to hold the ♥J bare then West and so took trick 12 with ♥10. Had he played the Ace instead, West would have taken the final three hearts.

So North, who looked to have a good hand, ended up with ten hearts. East, who looked to have a very poor hand, took no hearts at all. South, who played well, learned the perils of a long suit without the 2 and took one heart with his ♦3. And ironically West, who ditched his ♠K, Q early, and who could easily have led his ♠3 at trick 7, considered it safe to keep, but in the end collected two hearts with it. It was North's poor holding in the heart suit which did for him.

Variants

Domino Hearts In this game, for three to seven players, only six cards are dealt to each player, and the remainder are placed face down in the centre to form a stock. A player must follow suit to the card led if he can. If he is unable to he is not allowed to discard, even a heart. He must instead draw cards from the stock until he can play one. It follows that soon players will have an unequal number of cards, a situation which continues to the end.

When the stock is exhausted, the game continues but the rules change. Players must still follow suit if able, but may discard if unable to.

When a player's cards run out he drops out. If he wins a trick with his last card, then the next active player to his left leads to the next trick. The last player left in adds his remaining cards to those he has won in tricks.

Each heart taken counts one point. The game may end after an agreed number of games, or the winner may be the player with the lowest total when another player reaches 31 points.

Heartsette This variation, for three to six players, introduces a widow. If three or four play, the ♠2 is removed from the pack; if five or six play the full pack is used. With three players, each receives 16 cards, with three placed face down as a widow. Four players each receive twelve cards, with three in the widow. Five players each receive ten cards with two in the widow, and six players each receive eight cards with four in the widow.

The player to the left of the dealer leads to the first trick. The winner of the first trick takes the widow, discarding from his hand the same number of cards as he took up.

Play is as for the normal game.

Hoggenheimer

Hoggenheimer is merely an adaptation of the casino gambling game Roulette. Because it was invented in the UK it is sometimes called English Roulette.

Type	Gambling
Alternative names	English Roulette
Players	Any number
Special requirements	Chips or coins for staking

Aim

To win chips by betting on cards in the layout.

Cards

The standard pack of 52 cards is used, from which are removed the 6s, 5s, 4s, 3s and 2s and a Joker added, making a pack of 33 cards. The Joker must be indistinguishable in its condition from the rest of the pack; if it is cleaner from lack of use, then the ♣2, for example, could be used in its place.

Preparation

One player must be a banker. Should there be no volunteers, or if more than one wish to be banker, players draw a card from the pack and highest becomes banker (Ace high, 2 low). The odds later quoted for the game are true, so there is no advantage to holding the bank. A banker may relinquish the bank when he chooses. If there is competition for the bank, it should be agreed that a player holds the bank for a certain number of deals.

The banker has the right to shuffle last, and may ask any player to cut the cards. The banker lays out 32 cards face down in four rows of eight, laying aside for the moment the final card, face down.

The four rows represent the four suits: from the top, spades, hearts, diamonds and clubs. The eight columns represent the ranks: Aces on the left down to 7s on the right.

The players place bets upon whether a certain card, or combination of cards, will be exposed, ie turned face up, at the end of the game. The chips are placed in the same way that they are placed on a Roulette table.

Play

When the bets are placed, the banker turns over the odd card, and places it in its place on the layout, for example the ♠A goes in the top left-hand corner, the ♣7 in the bottom right-hand corner. The card in that place is turned over and put into its place, the card replaced going to its place, and so on. The game ends when the Joker is turned up, at which stage some cards will be exposed and others not. The banker then pays out those who made winning bets and takes for himself all losing bets.

An explanation of the various bets, and the odds they pay, is best made by referring to the illustration of a completed game that follows overleaf. The bets, and odds, are as follows:

On a single card	The stake is placed on the chosen card and the odds paid are evens, or 1–1.
	In the illustration, stake 1 on the ♥7 is successful, stake 2 on ♠9 loses.
On a pair of adjacent cards, either in a row or column	The stake is placed between the two cards. The odds paid are 2–1.
	Stake 3 on the two red Queens has won, stake 4 on the Queen and Jack of hearts has lost.
On any four cards, either in a column or a square	For a column the stake is placed below it, for a square it is placed in the centre. The odds paid are 4–1.
	Stake 5 is placed on the four Queens and has won, stake 6 on the square of ♦8, 7, ♣8, 7 has lost.
On any eight cards, either in a row or in two adjacent columns	The stake is placed either at the end of the row or between and at the end of the two columns. The odds paid are 8–1.
	Stake 7 is on the whole of the diamond suit and stake 8 is on all the Aces and Kings. Both have lost.

So in this particular game, where 20 of the 32 cards were exposed before the Joker appeared, there were eight bets of which three won. If all were of one chip, the banker ended two chips down.

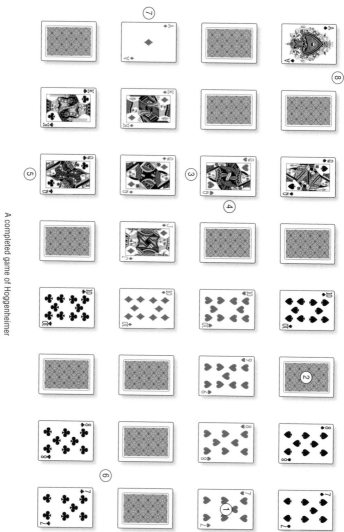

A completed game of Hoggenheimer

King Albert

This game is believed to be named after King Albert I of Belgium. In 1948 it was described by Basil Dalton, the distinguished writer on card games, as 'quite the best single-pack game of patience ever invented'.

King Albert rewards intelligent play, which makes a mystery of its alternative name, Idiot's Delight. Perhaps 50% of games should end in success.

Type	Patience
Alternative names	Idiot's Delight
Players	One
Special requirements	Playing surface large enough for nine columns of cards

Aim
To end with four piles of cards, one for each suit, in sequence from Ace up to King.

Cards
The standard pack of 52 cards is used.

Preparation
A row of nine cards is dealt face up to the table. A second face-up row of eight is dealt to the first eight cards, overlapping them. Further face-up rows are then dealt, of seven cards down to one, as shown in the illustration overleaf.

The seven remaining cards, the reserve, are laid face up in a row by the side. The four blank spaces are the foundations where the Aces will go when they become available.

Play
Aces should be released and played to a space on the table as foundations on which to build cards in sequence in their suits up to the Kings.

The cards available for play are the cards exposed at the base of each column, and the cards in the reserve. An available card may be played to a foundation of its own suit, in ascending sequence, or it may be packed on to an exposed card at the bottom of a column in descending sequence of alternate colours.

If a column becomes vacant, it may be filled by any exposed card.

Cards may be moved one at a time only; in other words, a sequence cannot be moved from one column to another as in many similar patience games.

Example game

In the layout opposite, the ♦A and ♥A can be played immediately to their foundations. The ♥2 can be played from the reserve to the foundation. The ♣2 can be packed on the ♦3, which empties a column, to which can be played the ♠K. This releases the ♣A to its foundation, and the ♣2 can be built on it. The ♣6 from the reserve can be packed on ♦7 and ♦5 packed on it. The ♥J can be played to ♠Q. The ♦Q can be packed on ♠K and ♠J packed on it. The ♠4 can be packed on ♦5 and the ♥6 on ♣7. The ♣10 can be packed on ♥J and ♥9 packed on it, releasing ♠A to its foundation, and so on.

This example appears hardly likely to go much further: the positions of the ♠2 and ♥3 are likely to block the building on these foundations for too long, especially as the ♣K is blocking the way to the ♠2. However, with care it can be played out.

King Albert

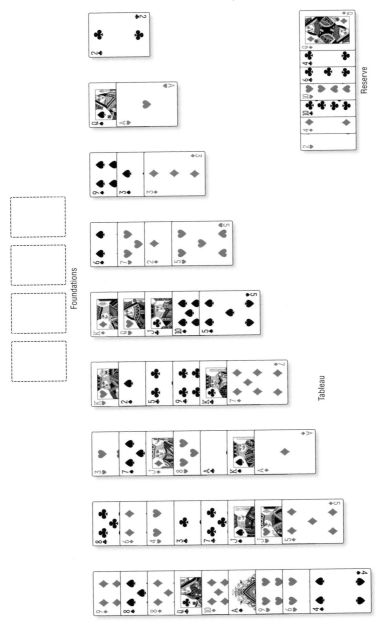

Reserve

Foundations

Tableau

173

Klaberjass

Klaberjass is a game widely played under different names and with slightly different methods in many European countries, but less so in the USA, although it was popular for a time in New York in the 1930s, and is mentioned in the stories by Damon Runyon that became the musical *Guys & Dolls*. The name comes from the German for the Jack of clubs.

Type	Trick-taking and melding
Alternative names	Clab, Clob, Clobby, Klab
Players	Two
Special requirements	Pen and paper for scoring

Aim
To have the highest total when one or both players have passed 500.

Cards
The standard pack of 52 cards is used, from which are removed the 6s, 5s, 4s, 3s and 2s, making a pack of 32 cards. In the trump suit the cards rank Jack (high), 9, A, 10, K, Q, 8, 7 (low). The Jack of trumps is called *jasz* (pronounced 'yahss'), the 9 is called *menel* and the 7 is called *dix* (pronounced 'deece'). In the plain suits the cards rank Ace (high), 10, K, Q, J, 9, 8, 7 (low).

Preparation
From a spread pack each player draws a card. The lower (with the cards in normal sequence from Ace down to 7) becomes the first dealer. The dealer shuffles last, and his opponent cuts.

The dealer deals six cards in bundles of three to each player, beginning with the non-dealer. The 13th card is laid face up on the table and the remainder of the cards, the stock, placed face down at right angles above it, so that the rank and suit of the card can be seen. This card is the 'turn-up' and its suit is the proposed trump suit.

Bidding The bidding is solely to determine the trump suit. There are two possible rounds of bidding.

First, the non-dealer bids and has three options. He may 'take it', which is to accept the proposed suit as trumps; he may *schmeiss* (pronounced to rhyme with 'mice'), which is to offer to abandon the deal; or he may 'pass', which is to reject the proposed suit as trumps.

If the non-dealer takes it, he becomes the 'maker' of trumps. If he says 'schmeiss', the dealer may accept the schmeiss by saying 'yes', or he may refuse the offer to abandon the deal by saying 'no' or 'take it'. This forces the non-dealer to accept the trump suit and become the maker.

If the non-dealer passes, the dealer then has the same three options as the non-dealer had. First, he may take it, in which case the suit of the turn-up becomes trumps with himself as maker. Second, he may schmeiss, in which case the non-dealer can accept, and the deal is abandoned; or the non-dealer can refuse by saying 'no', thereby forcing the dealer to be the maker, with the turn-ups suit as trumps. Third, he too may pass.

This round of bidding has four outcomes, therefore: that the proposed suit is trumps with the non-dealer as maker; that it is trumps with the dealer as maker; that the deal is abandoned; or that both players have passed. If both have passed, there is another final round of bidding.

The non-dealer again has three options. He may name one of the other three suits as trumps, he may schmeiss or he may pass. If he names a trump suit, then he becomes the maker with that suit as trumps. If he says 'schmeiss', the dealer has two options. He may accept, in which case the deal is abandoned, or he may refuse, which forces the non-dealer to name a trump suit and become maker. Should the non-dealer choose his third option, ie to pass, then the dealer again has two choices; he can name the trump suit and be the maker, or he can abandon the deal.

The whole process is simpler to perform than to describe, but the result is either that the deal is abandoned, or that one or other of the players is the maker in either the proposed suit or another.

Further deal When the trump suit is fixed, the dealer takes up the stock and deals three more cards, one by one, to each player beginning with his opponent. He then replaces the stock, but this time he exposes the bottom card and places it face up on the stock. This has no significance other than to show that this part of the game is complete. The stock is not used any more, but the exposure of this card might affect the tactics of the players.

Before play begins, if the trump suit is that proposed by the turn-up, a player holding dix (the 7 of the trump suit) is entitled to exchange it for the turn-up, which will, obviously, be a higher card of the trump suit.

Each player's hand now consists of nine cards. Before the trick-taking phase, points are scored for melds.

Melds A meld consists of a sequence of three or more cards of the same suit. For this purpose only (apart from deciding the dealer, as mentioned) the cards are in their normal sequence: A, K, Q, J, 10, 9, 8, 7, whether the suit is the trump suit or not.

Only one player can score for a sequence or sequences, and there cannot be a tie. A sequence of three cards counts as 20 points, a sequence of four or more 50.

The non-dealer announces the value of his highest sequence, either 50 or 20. If the dealer cannot beat or equal this he says 'good'. If he can beat it he says 'not good'. If he can equal it he says 'equal', or 'how high?', which asks the non-dealer to name the rank of the highest card in his sequence. The dealer then responds 'good', 'not good' or 'equal', as the case maybe. If the sequences are still equal, a player whose sequence is in the trump suit announces it, since of equal sequences that in trumps wins the points. If the best sequences remain equal, then the non-dealer scores for highest sequence. There is no tie.

Note that beyond four, the number of cards in a sequence is immaterial. A four-card sequence headed by Ace beats a five-card sequence headed by King.

A player who scores the points for the highest sequence may score additional points for any other sequence he holds. For example, a player who wins 50 points for a sequence of four, may also score 50 for any other four-card sequence he holds, or 20 for any three-card sequence.

The player who scores for sequences must show them to his opponent after the completion of the first trick in the play which follows. For this reason it is not compulsory to declare all or any sequences, and a player may decide not to do so for tactical reasons.

Play

The non-dealer leads to the first trick, and subsequently the winner of a trick leads to the next; see p383 for an explanation of tricks and trick-taking. The second player to a trick must follow suit if he can, and if he cannot he must trump if he can. If the lead is of a trump, the second player must not only follow suit but must win if possible. A trick is won by the higher trump it contains, and if it does not contain a trump, by the higher card of the suit led.

During the play, a player who holds the King and Queen of trumps may score 20 points for *bella*, provided he announces 'bella' when he plays the second of the two cards. It must be announced or it is not scored.

The object of the trick-taking phase is to win tricks containing cards which have a scoring value (see below). There is also a bonus of ten points for winning the last trick.

Scoring There are four ways to score, and each player's score is kept progressively as play takes place. They are:

i)   for melds of sequences

ii) for bella

iii) for winning the last trick

iv) for taking cards in tricks as follows:

Jasz (Jack of trumps)	20
Menel (9 of trumps)	14
Any Ace	11
Any 10	10
Any King	4
Any Queen	3
Any other Jack (not trumps)	2

When all the points scored in the deal are added, the final score for the hand is calculated. If the trump maker has the higher total, then each player scores the points he made. If the totals are the same, the maker does not score, but his opponent does. If the maker has the lower total, then he scores nothing, and his opponent adds the maker's points to his own. In this case the maker is said to be *bête*.

Game is to 500 points and the winner is the player with the higher total when one or both has passed 500.

Strategy It has been calculated that the combined score per deal of both players averages about 110. To make the trump suit, therefore, a player should hold cards which he expects to score about 60. But of course he makes his judgement when holding only six cards, not the nine of his final hand. With the six he should expect to make about 45, but bearing in mind the heavy penalty for making the trump and not winning the hand (the opponent scoring both sets of points) it is best to err on the side of caution.

The most important consideration when making is to hold jasz, which guarantees 20 points. Menel practically guarantees 14 and Aces are useful. A player holding the King and Queen of trumps (bella) is also guaranteed 20 points, since these cards score if they are played – they do not have to win. This is why bella has to be announced to score – a maker about to lose the hand will not announce bella, as he will be adding to his opponent's score.

A player holding ♠A, ♥J, ♣A, K, Q, ♦7, with hearts as the turn-up, should make. He will make 20 for jasz, possibly eleven each for the Aces, and possibly 20 for the sequence in clubs, giving him a possible 62 points even without his additional three cards. On the other hand, with more trumps but without jasz, such as (with hearts as turn-up) ♠J, 7, ♥ 10, Q, 8, ♣A, ♦A he would do better to pass. Although he holds three trumps, what could he win with them? His opponent might hold jasz and/or menel. If he passes, on the second round of bidding he could make spades trumps, when his hand would look much better.

So far as the intricate bidding system is concerned, it is not advised for the non-dealer to schmeiss on the first round. If he cannot take and says 'schmeiss', the dealer could have a hand in which he himself could take it. The dealer would then be better advised to refuse the schmeiss and force the non-dealer to take it. By winning the hand the dealer would score not only his points but his opponent's as well.

Example hand
The hands are dealt as shown below.

Dealer   Non-dealer

Turn-up and stock

The non-dealer passes, hoping that the dealer will do the same, in which case he would make spades trumps and hold jasz. The dealer, however, holds jasz with the turn-up as trumps and takes it.

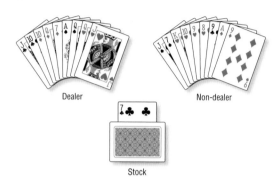

Dealer   Non-dealer

Stock

The illustration shows the hands with the addition of the three cards, and after the dealer has exchanged his dix (♣7) with the turn-up (♣10).

Before he did this, however, came the score for melds. The non-dealer, holding ♥10, 9, 8 announces 'twenty' for sequence, and the dealer, who doesn't hold a sequence, says 'good'. The non-dealer scores 20.

After the dealer has exchanged dix, the non-dealer leads his ♦A and wins the trick. He then shows the dealer his sequence, and leads to the next trick.

The play, with the scores each player makes by his captures in the trick shown in parentheses, goes as follows:

	Non-dealer	Dealer
1	♦A (11)	♦7
2	♥10 (12)	♥J
3	♥K (7)	♥Q
4	♥9	♣10 (10)
5	♠7	♠A (11)
6	♠J	♠Q (5)
7	♦9	♦10 (10)
8	♣9	♣J (34)
9	♥8	♦Q (13)

The dealer, on the last trick, make three for Queen and ten for last trick. The dealer scores 83 and the non-dealer (with his 20 for sequence) scores 50. Notice how the dealer could have gone badly wrong at trick 8. Had he decided to lead his ♦Q, to make sure of winning the last trick with jasz, he would have lost the hand 67–66, and the non-dealer would have scored 133 to nil.

Klondike

Klondike is a widely played patience game, perhaps the most widely played of all. It is often misnamed Canfield, which is really the name by which Demon is known in the USA, or sometimes simply Patience.

Type	Patience
Alternative names	Canfield (mistakenly)
Players	One
Special requirements	None

Aim
To end with four piles of cards, one for each suit, in sequence from Ace up to King.

Cards
The standard pack of 52 cards is used.

Preparation
The cards are shuffled and seven cards are dealt face down in a row. Six face-down cards are then dealt in a row underneath but one card to the right, each overlapping a card in the row above. Further rows, each shorter than the previous, are added until the tableau is completed, and the first card in each row is turned face up, as shown in the illustration overleaf. The four blank spaces are the foundations where the Aces will go when they become available. The cards not dealt form the stock.

Play
The cards available for play are those exposed at the foot of each of the columns, and they can be built to a foundation, or can be packed on each other in descending sequences of alternate colours. Cards can be packed from one column to another in units, for example a ♦7, ♣6 exposed at the foot of a column can be transferred as a whole to a ♣8 or ♠8 exposed at the foot of another column. Aces should be played to the foundations as soon as they become available.

When a card or group of cards is transferred from a column, the bottom card of the column is turned over and becomes available. If a column is emptied, it can be filled only by an available King, either with other cards attached to it in sequence, or alone.

When all the cards in the tableau have been played as far as possible, the stock is taken into the hand, and the top card is turned over and is available for play. If it cannot be played to the tableau or the foundations it is placed face up on the table to begin a waste-pile, or 'talon'. The card at the top of the talon is always available for play.

If the turned-over stock card can be played, all other moves which then become possible in the tableau can be made, including those resulting from the exposure of new cards at the foot of the columns. When all possible moves have been made, the next card is turned over from the stock to the talon, and so on.

It is not obligatory to play a card to its foundation immediately, but once it is built there it cannot be moved back into the tableau. The stock is turned over once only. The game is won if all the foundations are built up to the Kings.

Example game

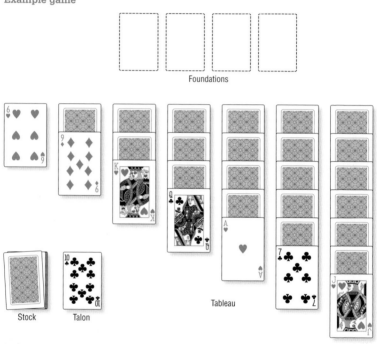

Foundations

Stock   Talon

Tableau

In the illustration, the ♥A is moved to a foundation, and the card below it faced; the ♥6 is packed on the ♣7; the ♥K is moved to fill the column from which the ♥6 was taken; the ♣Q is packed on the ♥K, followed by the ♥J; with each time the face-down card which finds itself at the foot of a column turned face up.

The first card turned from stock to begin the talon is the ♣10, but this can immediately be packed on ♥J, and the ♦9 can then be packed on to it.

Knaves

Knaves is said to have been invented by the late Hubert Phillips who, as well as being a writer on card games, was a humorous columnist of a national newspaper and a panellist on the BBC's *Round Britain Quiz*. He slightly immodestly described Knaves in one of his books as 'a good game for three'. It is based on an old game called Polignac. The Knave is the old name for the card which is now more usually called the Jack.

Type	Trick-taking
Alternative names	None
Players	Three
Special requirements	Pen and paper for scoring

Aim

To win as many tricks as possible to reach a total of 20 points, while avoiding taking tricks containing any of the four Jacks, which are penalty cards.

Cards

The standard pack of 52 cards is used, the cards ranking from Ace (high) to 2 (low).

Preparation

Each player draws a card from the spread pack, the drawer of the highest card being the first dealer.

The dealer deals 17 cards to each player clockwise one at a time, beginning with the player to his left. The final card is turned face up to denote the trump suit. The deal passes to the left with each hand.

Play

The eldest hand (the player to the dealer's left) leads to the first trick, and subsequently the winner of a trick leads to the next; see p383 for an explanation of tricks and trick-taking. The normal rules of trick-taking apply: players must follow suit to the card led if able, and may trump or discard if unable. The highest trump in a trick wins it, and if there are none the highest card of the suit led wins it.

The object is to win tricks, as each trick won scores a point. However, each Jack taken in a trick costs a point or more. To take the ♥J costs a player four points, the ♦J three points, the ♣J two points and the ♠J one point. Each deal therefore has seven points at stake (unless a Jack is turned up as the trump card): 17 for winning tricks, minus ten to be picked up in penalties.

A game is to 20 points.

Example hand

North, East and West are dealt the hands shown below, with the ♣3 turned up as the trump card.

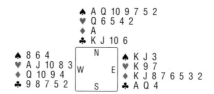

```
                      ♠ A Q 10 9 7 5 2
                      ♥ Q 6 5 4 2
                      ♦ A
                      ♣ K J 10 6
        ♠ 8 6 4            N            ♠ K J 3
        ♥ A J 10 8 3  W         E      ♥ K 9 7
        ♦ Q 10 9 4                     ♦ K J 8 7 6 5 3 2
        ♣ 9 8 7 5 2        S            ♣ A Q 4
```

West is on lead. The play proceeds as follows:

	West	North	East
1	♦ 10	♦ A	♦ J

An unpleasant surprise for North on the first round!

	West	North	East
2	♥ 10	♥ 6	♥ 9
3	♠ 8	♠ 10	♠ K
4	♦ Q	♣ 6	♦ 3
5	♠ 6	♠ 9	♠ 3
6	♠ 4	♠ 7	♠ J

East is forced into taking ♠J. He decides a small trump might be his safest lead at the moment.

	West	North	East
7	♣ 2	♣ 10	♣ 4
8	♥ 8	♥ 5	♥ 7
9	♣ 5	♣ K	♣ A
10	♦ 9	♠ 5	♦ 2
11	♦ 4	♠ 2	♦ K

East is in trouble. A diamond lead will almost certainly get him the ♥J, as will the lead of the ♥K, and ♣Q will get him ♣J. He must make ♣Q anyway, as it is the master trump. He decides to lead his diamonds, and see what happens.

	West	North	East
12	♥ J	♥ 4	♦ 8
13	♣ 7	♥ 2	♦ 7

14	♥3	♥Q	<u>♥K</u>
15	<u>♣8</u>	♠Q	♦6
16	♥A	♠A	<u>♣Q</u>
17	♣9	<u>♣J</u>	♦5

So West won five tricks and took no Jacks for a score of five. North took five tricks but took the Jacks of diamonds and clubs, for penalties of five points, so ending with zero. East took seven tricks, but these included the Jacks of hearts and spades, which took five points away, leaving him with two points.

At trick 16 North was helpless as the cards lay. He was sure to make ♣J whichever card he played. His only hope was that West held ♣Q, but he was unlucky.

Knockout Whist

Knockout Whist is only related to Whist in that it is a trick-taking game. It is very simple, and is often the game used to introduce children to the trick-taking principle.

Type	Trick-taking
Alternative names	None
Players	Three to seven
Special requirements	None

Aim
To win at least one trick in each round in order to stay in the game.

Cards
The standard pack of 52 cards is used, the cards ranking from Ace (high) to 2 (low).

Preparation
One player picks up the cards and begins dealing them, one to each player, until a Jack appears. The player dealt the Jack is the first dealer. The dealer shuffles, and the player to his right cuts.

The dealer deals seven cards to each player, one at a time, clockwise from his left. The remainder of the pack is placed face down in the centre and the top card turned face up to denote the trump suit.

Play

The eldest hand (the player to the dealer's left) leads to the first trick. The usual rules of trick-taking apply; see p383 for an explanation of tricks and trick-taking. Players must follow the suit led if they can, and if unable to follow may trump or discard. A trick is won by the highest trump it contains, or if there is none, the highest card of the suit led.

When all seven tricks have been played, any player who has failed to win a trick drops out and must wait for the next game to rejoin the action.

The player who won the most tricks deals the next round (if there is a tie, the players must draw cards from the pack to determine dealer; highest deals). The dealer on this and on subsequent rounds chooses the trump suit after looking at his hand, and the eldest hand leads. On the second round each player is dealt six cards.

The procedure is repeated as for the first round – any player who fails to win a trick is eliminated. The third round is of five cards each, the next of four, and so on until all players but one are eliminated, which must eventually happen as the last round, if reached, is of one card each.

The winner is, of course, the last player to survive.

Variants

Some people play that, instead of the first player who fails to win a trick dropping out, he receives a 'dog's chance' or 'dog's life'. This player is dealt a single card on the next round, and can choose to play it in whichever of the tricks he chooses. If he does not wish to play in the trick he knocks on the table when it would be his turn, including when it would normally be his turn to lead. He must play his card in at least one of the tricks in the round.

If the player wins a trick with his single card, he survives, receives a normal hand in the next round and is treated henceforth as a normal player. If he again fails to take a trick he drops out of the game in the usual way.

Just one dog's chance is available in a game, although if two or more players fail to win a trick in the same round each receives a chance in the next. Otherwise, once a player has been given a dog's chance, players who fail to win a trick in a subsequent round must drop out in the usual way.

A further variant for players who employ the dog's chance allows that if a player on a dog's chance loses again, he gains a 'blind dog's chance' in the next round. This is a single card dealt face down that may not be looked at by the player but which can be played in any of the round's tricks, as described above.

La Belle Lucie

La Belle Lucie is a very popular single-pack patience game with a pleasing layout. It rewards careful play, but is difficult to get out.

Type	Patience
Alternative names	Alexander the Great, Clover Leaf, Fan, Midnight Oil
Players	One
Special requirements	Playing surface large enough for 17 fans of cards

Aim
To end with four piles of cards, one for each suit, in sequence from Ace up to King.

Cards
The standard pack of 52 cards is used.

Preparation
The cards are dealt in 17 fans of three cards each, with one odd card, spread out on the playing surface. Traditionally the fans are themselves arranged in the shape of a fan, but this requires a very large table.

Play
The top (ie the right-hand) card of each fan, plus the odd card, are available for play. As Aces become available they are placed below the tableau as foundations, and other available cards are built upon them in ascending suit sequence. Available cards can also be packed onto each other in descending suit sequence, one at a time; once a card has another packed onto it, the sequence cannot then be moved elsewhere. If all cards in a fan are played, the fan is not replaced.

When all possible moves have been made, all the cards not built on a foundation may be picked up, shuffled, and re-dealt in fans of three. The last fan might consist of only one or two cards. Further moves are made until no more are possible, when the cards remaining in the tableau can again be picked up, shuffled and re-dealt as before.

Be careful when choosing where to play cards to fans, as the wrong choice can block play entirely in a situation in which an alternative could allow many more moves. This is especially important after the second re-deal (see below), as a block now will end the game.

Two re-deals only are allowed, and the game is lost if, after the second re-deal, it is impossible to build all the cards to the foundations.

Example game

Tableau of fans

Foundations

In the layout shown above, ♣A and ♣2 can be played to a foundation; ♣8 can be packed on ♣9; ♣7 on ♣8; ♥3 on ♥4. This allows both ♥A and ♠A to be played to their foundations. It is important now to pack ♥9 on ♥10 before ♥8 on ♥9, which would block the ♦A. By looking ahead, one can see how the 5s of all four suits can, with careful play, become very useful. The ♥9 is therefore packed on ♥10, allowing ♦A to be played to its foundation; ♥8 is packed on ♥9, ♦5 packed on ♦6; ♦4 on ♦5;

♦2 to foundation; ♣4 to ♣5; ♠3 to ♠4; ♠5 to ♠6; ♦8 to ♦9. The ♠2 is released to its foundation, which allows all the spades up to ♠7 to follow. Now the hearts up to ♥6 can be played to their foundation. The clubs up to ♣5 can follow. More thought is now necessary. Packing the ♠9 onto ♠10 to get at ♣6 would be a mistake, because it blocks ♠8. First it is ♠10 to ♠J; now ♠9 to ♠10. This releases the whole of the club suit to the foundation.

And so on. This game will be got out in one deal, an extremely rare occurrence. But one mistake with ♥8 early on would have ended the play on the first deal there and then, necessitating a second deal with only limited progress made. An excellent patience game.

Le Truc

Le Truc is an old French gambling game dating back to the 16th century. It is a simple, but not completely unskilful game, which can entail a degree of bluffing. However, unlike Poker, some enjoyment can be obtained by playing it for points rather than stakes.

Type	Trick-taking
Alternative names	None
Players	Two; four for variants
Special requirements	Pen and paper for scoring

Aim

To win the majority of tricks, ie two or three.

Cards

The standard pack of 52 cards is used, from which are removed the 8s, 5s, 4s, 3s and 2s, making a pack of 32 cards. The cards rank in the order of 7 (high), 6, Ace, King, Queen, Jack, 10, 9 (low). The suits are of no significance.

Preparation

Players cut for first deal, and the player holding the lowest card deals, cards being in their usual order from Ace (high) to 6 (low). Subsequently the deal alternates.

The dealer shuffles, and the non-dealer cuts. The dealer deals three cards to each player, one at a time, beginning with the non-dealer.

The non-dealer studies his hand and has two options. He may say 'I play' in which case the play starts, or he may request a new deal, in which case the dealer may agree or refuse. If he agrees, the hands are laid aside face down and the dealer deals two fresh ones. If the dealer refuses a new deal, the players start with the hands dealt to them.

Play

Suits are immaterial, so there are no trumps and no obligation to follow suit. Players can play whichever cards they like to each trick; see p383 for an explanation of tricks and trick-taking. A trick is won by the higher card it contains. If both players play a card of equal rank, the trick is 'spoiled', and is claimed by the player who won the first trick. If the first trick is spoiled, then it is claimed by the player who wins the second trick, and if both are spoiled, they are claimed by the player who wins the third. If all three tricks are spoiled, the hand is tied and the deal passes. The leader to a trick which is spoiled leads to the next.

Each deal is worth one point to the winner of the majority of the three tricks, but the attraction of the game (which introduces the possibility of bluffing) is the opportunity to double. A player, before playing a card at any time, whether leading or following to any of the three tricks, may offer to double the value of the hand. His opponent may either decline in which case he concedes the hand at the value before the offered double, or he accepts. A hand may be doubled a maximum three times, making its value eight points (1, 2, 4, 8), but a player cannot double the hand beyond a value which would take his score past the 12 needed to win (hence a double to 16 is impossible). If he wishes, however, he can increase the stake to the level where, if he won the hand, he would have the necessary twelve points. He does this by saying 'my remainder'. For example, if the value of the hand is four and a player's s existing score is six, he cannot propose doubling the value of the hand to eight, because that would take his score past 12, but he can win the six points necessary for him to win the game by proposing 'my remainder'. There is a drawback to this proposal, however, because if the opponent accepts, the points at stake represent his remainder too, no matter what his current score, so that if he wins the hand he wins the whole game.

A player offers to double by stating the new proposed value for the hand, for example if the hand is worth one, he will say 'two if I play'. His opponent accepts by saying 'yes', and the doubler proceeds to lay his card. The opponent declines by laying aside his hand face down.

A game ends at 12 points exactly (it cannot be doubled beyond).

Strategy In the question of deciding to play, a player with a poor hand may occasionally offer to play, and even double in the hope of forcing his opponent to throw in his hand. His opponent, of course, must use judgement in accepting or refusing such offers.

In the play, it is generally considered necessary to try to win the first trick, because that ensures one will win the hand if either subsequent trick is spoiled. However, this doesn't always apply. The order in which the player plays his cards can be vital, as the example hand will show.

Example hand
Suppose the hands are as illustrated.

Non-dealer

Dealer

If the non-dealer decides to make certain of not losing the first trick, to ensure he wins the hand if a subsequent trick is spoiled, he will lead ♦7. The play will proceed:

	Non-dealer	Dealer
1	♦7	♣K
2	♣A	♠6
3	♥K	♦A

The dealer wins the hand 2–1.

If the non-dealer leads his Ace, the outcome will be the same. The dealer will win the first trick with his 6, and must win another whichever card he leads: if he leads his King he wins the third trick with his Ace. If he leads his Ace at the second trick, he again wins the third trick, which will be spoiled, with his King, by virtue of having won the first.

But suppose the non-dealer leads his King. He is now sure to win the hand, whatever the dealer plays. The likeliest outcome is:

	Non-dealer	Dealer
1	♥ K	♦ A
2	♦ 7	♠ 6
3	♣ A	♣ K

The non-dealer wins the hand 2–1.

Experience is the best teacher in deciding what is a good hand, what to lead and when to double.

Variants

Le Truc for four players The game is played by four players in partnerships of two. Unless agreed otherwise, players cut to determine partners and the dealer. The two highest (cards in their usual sequence Ace down to 7) play the two lowest, with the lowest of all being the first dealer.

On each hand, the dealer and the eldest hand (the player to the dealer's left) are the 'captains' of their sides, and they are the two who decide whether to play or to deal new hands (without any collusion from their partners). Only the captains are dealt new hands; their partners keep theirs.

A trick is spoiled if the equal high cards are played by both partnerships. A trick is not spoiled if the same partnership plays the equal high cards. If three or four cards are equal highest the trick is spoiled, as both sides have contributed.

The player who wins a trick leads to the next, and if two players from the same side play equal high cards to win a trick, the player who played the first of the two leads to the next trick.

Only the captain of a side may double or remainder, and he must do so before his side plays its first card to a trick. Only the opposing captain may respond. The rules for the two-handed game apply in all other respects.

It must be emphasized that when four are playing in partnership, especially if the game is being played for stakes, there must be no passing of information or hints from any player to his partner.

Limited

Limited is not a particularly well-known patience game, but it can be a very satisfactory one, in that it sometimes produces runs of success which enable it to be got out from what appear to be hopeless positions. It is an improvement on a more popular two-pack patience which goes by a variety of names, the most popular of which is Napoleon at St Helena.

Type	Patience
Alternative names	None
Players	One
Special requirements	Two packs of cards; playing surface large enough for three rows of twelve cards

Aim
To end with eight piles of cards, two for each suit, in sequence from Ace up to King.

Cards
Two standard packs of 52 cards, shuffled together, are used, making a pack of 104 cards.

Preparation
The cards are shuffled and three rows of twelve cards are dealt, face up, forming the 'tableau'.

Play
The cards in the bottom row are available for play. Any Aces in the bottom row are immediately played to a new row above the tableau, forming the 'foundations', where they can be built upon in ascending suit sequences. When a card is taken from the bottom row, the card in the middle row above it becomes available for play, and when that is played, the card above in the top row is available.

Available cards can also be packed upon each other in descending suit sequence. The card moved should be overlapped onto the other, to establish that the two are a pair. A pair cannot be moved again or have a third card packed upon it: it must remain where it is until the cards can be played to a foundation (it is not compulsory to play the two cards to a foundation together – for tactical reasons it might be preferable to play one but not the other, in which case the card remaining in the tableau ceases to be part of a pair). It is not compulsory to pack on other cards, and it may be advisable not to.

It will be clear why the game is called Limited – the moves are very limited.

The remaining cards are the 'stock'. Once all initial moves have been made, the stock is turned over one card at a time. In practice, since the stock is of 68 cards, it is usual to put half aside, while taking the other half face down in hand and turning them one at a time face up to the table. If a card can be played to a foundation or packed on an available card, it can be, but the latter is not compulsory. If a card turned over from the stock is played to a foundation, all subsequent desirable moves in the tableau can be made before the next card is turned over from the stock. A card that is not played to the tableau or a foundation is played face up to a waste heap. The card on top of the waste heap is always available for play.

If a column in the tableau is emptied, it is replaced by any available card, ie by a card from the top of the waste heap or from the bottom row of the tableau. Vacancies need not be filled immediately, and it usually pays to wait for a suitable card to appear from the stock. A suitable card would be one which would enable a card from another column to be packed on it, thus releasing an Ace or other vital card which was blocked.

When the whole stock is exhausted, the player is allowed a second turn, though that itself is a limited one. In this, the waste pile is turned over and the first four cards are dealt in a line, face up, below the tableau. These are called 'grace cards', and are available to be played to a foundation, packed on a card at the foot of a column or used to fill a vacant column. If a card is played, it is replaced by the next card of the stock, so the grace cards remain at four.

If a stage is reached when no cards are playable, even the four grace cards, there is one last move. A fifth card is added to the grace cards from the stock. If that cannot be played, the game is lost. A fifth card can only be added once.

This game sounds almost impossible to get out, and newcomers to it will be convinced of this as the waste pile builds up alarmingly. But sudden turns of fortune occur, and once several Aces are released to foundations it speeds up. In fact, about one in five games will be successful.

Example game

In the tableau illustrated opposite, the ♦A and ♥A can be played to foundations, and the ♥2 can follow. The ♣5 can be packed on ♣6 and ♠2 on ♠3. Now the ♦10 can be packed on ♦J, releasing ♠A to a foundation. The ♠2, 3 can go to the foundation. The ♠6 can be packed on ♠7, allowing ♦2 to be played to a foundation. With three foundations established and a vacant column, this is an excellent start.

You might now consider playing ♣Q to the vacant column, thus releasing ♦3 to a foundation and the ♥Q to the ♥K, or you may turn a card or two of the stock to see what might become available.

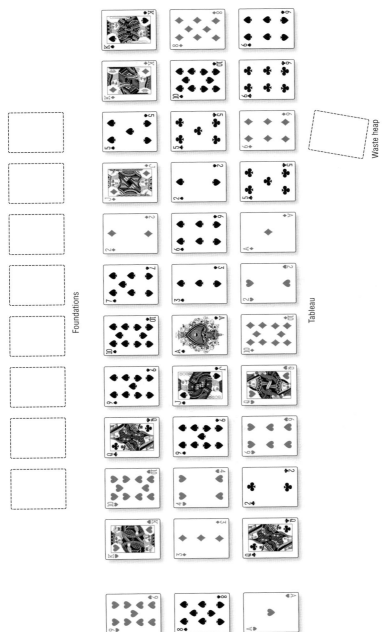

Foundations

Tableau

Waste heap

Loo

Loo dates from the 17th century, and for more than 100 years was one of the most popular card games in Britain. It was originally called Lanterloo, from the French *lanterlu*, which has been translated as 'fiddlesticks' and was the chorus of a popular song. It was supplanted in the late 19th century by the similar game of Napoleon. There are three-card and five-card versions, and limited and unlimited versions. The main description here is of three-card limited Loo.

Type	Trick-taking and gambling
Alternative names	None
Players	Three to seventeen; six or seven is best
Special requirements	Chips or coins for staking

Aim
To win at least one trick in each hand, thus winning chips.

Cards
The standard pack of 52 cards is used, the cards ranking from Ace (high) to 2 (low). For fewer than five players it's preferable to reduce the pack to 32 cards by removing the 6s, 5s, 4s, 3s and 2s, the cards ranking from Ace (high) to 7 (low).

Preparation
Any player may pick up the cards, shuffle and begin to deal cards one at a time to each player round the table until a Jack appears. The player dealt the Jack becomes the first dealer. The deal subsequently passes to the left.

Before each deal, the dealer must put an agreed stake into a pool. It must be divisible by three, as a third of it is taken by the winner of each trick, so the pool could be of three chips.

The dealer shuffles the cards and the player to his right cuts. Beginning with the 'eldest hand' (the player to the dealer's left), the dealer deals one card at a time clockwise to each player and one to an extra hand, called 'miss', until each has three cards. He then places the remaining cards face down in the centre with the top card turned face up. The suit of this card is the trump suit.

Play
The players examine their hands and, beginning with the eldest hand, each has three choices. First, he may play with the hand dealt him. Second, he may exchange his hand for 'miss' and play with that, discarding the hand he was dealt face down. Third, he may decline to play, in which case he again discards his hand face down. Of course, once a player decides to play with miss, subsequent players have only two choices: to play or to decline.

The player who first decides to play leads to the first trick; see p383 for an explanation of tricks and trick-taking. A trick is won by the highest trump it contains, or the highest card of the suit led if it does not contain a trump.

However, the normal rules of trick-taking do not apply, and Loo's trick-taking rules are quite eccentric:

i) A player must follow suit, if able, and if 'void' (ie if he does not hold any cards in that suit) must trump, if able. In either case, he must 'head' the trick if able, ie play a card to beat the previous highest card in the trick.

ii) If the player leading the trick holds the Ace of trumps (or the King if the Ace was the turn-up) he must lead it.

iii) If the player leading the trick holds two or more trumps he must lead one, and if there are only two players left in the game he must lead the higher or highest of his trumps.

If a player fails to observe these rules and this 'revoke' is not discovered and put right before the next player plays, the hand is abandoned and the pool shared between all those playing except the revoker, any odd chips being left in for the next deal. The revoker must additionally provide six chips for the following pool.

When the hand is finished, each player takes one third of the pool for each trick won (which is why the initial pool is of a multiple of three chips). A player who played but failed to win a trick is 'looed'. He must put three chips into the next pool (this is why players may choose not to play – they lose the chance of a share in the pool, but they avoid the risk of having to put in three chips for being looed). The chips put in by looed players form the succeeding pool, and the dealer avoids needing to provide the pool. If no player is looed, the dealer puts in three chips as usual.

If all the players refuse to play on any deal, the dealer takes the pool (he may or may not have provided it himself) and the deal passes. If only one player has chosen to play by the time the choice reaches the dealer, then the dealer must play. He can, however, protect himself from being penalized for being looed by announcing that he will play for the pool instead of for himself. This means any chips he might be entitled to for winning tricks remain in the pool.

Example hand

Suppose five players have chosen to play and there are nine chips in the pool. The hands are as illustrated, with clubs the trump suit.

Player A   Player B   Player C   Player D   Player E

Player A is the eldest hand and leads. The play proceeds:

	Player A	Player B	Player C	Player D	Player E
1	♦K	♦5	♥K	♦Q	♣J
2	♣5	♣A	♠Q	♣6	♠A
3	♦J	♥8	♥A	♣8	♠5

Player B, Player D and Player E each collect three chips from the pool, and Player A and Player C must each put three chips in to form a pool of six chips for the next hand.

Variants

Loo has been played for hundreds of years and from time to time minor variations to the above have been popular. The biggest variation is in the number of cards in the hand. The differences between three-card Loo, as described above, and five-card Loo are as follows.

Five-card Loo Each player is dealt five cards. The maximum number of players is therefore ten. The pool must consist of five chips, and a player looed must put five chips into the pool for the following hand.

There is not a miss hand.

A player who has decided to play may exchange any number of cards from his hand with the same number from the top of the stock. He cannot subsequently decide not to play, nor can he exchange before deciding to play. This option is available only while cards remain in stock.

The ♣J is the highest trump no matter what suit is trumps. It is known as 'pam'. The holder of pam must obey the rules which the holder of the Ace faced in three-card Loo, with one exception. If a player leads the trump Ace and announces 'pam be civil', then the holder of pam is barred from playing it on that trick. He must otherwise obey the rules, ie he must play another trump if he holds one.

Should a player hold five cards of the same suit or four plus pam, he has a 'flush' and exposes it, automatically winning the pool, with all other players looed. A player may find he holds a flush after exchanging cards and may declare it then. All other players are looed even if they have already declined to play. The hands are not played out. Should two or more flushes be held in the deal, a flush in the trump suit takes precedence over one in a plain suit. Otherwise the highest card in the suit decides precedence, if equal the second highest and so on. Exactly equal flushes share the pool equally.

Irish Loo This is played as three-card Loo, with two differences. Firstly, there is no miss, but a player who decides to play may exchange any number of cards by discarding and drawing the same number from the stock. Secondly, if clubs are trumps, no player may drop. This leads to more players being looed and consequently bigger pools.

Unlimited Loo All versions of the game described are known as 'limited' games. They can all also be played as 'unlimited' games. 'Limited' refers to the obligation of a player looed to put chips into the pool for the following deal, which in the games above is limited to three chips for three-card Loo and five for five-card Loo.

In unlimited Loo a player who is looed puts into the next pool the amount of the pool at the beginning of the deal. Thus if two players are looed in a game where the pool is nine units, as in the example hand above, they each put nine chips into the next pool, making a pool of 18 chips. If two are looed in this deal, the pool reaches 36 chips. The pool can soon reach such large amounts that only very rich gamblers play unlimited Loo.

Miss Milligan

Miss Milligan has correctly been described as 'maddening'. But this refers to the game, not the person. The real Miss Milligan, although her name has graced this game for years, is elusive; no one knows who the original Miss Milligan was, if indeed she existed at all.

Miss Milligan is a very difficult patience to get out. Probably fewer than one in 20 games is successful, so it is a patience for those who enjoy a rare triumph, rather than for those who like to succeed at least once each time they sit at the table to play.

Type	Patience
Alternative names	None
Players	One
Special requirements	Two packs of cards

Aim
To end with eight piles of cards, two for each suit, in sequence from Ace up to King.

Cards
Two standard packs of 52 cards, shuffled together, are used, making a pack of 104 cards.

Preparation
The cards are shuffled and eight cards are dealt face up in a row. The remaining 96 cards are set aside, face down, for the time being.

Play
The eight cards dealt are all available for play. Aces are played to a foundation row above the initial eight cards as they become available, and the Aces should be built up with cards of the same suit, in sequence up to Kings, as they become available.

All available cards can also be packed on each other, one at a time, in downward sequences of alternate colours. A complete sequence can also be packed on another column in the same way.

When no further moves can be made, the pack is taken face down into the hand and another eight cards are dealt face up to the foot of the columns, from left to right, overlapping any cards which might be in the column. Again all possible moves are completed, and then another eight cards are dealt in the same way. Only the cards at the foot of each column are available for play. No packing or building can be done until all eight cards have been dealt to the row; in other words, it is not allowed to pack or build on a foundation, or place an Ace to a foundation, in the middle of dealing.

Should a column become vacant, it can only be filled by an exposed King, or an exposed sequence headed by a King.

There is one extra help for the player. When all the cards in the stock have run out (which they will do exactly after thirteen deals, there being thirteen eights in 104), the player may temporarily take into his hand any exposed card which is preventing him from making any moves. This is called 'waiving'. He can then make all the moves made possible by the removal of the card. However, once he has made these moves, he must be able to replace the waived card legally into the tableau, either by building to a foundation or packing. If he cannot, the game is lost.

If he can replace the card, then he may waive another card on the same conditions. He can waive as many cards as he likes, but only one at a time, and only if he can replace the waived card after making the moves available to him.

Example hand
Suppose the eight cards dealt are as illustrated.

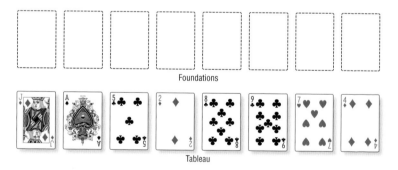

Foundations

Tableau

The ♠A is played to a foundation; ♥7 packed on ♣8; ♦4 packed on ♣5. That is all the moves that can be made at the moment. The tableau as it now stands is shown in the illustration that follows. You will notice that there are three blank columns. A blank column is always useful because an available King (but only a King), which later in the game might block a column, can be played to a blank column.

As no further moves can be made, another eight cards are dealt face up to the columns. Suppose these eight cards are ♦A, ♠6, ♥K, ♠10, ♠A, ♠Q, ♦8, ♦Q.

Now ♦A and ♠A (the second one) are played to foundations; ♠Q packed on ♥K, followed by ♦J and ♠10; ♦2 is built on its foundation; ♠6 is packed on ♥7; ♦8 is packed on ♣9. This ends the activity, but, as explained above, the sequence headed by ♥K can be moved to a blank column – let's say column 1. Another eight cards are now dealt from left to right. Suppose they are: ♥5, ♣8, ♥A, ♠9, ♣J, ♣K, ♦3, ♦10.

Now ♥A can be played to a foundation, ♦3 can be built on ♦2 in the foundation, followed by ♦4; ♦10 can be played to ♣J; thus allowing ♦Q to be packed on ♣K, followed by ♣J, ♦10 as a unit; now the whole sequence headed by ♣K can be played to a blank column; ♠9 can be packed on ♦10; ♥5 can be packed on ♠6.

The illustration above shows the tableau as it now stands. There are still two valuable blank columns. A further eight cards are now dealt, and so on. This game is going well – better than most.

Monte Bank

Monte Bank is a simple gambling game that depends upon the turn of a
single card. There is an advantage to the banker.

Type	Gambling
Alternative names	None
Players	Any number
Special requirements	Chips or coins for staking

Aim
To win money by betting on the suit of a turned up card.

Cards
The standard pack of 52 cards is used, from which are removed the 10s, 9s and 8s,
leaving a pack of 40 cards.

Preparation
A banker must be chosen. In friendly games, it could be agreed that the bank passes
to the left with each deal. Minimum and maximum stakes should also be agreed.

The banker shuffles and the player to his right cuts.

Play
The banker draws the bottom two cards from the pack and lays them face up on
the table side by side. This is the bottom layout. He then draws the top two cards
from the pack and lays them face up above the other two. This is the top layout. The
pack is placed face down on the table. No one at any stage should be able to see
the bottom card.

The players bet on whichever layout they choose. The banker then turns over the
whole pack, exposing what was the bottom card, which is known as the 'gate'.

If either layout shows a card of the suit of the gate, then those who backed that
layout are paid out at even money, or 1–1, ie they receive the amount of their stake
plus their stake back. If both cards of a layout are the same as the gate, backers of
that layout are paid at 3–1, ie they win three times the amount of their stake and
receive their stake back.

Players who bet on a layout which does not include the suit of the gate lose.

There is a slight advantage to the banker if the layouts contain two or more cards of
the same suit. For example, suppose in the illustration that follows under Example
game that the spade in the bottom layout had been a club, making two clubs in the
layouts. There would then be only eleven clubs in the pack, making the odds of a
club being the gate 37–11 against, and the overall chance of a bet on either layout

winning 25–23 against. The banker would win both bets on 13 occasions (when a spade was the gate), lose both on eleven (a club) and win one and lose one on 24 (a diamond or a heart). If there is one card of each suit in the two layouts, then the game is fair to both sides. It follows that players hoping not to lose money would be advised to bet only on a layout that did not duplicate a suit from the other layout.

It would be a better game, in fact, and the suggestion is put forward, that the two layouts should be dealt face down. Players make their bets, the gate is revealed, and only then are cards in the two layouts exposed and settlement made.

Example game
In the illustration, the pack was turned over to reveal ♥A as the gate.

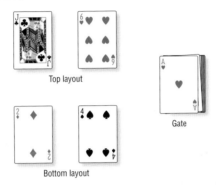

Top layout

Gate

Bottom layout

The backers of the top layout therefore won, as it included ♥6. The backers of the bottom layout, which did not include any hearts, lost.

Napoleon

Napoleon (or Nap, as it is almost always known), is the British representative of the many five-card trick-taking games, the earliest known of which is Triomphe which was played in the 17th century. Games of the same type which became popular in other parts of the world are Euchre, Écarté and Spoil Five, all described in this book.

The name Napoleon was not given to the game until the late 19th century, and it is therefore not thought to be linked to the most famous Napoleon, although the later introduction of bids called 'wellington' and 'blücher' have established a link.

Type	Trick-taking and gambling
Alternative names	Nap
Players	Two to eight; five is perhaps best
Special requirements	Chips or coins for staking

Aim
To win a contract to make a certain number of tricks, and then fulfil that contract in the play.

Cards
The standard pack of 52 cards is used, the cards ranking from Ace (high) to 2 (low).

Preparation
Players draw cards from a spread pack to determine the first dealer. The drawer of the lowest card deals. A peculiarity is that Ace counts low for this purpose only. The deal subsequently passes to the left with each hand.

The dealer deals five cards face down to each player, one at a time, clockwise to his left.

Bidding Each player, beginning with the 'eldest hand' (the player on the dealer's left) has one opportunity to bid or pass. A bid is an offer to make a stated number of tricks with the trump suit of the bidder's choice. The bidder states only the number of tricks, and does not reveal the intended trump suit. The lowest bid is two, except if all the players pass, leaving only the dealer, he must bid at least one.

Each successive bid must be higher than a previous bid.

A bid to win all five possible tricks is called 'napoleon' or 'nap', and the bidder usually says 'nap'. A further bid is allowed, which is 'wellington'. It, too, is a bid to make all five tricks, but it can be called only after a previous player has bid nap.

Play

The highest bidder, called the 'declarer', leads to the first trick; see p383 for an explanation of tricks and trick-taking. He does not need to name trumps, because the first card led indicates the trump suit. The usual rules of trick-taking apply: players must follow suit to the card led and, if unable, may trump or discard. A trick is won by the highest trump it contains, or if it does not contain a trump by the highest card of the suit led.

The object of the declarer is to win enough tricks to make the contract, and of his opponents to prevent him. There is no bonus for making tricks in excess of the contract, and once the contract is made it is usual not to play out remaining tricks (but the declarer should show the remaining cards in his hand to prove he has not 'revoked').

Scoring It is not customary to keep a running score, but to settle after each hand. A declarer successful in making his contract is paid by each opponent the number of chips corresponding to the number of the bid. If the declarer fails, he pays each opponent the same amount.

There are two exceptions. A successful bid of nap earns ten chips from each opponent, but failure costs only five chips to each. A successful bid of wellington earns ten chips from each if successful, and failure also loses ten chips to each.

Strategy Players should appreciate how many cards are 'sleeping' (ie not in play). With up to five players, there are more cards sleeping than in play, so if a player holds a King, it is more likely than not to be the 'master' (ie the highest card in the suit, as the Ace has more chance to be sleeping than 'active'. So bidding includes an element of working out probabilities. The fewer the players, the more luck enters the game.

However, no matter how many players there are, each one will have a hand which includes a suit of at least two cards. So, holding Ace and a small trump is a long way from guaranteeing two tricks in trumps.

Similarly, even holding three high trumps including the Ace plus a 'side suit' with an Ace and a small card is no guarantee that, having forced out all opposing trumps and won the Ace, the small side-suit card will make the fifth trick and ensure success if bidding 'nap'. This is because opponents discarding on the three trumps will note the discards of the other players, and each will attempt to keep a 'guarded' high card in a suit that the others are discarding, purposely to defeat a declarer trying to make two tricks in the same suit at the end. When trying to defeat a contract, a guarded King, for example, is usually a better combination to keep for the last two tricks than a pair of Kings. If fellow defenders take the same line, and keep two cards of the same suit, then the declarer is unlikely to win the last two tricks with Ace and another by expecting the Ace to make all opponents void in the suit.

Example hand

Five hands are dealt to five players as shown.

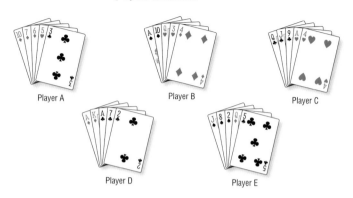

Player A

Player B

Player C

Player D

Player E

Player A is the eldest hand and bids first. He passes. Player B bids two. With spades as trumps he will make ♠A, could expect to make ♠10 by trumping a club, and if not will hope ♥Q is the master. Player C bids three on the strength of expecting to make at least two club tricks as trumps and the ♥A. Player D bids four, with ♦A, K certainties. He plans to keep back ♦K to trump in and make his third club on the last trick. Player E passes. Player D is therefore the declarer and leads to the first trick. The play goes as follows:

	Player A	Player B	Player C	Player D	Player E
1	♦6	♦4	♣9	<u>♦A</u>	♦Q
2	♣3	♠10	♣J	<u>♣A</u>	♣5
3	♥5	♥3	<u>♣Q</u>	♣2	♠2
4	♦7	♥Q	♥A	<u>♦K</u>	♠8
5	<u>♦10</u>	♠A	♥4	♣7	♠J

So Player D went down. It was a very optimistic bid. Even without Player A's trumps, Player C could have foiled him by not discarding ♣9 on the first trick. Player A did well not to trump on trick 3, but would have foiled the contract anyway – he had a trump to spare. Had Player D, the declarer, led his King of trumps at trick 2 and ♣A at trick 3, he would still have lost, as Player A would have trumped at trick 4 and led a heart at trick 5.

Had Player B been allowed originally to buy the contract with his bid of two, he would have failed as well, because of Player E's three spades. Had Player C been allowed the contract with his bid of three, he, too, would have failed. Player D ends by paying his four rivals four chips each.

Variants

Bidding Some players allow two additional bids. 'Blücher' is a bid to win all five tricks, and can only be bid if a previous bidder has bid wellington. It is very rare. The contractor receives ten chips from each player if successful (as for napoleon and wellington), but pays out 20 to each if he loses. The other bid is '*misère*'. This is a bid to lose all the tricks, without a trump suit (although some players treat the opening lead as a trump indicator as usual). The bid ranks between three and four, and is worth three chips to or from each player.

Short pack Some players like to shorten the pack to suit the number of players, thereby increasing the skill factor as, with fewer sleeping cards, chance plays a smaller part. This is done by stripping the pack of the smaller denomination cards. Thus for four players the lowest cards might be the 9s, for five players the 7s, for six players the 6s and for seven players the 5s.

Newmarket

Newmarket is a mild gambling game, the modern version of Pope Joan. It takes its name from the famous racecourse, but there are many other names for it and, wherever it is played, there are likely to be minor deviations from the description below. As a gambling game it is more popularly played among families for pennies than among serious gamblers.

Type	Gambling
Alternative names	Boodle, Chicago, Michigan, Saratoga, Stops
Players	Three to eight
Special requirements	Four cards from another pack; chips or coins for staking; a bowl or similar receptacle for use as a kitty

Aim
To make money by getting rid of your cards, thus winning the kitty, and also to play one or more of the 'boodle' cards, thus winning the stakes placed upon them.

Cards
The standard pack of 52 cards is used, the cards ranking from King (high) to Ace (low). Four cards from another pack are also required; a King, a Queen, a Jack and a 10, each of a different suit.

Preparation
The four cards from the other pack (called 'boodle' cards) are laid out in a row upon the table, with a bowl beside them to hold the chips contributed to a kitty.

Any player may pick up the cards, shuffle and begin to deal cards one at a time to each player round the table until a Jack appears. The player dealt the Jack becomes the first dealer. The deal subsequently passes to the left.

Before the deal, each player must place five chips to the centre. One goes into the kitty, and the other four are distributed among the boodle cards as the player wishes; he may place one on each card, all four on one card, or distribute his stake in any other combination.

The illustration opposite shows a layout as it might be with five players, before the deal.

The dealer then deals the cards one at a time face down to each player and one to a spare or 'dead' hand, which is not used. It does not matter if some players receive a card more than others, as the deal rotates.

Play
The 'eldest hand' (the player to the dealer's left) plays face up to the table in front of him a card of whichever suit he prefers, but it must be the lowest card he holds

Boodle cards

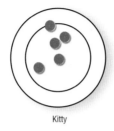

Kitty

in that suit. He announces its rank and suit. The player who holds the next higher card in that suit then plays it face up to the table in front of him and announces it in the same manner, and so on. The playing of the cards is 'stopped' either by the sequence reaching the King, or by it reaching one of the cards in the dead hand. When the sequence is stopped, the player who played the last card begins a new sequence. Like the opening leader, he may lay a card of any suit, but it must be the lowest card he holds in that suit. It may be of the same suit as was stopped, if he wishes, in which case the sequence may also be stopped by reaching the point at which the previous sequence in that suit began.

When a player lays a card matching one of the boodle cards, ie the identical card in both suit and rank, he collects the chips on that card. The first player to get rid of all his cards collects the kitty and play ends. Should any chips be left on the boodle cards, they remain there for the next deal. All players distribute five chips again as before, and the previous eldest hand becomes the dealer for the next hand.

Variants

Michigan Michigan is the most popular name for the game in the USA, where the standard version varies from that described above in the following respects:

Boodle cards   These are A, K, Q, J of different suits (ie Ace is included, not 10).

Rank of cards   The cards rank from Ace (high) to 2 (low).

Staking   The dealer places two chips on each boodle card, while the other players put one (ie there is no choice and the boodle cards are evenly staked). There is no kitty.

Dead hand   The cards are dealt as in Newmarket, except that cards to the spare or dead hand are dealt first rather than last, ie the dead hand is between the dealer and the eldest hand. Moreover, it is not dead, but a 'widow', which belongs to the dealer. After looking at his hand, the dealer may, if he wishes, exchange it with the widow. He is not allowed to look at the widow first, nor is he allowed to change back if he decides he prefers his original hand to the widow. Some players agree that, if the dealer is happy with his dealt hand, another player may buy the widow. Whoever offers most for it, takes it and pays the dealer for it. He may not change his mind after buying it. The original hand of the player who takes the widow is discarded face down and becomes the dead hand.

Stopped suits When a suit is stopped, the player whose card stopped it must change the suit to restart play, ie he cannot begin a new sequence in the suit that was stopped. Some players restrict this even further, and the new suit must be of the opposite colour to the stopped suit. In either case, if the player due to start the new sequence does not hold a card with which he may legitimately do so, the player on his left begins the new sequence, subject to the same restrictions.

Kitty In the absence of a kitty, the player who goes out collects one chip from all the other players for each card still held in their hands at the end of the play.

General Although Newmarket and Michigan are basically the same game, the number of variants listed are numerous. However, neither game is always played as stated, and many players play the game with elements of one and elements of the other. It is not a question of which rules are correct, but of which the players choose to apply. All should agree before play starts, of course.

Nomination Whist

Nomination Whist is the name given here to an enjoyable trick-taking game not usually found in books, in which the name is instead reserved for a kind of off-shoot of Solo Whist in which a declarer nominates a card and the holder of it becomes his secret partner. The game described here is played by up to seven players, without partners, secret or otherwise.

Type	Trick-taking
Alternative names	None
Players	Three to seven
Special requirements	Pen and paper for scoring

Aim
To score points by correctly forecasting the number of tricks you will make on each deal.

Cards
The standard pack of 52 cards is used, the cards ranking from Ace (high) to 2 (low).

Preparation
Any player may pick up the cards, shuffle and begin to deal cards one at a time to each player round the table until a Jack appears. The player dealt the Jack becomes the first dealer. The deal subsequently passes to the left.

It is necessary to agree a scorer.

The dealer shuffles the cards, and the player to his right cuts. The dealer deals seven cards face down to each person, one at a time clockwise. The remaining cards are placed face down on the table and the top card is exposed to indicate the trump suit.

Play
Beginning with the 'eldest hand' (the player to the dealer's left), each player nominates the number of tricks he intends to make, out of the potential seven in the first deal, and these are noted on the score sheet. When it is the dealer's turn to nominate, he is not allowed to bring the total of tricks nominated to seven (this prevents the possibility that, with seven tricks nominated and seven to play for, every player will get his forecast correct).

The eldest hand leads to the first trick. The normal rules of trick-taking apply. Players must follow suit to the card led, and if unable to may trump or discard. The trick is won by the highest trump it contains, or if it is without trumps by the highest card in the suit led; see p383 for an explanation of tricks and trick-taking. The hands are played out, and each player whose forecast was exactly correct scores ten points (to score too many tricks is as wrong as to score too few). In addition, each player scores one point for each trick he makes. The scores are noted down and a cumulative total kept for each player.

The deal passes to the left for the second round, and the process is repeated, except that each player is dealt only six cards. The number of cards dealt is reduced by one at each deal. As before, the dealer is not allowed to bring the total of tricks nominated to six, then to five, and so on.

There is one restriction on the number of tricks a player may nominate to win. Because nominating zero is often an easy option (especially when the hands are of only one or two cards), it is forbidden to bid zero more than twice running.

On the seventh round, the hands consist of one card only. On the eighth round, the hands are increased to two cards, and from then on the hands increase by one card each round until on the thirteenth round the hands are again seven cards each. After this round the game ends and the player with the highest score wins.

Example hand

Suppose there are seven players and it is the fourth round, in which each player holds four cards only. The seven hands are as illustrated.

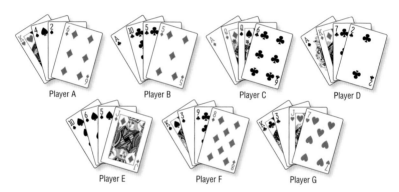

Player A   Player B   Player C   Player D

Player E   Player F   Player G

Player G dealt, so Player A is the first to bid. Hearts are trumps.

Player A bids one. The only threat against him getting one is if the Ace of trumps is led and he loses his King. He is unlikely to make a trick with any other card.

Player B bids one, his main threats being that clubs are not led, or are trumped, or that having made the ♣A he has to lead another club, which also wins a trick.

Player C bids one, expecting to make either ♦A or ♠Q and hoping to be able to discard the others.

Player D bids one on the same principle, expecting to make either ♠A or ♦K, and not expecting to make both, as all three of the previous bidders have bid one. His bid of one means that all four tricks are now accounted for.

Player E knows this and is fairly confident in bidding zero.

Player F also bids zero.

Player G, the dealer, is barred from bidding zero as four tricks have already been bid. However, with two trumps and a King he might well have bid two had he been first bidder, so now he is happy to bid one, expecting, with all the other bidding, that he will lose one of his trumps, and hoping to discard his ♣K.

There are five tricks bid for, so each of those who bid one knows he has to fight for his trick.

Player A, who leads, will not lead his King of trumps, in case another player holds the Ace. It would be safer for him to trump on a club lead, say. He decides to lead ♠4. Play proceeds as follows, with the number of tricks bid by each player shown in brackets:

	Player A (1)	Player B (1)	Player C (1)	Player D (1)	Player E (0)	Player F (0)	Player G (1)
1	♠4	♣10	♠Q	♠A	♠10	♠K	♥J

Player G plays his larger trump, as he wants only one trick. He then leads his other trump, feeling confident that somebody would over-trump. Had he kept it he might have been forced to win with it later (as the cards lay, he was right).

2	♥K	♣5	♦Q	♣7	♦J	♦8	♥7
3	♠2	♦5	♣6	♣2	♠5	♠3	♣K

Disaster for Player E. Who could have thought that with players fighting for tricks, he would win a trick with ♠5? Worse was to follow:

4	♦6	♣A	♦A	♦K	♠6	♣9	♣3

So Player E, who did not want a trick, made two with ♠6, 5. Three players who nominated one trick did not make a trick at all. And none of the three Aces dealt made a trick.

Player A and Player G each score eleven points (ten for a correct forecast and one for a trick), Player F ten (for a correct forecast), Player E two (for his two tricks) and Player B, Player C and Player D nil. Each player's bid was reasonable, and all played as well as possible.

Readers can set up the hands as shown, and see what happens if Player A's opening lead is ♦6 (as it would be with many players). Six of the seven players would have got their forecasts correct, had everybody played well.

Variants

Because the restriction on bidding zero more than twice running gets very trouble-some over the run of deals when the hands are of one or two cards only, some players ignore this rule.

Some players, instead of turning up a card to indicate trumps, prefer the trump suit to be rotated, for example hearts, clubs, diamonds, spades.

Oklahoma

Oklahoma is a game which rests between Rummy and Canasta, having some of the properties of the latter in that big melds can be made and large numbers of cards can be held by picking up the whole of the discard pile. However, it is without most of Canasta's complexities. It is not to be confused with Oklahoma Gin, which is a variant of Gin Rummy and is included in this book under that heading.

Type	Melding
Alternative names	Arlington
Players	Two to five; three is best
Special requirements	Two packs of cards; pen and paper for scoring

Aim

To be the first player to reach 1,000 points; points are won by making melds of cards of the same suit in sequence, or of the same rank irrespective of suit.

Cards

Two standard packs of 52 cards, shuffled together, are used, plus one Joker, making a pack of 105 cards.

Cards rank from Ace (high) to 3 (low), with the Joker and all deuces (2s) being 'wild', ie they can represent any cards that their holder wishes. Sequences are a feature of the play, and an Ace can be part of a high sequence (A, K, Q, J, etc) or a low sequence (A, 2, 3, 4, etc), but cannot be used 'round the corner' (ie Q, K, A, 2, 3 is not a legitimate sequence).

Preparation

The players draw cards to decide the first dealer. For this purpose Ace is high, 2 is low and Joker ranks below 2. The drawer of the lowest card deals the first hand. The deal subsequently passes to the left.

Both packs are shuffled together thoroughly. The dealer is entitled to the last shuffle, and the player to his right cuts. The dealer deals 13 cards to each player, face down one at a time. The remainder of the joint pack is placed face downwards in the centre to form the 'stock'. The top card of the stock is turned face up (the 'upcard') and placed next to the stock to begin a 'discard pile'.

Play

Players try to form 'melds'. A meld consists of three or more cards of the same suit in sequence (this could be as long as 14 cards – a complete set with an Ace at each end) or three or four cards (but not more) of the same rank. A meld of cards of the same rank need not be of cards of different suits; for example, the two ♥5s may be included in the same meld.

When the cards are first dealt, the 'eldest hand' (the player to the dealer's left) may take the upcard into his hand or refuse it. The next player clockwise has the same option, and so does each player in turn while the card is refused.

To take the card, a player must immediately meld with it. This means he must lay on the table a meld which includes the upcard. This meld may include any number of wild cards (ie the Joker and the 2s).

If a player takes the upcard and melds, he completes his turn by discarding, beginning a new discard pile.

This allows the next player a different choice: to take the upcard (under the same conditions) or to take into his hand the top card of the stock. He may then meld, if he wishes, or not. In either case he completes his turn by discarding onto what becomes, rather than a single upcard, a discard pile.

From then on, and throughout the game, a player has the choice of taking into his hand the card heading the discard pile (with the proviso that he must meld with it, or add it to an existing meld), or of taking the top card of the stock.

A player who takes the top card of the discard pile and melds with it, must then take into his hand the remainder of the discard pile, and can continue melding with the cards so obtained. His turn must always end with a discard.

If on the first round of play, nobody takes the upcard and the turn comes round again to the eldest hand, who has already refused it, the eldest hand then takes the top card of the stock and play resumes as described.

When melding with the Joker or a 2, the player must announce the card it represents. This prevents a wild card being used as a card at one end of a sequence and then switched to the other end at the holder's convenience. However, a player may replace the Joker in a meld with the card it represents if he should acquire that card on a future turn. He can then take the Joker into his hand and use it again as he sees fit. This concession applies only to the Joker and not to a 2. By this means a player can take the discard pile if the card that the Joker in his meld represents appears at the top of it. He merely replaces the Joker with the card and takes the discard pile. A Joker can only be replaced in a meld by the player whose meld it is.

A player when discarding can discard any card he likes except ♠Q. This can be discarded only if it is the last card in the player's hand (ie if the player 'goes out', by getting rid of all his cards).

A deal ends when a player goes out or when a player draws the last card of the stock and discards without going out.

A player must discard before going out. He cannot meld all the cards in his hand and go out without a discard. It follows that if he holds two cards in his hand, he cannot meld with them because he would not have a card remaining to discard. He can go out only by adding each card to his existing melds.

Scoring At the end of the deal the cards in a player's melds are scored for him, and those cards still in his hand are scored against him, as follows:

Card	Plus score when melded	Minus score in hand
Joker	100	200
♠Q	50	100
Each Ace	20	20
Each high card (8–K) (excluding ♠Q)	10	10
Each low card (3–7)	5	5
Each deuce (2)	value of card represented, although a deuce representing ♠Q counts 10, not 50	20

A player who goes out receives a 'going out bonus' of 100 points. A person who goes out without having previously melded is said to go out 'concealed', and receives 100 points plus an extra bonus of 150 points, but does not get the extra bonus if he goes out on his first turn. This extra bonus is added to his total at the end of the game, and does not count towards reaching the game score.

The game score is 1,000 points, and the game ends when one player's cumulative score passes this total. If two or more pass 1,000 points on the same deal, the winner is the player with the most points. The winner receives an additional bonus of 200 points.

For settlement purposes, each player's score is rounded up or down to the nearest 100 (50 is rounded upwards), and if played for stakes, settlement is made at an agreed rate per 100 points.

Example hand
The illustration opposite shows a game in progress.

If it were the turn of either Player A or Player B (as it must be, because only Player C would have discarded the ♠5), the card would probably be taken in hand and melded with. However, this might depend on the size of the discard pile and the cards it contains, because both players know that Player C wants only one card to go out, so to hold a large hand of unmelded cards could count against them. Player C needs to draw from stock a Jack, 9, 4, Ace or wild card to add to his melds and go out by discarding ♥5.

Hand

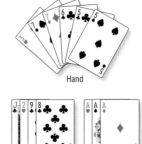

Hand

Melds   Player A

Melds   Player B

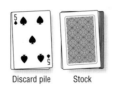

Hand

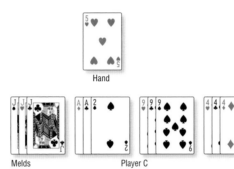

Melds   Player C

Discard pile   Stock

Old Maid

Old Maid is a game for children in which there is not a winner but a loser. The loser is the Old Maid, and is subject to derision – if it were a recently invented game, it would no doubt have a less politically incorrect title. It is not necessary for the penalty card to be a Queen, and in France it is a Jack.

Type	Children's
Alternative names	None
Players	Any number of three or more
Special requirements	Two packs of cards if more than six players

Aim
To avoid being left at the end holding the odd Queen.

Cards
The standard pack of 52 cards is used, from which is removed one Queen. If more than six play, it is better to use two packs of cards shuffled together, but again only one Queen is removed.

Preparation
Anybody may pick up the cards, shuffle them and deal them one at a time face down to all the players until the pack is exhausted. It does not matter if some players get a card more than others.

Play
The players look at their cards and discard face down on the table before them any pairs they may hold. If they hold three cards of the same rank they discard two of them and keep the third. Four of a kind are treated as two pairs.

The player to the dealer's left shuffles the cards remaining in his hand, and offers his hand as a fan face down to the player on his left. That player selects one card and adds it to his hand. If it matches a card he already holds, he pairs them together and discards them to the table. In any case, he then shuffles his hand and offers it face down as a fan to the player on his left, who selects a card, checks if it pairs with one of his, and if so discards them. He then offers his hand to the next player, and so on.

As play proceeds, and pairs are made, the players' hands will get progressively smaller, and players will drop out as all the cards in their hands are paired and discarded to the table. If a player holds only one card in his hand after pairing, the player on his left of course has no choice when it comes to receiving a passed-on card and the first player goes out of the game.

Eventually, all the cards will be paired except the odd Queen, and the player holding it is the loser, or 'old maid'.

Young children holding a Queen in their hand sometimes do not conceal their excitement when they manage to pass it on, and so the whereabouts of the Queen or Queens becomes the knowledge of all. This, if anything, usually adds to the general enjoyment.

Ombre

Ombre is an old Spanish game which dates back to the 14th century, and which was very popular in Europe for some 400 years until finally almost extinguished by Whist. It was introduced to England in the late 17th century by Catharine of Braganza, who married Charles II. Versions of it may still be found in Spain and Latin America, and in the USA a simplified form for four players is known as Solo (not to be confused with Solo Whist).

The simplest form of the three-handed game, with its complex ranking of the cards, is described here for those who wish to experience a game of a more leisurely (at least among the aristocracy) age. It is actually a good game.

Type	Trick-taking
Alternative names	Hombre, Rocamber, Tresillo
Players	Three
Special requirements	Chips or coins for staking, or pen and paper for scoring

Aim

If playing as 'ombre', to win more tricks than each of your opponents; if opposing ombre, to win more tricks than ombre or to help the other player opposing ombre to win more tricks than ombre.

Cards

The standard pack of 52 cards is used, from which are removed the 10s, 9s and 8s, leaving a short pack of 40 cards equivalent to the Spanish pack.

In 'plain' (non-trump) suits, the cards rank in different orders according to whether they are red or black. In red suits they rank, unusually, as K, Q, J, A, 2, 3, 4, 5, 6, 7. In black suits they rank normally, ie A, K, Q, J, 7, 6, 5, 4, 3, 2.

In red trump suits the cards rank ♠A (*spadille*), 7 (*manille*), ♣A (*basto*), A (*punto*), K, Q, J, 2, 3, 4, 5, 6. In black trump suits, the cards rank ♠A (*spadille*), 2 (*manille*),

♣A (*basto*), K, Q, J, 7, 6, 5, 4, 3. The three top trumps – spadille, manille and basto – are called the 'matadors'. Hence, when a red suit is trumps, there are twelve trumps (including ♠A and ♣A) and when a black suit is trumps there are only eleven trumps.

Preparation

In Spanish games the normal direction of play is anti-clockwise. Any player takes the pack and deals a card face up anti-clockwise to each player, beginning with the 'eldest hand' (in this case the player to the dealer's right), until a black Ace appears. The black Ace indicates the dealer. Each deal is a game in itself, and the dealer is decided in the same way.

Each player puts an agreed stake into a pool.

The dealer shuffles and the player to his left cuts. The dealer deals each player nine cards, in three bundles of three, in an anti-clockwise direction. The remaining 13 cards are placed face down in the centre of the table.

Bidding The bidding is to determine 'ombre'. Ombre has the right to name the trump suit and to exchange cards by discarding and drawing from the stock. There is one round of bidding.

The eldest hand (remember, this is the player to the dealer's right) has the first choice to be ombre. A player announces his willingness to be ombre by saying 'I play'. Otherwise he says 'I pass'. If only one player says 'I play', he becomes ombre. A player who says 'I play' might, however, be overcalled by a subsequent player saying 'I play'. The second player is announcing that he is willing to be ombre without exchanging any cards with the stock. The first player who called still has the option to become ombre, but he must state that he also is prepared to play without exchanging any cards. If so, he has precedence over the second bidder.

If all three players pass, the deal is abandoned, and a further deal is made, with the new dealer being decided as above, and the pool remaining where it is for the new deal.

Play

Ombre announces the trump suit. If ombre was unopposed (ie he has the right to exchange cards), he discards as many cards as he wishes, and places them face down to one side. He then draws from the top of the stock the same number, so that his hand remains at nine cards. The player to his right then has the opportunity to change cards, and finally the third player may do so. If there are any cards remaining the third player has the right to decide whether they shall be shown to all players or remain face down. If ombre did not exchange, then the other players do not either.

When the final hands are determined, ombre leads to the first trick; see p383 for an explanation of tricks and trick-taking. The normal rules of trick-taking apply (with one exception, mentioned later). Players must follow suit to the card led and, if unable, may trump or discard as they wish. The trick is won by the highest trump it contains, or if it doesn't contain a trump, by the highest card in the suit led.

The exception to the need to follow suit concerns matadors. If a non-matador trump is led, a player holding only matadors in the trump suit need not follow suit, but can 'renege', ie discard from a non-trump suit. However, if the lead itself is a matador, he must follow suit even if it means playing a lower matador, but he is not forced to beat the lead with a higher matador, so that if he holds only higher matadors, he can renege. The simple effect is that matadors cannot be forced out by the lead of lower trumps, but must be played (if no lower trumps are held) if a higher matador is led.

The winner of a trick leads to the next. The object of each player is to win the most tricks, but a secondary object of the two players opposing ombre, as the settlement details below will make clear, is to attempt to prevent ombre from making the most tricks. It might pay for a player opposing ombre not to win a trick in which the other player opposing ombre has already played a higher card than ombre. This could diminish ombre's chances of winning the most tricks.

To win, ombre does not need to take the majority of the tricks, but only to take more than either of his opponents (ie four tricks will be sufficient if his opponents split the others 3–2). If ombre wins the most tricks, he takes the pool. This is called *sacardo*.

If one of his opponents wins more tricks than ombre, then ombre pays that player a sum equal to the amount in the pool and the pool remains for the next deal. This is called *codille*.

If one or both of his opponents wins the same number of tricks as ombre, ombre doubles the amount in the pool and the doubled pool is carried forward to the next deal. This is called *puesta*.

It follows that an opponent who can win only one or two tricks should concentrate on trying to win tricks which would otherwise be won by ombre, rather than tricks which the other partner opposing ombre might win.

Example hand
The cards are dealt as illustrated, using the Bridge convention of calling the players North, East and West (South not being used as this is a three-player game).

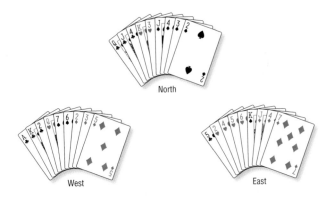

North

West

East

North was the dealer, so West is the eldest hand. West can see that with clubs as trumps, he will hold three of the top four, so is certain of two tricks, and has a good chance, by exchanging his other six cards, of raising this to four or five, so he says 'I play'. If another player says 'I play' he will back down, since his hand is much too poor as it stands for him to be ombre. As it happens, neither East nor North have good hands, so West is allowed to be ombre.

West discards his six non-trump cards, and picks up two small trumps and the master King of diamonds – not bad, and he probably thinks his chances are at least even.

East, who suspects trumps will be black, decides to ditch his two smallest diamonds. His hand is so poor that he wants to leave North as many cards as possible to exchange, in the hope that he may stop ombre. As it happens, he picks up spadille and the ♦A, thus depriving North of spadille, which he would have liked.

North, who thinks diamonds is much the likeliest trump suit, decides to discard all his spades and the ♥3, which was a good choice – if there had been more cards in the stock, he would have discarded some clubs, too. So the exchange was just about even in its fortunes.

The new hands are shown below, arranged with the trumps to the left of each hand.

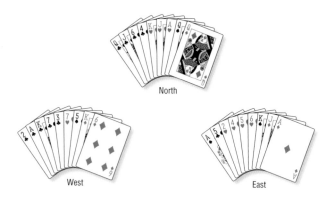

West leads manille. He expects to win four trumps and the ♦K which will be sufficient to score sacardo. East decides to take the trick with spadille (although if he held it back, West would not be able to force it out by leading trumps again). East leads his master spade and then hearts, hoping that North might eventually be able to trump them.

The play goes as follows:

	West (ombre)	East	North
1	♣2 (manille)	♠A (spadille)	♣4
2	♠5	♠K	♠Q
3	♥7	♥6	♥K
4	♣7	♥5	♥J
5	♣A (basto)	♣5	♣6
6	♣K	♥2	♣J
7	♣3	♥4	♣Q
8	♦6	♦A	♥A
9	♦K	♦J	♦Q

West, in the end, was lucky. After losing the first three tricks and then his long trump, he was lucky that North had ♦Q to lead on the last trick. So West takes the pool as sacardo.

Readers might like to work out what might have happened if East had held back spadille on the opening lead.

Omnibus Hearts

Omnibus Hearts is a game which combines many of the elements of Black Maria and Hearts, and is regarded as the best version of the game by many players.

Type	Trick-taking
Alternative names	Hit the Moon
Players	Three to six; four is best
Special requirements	Pen and paper for scoring

Aim

To avoid taking tricks which contain penalty cards (♠Q and all the hearts) and to win the trick containing the bonus card (♦10).

Cards

The standard pack of 52 cards is used, the cards ranking from Ace (high) to 2 (low). For four players the full 52 cards are used. For three players, the ♣2 is removed, to give hands of 17 cards each. For five players, both black 2s are removed, and hands are of ten cards each. For six players, ♣ 2, 3, ♦2, ♠2 are removed, and hands are of eight cards each (the ♥2 is retained as it is a penalty card).

Preparation

Players draw cards from a spread pack to determine the first dealer. The drawer of the lowest card deals. The deal subsequently passes to the left.

The dealer shuffles and the player to his right cuts. The dealer then deals the whole pack clockwise, one at a time face down, to each player, beginning with the player to his left.

Players examine their cards and each passes on three cards face down to his righthand neighbour. A player cannot pick up the cards passed to him until he himself has already passed on. With more than four players only two cards are passed.

Play

The 'eldest hand' (the player to the dealer's left) leads to the first trick; see p383 for an explanation of tricks and trick-taking. There is no trump suit. Players must follow suit if able, and if unable may discard any card they wish. The trick is won by the highest card in the suit led, and the winner of a trick leads to the next.

The object is to avoid taking in a trick the ♠Q, which counts as –13 points to the player taking it, and any hearts, which count as –1 point each. On the other hand, to capture ♦10 is worth ten points.

A player who takes all fifteen counting cards (♠Q, ♦10 and all the hearts) scores 26 points instead of –16 as they would if counted normally. This is known as 'hitting the moon', 'take-all' or 'slam'.

The game ends when one player reaches a score of –100. The winner is the player with the smallest minus score (or, rarely, the highest plus score).

Example hand
The hands are dealt as illustrated, using the Bridge convention of calling the players North, South, East and West.

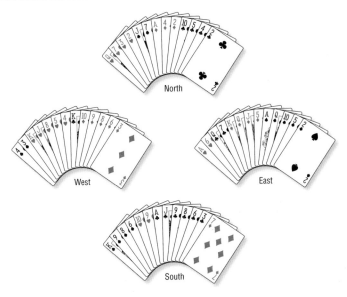

North

West

East

South

South is the dealer, and West the eldest hand. West would like diamonds to be led often so that he could win a trick with ♦10. He passes on the dangerous ♥K, J and ♣K. South keeps his clubs, as being relatively safe, and if he establishes them he might pick up ♦10. He passes ♥10, 9 and ♠K. East sees a chance of picking up ♦10 with his diamond court cards, and passes on ♠A, Q and ♥A. North has a hand which might not win a dangerous trick and passes on ♥Q, 7 and ♣10. The hands are now as shown below.

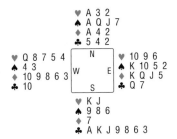

```
                    ♥ A 3 2
                    ♠ A Q J 7
                    ♦ A 4 2
                    ♣ 5 4 2
        ♥ Q 8 7 5 4    N      ♥ 10 9 6
        ♠ 4 3                 ♠ K 10 5 2
        ♦ 10 9 8 6 3  W   E   ♦ K Q J 5
        ♣ 10           S      ♣ Q 7
                    ♥ K J
                    ♠ 9 8 6
                    ♦ 7
                    ♣ A K J 9 8 6 3
```

West begins by leading his ♦9, and play proceeds:

	West	North	East	South
1	♦9	♦4	♦K	♦7
2	♣10	♣5	♣Q	♣J
3	♥Q	♣4	♣7	♣6

A slight shock for East who decides to exit with ♦5.

4	♦3	♦2	♦5	♥K

Another shock! East's best bet now seems to be to lead ♠5.

5	♠4	♠J	♠5	♠9
6	♥8	♣2	♠K	♣A

South now holds all the clubs. He leads ♠6.

7	♠3	♠7	♠10	♠6
8	♥7	♠A	♠2	♠8

With relief, North knows that his ♠Q is the only spade left, and he will not be caught with it, unless he is forced to lead it. He exits with ♥3.

9	♥5	♥3	♥6	♥J

South has only clubs left, and must make the rest of the tricks, which include both the ♦10 and the ♠Q.

The final scores are West 0, North –1, East –2 and South –13.

Variants

Omnibus Hearts is itself a variant of Hearts, but players who wish to take in even more variants to the basic game might give minus values to the hearts suit of Ace –5, King –4, Queen –3, Jack –2 and the spot cards –1 each.

Some players prefer the ♦J or ♦8 to be the bonus card.

Panguingue

Panguingue is a game which uses a lot of cards – 320 is about average – and is popular in the south-west of the USA, in Nevada and along the Pacific coast, where there are casinos devoted to it.

It is a game of the Rummy family, descended from Conquian or Coon Can, and is of Spanish origin.

Type	Melding and gambling
Alternative names	Pan
Players	Up to 15; six to eight is best
Special requirements	Eight packs of cards; chips or coins for staking

Aim
To meld all your cards and thus go out.

Cards
Eight standard packs of 52 cards are usually used, but sometimes as few as five or as many as twelve are used. From the packs are traditionally stripped the 10s, 9s and 8s, but as sequences are a vital part of the game, it is logical to strip the Kings, Queens and Jacks instead, which avoids the awkwardness of sequences of 6, 7, J. The amalgamated pack is therefore of 320 cards.

With the court cards stripped, the ranking of the cards is 10 (high) to Ace (low). The following description assumes that the cards used are the 10s down to Aces.

Preparation
All players shuffle part of the pack, and the pack is then brought together again. Each player draws a card to determine the dealer and the 'eldest hand': the drawer of the lowest card becomes the eldest hand, and the second lowest the dealer. The dealer sits on the eldest hand's left. This is contrary to usual practice in Britain and North America, but it conforms to Spanish tradition where the play is anti-clockwise.

On following deals, the deal does not rotate, either to right or left. The winner of a hand becomes the eldest hand for the next, so the next dealer is the player sitting to the left of the winner. The player to the left of the dealer has the final shuffle. Rarely do all the cards get used during one hand, and between hands it is customary to shuffle only the cards used, together with part of those not used, these then being put at the bottom of the total pack.

Play
The dealer takes roughly as many cards in his hand as will be needed to deal ten cards to each player, with a few over. The cards are dealt anti-clockwise in two bundles of five. The remaining cards are added to the others and are placed face

down in the centre to form the 'stock'. It is customary to divide the stock in two, the upper part, called the 'head', being used, while the lower part, the 'foot', is put to one side in case of need.

The top card of the stock is turned face up and placed to the side of the stock to be the 'upcard', which, as other cards are placed on it, becomes a 'discard pile'.

Beginning with the eldest hand, each player in turn to the right of the dealer, after looking at his hand, announces whether he will play or drop out. If he drops out, he must put two chips into a pool. These chips are placed on the part of the stock called the foot, the player who drops out saying he is 'going on top'. He places his cards face down at right angles to the foot. They are not used in the play.

The players who stay in, again in an anti-clockwise direction beginning with the eldest hand, draw a card either from the discard pile or from the top of the stock. To draw from the discard pile requires that the card taken is immediately melded. A meld is usually called a 'spread', and it consists of exactly three cards. There are two kinds: a 'group' and a 'sequence'.

A group is a spread of three cards of the same rank, but there are restrictions in some cases. There are no restrictions to a group of 10s or Aces; they can be made up of any suits. However, for other ranks they must either all be of the same suit, or each of a different suit.

A sequence is usually called a 'stringer', and it consists of three cards of the same suit in sequence.

To meld, a player on his turn lays down before him the three cards of the meld. He may have drawn from the discard pile (in which case, as stated, he must use the card drawn in his meld), or he may have drawn a card from the stock which allows him to meld, or he may have been dealt with a meld.

On his turn, a player may 'lay off' onto his own melds, ie he may add a card or cards to his existing meld or melds. To lay off to a sequence he adds additional cards to the sequence. A group of the same suit may be added to by laying off another card of the same rank and suit. A group of different suits may be added to by laying off cards of any suit (otherwise the group would be limited to four cards, which it is not). Groups of 10s and Aces can also be added to without restriction.

A player can take the top card of the discard pile to lay it off to one of his melds, if he wishes. If he doesn't wish to, he can be forced to lay it off by any other player who demands he do so. This is often done in practice, as it could disrupt a player's hand, especially if he is near to going out, as will be seen later.

Conditions A player who makes certain melds called 'conditions' immediately collects chips from the other active players according to the meld's value. So far as conditions are concerned, certain ranks of cards are known as '*valle* cards' (ie value cards). The valle cards are 7s, 5s and 3s; the other ranks are 'non-valle' cards. The five classes of conditions melds, and their appropriate payments from each player, are shown in the table that follows.

Three valle cards of different suits	one chip
Three valle cards of the same suit	four chips in spades, otherwise two chips
Three non-valle cards of the same suit	two chips in spades, otherwise one chip
Low sequence (Ace, 2, 3)	two chips in spades, otherwise one chip
High sequence (10, 9. 8)	two chips in spades, otherwise one chip

A player who lays off on a condition, collects the same amount again from each active player, except in the second case above (three valle cards of the same suit), when he collects two chips in spades and one in other suits.

Splitting If a player lays off onto a meld, he may later split off cards from it to make another meld, provided he leaves a value meld. For example, if his original meld was a sequence of ♥ 5, 4, 3, he can on subsequent turns add, say, ♥6 and ♥2. If, on a later turn, he acquires ♥A, he may add ♥A and split the meld into two, ♥ 6, 5, 4 and ♥ A, 2, 3. In this example, he has created a condition (low sequence) and he collects one chip from each player for it. Later, if he added ♥7 to his ♥ 6, 5, 4 sequence he could 'borrow' the ♥4 (because it leaves a valid sequence of ♥ 7, 6, 5) and add the ♥4 to his condition and collect a chip from each player again.

Going out A player's turn consists of drawing a card (either from the discard pile or the stock), melding and/or laying off if he is able to and wishes to (it is not compulsory) and discarding. Throughout the game until the end, therefore, his hand, including cards in hand and those melded on the table, consists of ten cards.

However, when going out, a player is not allowed to discard, and must therefore have eleven cards melded on the table.

A player with three melds on the table and one card in his hand therefore needs to find two cards to lay off. He might pick up from stock a card which he can lay off, but when he discards he will still not have eleven cards melded, so cannot go out, even though he has no cards in his hand. He must continue to draw on his turn until he draws a card he can lay off, in which case he can legitimately go out. (This is where it could be profitable to force a player to take a discard and lay off with it, if it reduces his hand to one card.)

If a player is in the situation where he is waiting for a card to lay off, with ten cards melded, the player to his left must not discard any card which allows him to take it and go out, unless he has no safe card which will prevent it.

The player who goes out wins the game and collects one chip from each active player (an optional rule stipulates two chips from any player who has not melded), plus the values of any conditions he has (thereby being paid for them twice, as he has already collected once for them during play) and also the chips stacked on the foot of the stock from those players who dropped out.

If both halves of the stock (head and foot) are exhausted before a player has gone out (a very rare occurrence), the discard pile is turned over and play continues.

Strategy The initial decision is whether to play or pay two chips to drop out. Because the topmost card of the discard pile cannot be taken without melding, it is difficult to build a hand; one can improve it only by the draws from the stock.

Therefore a hand with several unconnected cards in it should be discarded. The hand illustrated is a hand in point.

There are two pairs and six cards which bear very little relation to each other. The prospects of melding conditions or going out are so remote that this hand should be ditched.

On the other hand, the hand illustrated below is ripe with possibilities.

There are two cards towards several melds: a condition of three valle cards of the same suit, conditions of low sequence and high sequence in diamonds; other sequences in clubs and diamonds; and pairs of 8s, 6s and 3s. There is not an unmatched card and excellent prospects of going out. With a hand like this, with a number of cards which can be melded in two different ways, it would be a mistake to lay down melds too early. The cards held in the hand when an opponent goes out are not penalty cards. Of course, a condition should be laid down, and the chips collected for it, because they would be forfeited if an opponent went out.

Pelmanism

Pelmanism requires concentration and a good memory. It is popular with children, but should be played by those of similar ages, because older children will usually beat younger children, to the younger's frustration.

Type	Children's
Alternative names	Concentration, Memory, Pairs, Picking Pairs
Players	Two or more
Special requirements	Playing surface large enough to lay out 52 cards

Aim
To collect as many pairs (two cards of the same rank) as possible.

Cards
The standard pack of 52 cards is used.

Preparation
The cards are shuffled by any player and laid out face down on the table. Some players prefer neat rows, but others think the game is improved if the cards are scattered haphazardly. The main requirement is that they do not touch each other.

Play
One player begins the game by turning over any two cards, one at a time, so that all the other players can see them (there is no advantage to going first). If the two cards turned over are a pair, he removes them and puts them to one side to form his own individual pile. If not (and he must allow a moment or two for all players to note what ranks the cards are), he turns them face down again, without altering their position in the layout in any way.

If a player collects a pair, he has another turn and turns over two more cards. If he fails to collect a pair, the turn passes to the player on his left, who turns over two cards in the same way, adding any pairs to his own individual pile, and so on. When all the cards have been paired, and none remain on the table, the player with the highest number of pairs is the winner.

Good play consists of remembering the rank and position of all the cards previously turned over, so that when a player turns over a card of a rank equal to one which has been turned previously, he knows where that other card is, and can make a pair.

Variants
For two or three players, a shorter game can be had by using a 40-card pack (by removing the court cards) or a 32-card pack (by removing cards of ranks lower than 7). Older children, or adults, who think the game is rather simple and somewhat easy, can try turning up four cards at a time, and instead of collecting pairs can collect 'books', sets of all four cards of the same rank.

Pig

Pig is a rather curious game which, according to a respected US card game rule book, is a simplification of an old game called Vive l'Amour ('Long Live Love'). Nevertheless, Pig is a children's game which is suitable for parties, and is not to be taken too seriously.

Type	Children's
Alternative names	Donkey
Players	Three to thirteen; four to seven is best
Special requirements	None

Aim
To collect four cards of the same rank, or to notice when another player does so.

Cards
The standard pack of 52 cards is used, but is reduced to the number of cards equal to the number of players multiplied by four: four players use a 16-card pack, five players a 20-card pack and so on. This is achieved by removing as many ranks as necessary from the pack to make the total; for example, four players might strip everything but Aces and court cards from the pack, five players might strip everything except Aces up to 5s. Thirteen players would use the full pack.

Preparation
Once the pack is of the required number of cards, any player may deal (there is no advantage to dealing, and the position of the players round the table is of no consequence). Four cards are dealt to each player, which exhausts the pack.

Play
Players look at their cards. Simultaneously each then passes a card face down to his left for his left-hand opponent to take, at the same time taking into his hand the card passed to him by his right-hand opponent. This exchange must be synchronized, as no player must see the card he is receiving before he has passed his card on. Once this exchange has been made there is a brief pause for players to look at their cards and then it is repeated; the process continues to be repeated until one player has managed to acquire four cards of the same rank, called a 'book'.

Once a player manages this, he quietly and without any fuss stops exchanging and puts his finger to his nose. Other players, on noticing this, quietly do likewise. The last player to put his finger to his nose is the loser, and thus the Pig.

How this game arose from one called Vive l'Amour can only be imagined.

Pinochle

Pinochle is derived from Bezique, and is practically the same game; Pinochle is the version which took hold in the USA in the late 19th century and became one of that country's most popular games. It is thought that it gets its name from the French and German word *binocle*, meaning pince-nez (*besicles* in French also means 'eye-glasses'). Binocle was an early name for Pinochle and even now nobody can explain the intrusive 'h' in its name; some experts still ignore it and spell the game Pinocle.

The game which took hold in the USA is technically Auction Pinochle with Widow, which is a game for three players. Although the traditional European game is for two players, it is sensible (since the main description of Bezique in this book is for two players) to describe here the three-player version most widely played in the USA, with the two-player version as a variant.

Type	Trick-taking and melding
Alternative names	None
Players	Three; two, four, five or six for variants
Special requirements	Two packs of cards; chips or coins for staking, or pen and paper for scoring

Aim
To score points by melding and by winning in tricks cards with certain scoring values.

Cards
Two standard packs of 52 cards, shuffled together, are used, from which are removed the 8s, 7s, 6s, 5s, 4s, 3s and 2s, leaving a combined pack of 48 cards. The cards rank Ace (high), 10, King, Queen, Jack, 9 (low).

Preparation
Each player cuts, and shows the bottom card of the portion he cut. With the cards ranking as above, the player who draws the lowest card chooses where to sit and becomes the first dealer, with the next lowest sitting to his left. The deal subsequently passes to the left.

The dealer shuffles the pack, and the player to his right cuts. The dealer deals a bundle of three cards, face down, to each of the players clockwise, then three more face down to the centre to form a 'widow'. He then continues to deal to the players four more rounds of cards in bundles of three, so that each player has 15 cards and the widow three.

Bidding Each player in turn, beginning with the 'eldest hand' (the player to the dealer's left), has an opportunity to bid, which is an offer to make a certain number of points. He does not name the trump suit. He may bid or pass, but if he passes he cannot re-enter the bidding later. Bids are expressed in multiples of ten points, and the lowest bid is of 300. Each bid must be higher than the last. The bidding is continuous and ends when two players have passed, the third player who remains becoming the 'bidder'. The bidder will play against the other two players combined, who are the 'opponents', with the object of making the number of points of his bid. If all three players pass, the deal is abandoned, and the deal passes to the left.

Widow When the bidding has finished, the bidder turns over the three cards in the widow so that the opponents can see what they are. He then takes them into his hand.

Melding Only the bidder melds. He announces his melds and then scores for them, and the scores are noted. It is not in the rules for the bidder to be obliged to show his melds, but he must if an opponent asks him to, and in practice it is customary, and common sense, for the bidder to show them. He may change his melds any time before he leads to the first trick.

Burying After melding, the bidder lays away face down any three cards that he has not used in a meld (which makes it sensible that he should lay his melds on the table, so that the opponents can see that the buried cards were not used in melds). This is called 'burying', and it brings his hand back to 15 cards. At the same time, he announces the trump suit. He is not obliged to state whether or not he has laid away a trump. He is permitted to change his mind about the trump suit and the cards he is burying (as well as his melds) any time before he makes the first lead. When the bidder has decided on the trump suit and his melds, it is customary, rather than to note the points of his melds, to note the points he needs in play to make his bid. For example, if he has bid 350, and his melds total 210, he is said to need 140. As there are 250 points at stake in the trick-taking, his opponents need 111 to defeat him.

Concession The bidder (possibly disappointed with the widow) may concede defeat without even leading to the first trick, whereupon he pays to each opponent chips to the value of his bid. This is called a 'single *bête*' (see Scoring, below). At the same time, either opponent can propose that the opponents concede, and if the other opponent agrees, the contract is considered made. This might happen if the bidder's melds bring him so close to his contract that it is obvious he must make it. Both opponents must agree, however, before they can concede.

Play

The bidder leads to the first trick, and may lead any card he likes; see p383 for an explanation of tricks and trick-taking. The rules of play are not the usual trick-taking rules, however. A player must follow suit if able. If he is unable to follow suit, and holds a trump, he must play a trump. If another player has already played a trump to the trick, he must still play a trump, but he need not try to win the trick. On the other hand, if a trump is led, each player must, if able, play a higher trump than any previously played. This is called 'playing over'.

A trick is won by the highest trump it contains. If it does not contain a trump it is won by the highest card of the suit led. If two cards identical in suit and rank are the highest cards in a trick, the first played wins the trick. The winner of a trick leads to the next.

The bidder collects all the tricks he wins and adds them face down to the cards he buried – they will all count for him in the final settlement. The opponents' tricks are collected into a single pile, and at the end of the deal the two sides agree on the number of points the bidder has made, in melds and tricks.

If he has made as many points as he bid, he has made his contract. If he has scored fewer points he has lost. This is called a 'double *bête*' (see Scoring, below).

Scoring

The scoring values of cards taken in tricks are:

each Ace	eleven points
each 10	ten points
each King	four points
each Queen	three points
each Jack	two points
each 9	no value

Only the 9s have no value when taken in tricks. The winner of the last trick scores a bonus of ten points. The number of points available in trick-taking is therefore 250 points per deal.

The melds and their values are as follows:

Sequences	
Flush (A, 10, K, Q, J of trumps)	150
Royal marriage (K, Q of trumps)	40
Common marriage (K, Q of any other suit)	20
Groups	
Hundred Aces (one Ace of each suit)	100
Eighty Kings (one King of each suit)	80
Sixty Queens (one Queen of each suit)	60
Forty Jacks (one Jack of each suit)	40
Special	
Pinochle (♠Q, ♦J)	40
Dix (9 of trumps, pronounced 'deece')	10

A card used in one meld may not be used as part of another meld in the same category, but may be used as part of a meld in another category. For example, a King or Queen used in a flush, cannot be scored also as a royal marriage, since both melds are in the category of sequences, but both could be used in melds of eighty Kings or sixty Queens, since these melds are in the category of groups. If spades were trumps, ♠Q could be used in all three categories.

If chips are used, each player settles with each other at the end of each deal. Players use various scales of payment, some quite unrelated to others. A popular method values the making of a contract from one chip from each opponent for a contract of 300–340, to 19 chips for a contract of over 600. The full scale is:

Contract	Chip value
300–340	1
350–390	3
400–440	7
450–490	10
500–540	13
550–590	16
600+	19

Most players agree that the chip value of the contract is doubled if the trump suit is spades.

The bidder receives from or pays to each opponent according to whether he makes his contract. If the bidder is double bête he pays double.

If the game is played for interest only, with scores kept on paper, the above table can be used, with the winner the first player to score 21, and if two pass 21 on the same hand, the higher scorer of the two wins.

Alternatively, a simpler method is merely to score the number of the contract: to the bidder if he makes it, to his opponents if he fails, not forgetting to double it for double bête. In this case, the first player to 1,000 points is the winner, or the higher scorer of the two if two players pass 1,000 on the same deal.

Strategy The strategy begins with what to bid. It is best to employ a cautious outlook in bidding. Playing and failing to make a contract costs twice as much (because of double bête) than is gained in making it, therefore one needs at least a 2–1 on chance of making a contract before it is worth bidding it. Generally speaking, bidding more than what can almost certainly be made is dangerous.

The first step in evaluating a hand is to count the points to be made from melds. To this must be added the expectation to be made from tricks. It is necessary to hold six or seven trumps, or at least no fewer than five top trumps. There are twelve trumps in all, including two of each rank, including Aces. It is reasonable to expect 10–15 points to be won from each trick won (there being 250 points at stake over 15 tricks, but the two opponents will try to play high-value cards to tricks won by each other). Around 20 points could be added for improvement which might come from the exchange.

The hand illustrated has 280 points in melds (with hearts as trumps): 150 for flush, 100 for hundred Aces, 20 common marriage and 10 for dix. If to this is added about 100 for tricks and 20 for the exchange, a total of 400 points is reached, which would be a possible bid, but 450 would be extravagant.

The discard is the next thing to consider. It is reasonable to seek a two-suited or three-suited hand – a long side suit beside a long trump suit is a good way to ensure making plenty of points for tricks, as opponents use their trumps on your long suit, and you can trump their Aces in a void suit. In the hand above, it is impossible to make a void suit, because that would lose the 100 points for Aces (one cannot discard cards used in melds), but the spade suit is ideal for an attempt to hold a bare Ace in a suit, which is equally good.

Suppose you held the hand above, and picking up the widow found ♣10, ♦10, 9. The discard of the two spade Jacks and ♦9 would improve the hand considerably.

It is possible that the widow will change a player's view of which suit to choose as trumps. For example, suppose the holder of the different hand illustrated below has become bidder with a bid of 350, on the strength of holding 250 in melds, with a flush (hearts as trumps), eighty Kings and a common marriage. The widow holds ♠Q, ♦A, ♣9. By taking ♠Q and ♦A in hand, in exchange for ♣J and ♦9 he will immensely improve his hand. He will now make spades trumps. He gains an extra trump (now six) and another ten points in melds, by virtue of dix, making his meld 260. He needs 90 from tricks to make his contract, and will almost certainly do so, and with spades as trumps will score double for it.

In the play, it is not usually desirable to lead trumps, unless the declarer has a solid side suit, containing, say, both Aces and 10s. In this case leading trumps to exhaust those of the opponents, in order to make the tricks from the side suit at the end, without fear of trumping, might be the policy. With the hand as above, the side suit of hearts is not solid enough, so it would be best to lead the ♦A, then ♥A, followed by, if they win, the ♥J, to try to clear the opponents of hearts and win a long heart or two after winning tricks with the trumps.

Variants
Pinochle for four, five or six players The game can be played by four players by means of one player dropping out in turn and becoming the dealer. The dealer's function is merely to deal the cards for the other players. He does not have cards himself and takes no further part. He is an inactive player, and may not advise either side. The player to his left becomes the eldest hand, and the game proceeds as above. The inactive player does, however, take part in the settlement. The bidder pays to him or collects from him when he wins or loses as he does with the other opponents.

This is a popular version of the game in the USA. In fact, many players regard it as better than when played by three only; perhaps the inactive role of the dealer enables him to attend to his personal needs and maybe to oversee the beer. It is also not unknown for five or six to play this way, with two or three being inactive on each deal. The dealer misses out the player or two to his left when dealing. However many players there are, active and inactive, each player's turn in dealing, bidding and playing comes to him clockwise from his right.

European Pinochle for two players This variant details the game as usually played in Europe, without the auction. It is normally a game for two players. Players aim to win the majority of the points. The cards, their ranking, their values when won in a trick and the melds and the values thereof are as in the basic game.

The dealer deals twelve cards to each player in bundles of either three or four at a time, whichever he prefers, and turns the next card face up on the table to indicate the trump suit. The remaining 23 cards are placed face down in a pile above the turned-up card but at right angles to it and half covering it, so that it remains visible to both players.

The non-dealer leads to the first trick, and subsequently the winner of a trick leads to the next; see p383 for an explanation of tricks and trick-taking. The trick-taking phase of the game is in two halves, with different rules governing. For the first twelve tricks (ie until the stock is exhausted) players may play any card they like to a trick. It is not necessary to follow suit or to trump.

A trick is won by the higher trump it contains, or if it does not contain a trump, by the higher card in the suit led. The winner of a trick takes the top card of the stock, and the loser the next card. Winners of tricks keep their tricks face down to one side.

On his turn, a winner of a trick may meld any of the combinations listed in the main description above, and his score is noted on a score sheet. To meld, he lays the cards face up on the table before him, where they remain a part of his hand, and are available to be played to tricks if required. There are three rules to melding:

i) One meld only may be made at a turn. A player must win another trick to enable him to make another meld.

ii) At least one card must be played from the hand to make a meld. In other words a player cannot rearrange melds on the table to form new ones without adding a card.

iii) A card already melded may be melded again if the new meld is in a different category to the original one, or if it is a higher-scoring meld in the same category of the original one.

The categories of meld are as in the table described earlier: sequences, groups and special. Thus, a ♠Q melded in a pinochle can also be melded in a group of sixty Queens, the other three Queens being played from hand to it, because the two melds are in different categories. Also, a royal marriage can have the Ace, 10 and Jack added to it to become a flush, because a flush is a higher scoring meld in the same category. However, if the flush were melded first, a player cannot remove the K, Q from it and score for royal marriage, because this is a lower-scoring meld in the same category.

If the dealer turns up the 9 (the dix) as the trump card, he scores ten for it. Otherwise, a player holding or drawing a dix scores for it merely by showing it (but only on winning a trick, although on this occasion he may make another meld at the same time). On winning a trick a holder of a dix may exchange it if he wishes for the turn-up (very valuable if the turn-up were an Ace).

A player who wins the twelfth trick may meld if he can (it will be his last chance) and then he takes the last face-down card of the stock, which he must show to his opponent. His opponent then takes the turn-up, which will probably be a dix (he does not score for it).

Once the stock has gone, players take any cards which may be on the table in melds, and return them to their hands. As mentioned earlier, the last twelve tricks are played under different rules. A player must now follow suit when able, and if he cannot he must trump if he can. He can discard only if he cannot follow suit or trump. If a trump is led, a player must not only follow suit, but must win the trick if possible. There is no further melding during this stage. The winner of the last trick scores ten points.

Scores for melds, dix and the last trick are added to the score-sheet as they occur. The points for the cards won in tricks are added after the game, when the players examine their tricks and sort out the value cards. The two players' scores for cards should add up to 240 (this is not counting ten for last trick). When each player's scores for melding and cards are added, it is customary to round the last digit, if it is seven, eight or nine, up to the nearest ten, and to round down if it is six or lower.

Players may treat each deal as a separate game, and if playing for stakes settle up accordingly at a previously agreed rate. In this case the winner of the game deals the next. Players who prefer to play a series of games until one player's score reaches a target (1,000 is the usual figure) just keep a running score. In this case, the deal alternates between the players.

European Pinochle for four players This variant details the four-handed game as usually played in Europe. Pinochle for four players is played in partnership, two against two. It is played differently to the two-handed game just described, because there is no stock. The differences are as follows.

Each player is dealt twelve cards each in bundles of three (this takes the whole pack). The last card (the dealer's last card) is turned face up to show trumps. Beginning with the player to the left of the dealer, a player holding a dix (there are two in the pack) may exchange it for the turned-up card. Each player who is dealt a dix (whether it is exchanged or not) scores ten points for it. If the dealer turns up a dix, he keeps it and scores ten points.

All players expose their melds in front of them on the table, individually, before the trick-taking phase. In addition to the melds listed under the first description above, there are additional ones, as follows:

Double trump sequence (A, 10, K, Q, J)	1,500	All eight Kings	800
Double Pinochle	300	All eight Queens	600
All eight Aces	1,000	All eight Jacks	400

These melds are very rare, and since the partner's hands aren't combined, no more likely to occur then in the two- or three-handed game, so their existence is puzzling. Melds are calculated immediately, but the scores for them do not actually count until the partnership wins a trick, when each partner's score for melds becomes 'official'.

When the melds have been shown, all players return their cards to their hands, and the play for tricks begins, the eldest hand leading first. The rules are as in the basic game, ie players must follow suit if able, and if unable to follow suit they must play a trump if able, but are not obliged, if a trump has been played earlier, to try to win the trick. If a trump is led, however, each player in turn must not only follow suit if able, but must try to win the trick, if possible, by playing a trump higher than any previously played. Only if a player cannot conform to these rules is he allowed to discard any card he wishes.

As in the other games described, players try to win tricks containing scoring cards, but the scoring is simplified. Each partnership's tricks are combined.

When all twelve tricks have been played, each partnership counts the values of the scoring cards won. For every Ace and 10 taken, ten points are scored; for every King and Queen five points. Jacks join 9s in having no value. The winner of the last trick scores ten points. The total amount of points available in the trick-taking phase is therefore, as in the other games, 250. The winning partnership is the first to reach 1,000 points. If at the end of a deal, both sides have passed 1,000, play continues till one side has 1,250, and if necessary to 1,500 and so on.

However, at any time and at any point in play, any player may declare his side to be 'out', ie to have reached 1,000 points, or 1,250 or whatever the target happens to be. In that case, play ceases and the points of the claiming side are calculated. If the claim is found to be correct, that side wins the game, if not it loses. This is irrespective of the total of the other side, which may, in fact, have more points, but still loses if the claiming side is correct. A side may not claim to have won before the play of cards begins, because it has to win a trick before its melds become official and are scored, nor can it claim between deals, while the points are being totalled.

Piquet

Piquet has been played, practically without alteration, for about 500 years. The reason? It is the perfect card game, the best for two players. It is a unique game which combines trick-taking with other aspects of card play, such as scoring points for forming certain combinations.

It was known originally as Cent, Sant, Saunt or Saint. The name Piquet first appeared in the 17th century, and although modern English-speaking players prefer to retain many French terms when playing, it is not absolutely certain that the game is of French origin, and it might even be Spanish. The use of French was not always followed, and the game itself became known as Picket in English. Under its current spelling, it is still 'properly' pronounced 'pick-et', although at least one modern English dictionary has 'pee-kay' as an alternative pronunciation, and *Chambers's Twentieth Century Dictionary* retained 'a game at cards' as one definition of Picket as late as 1950. The game has declined, like nearly all others, with the advent of Bridge, but there are enough connoisseurs playing it to keep it going.

Type	Trick-taking and melding
Alternative names	Picket
Players	Two; three or four for variants
Special requirements	Pen and paper for scoring

Aim

To score more points than your opponent over six deals, six deals constituting a game; points are scored in a count before the trick-taking phase, during the trick-taking and also in certain extraordinary scores.

Cards

The standard pack of 52 cards is used, from which are removed the 6s, 5s, 4s, 3s and 2s leaving a short pack of 32 cards. The cards rank from Ace (high) to 7 (low).

Preparation

The players draw cards from a spread pack for the privilege of having the choice of first deal, the drawer of the higher card having the choice. It is always better to choose to deal first, as there is an advantage to being the non-dealer on the sixth and final hand.

The dealer deals twelve cards to each player in bundles of two or three as preferred. The remaining eight cards are placed face down to form a 'talon', cards reserved for later use. Some players like to separate the top five cards of the talon from the bottom three, for a reason which will become apparent later.

After each player picks up his cards and examines them, one of the extraordinary scores in Piquet comes into play. This is *carte blanche*. If either player is dealt a hand that does not contain a court card (King, Queen or Jack), he may score ten points for carte blanche. It must be declared before a player exchanges cards (see below). Thus, the elder must declare carte blanche upon picking up his hand. The younger must declare it when the elder has exchanged cards with the talon, and before he himself does so. A player claiming points for carte blanche must show his hand to his opponent before drawing. It is not compulsory to declare it, but the ten points cannot be scored otherwise.

Exchanging The 'elder' (the non-dealer, or *majeur* in French) is entitled to exchange from one to five cards with cards from the talon (hence the separation of the talon mentioned above). He discards first to a waste pile. Unless he is dealt a very good hand, it is common for the elder to exchange the maximum five cards. First, he discards the number chosen face down to a waste pile (he must exchange at least one). If he exchanges fewer than five, he may look at those to which he was entitled, and does not show them to the 'younger' (the dealer, or *mineur*).

The younger is now entitled to exchange cards up to the number remaining in the talon (which will be three plus any that elder was entitled to but didn't take). He, too, must exchange at least one card. If the elder has left in the talon any of his entitlement, these cards remain as the top cards of the talon and the younger takes these before the bottom three which were reserved for him. If the younger leaves any cards in the talon, he has the option of looking at what they are, but if he does so, he must show them to the elder, too. The players do not mix their discards, and they are entitled to glance at their own discards during play to refresh their memories.

During this phase of the game, players are attempting to improve their hands by exchanging cards with the talon. It helps therefore if the players are familiar with the scores, as set out below, before deciding which and how many cards to exchange.

Scoring The count before the trick-taking is in three sections:

Point   Points are scored by the holder of the 'longest suit'. The elder announces the number of cards in his longest suit. If this is better than the younger's longest suit, the younger says 'good' and the elder scores one point for each card in the suit. If the younger has a longer suit, he will say 'not good' and scores the points himself. If the younger's suit is equal in length to the elder's, he says 'making?'. This asks elder for the pip value of his suit, with Ace counting eleven and court cards ten each. The elder announces his total, and the younger responds either 'good', 'not good' or 'equal'. The player with the higher total scores for 'point', and if both are equal neither scores.

Sequences   Points are scored for the longest sequence in a suit. A sequence must consist of at least three cards. The elder announces his longest sequence. The terms are 'tierce' (a sequence of three), 'quart' (a sequence of four), 'quint' (five), '*sixième*' (six), '*septième*' (seven) and '*huitième*' (eight). The younger replies as before: 'good', 'not good' or 'how high?' The last asks for the highest card of the sequence. The answers are the same: 'good', 'not good' or 'equal', and the player with the best sequence scores for it. Neither scores if they are equal. The points scored are one point for each card in the sequence, but a sequence of quint or more scores a bonus of ten points; for example, quint is worth 15 points, sixième 16 points and so on.

A further bonus for winning sequence is that the winner may score for other sequences he holds, too. He must announce what they are, for example 'plus six for two tierces'.

Quatorzes and trios — Points are scored for the highest '*quatorze*' held (four cards of the same rank), or if neither player holds a quatorze, for the highest 'trio' (three cards of the same rank). The elder announces his best, for example 'quatorze of Queens', and the younger replies either 'good' or 'not good'. There cannot be a tie, and neither scores if neither holds a quatorze or trio. A quatorze scores 14 points and a trio three. As with sequences, the winner may score for any other quatorzes or trios held by announcing them.

Points for these categories are scored in the order set out. The tradition in Piquet is to keep your score in your head during a hand, continually announcing it as you add to it, but some might prefer to enter scores on a score-sheet as they are made. A player may forfeit a score by not announcing it. He might do this purposely to deceive his opponent as to what he holds in his hand. He might also understate his holding; for example, in point he might announce a suit of six cards when he holds seven, thus forfeiting a point for his deception. This is called 'sinking'.

Repique — There is a further extraordinary score, which may occur before the trick-taking phase. A player who scores 30 points in the combination categories alone, before his opponent scores a point, scores 'repique', which gives him a bonus of 60 points. For example, if a player scores six for point, 15 for quint and 14 for quatorze, making 35, he scores an extra 60. Points are taken in the order: carte blanche, point, sequences, quatorzes and trios.

Play

It is traditional for the elder, before leading to the first trick, to announce his score for the categories above, and then add one to it for leading, and for each player to announce his cumulative score with each card he plays. However, players with poor memories (and it is not difficult to forget your cumulative score as play progresses) who have noted the scores for the categories so far on paper, might begin to score for trick-taking separately, announcing the first point as 'one'.

See p383 for an explanation of tricks and trick-taking. Players must follow suit to the card led, and if unable to must discard. There are no trumps. The higher card of the suit led wins the trick. The winner of a trick leads to the next.

A player scores a point each time he leads to a trick. He also scores a point each time he wins a trick to which his opponent led. Therefore it is not unusual for both players to win a point on the same trick.

The player who makes the majority of the tricks (ie seven or more) scores an extra ten points for 'cards'. If the tricks are divided six each, neither player scores for cards. If a player takes all twelve tricks, he scores 40 points for *capot* instead of ten for cards.

Pique If a player fails to reach 30 points for categories (see Repique, above) but does so during the trick-taking phase before his opponent has scored at all, he scores a 'pique', which gives him a bonus of 30 points. For example, a player who scores six for point, 15 for quint and three for trio, making 24, and then leads to the first six tricks, will reach 30 before his opponent scores and earn another 30 for pique. It follows that pique is open only to the elder, because he leads to the first trick and always takes the first point in the trick-taking phase.

Partie A game consists of six deals, three by each player. It is known as a 'partie'. The winning margin is the difference between the two totals plus 100 points. If one or both players fail to reach 100 points, however, the two totals are added together and 100 is added to determine the winning margin. This method of scoring, in which it is vital for a player to 'cross the Rubicon' of 100 points, leads to the game often being called Rubicon Piquet.

Strategy The strategy begins with the discarding, which is very important. Each player will have different aims in the discarding (one of the beauties of Piquet). The elder is the aggressor because he does not have to worry about pique, and because he has the first lead, which means if he can build a long solid suit he might be able to take the first six or seven tricks. Also, he can exchange five cards. So the elder will usually exchange all five cards and attempt to win points in the combinations for point and sequence.

The younger, on the other hand, is on the defensive. A long suit to him might be useless in trick-taking, as he might not get the lead early enough to cash in on them. He might have to discard most as the elder leads his long suit.

Example hand
Suppose the two hands are dealt as shown.

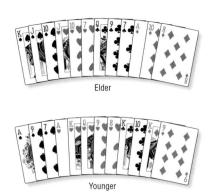

Elder

Younger

The elder has a poor hand and will change his maximum five cards. His best chance of sequences lie in spades and hearts, so he will keep his ♦A and ditch all his other diamonds and clubs.

The younger must think defensively. He stands a good chance of winning cards, but must keep his guarded ♣K and ♦K to do so, and his long hearts. He might exchange only two cards, his low spades.

The elder, remarkably, draws all diamonds and clubs, but much better ones than he discarded. He draws ♦Q, J, 7 and ♣A, J. He has a quatorze of Jacks.

The younger does not do so well, getting ♠Q, 8. He decides not to expose the unused card, as it will not affect his play.

The new hands are shown.

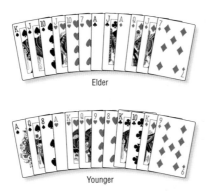

Elder

Younger

The first thing to be decided is point, as neither player has claimed carte blanche. The elder says 'point of four', and the younger replies 'not good'.

The elder now admits that he does not have a sequence, so the younger claims his sequence of three. The elder then announces 'quatorze', to which the younger replies 'good'.

Traditionally the elder would now announce his scores thus: 'quatorze fourteen'. He would then lead to the first trick and announce 'fifteen', since there is a point for each lead. The younger would then announce his score: 'point five, tierce three, I start with eight'. The players would then announce their running scores with each card they played, whether it won a trick or not.

Players may follow this tradition or, if scoring on paper (or on a Cribbage board, as some prefer; see the illustration at Cribbage), write down or enter their scores for combinations and begin the trick-taking sequence at 'one'.

The play of the tricks might go as follows (with the running scores announced as shown):

	Elder	Younger
1	♦ A '15'	♦ 9 '8'
2	♦ Q '16'	♦ K '9'
3	♥ 7 '16'	♥ A '10'
4	♥ 10 '16'	♥ K '11'
5	♥ J '16'	♥ Q '12'
6	♣ J '16'	♥ 9 '13'
7	♠ 10 '16'	♥ 8 '14'
8	♠ J '16'	♠ A '15'
9	♠ K '17'	♠ Q '16'
10	♣ A '18'	♣ 10 '16'
11	♦ J '19'	♠ 8 '16'
12	♦ 7 '21'	♣ K '16'

There is an extra point for winning the last trick, which is why the elder announced his score as '21' and not '20'. The winner of the majority of tricks scores ten points, so the younger, with seven of the tricks, scores 26 points in the deal to the elder's 21.

It was explained under Strategy, above, that a long suit might be useless to the younger as he might have to discard most as the elder leads his long suit. The example hand above was an exception, however, which arose because the elder was unlucky in the draw, and did not obtain a long suit, and moreover the younger was able to guard all four suits, which is rarely possible. In fact, his hearts turned out to be the longest suit. Generally the younger must keep stoppers in at least two suits, or he might find the elder scoring 40 for capot.

The hand above shows how the two players might look at the same hand differently. The elder will see the club suit as the likeliest to win him point and sequence, and if he acquired one more club in the exchange would be certain to win him the majority of tricks, so he will concentrate on building up the club suit. He will certainly exchange ♥Q, 10, 9 and ♠10, and his only question is whether to discard ♠K as well, or keep it in the hope of getting a fourth King for quatorze.

The younger will note that he has guards in all four suits, and that at the moment, whatever suit the elder leads, the elder cannot win more than three tricks before the younger gets the lead. By exchanging ♣J, 9, 7 he will retain this situation, but will still need an additional trick or two from the exchange to make the majority of tricks, and the only hope he has in combinations is to draw a King for quatorze (he knows he will score at least trio for his Kings). On the other hand, he can exchange his three hearts, hoping that the elder might also ditch hearts, and that his (the younger's) club suit might fill out. If he does this, he knows that the elder will not be able to make more than five heart tricks and the ♠A before the younger has the lead and the prospect of tying at least for cards. Exchanging the hearts might be his best play, but who knows?

The state of the game might be the younger's guide here. If it is the last deal and he is winning he might play safe. If he needs a big score, ditching the hearts and hoping for the best might be his preferred option.

Variants

Piquet Normand This is a version of Piquet for three players, each playing for himself. Each player has ten cards, and there is a talon of two. Only the dealer (the youngest) may exchange cards with the talon. The 'eldest hand' (the player to the dealer's left) begins the play by announcing the number of cards in his longest suit, the other players in turn responding 'good', 'not good', or 'making?' as before. The same method is used for deciding who scores for other combinations. Only one player may score per category – nobody scores when there's a tie. A scorer in sequence or quatorze and trio also scores for other or lesser combinations in the same category. To score pique or repique a player must score 20 (not 30) before either opponent has scored. The bonuses are the same as in the parent game (30 and 60). A player scores 40 for capot, and 10 for cards as in the parent game, but if two players take five tricks each they score 20 each for capot, and if two tie for the majority of cards (ie four each) they score five points each. Game is to 100 points.

Piquet Voleur This is a version of Piquet for four players, playing in two partnerships. Partners sit opposite each other. Each player is dealt eight cards, and there is no talon. Points for combinations are scored as before, with the eldest hand being the first to announce his holding in each category. However, in point, the value of the cards must be 30 or more in order to score. A side which scores in a category may score for lesser combinations in the same category as well, and both partners can score for these. Two players of the same side who tie in a category both score, but if players from opposite sides tie, neither scores. Pique and repique are scored if one player (not one side) can score 20 before his opponents score – they carry the same bonuses of 30 and 60 points. The side taking the more tricks scores ten points, and if they take all eight, they score 40 for capot. Game is to 100 points.

Pitch

Pitch or, to give it its full title, Auction Pitch is of the All Fours family, and in the USA became the most popular form of the family, particularly around New England.

Type	Trick-taking
Alternative names	Setback
Players	Two to seven; four is best
Special requirements	Pen and paper for scoring

Aim

To score seven points to win the game; points are scored by capturing certain cards in tricks.

Cards

The standard pack of 52 cards is used, the cards ranking from Ace (high) to 2 (low).

Preparation

Players draw cards from a spread pack to determine the first dealer. The drawer of the highest card deals.

The dealer has the final shuffle and the player to his right cuts. The dealer then deals six cards face down to each player in bundles of three, clockwise beginning with the player to his left. The remaining cards are placed face down to one side and are not used in the game.

Bidding One player, the 'pitcher', plays against all the other players, who play in temporary partnership. To determine the pitcher, a round of bidding takes place. There are four points (sometimes only three) to play for in each hand, and a bid is an offer to make a certain number, from one to four. Each player, beginning with the 'eldest hand' (the player to the dealer's left) has one opportunity to bid or pass. Each bid must be higher than the previous bid. The highest bidder becomes the pitcher.

The pitcher has the advantage of deciding a trump suit and of leading to the first trick. He does not name the trump suit in his bid, the trump suit being indicated by the card he leads to the first trick. If a player wishes to bid four, all he need do on his turn is to lead (called 'pitching') since a bid of four (called a 'smudge') cannot be beaten.

Play

Points are won by capturing certain cards in tricks. The tricks themselves are of no significance. One point is scored for each of the following:

High	for winning the highest trump card in play;
Low	for winning the lowest trump card in play;
Jack	for winning the Jack of trumps;
Game	for the highest total of points taken in tricks, the scoring scale being

Ace	4
King	3
Queen	2
Jack (except the Jack of trumps)	1
10	10

If only one trump is in play, it counts as high and low, so the points for these are always counted. However, the Jack of trumps might not be in play, in which case there will be only three points at stake, so a player would be foolish to bid four unless holding the Jack of trumps. Game is not scored if two players tie with the value of cards taken in tricks.

The pitcher leads to the first trick, and the trick led is trumps; see p383 for an explanation of tricks and trick-taking. Players must follow suit to a trump lead if able. When a side suit is led, a player holding a card in the suit may follow suit or trump as he wishes, but he cannot discard. A trick is won by the highest trump it contains or, if there are no trumps, by the highest card in the suit led. The winner of a trick leads to the next.

Scoring If the pitcher scores at least as many points as he bid, he scores all the points that he makes. If he scores fewer points than he bid, the amount of his bid is subtracted from his score. It is possible therefore for a player to have a minus score. In this case his score is circled on the score-sheet and he is said to be 'in the hole'. The opponents of the pitcher also score any points they make individually.

The first player to score seven points wins the game. If two reach seven on the same deal, the pitcher's points are counted first, and among the other players points are scored in the order high, low, Jack, game to ascertain who reached seven first.

The winner collects one chip from each of the other players, or two chips from any player who is in the hole at the end.

A player who bids and makes a smudge (four tricks) wins the game immediately, unless he was in the hole. If in the hole he scores the four points as usual.

Example hand

The hands are dealt as in the illustration, using the Bridge convention of calling the players North, South, East and West. South is the dealer.

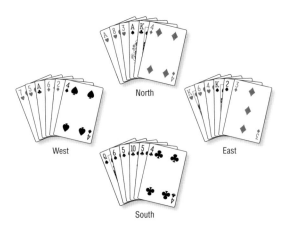

North

West

East

South

It is the first hand. West must pass. North, with hearts as trumps, will certainly make high, possibly low and has a excellent chance of game. He is an adventurous player and bids three. East cannot bid more than three and nor can South, so North becomes the dealer. The play goes as follows:

	North	East	South	West
1	♥A	♥6	♣4	♥5
2	♥8	♥K	♠5	♥7
3	♥3	♦3	♠6	♦6
4	♣K	♠2	♣5	♣A
5	♠A	♥4	♠Q	♠4
6	♦4	♠K	♣10	♦2

North won high and low as expected, but East easily won the point for game, even without the ten points for ♣10 in the last trick. North was unlucky to find East with three hearts. East played well to trump North's ♠A at trick 5, rather than to follow suit. South, however, should have played ♣10 at trick 2, which would have made it difficult for North to get the point for game, even if East had not held the third trump. He also missed a chance at trick 4 to give it to West.

So after the first hand, East has a point, South and West none, and North is three points in the hole.

Strategy Length in the trump suit is important for bidding. Three trumps are usually sufficient, as it is unlikely that an opponent will hold more than two, and

Ace and another will get rid of opposition trumps. This is what North was hoping for in the example hand. After two rounds he expected to hold the only trump, with ♠A certain to win a trick and ♣K a slight odds-on chance to win, too.

Players opposing the pitcher should be careful when discarding valuable cards to give them to the right players. As mentioned, South missed a chance with his ♣10 in the example hand to prevent the pitcher winning it. As the game develops, the situation might arise where he might want to give it to the pitcher. For example, if in the example hand East had six points towards winning the game, needing one more, South would have been anxious not to allow East the ♣10, and his play at trick 2 would have been correct.

In Pitch, when four are playing, players should remember that there are 24 cards dealt and 28 'sleeping', making the odds of any particular card being in the deal 7–6 against. A player well behind who sees a chance of a smudge if a particular Ace is sleeping might think it worth taking a chance at those odds.

Poker

Poker is often referred to as the national card game of the USA, where its popularity grew from its first mention in reference books in the 1830s to its current ubiquity on the Internet and television screens. The early references to Poker place it as being played around New Orleans, which was French territory until sold to the USA by Napoleon Bonaparte in 1803, leading to the belief that the direct ancestor was the French game Poque. There are now many forms of Poker.

Type	Gambling
Alternative names	None; the main varieties are Draw Poker, Omaha, Stud Poker and Texas Hold 'Em
Players	Any number; five to seven is perhaps best
Special requirements	Chips or coins for staking

Aim

To win money, or chips representing money, by holding the best hand at the end of the deal.

Cards

The standard pack of 52 cards is used, the cards ranking from Ace (high) to 2 (low). The Ace may be used in sequences, called 'straights', as either high or low; for example, A, K, Q, J, 10 and A, 2, 3, 4, 5 are both valid sequences, but Q, K, A, 2, 3 is not.

Preparation

Each player in each deal is dealt a hand of five cards. In some games, for example Seven-card Stud Poker, a player selects his five-card hand from a larger number dealt to him, and in others, such as Texas Hold 'Em, a player will select his hand from cards dealt specifically to him and from others which are communal cards, available to all players. In every case, however, the hand which counts consists of five cards.

Play

In successive rounds of betting, each player has the opportunity to bet that his hand is the best or to 'fold' (ie drop out). Bets are made by players placing their stakes towards the centre of the table, the accumulated stakes forming the 'pot'. At any time during the betting a player may fold, but he loses the stakes he has contributed to the pot. Any player may raise the stakes during the betting, and the other players must equalize the stakes or fold.

The deal is complete when all but one player has folded, in which case he takes the pot, or when all the players remaining have equalized their bets and none wishes to raise the stake higher. In this case there is a 'showdown', when the players reveal their hands and the player with the highest ranking hand wins the pot. If two or more players have equal hands at the showdown, the pot is shared.

Each Poker deal is complete in itself, and settlement is made after each.

Ranks of Poker hands There are nine classes of Poker hand. They are ranked in the following order, along with the number of such possible hands in a 52-card pack, and the probability of being dealt such a hand straight from the pack.

Straight flush   (40; 1 in 64,974 or 0.0015%)
Five cards of the same suit in sequence. Between two straight flushes, that with the higher top card wins. A tie is possible. The highest straight flush of all (A, K, Q, J, 10), of which there are only four in the pack, is called a 'royal flush', and in some books this is unnecessarily listed as a class of hand on its own.

Four of a kind   (624; 1 in 4,165 or 0.0240%)
Four cards of the same rank, with an odd card. Of similar hands, that with the higher ranking four cards wins. A tie is not possible, so the rank of the odd card is of no consequence.

Full house   (3,744; 1 in 694 or 0.1441%)
Three cards of one rank (a 'triple') with two of another (a 'pair'). Between two full houses, that with the higher ranking triple wins. A tie is not possible.

Flush   (5,108; 1 in 509 or 0.1967%)
Five cards of the same suit, but not in sequence. Between flushes, that containing the highest card wins, if equal the second highest and so on. A tie is possible.

Straight   (10,200; 1 in 255 or 0.3925%)
Five cards in sequence, but not of the same suit. Between straights, that with the highest card at the top of the sequence wins, thus A, K, Q, J, 10 is the highest straight and 5, 4, 3, 2, A the lowest. A tie is possible.

Three of a kind   (54,912; 1 in 47 or 2.1129%)
Three cards of the same rank with two unmatching cards. Between similar hands, that with the highest ranking triple wins. A tie is not possible.

Two pairs   (123,552; 1 in 21 or 4.7359%)
Two cards of one rank, two of another and an odd card. Between similar hands, that with the higher ranking, top pair wins, if equal that with the higher ranking second pair, if equal the higher ranking odd card. A tie is possible.

One pair   (1,098,240; 1 in 2.3665 or 42.2569%)
Two cards of one rank plus three unmatching cards. Between similar hands, that with the highest ranking pair wins, if equal the highest ranking odd card, if equal the highest ranking second odd card, and so on. A tie is possible.

High card   (1,302,540; 1 in 1.9953 or 50.1177%)
This hand lacks an accepted name and is sometimes called 'nothing' or 'no pair'. These hands are ranked by the highest ranked card they contain, if equal the second highest ranked, and so on. A tie is possible.

It will be noted that almost exactly half of hands do not contain even one pair, and that over 92% of hands are not better than one pair. However, it should be appreciated that in Draw Poker, with its chance to improve the hand, these percentages are very different after the draw, and in other forms of Poker, where the hand is chosen from, say, seven cards, the percentages also do not apply. The nine classes of hand, with the highest and lowest hands in each class, are shown below.

Ranks of Poker hand

Blank cards are immaterial since they cannot affect ties

Example of highest possible		*Example of lowest possible*
Royal flush	Straight flush	
	Four of a kind	
	Full house	
	Flush	
	Straight	

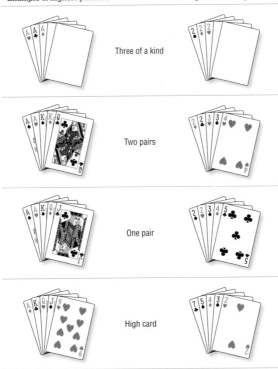

Example of highest possible | Example of lowest possible

Three of a kind

Two pairs

One pair

High card

Draw Poker

Draw Poker is the simplest form of Poker played today. It is best for between five and seven players.

Preparation Players should first agree on a time limit. This avoids ill-feeling, when a losing player will not agree to a game ending. After the time limit is passed, any player can announce that the next deal will be his last. Play should end when the deal arrives back at the first dealer.

Agreement should also be reached on minimum and maximum stakes; for example, a minimum of one chip and a maximum of five chips. If they wish, players might also agree on the maximum number of raises any player might make in one betting interval.

To decide the first dealer, and where players are to sit, the cards can be shuffled by one player and cut by another, prior to any player dealing a card face up to all players. The player dealt the highest card is the first dealer and can choose his seat. The next highest chooses his seat, and so on. Players dealt equal cards are dealt a second to break the tie.

Before the deal, each player puts one chip into the centre to form a pot. This is called an 'ante'. If preferred, to streamline matters, the dealer can put in the whole amount of the ante himself.

The dealer shuffles and the player on his right cuts the cards. The dealer then deals five cards to each player one at a time face down clockwise to his left. The dealer places the remainder of the pack face down in front of him.

First betting interval After examining their hands, players have an opportunity to bet, the 'eldest hand' (the player to the dealer's left) first. He has three options: to fold, to 'check' or to bet. To fold, he places his hand face down before him and takes no further part in the deal. To check, he stays in the deal but without staking anything. He announces 'check', but in established games the player usually just taps his fingers on the table. He bets by pushing a stake between the minimum and maximum agreed towards the centre of the table and announcing its amount. At all times players must keep their stakes visible and separate from those of other players so that it is clear how much they have staked.

Each player round the table has the same options until one of them bets. The options then become: to fold, to 'call' or to 'raise'. To call, a player puts in a stake equivalent to the amount of the previous bet. To raise, he puts in the amount needed to call, ie to equal the previous stake, plus a further amount to raise the stake higher. For example, if he needs to put in two chips to call, he can announce 'call for two, and raise two more', placing four chips towards the centre.

Play continues with all players folding, calling or raising until all the players remaining have equal stakes on the table, when the first betting interval ends.

If nobody bets, the deal is abandoned, the cards are collected and the deal passes to the left. The chips in the pot remain for the next deal, and are added to by the players putting in their antes for the next deal.

Draw Placing his own hand face down on the table, the dealer takes up the pack and asks in turn each active player, beginning with the one nearest his left, how many cards he wishes to draw. If he does not wish to draw any he 'stands pat'. Otherwise, he may draw any number from one to three; if there are fewer than six players, he may discard and draw four. He announces how many he wishes, and discards the equivalent number from his hand by passing them face down to the dealer who begins a discard pile to one side of him. He then deals face down to the player the number of cards needed to being his hand back to five cards. All players are dealt with in the same manner, and if the dealer is still active he deals with himself last, showing all other players how many cards he is exchanging.

Before a bet has been made in the second betting interval, any player may ask another how many cards he drew.

Second betting interval When all the players have what is now their final hand, the second betting interval takes place. The first player to speak is the player who opened the betting on the first betting interval, or if he has since folded, the first active player to his left. The procedure is exactly the same as the first betting interval. When all players still active have contributed the same amount to the pot, the betting ends.

Showdown Starting with the last player to raise, and continuing clockwise, the players reveal their hands and the player with the best hand takes the pot. If there is a tie, the pot is shared. If all players fold except one, the winner may take the pot without being obliged to show his hand.

Example hand Hands are dealt to six players as shown.

Player A was the dealer, and has put six chips into the pot. The first betting interval proceeds as follows:

1	Player B checks
2	Player C checks
3	Player D bets one chip
4	Player E calls
5	Player F calls
6	Player A calls
7	Player B calls
8	Player C calls

The first betting interval ends with all players active and six chips staked (plus six in the pot). The draw now takes place:

9	Player B keeps ♦ A, J and draws three: ♣ A, 2, ♥ J
10	Player C keeps his pair of 2s and draws ♣ 3, ♥ A, 3
11	Player D keeps his pair of 9s and draws ♦ 7, 4, ♣ 5
12	Player E keeps his pair of 10s and draws ♣ K, ♠ K, 9
13	Player F keeps ♠ A, J, ♦ Q and draws ♦ 10, 8
14	Player A keeps his pair of 8s and draws ♥ Q, ♦ 9, ♣ 4

The new hands are shown below.

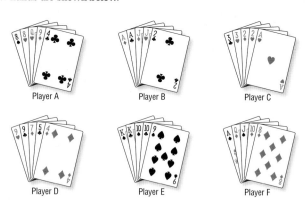

Player A   Player B   Player C

Player D   Player E   Player F

In the second betting interval, Player D, as the first to bet on the first betting interval, has the first opportunity to bet:

15	Player D, disappointed at not improving his hand, checks
16	Player E, with two pairs, bets one chip; he is willing to bet more, but does not wish to scare his opponents into folding
17	Player F folds
18	Player A, who also did not improve his pair of 8s, decides to call
19	Player B, with two big pairs, calls one and raises one
20	Player C, who also has two pairs, calls, pushing forward two chips
21	Player D now thinks he is beaten, and folds
22	Player E likes the way things have gone, calls one and raises two
23	Player A now folds
24	Player B calls two and raises a further three
25	Player C, thinking the other two might have only a big pair each, decides to call, thinking this might be his last bet if the others press on; it costs him five chips to call
26	Player E, still thinking he might have the best hand, calls three and raises three more
27	Player B, now fearing Player E has a triple, calls for three
28	Player C has a Poker player's typical dilemma; he fears he has lost but is unwilling to give up when it will cost him only three to call and end the betting. He calls.

As the players have equalized their stakes, Player E shows his hand first, only to find that Player B has beaten him. As he feared, Player C is also beaten and sacrificed his last three chips for nothing. So Player B picks up 43 chips, including the pool of six.

There are many variants of Draw Poker, the most common of which are explained below.

Jackpots Of the many variations on Draw Poker, Jackpots must be mentioned because it is the most popular, and in the USA in particular is often described as if it were the parent game. The difference is that before any player can make a bet, he must hold a pair of Jacks or better. Once a player has opened the betting, other players may call, bet or raise as they wish.

A player who opens the betting must retain his discards and, if he folds, his hand, since at the end of the deal he might be required to prove that he had the requisite two Jacks or better to open. If nobody opens, the hand is abandoned and the deal passes to the next player, with the pot remaining in the centre and being added to by another round of antes.

Progressive Jackpots This is played as Jackpots, except that if a hand is abandoned because nobody can open the betting, the requirement to open on the next hand is a pair of Queens or better ('Queenpots'). Further abandonments lead to the minimums becoming a pair of Kings, then Aces. If the succession of abandoned hands continues after 'Acepots', the minimum requirement to open reduces, to a pair of Kings, then Queens, then Jacks, and then back upwards again... and so on, up and down. Meanwhile, the pot continues growing with each abandoned hand.

Wild cards In all forms of Poker, 'wild cards' can be used. A wild card is a card which can represent any card its holder wishes. At one time, a Joker was added to the pack as a wild card. In modern times it is more usual for a whole rank to be wild, and this is usually the 2s ('deuces wild'). If only two wild cards are required, they can be the black 2s, or some prefer the 'one-eyed Jacks' (♥J and ♠J).

Wild cards are introduced to allow players to hold higher-ranking hands, but they are not recommended, and decisions must be made as to how they are used. For example, can a hand of five of a kind be allowed? Or a flush headed by two Aces, which might be claimed by a player holding ♦A, 9, 7, 4 plus a wild card? These dilemmas can be solved by a rule which prevents a wild card duplicating a card which is already held. This would rule out five of a kind and a doubled-Aced flush.

There is also the question of whether a hand without a wild card beats a hand in the same category which uses one. For example, the straight J, 10, 9, W, 7, where W represents a wild card, would beat the straight 8, 7, 6, 5, 4 unless there were a rule to the contrary. Players must agree these side issues if they wish to play with wild cards.

Spit in the Ocean The distinguishing feature of this form of Poker is that players are dealt four cards each face down, and their hands are completed by a final card which is dealt face up to the centre of the table. This is a card common to all players. However, this card (called the 'spit') is a wild card, as are all three other cards of the same rank. So all players have at least one wild card in their hands, and some may have two, three or four.

The game is usually played with only one betting interval, ie without a draw. However, it can be played as Draw Poker, with betting intervals before and after a draw. Players must decide beforehand the rules governing wild cards.

Lowball Lowball is played as Draw Poker, but with the great difference that it is the lowest-ranked hand which wins. The ranking of the hands is different. Flushes and straights are ignored, and Ace counts low in all respects.

Thus the lowest hand (and therefore a winning hand) is 5, 4, 3, 2, A, the lowest ranked cards in the pack. It does not count as a straight, and if all the cards were the same suit, it would not count as a flush.

Where unmatched hands are concerned (ie those not containing a pair, a triple or a four, the highest-ranking card determines the precedence and, if equal, the next highest and so on (exactly as it does in Draw Poker). For example, 9, 6, 5, 4, 3 beats 9, 8, 4, 3, 2 in Lowball, because the 6 is lower than the 8.

All the procedures, for example the two betting intervals, one each side of the draw, are the same as in Draw Poker.

High-Low Poker This form of Poker is a combination of the standard game in which the highest-ranked hand wins, and Lowball, in which the lowest wins. The pot is shared by the highest hand and the lowest (an odd chip going to the highest) and players can go for either, or even for both, as the same hand can win both (as will be explained).

Players do not declare until the showdown whether they are trying to win high or low. A player drawing two cards to 3, 2, A, hoping for low, might draw two Aces, and immediately be hoping to win high.

High hands are ranked as in Draw Poker, and low as in Lowball, which accounts for the possibility of one hand winning both, for example ♥A, 7, 6, 4, 2 would have an excellent chance of winning high as an Ace flush, and of winning low as 7 high.

At the showdown, before exposing their hands, players must indicate simultaneously whether they are trying for high or low. The simplest way of doing this is for each player to hide a chip in his fist under the table, say blue for high, white for low, one of each for high-low (ie high and low). Players then unclench their fists at the same time to indicate which pot they are aiming at.

If only one player is trying for high or low, he wins his half of the pot automatically. If all the players try for the same pot (for example if there are three in the showdown and all go for high) then the winner takes the whole pot. This, obviously, leads to some interesting choices for players. A player aiming for high, for example, but judging from the betting that he is unlikely to win, might at the showdown opt instead to go for low, hoping that he will be the only one who does.

A player who competes for high-low must have the best hand in both categories to win. If he holds the highest hand but not the lowest, or vice-versa, he loses both. The other players take the pots as if he hadn't bet.

Dealer's Choice Poker is a rapidly evolving game in which dozens of variants have been recorded (and no doubt thousands unrecorded). One of the popular versions in social games, where the players know each other and all the variants, is to have a session of Dealer's Choice. In this, each dealer chooses which variant will be played on his deal. It introduces variety and keeps everybody on their toes.

Stud Poker

The main difference between Stud Poker and Draw Poker is that in Stud Poker most of the cards are dealt face up and there is no draw. There are two forms, five-card and seven-card.

Five-card Stud Poker It is possible for up to ten people to play Stud Poker, but it is better for up to six. Even as few as two can play, as the marathon match which was at the centre of the film *The Cincinnati Kid* showed.

As with Draw Poker, the seating, first dealer, time limit and stake limits for Stud Poker should be agreed beforehand. It is not usual to have an ante, but some players like to have one. A way of limiting stakes is to make the lowest bet of one chip, with high limits varying with the betting intervals, say two for the first, three for the second, four for the third and six for the fourth and last. It is usual for the high limit to come into force on any round after a player has an 'open pair', ie a pair among his cards face up on the table.

After the shuffle and cut, the dealer deals one card face down to each player (his 'hole card'). He then deals one card face up to each, and the first betting interval takes place. The player with the highest face-up card is the first to bet. If there are equal highest cards showing, the holder of the one nearest the dealer's left bets first. This player has no option. He is obliged to bet within the staking limits agreed. Thereafter, each player in turn may fold, call or raise. Betting continues until all the stakes of those still active are equalized. A player who folds must turn his face-up card (or later, cards) face down and place it on his hole card. At no time may other players see these cards.

The dealer then deals a second face up card to each active player. There is then a second betting interval. Again the player whose face-up cards show the highest Poker combination has first opportunity to bet. For this purpose, straights and flushes do not count, so in the second betting interval a pair is the highest combination possible (on later rounds, it might be a triple or four, but flushes and straights never count). From the second betting interval onwards, the first player, and subsequently others, may 'check', ie stay in without betting, but once a player has bet, that option disappears and players must fold, call or raise.

When stakes are equalized again, a third card is dealt face down, followed by a betting interval, and then a fourth, followed by the last betting interval.

When dealing the face-up cards, the dealer should announce the rank of the receiving player's hand, for example he should say 'Queen high' or 'pair of 9s', etc, and at the end of that round of dealing point out which player must speak first in the betting interval. If he makes a mistake, other players may correct him. On the third and fourth rounds, he should also announce possible flushes or straights, for example dealing a 10 to a hand consisting of a Jack and 9, he should say 'possible straight'. He is not liable for any errors he makes and players can correct him if he makes one.

If, before the final cards are dealt, all players have folded except one, then that player takes the pot without the need to show his hole card. If after the fourth betting interval there are two or more players remaining, there is a showdown in which each player turns over his hole card, the hands are compared, and the player with the best takes the pot.

Seven-card Stud Poker Seven-card Stud Poker (also known as Seven-toed Pete or Down the River) is very popular, and perhaps the most interesting form of Poker for home play. Seven players is the maximum.

The preparations are as for Five-card Stud, except that the betting limits are not affected by the appearance of a pair among a player's cards.

After the shuffle, the dealer deals one card face down to each player, then another, and then one card face up. Each player has two hole cards. As with Five-card Stud, the player with the highest face-up card is obliged to bet, and subsequent players to fold, call or raise. After the bets are equalized, a second face-up card is dealt to all players, and a second betting interval takes place, with this time the player with the highest combination showing having the right to check, as in Five-card Stud. Play proceeds as in Five-card Stud, with face-up cards being dealt one at a time, followed by a betting interval, until each player has two hole cards and four face-up cards. After this betting interval, a seventh card is dealt to each player face down, giving each player three hole cards. There follows the final betting interval and the showdown, if necessary, during which each player reveals his hole cards and makes the best Poker hand he can from the seven available to him. The player with the best hand takes the pot.

Variants on Stud Poker There are many variants on Stud Poker. The game can be played Lowball, and High-low, with the rankings for the low hands being as described in Lowball and High-Low Draw Poker, with the players making their calls of high or low or both in the same manner, with chips of different colours.

Seven-card Stud, High-Low This is a very interesting game, guaranteeing plenty of action, and an example hand is given below. Five hands are dealt as shown:

Player	Hole cards		Face-up cards 1	2	3	4	Final hole card
A	♣8	♦7	♠6	♦6	♦J	♣5	♦A
B	♠K	♦8	♣K	♦3	♦10	♥3	♦K
C	♠5	♥5	♠9	♦4	♣Q	♥A	
D	♥K	♠10	♥10	♣6	♥2	♦5	
E	♠Q	♥7	♠J	♦Q	♠A	♣3	♣7

The limits are one chip minimum, three chips maximum for the first three betting intervals and five for the last two.

After the first face-up card is dealt, Player B with a King showing is the first to bet, and he must bet, so he bets one chip. All players call. Three players have pairs already, Player C's being concealed. Player A has every chance of a straight, and with 8 high is best placed at the moment for low.

The second face-up card leaves Player A with a pair showing, so he speaks first. He is allowed to check, but decides to bet one chip, as he likes the look of his hand. Again, all the players call. Three of them have pairs higher than Player A's 6s, and Player C, who was dealt a pair, is actually last on the current ranking of the hands. Of course, each player can see only the face-up cards of their opponents, and no hand looks impressive yet, judging by the cards on the table. Even Player A's exposed pair of 6s does not look very good, as a third 6 is already exposed on the table in Player D's hand.

The third face-up card leaves Player A, showing two 6s, the first to bet again. Nobody has improved on this round, so betting is cautious. Players B and D have three cards towards a flush. Player A checks. Player B raises one chip and all others call.

The fourth face-up card leaves Player A still the first to speak. His straight is still a possibility and if his last hole card is 3, 2, or Ace he will have 8 high for low. He decides to check.

Player B now has two pairs, and there isn't another King on the table. He decides to bet five. It is something of a bluff. He doubts if another holds a triple, and hopes to scare off all high contenders. Player C decides low is his only chance, and he cannot do better than 9 high, so he folds. Player D also folds, thinking his pair of 10s will not win high and not fancying his chance of low. Player E decides to call. He could go high if he gets an Ace or a Queen, or try low with Jack high if he gets a low card. Player A, with only two others remaining in, and possibilities of high or low, also calls.

The final hole cards were excellent for Player A and Player B. Player A, certain he thinks of low, bets five. Player B cannot see himself beaten for high with a full house, calls and raises five. Player E, despite getting ♣7 and thus two pairs, guesses that Player B has cards on the table to beat his hand for high and is not going to bet ten more chips on low as Player A is almost certainly going to call low, so he folds. Player A calls.

Player A calls low and Player B high. They do not have to show their hands to share the pot, each taking 25 chips, and each therefore winning seven chips on the deal. It might not seem much, having put 18 each in themselves, but once they began staking in five chips at a time, they were pretty sure of winning.

English Seven-card Stud This interesting version of Stud introduces a drawing element. It is played as Seven-card Stud described above until the stage when all players have five cards, two 'in the hole' and three face up. At this stage, players reject one card before receiving their sixth card from the dealer. They may reject a hole card or a face-up card. If they reject a hole card, the sixth card is dealt to them face down, but if they reject a face-up card, the sixth card is dealt face up. After the betting interval, the seventh card is dealt to them in the same way. Therefore a player's hand is never more than five cards, two face down and three face up. On the sixth and seventh rounds, a player happy with his hand need not draw a new card at all – he can stand pat with the five cards he has. If he stands pat on the sixth round, he must do so on the seventh round as well.

Texas Hold 'Em

This is the form of Poker which has had the greatest explosion in popularity since the 1980s, when World Championships began to be played in US casinos, in particular Binion's Horseshoe in Las Vegas. Once television channels on both sides of the Atlantic began hosting big-money tournaments, and then celebrity tournaments, the public took to the game in a big way and now thousands play on the Internet.

Texas Hold 'Em, often just called Hold 'Em, can be played in theory by up to 22 players (ie there are enough cards in the pack to accommodate 22 players), but in practice six to eight is best. In this form of Poker, each player's object is to make the best possible Poker hand from the two cards he holds and the five common cards, called 'community cards', which are dealt in stages to the table. A player may use both his cards, or one, or none, as he prefers. Of course, if he uses none (called 'playing the board') he cannot do better than tie, since all the other players have the same option to use all five community cards as their hands.

Preparation The first dealer and the seating arrangement are decided in the manner described for Draw Poker.

Stake Limits Before each deal the first two players to the left of the dealer put towards the centre small stakes known as 'blind bets' or 'blinds'. The first player puts in a 'small blind', which would be one chip. The next player puts in a 'big blind', which might be any multiple of the small blind, and is usually three chips. This will make the minimum stake for betting and raising three chips. The maximum bet and raise can be what players decide. It is best to have a maximum, say ten or twenty chips, or the richest player will be able to steamroller his opponents with huge bets.

In televised tournaments there is no limit, but all players start with the same amount of chips and retire when they lose them. These are knockout tournaments, and allowing each player the same amount of chips to start makes it a fair tournament. In tournaments of this kind, the blind bets get progressively bigger. This speeds up the betting, in effect forcing players to bet more than they would otherwise, and ensuring a result in a reasonable amount of time. Social players can play like this, but generally prefer a game where some win and some lose, rather than a winner-takes-all game.

When the two players to the dealer's left have made the blind bets, the dealer shuffles and the player to his right cuts. The dealer deals clockwise one card at a time face down to each player, including himself, until all players have two cards.

In casinos, and televised tournaments, a dealer, who does not take part in the game, is provided, so that the players do not have to deal themselves. In effect, the dealer deals for each player in turn. A disc, or 'button', is moved round the table on each deal to indicate which player is the 'dealer', and thus which players must put in the blinds.

Play The first player to speak is the player to the left of big blind. He cannot check, because the blind bets are regarded as normal bets, so he must fold, call or raise. All players in turn have the same options, including the blind bettors. Small blind must obviously add to his stake if he wishes to stay in, since he contributed only one chip to the pot. Big blind will have to increase his stake to stay in too, if the stake has been raised before his turn comes round.

When all the stakes are equalized, the dealer deals three cards face up to the table in a row. These are known as the 'flop', and are common to all players, who now have five cards each. There is now a second betting interval, in which the first to speak is the nearest active player to the dealer's left, as is the case on subsequent betting intervals. A player may check on this round, as all the stakes are equal, but as soon as a player bets, then all others must either fold, call or raise.

When stakes are equalized, a fourth card is dealt to the row on the table. This is called the 'turn', or 'fourth street'. A third betting interval takes place, after which a final card is dealt to the row of community cards. This is 'fifth street' or 'the river'.

The final betting interval takes place, and if necessary there is a showdown.

Tournament play In the tournaments, as widely televised, the only limit is the amount of chips a player has, and often a player's best policy is to go 'all in', ie to bet all his chips at once. Any active players can now only fold or call, and if anyone calls there is a showdown, which will result in the player who went all in being eliminated if his hand is not the best.

Example hand Six players are dealt two hole cards each, as in the illustration that follows.

Small blind is one chip, big blind three and the maximum bet and raise is twelve chips. Player A is the dealer, so Player B stakes one chip as small blind and Player C three chips as big blind.

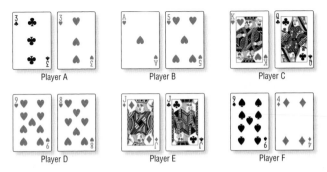

| Player A | Player B | Player C |

Player D speaks first, and with 9, 8 'suited' (ie of the same suit) he calls with three chips. Player E has a good hand, a medium pair (Jacks) and also calls. Player F folds. Player A calls with his small pair. He will be hoping for a third 3 on the flop, as a small pair is not likely to win anything unless it improves. Player B has a suited Ace, a reasonable hand, and calls. As he has already staked one chip, it costs him two chips to call. Stakes are equalized, and the dealer deals the flop. This is shown below.

Flop

Player B speaks first on the next betting interval. He has not improved, but has three hearts towards a flush. He checks. Player C has a pair of Queens and a Jack on fourth or fifth street would give him a straight. He bets three chips. Player D has a pair of 9s, not too impressive in itself, but he also requires a Jack for a straight, and calls. Player E, who has two Jacks already, also has four cards to a straight, but his is open-ended, and he needs a King or an 8 to complete it. He, too, calls. Player A, with four players still in, decides his two 3s are going nowhere and folds. Player B now has to decide whether to risk three more chips on seeing fourth street, and being adventurous, he calls and stays in.

The dealer adds the turn, or fourth street, to the flop. It is ♥10, and the community cards are as shown below. The pair of 10s in the community cards make everybody's hands look better, but in fact, everybody has this pair.

Flop and turn

Player B speaks first. His only realistic chance of winning this hand is if a fourth heart appears on the river. He would then have an outstanding chance of winning, as he would hold the best possible flush, as he has the Ace. The best possible flush, as the cards lie, is known as the 'nut' flush. He would beat any straight that another might hold. But, in reality, he has only a pair of 10s at the moment. He decides to check. Player C has two pairs (although everybody has the 10s) and stakes another three chips on his hand. Player D needs only the ♥J on the street to hold every player's dream, a straight flush. From his point of view, the odds against him getting it on the river are 45 to 1 (he knows where six cards are, so there are 46 that could appear on the river). Otherwise he holds two pairs and a chance of a straight. He, too, calls. Player E has two pairs, Jacks and 10s, but knows this would be beaten by an opponent whose hole cards included a Queen. He still has a chance of a straight and decides to call. Player B now assesses his chances. There are 46 cards he knows nothing of, of which nine could be hearts. The odds against him getting a heart on the street are 37–9, or roughly 4–1. There are 36 chips in the pot to win, and he needs to put in three to stay in with a chance. As he would be paid out at 12–1 for a 4–1 shot, he decides to call (although, of course, even if a heart appears on the street, he could still lose to a full house which, as the cards lay, and the betting has progressed, is far from an impossibility).

So with four players still in, the dealer turns up the last of the community cards, the river. It is ♠4, which helps nobody. The five common cards are shown below.

Flop, turn and river

Player B checks but is not going to add to the pot. Player C bets three more, on the strength that if two pairs wins, he probably will, as he can be beaten only by a player with A, A, or K, K, or A, Q as his hole cards. As it happens, Players D and E each have two pairs, and both are reluctant to fold their hands when with three chips they could stay in, so both call. Player B folds. There is a showdown, and Player C discovers he judged his last bet very well, and won an extra six chips from it. He picks up 48 chips, a profit of 36.

Omaha

Omaha is a similar game to Texas Hold 'Em, and in fact the names of these games aren't yet set in stone, and not all books would agree that Omaha is played as described below, or that the game described is Omaha. The main difference to Texas Hold 'Em is that each player has four hole cards instead of two.

Preparation The choice of dealer, shuffle and cut are as described in Texas Hold 'Em. The anteing can be the same (ie small blind and big blind), or the method described under Draw Poker can be used, with each player contributing an ante or the dealer putting in a chip for each player.

The dealer deals four cards face down to each player one at a time clockwise. Players examine their cards and a betting interval takes place. The first to speak at this and succeeding betting intervals is always the first active player to the left of the dealer, except when the small and big blind system of antes is used when, at the first betting interval only, the player to the left of big blind speaks first.

When all bets are equalized, the first three community cards, the flop, are dealt in a row. A second betting interval takes place, then the turn is revealed, followed by a third betting interval, which is followed by the exposure of the river and the final betting interval. These procedures are exactly the same as described for Texas Hold 'Em.

There is now a showdown, which is where there is a further difference to Texas Hold 'Em. Each player has nine cards from which to select his best hand, but there is a vital restriction. Each player must use two of his four hole cards to build his hand, together with three of the five community cards. The holder of the best hand at the showdown wins the pot.

Example hand The need to use precisely two hole cards and three community cards causes problems which can spoil promising hands.

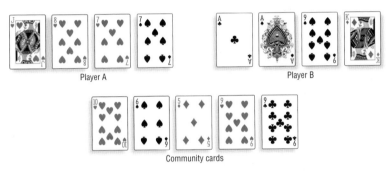

Player A   Player B

Community cards

Suppose two players remain for the showdown, with the hands shown above. Player A, could he use all nine cards available to him, would hold a straight flush, with ♥J, 10, 9, 8, 7. But he can use only two of ♥J, 8, 7 which he holds in his hand. Player B, with unrestricted choice of the nine cards, could have a full house, with ♠9, ♣9, ♥9, ♣A, ♠A. But he cannot use both Aces plus a 9 from his hand.

The best hands the players can make are shown below, with Player A having the better: a straight opposed to a triple.

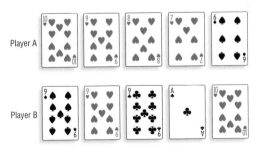

Omaha High-Low Eight This variant of Omaha is an interesting game. It is played as other High-low Poker games, with half the pot going to the high hand and half to the low hand. The number of cards to choose from, plus the restriction of having to use two hole cards and three community cards in each hand, make for many permutations of hands and the fact that a player can go for high or low with completely different hands makes it fascinating. The 'Eight' in the title refers to another restriction: that the low hand has to be no worse than 8 high in order to compete, ie a 9-high low hand is ineligible.

In the assessment of low hands, flushes and straights do not count, and Ace is low, so that 5, 4, 3, 2, A is the lowest possible hand. A player does not need to specify at the showdown whether he is aiming at high or low, and all players remaining at the showdown provide a hand for each. If no players in the showdown can compete for low because they do not have a hand which qualifies, then the winner of high takes the whole pot. In the hands shown previously in the example game at Omaha, neither player would have been able to compete for low because there are not three cards among the community cards below the rank of 8.

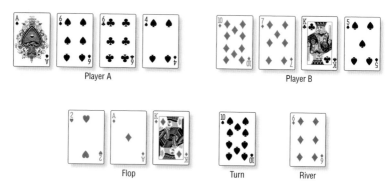

Player A   Player B

Flop   Turn   River

The illustration shows the four hole cards of two players at the showdown, together with the community cards. Player A, because of the restriction of having to use two hole cards only, cannot make a full house for high despite having three 6s and two Aces in his total of nine cards. His best hand is a triple of 6s. Player B wins high on the strength of his flush in diamonds.

Player A is even more unlucky when it comes to low. Despite his nine cards including no fewer than seven with a rank of 6 or under, he cannot make a hand eligible for low, as he has only four cards of different ranks below 8 in 6, 4, 2, A. He cannot use another Ace or 6 because that would give him a pair. Player B, on the other hand, can win low with ♦7, ♦6, ♠5, ♥2, ♦A. Not that he needed to; he would take the whole pot anyway by virtue of winning high, and Player A failing to win low.

General strategy in Poker

Psychology and bluff probably play bigger roles in Poker than in any other card game, but it would be wrong to believe, as many non-players might believe, that bluffing and a 'poker face' are the main elements of the game. It is possible to win at

Poker without bluffing, but it is impossible to win without a grasp of the arithmetic possibilities of the game: the value of a hand, the probabilities of improving it, what might be inferred from the number of cards opponents draw and how they bet. A knowledge of the ranks of the combinations of two cards that might be held as the hole cards – for example that a pair of Aces is much better than a pair of Kings, which is considerably better than a pair of Queens, and that Jacks, 10s and 9s should be considered only as medium pairs, and that an Ace with a high kicker, particularly if suited, is more valuable than a small pair – is worth more to a player than any supposed skill at bluffing.

So far as bluffing is concerned, there are two main objectives. One is to mislead your opponents into believing that your hand is better than it is. The object is to persuade them to fold, so that you win without a showdown. This is more likely to succeed if there is only one opponent to beat, therefore is best practised by a player speaking last when all but one have folded. To bluff with a poor hand when speaking first, and then finding two or three opponents calling or raising, is a good way to lose money pointlessly.

The other objective in bluffing is more subtle, and probably more used and more successful. It is used to fool opponents into believing that your hand is not so good. Should a player on receiving a good hand bet the maximum, or make the maximum raise, players with a middling hand will fold. On the other hand, should he merely call and generally give the impression that he is staying in to see what develops, other players will be encouraged to stay in too, and the pot will grow to a size more worth winning.

There are points to remember about bluffing. One is that one should not become stereotyped. Players who play regularly together will get to know something of each other's habits; it will be noticed if a player always tends to bluff in certain situations, and the bluff will become increasingly less effective. Another is to be decisive. In trying to persuade an opponent your hand is better than it is, there is no point in making a small raise, thinking you'll cut your losses if he calls – a sort of 'each-way' bet. A bluff should be sufficiently high to say to the opponent: 'It will cost all that to see what I've got – are you prepared to risk it?'

The best advice with regard to bluffing is that all bluffs should have a definite purpose, which is winning the pot, and as large a pot as possible. It is a recipe for disappointment to bluff in hope, or in desperation during a run of bad hands.

Polignac

Polignac is a French game, dating back to the early 19th century, and is an ancestor of Knaves. The German game of Slobberhannes is also mentioned here as a variant.

Type	Trick-taking
Alternative names	Four Jacks, Quatre Valets
Players	Three to six; four is best
Special requirements	Pen and paper for scoring

Aim

To avoid taking tricks containing the four Jacks.

Cards

The standard pack of 52 cards is used, from which are removed the 6s, 5s, 4s, 3s and 2s, leaving a pack of 32 cards. If three, five or six play, the two black 7s are also removed, making a pack of 30 cards. The cards rank from Ace (high) to 7 (low).

Preparation

Any player may pick up the cards, shuffle and begin to deal cards one at a time to each player round the table until a Jack appears. The player dealt the Jack becomes the first dealer. The deal subsequently passes to the left.

The dealer deals one card at a time to all players, clockwise, until the pack is exhausted. Four players therefore receive eight cards each, three receive ten cards, five receive six cards and six receive five cards.

Play

The 'eldest hand' (the player on the dealer's left) leads to the first trick; see p383 for an explanation of tricks and trick-taking. He can lead any card he wishes. Players must follow suit if able, and can discard any card if unable. There are no trumps. The highest card in the suit led wins the trick, and the winner of a trick leads to the next. The object is to avoid taking a trick containing a Jack, in particular the ♠J (called the *polignac*). The ♠J carries a penalty of two points, and the other three Jacks carry penalties of one point each.

Scoring At the end of the deal, the players' penalties are entered onto a score-sheet. A cumulative score is kept, and the winner is the player with the fewest penalty points after an agreed number of deals, say three per player.

Variants

A variant which might come to the rescue of a player dealt a very poor hand (ie one with which he will win tricks) is called *capot* or 'general'. Before the first card is led, a player may declare capot, which announces his intention to win all the tricks. If he succeeds, five points are added to each opponent's minus score, but if he fails he is debited with five penalty points himself.

Slobberhannes Slobberhannes is played exactly as Polignac, but the penalties are entirely different, making it an interesting game quite unlike most of those games where the intention is not to take certain tricks. There are three ways of acquiring a penalty point. One is to win the first trick, a second is to win the last trick, and a third is to win the trick containing the ♣Q. A player who incurs all three of these penalties gets another one as a bonus.

Example hand

Suppose the hands for Slobberhannes are as illustrated, using the Bridge convention of calling the players North, South, East and West. West dealt, so North has the first lead.

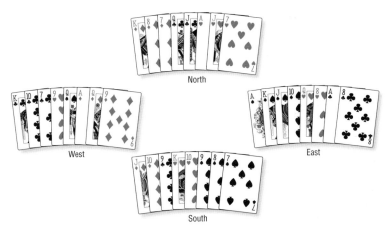

North sees the ♣Q as a big danger card. He hopes he can unload it on a spade lead. East has a terrible hand, with the void in diamonds his best chance of not taking ♣Q with his ♣A. South has a reasonable looking hand, and West must beware ♠Q.

North decides to lead ♦7 (to East's great relief), because he retains the lowest card in the suit, the ♦8. The play might proceed:

	North	East	South	West
1	♦7	♣A	♦10	♦9

South picks up the penalty point for first trick.

	North	East	South	West
2	♣J	♣8	♣9	♣7
3	♥A	♥Q	♥K	♥9

North, knowing that he cannot take ♣Q, as he holds it, unless another player leads a club, decides to unload some big cards.

4	♦ K	♠ A	♦ J	♦ A

Unfortunately for North, West knows that the only club remaining in the other hands is the ♣Q, so promptly leads ♣10.

5	♣ Q	♠ K	♥ 10	♣ 10

North knows there's only one diamond left, so:

6	♦ 8	♠ J	♠ 9	♦ Q

Now West must make the last two tricks, and pick up the penalty point for last trick. So North with ♣Q has two penalty points, West and South one each, and East, with his poor hand, has no penalties.

Pontoon

Pontoon is probably a corruption of the French *Vingt-Un*, through the intermediate stage of Van John, which it was also called. It is likely that British soldiers of World War I picked up the name of the French version. This popular family gambling game often appears in British card books as Vingt-et-Un, although 99% of Britons actually know it as Pontoon. Blackjack is the much less interesting commercial version played in casinos, particularly in the USA. As with many games popular in pubs and houses, rules differ everywhere. Described here is a standard version.

Type	Gambling
Alternative names	Blackjack, Twenty-one, Vingt-et-Un, Vingt-Un
Players	Three to ten; five or six is best
Special requirements	Chips or coins for staking

Aim
To build a hand to beat the banker, which, apart from special hands, is a hand with a count nearer to, but not exceeding, 21.

Cards
The standard pack of 52 cards is used. Cards have their pip values, with court cards counting as ten, and Aces as one or eleven at their holder's discretion.

Preparation

Any player may pick up the cards, shuffle and begin to deal cards one at a time to each player round the table until a Jack appears. The player dealt the Jack becomes the first dealer, who is also the banker.

There is an advantage to holding the bank. The bank passes from one player to another on the occurrence of a special hand called a 'pontoon', as will be explained below.

It is as well to agree a minimum and maximum initial stake which can be bet on a hand.

Play

The banker deals one card face down to each player, including himself. The players look at their cards but the banker does not. Each player announces a stake and places it before him. It should be between an agreed minimum and maximum. The banker then gives each player, and himself, a second face-down card. Again, the players look at their cards but the banker does not.

Players try to build a hand with a pip value of 21, or as near to it as possible without exceeding it. If a player holds a 'pontoon' (a two-card hand of 21, consisting of an Ace and a 10-count card) he declares it immediately and lays it on the table, usually with one card exposed. This is the highest hand and cannot be beaten, except by the banker also holding a pontoon.

The banker then deals with each player in turn, beginning with the player to his left.

A player who has been dealt a pair of Aces may 'split' them. He separates the cards and puts the same stake on the second card as on the first. The two cards now represent the first cards of two hands, so the banker deals a second card to each hand and deals with them separately. A player splitting Aces who receives another Ace to either hand can split further, and could (very rarely) hold four separate hands.

Each player has three choices when the banker comes to deal with him. He may:

Stand or stick	This means he is happy with his count and stands or sticks with it, taking no more cards. He may not stand on a total lower then 16.
Buy	He may buy a further card face down, for a stake not exceeding his previous stake. He can buy further cards if he wishes, but always for a stake not exceeding his previous one. He may continue to buy until he has five cards, which is a special hand. A five-card hand, no matter what its total, beats all other hands except a pontoon. A player cannot buy a fifth card if his four-card total is 11 or lower. This is because he cannot lose, as he cannot exceed 21. He may, however, 'twist', which is to receive another card without buying it.
Twist	This is a request that the dealer twist the player a card face up, for which he does not pay. A player may twist at any time, whether or not he has previously bought a card, but he cannot buy a card after he has twisted.

If while receiving cards a player's count exceeds 21, he has 'busted' and loses his stake. He passes his hand to the banker, who puts it face down on the bottom of the pack. He also passes over his stake.

When all the players have been dealt with (they do not show their hands), the banker turns over his two cards. If he has a pontoon, he immediately takes all the stakes of the players remaining in the game, including any players who also have a pontoon. Otherwise he may stand, or deal himself extra cards, standing when he wishes to. There is no restriction on when he may stand.

If the banker has a five-card hand, he loses to a pontoon but beats all other hands, including a player's five-card hand. Thus, should his count be 21, he will announce he is paying pontoons and five-card tricks only.

The banker wins on all ties.

Should the banker's count exceed 21, he busts and pays all players still in the game.

A player who holds a pontoon is paid double by the banker, except when the pontoon was part of a split hand. The banker is not paid double when he holds a pontoon, nor is a banker allowed to split Aces (he may still count them as 1 or 11).

The banker holds the bank until a player beats him with a pontoon, when that player may take over the bank if he wishes (he should, as it is usually profitable). Should two or more players hold a pontoon on the same deal, the player nearest to the banker's left has precedence.

The reason the bank is usually profitable, despite the fact that the players can choose their stakes according to their hands, is that the banker wins all tied hands, and wins from all players who bust, even though he might bust himself.

Example hand

The illustration opposite shows how a deal with seven players might progress.

Player A stood on a two-card hand of 19.

Player B bought another card with a two-card total of 10, hoping for a 10-count card, but had to stand with 17.

Player C kept buying cards and was rewarded with a five-card hand.

Player D twisted (he is not allowed to stand) with the nasty count of 15, and bust.

Player E bought a second card with a count of 11 and was rewarded with a 10-count card for a total of 21.

Player F stood on a two-card hand of 18.

Player G split his Aces and eventually stood on both hands with disappointing counts of 16 and 20. He might have stood on the first, by counting his Ace as 11, with a total of 17, but twisted another card in the cope of a five-carder, only to get a 9 and settle with a count of 16, not risking busting in an attempt to get a five-carder.

The banker paid out on hands of 19 and over. So Player A won three units, Player B lost two, Player C won four, Player D lost three, Player E won two, Player F lost one, and Player G lost six on one hand, and won six on the other. The banker lost three units on the deal.

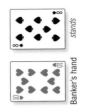

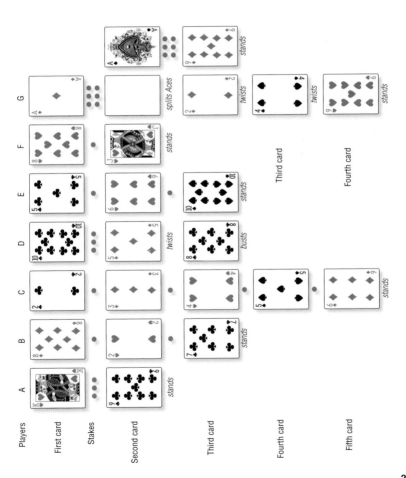

Variants

i) A common variant is to allow a third category of hand, a 'prial' of 7s, ie three 7s. This hand beats all. When held by a player the banker pays treble, but not vice-versa. Some regard this as unnecessary and feel it detracts from the best hand, pontoon, which after all is the name of the game.

ii) The banker looks at his first card when all players have staked on theirs, and may if he wishes demand all players double their stakes. This just gives him an additional advantage and is not recommended.

iii) An Ace and 10 is not regarded as a pontoon, which is limited to Ace and court card. Ace and 10 count as a normal 21.

iv) The banker is paid double when he holds a pontoon, except by a player holding a pontoon, who just loses his stake. This is not recommended for the same reason as ii) above.

v) Any pair may be split like Aces. This generally favours the Banker, as it is not a good policy for the player to split cards other than Aces.

vi) The banker looks at his two-card hand before dealing with the players, and if he holds a pontoon exposes it and collects all stakes immediately. This is greatly in favour of the players, who avoid buying cards or splitting Aces in situations when they cannot win.

Pope Joan

There is a reference to the game Pope Joan as far back as 1732, and it is the forerunner of Newmarket. Pope Joan was once believed to have been a female pope of the ninth century, and she is represented in the game by the ♦9. The game was very popular in Scotland, and the fact that Scottish feeling against Catholicism was so strong is one of the most widely held beliefs for the fact that the ♦9 is still known as the 'curse of Scotland'.

Type	Stops
Alternative names	None
Players	Three to eight
Special requirements	Chips or coins for staking; a board or eight labelled saucers to hold the stakes

Aim
To win the chips in each of the eight divisions on the board by playing the relevant cards or by playing all your cards to the table.

Cards
The standard pack of 52 cards is used, from which is removed the ♦8. Cards rank from King (high) to Ace (low).

Preparation
Pope Joan was traditionally played with an elaborate and highly decorated wooden board, a few of which are still around in museums or maybe antique shops. The circular board contained eight hollows into which chips or counters could be placed as stakes. Nowadays, unless one is lucky enough to own such a board, one must either draw on a sheet of cardboard eight spaces labelled Ace, King, Queen, Jack, Pope (or ♦9), Matrimony, Intrigue and Game, or perhaps place eight saucers on the table carrying those labels. These are spaces into which chips or coins are placed.

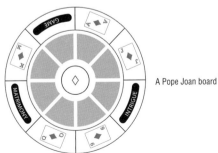

A Pope Joan board

Before the deal, the dealer places chips (or coins) onto the board (or into the saucers) as follows: six in that labelled Pope, two each in Matrimony and Intrigue, and one each in Ace, King, Queen, Jack and Game. This is called 'dressing the board'. It follows that, to be fair, the game should continue until all players have dealt an equal number of times.

Any player may pick up the cards, shuffle and begin to deal cards one at a time to each player round the table until a Jack appears. The player dealt the Jack becomes the first dealer. The deal subsequently passes to the left.

The dealer deals the cards one at a time clockwise to each player. The number of cards each player receives depends on the number of players. Some cards must be left over for a 'widow'. The number of cards to each player and to the widow (spare cards not used) are as follows:

Number of players	Cards each	Widow
3	15	6
4	11	7
5	9	6
6	8	3
7	7	2
8	6	3

The widow is placed face down in the centre and the top card is turned over to denote the 'trump' suit. This is not a trump in the normal sense of the word. It indicates that whoever plays the Ace, King, Queen or Jack of that suit during the game wins the stakes in the appropriate space on the board, or from the appropriate saucer.

If the turn-up is the ♦9, the dealer collects the chips in the space labelled Pope or ♦9, and the chip for game. The hands are not played out. The cards are collected and re-shuffled with the next dealer dressing the board in full before dealing.

Play

The 'eldest hand' (the player to the dealer's left) makes a lead by placing a card in front of him and announcing it. It can be of any suit he chooses, but it must be the lowest card he holds in that suit. The player holding the next card in that suit in ascending sequence then plays it and announces it, then the player with the next card, and so on. For example, if the lead is ♥2, the player with ♥3 plays it, then the player with ♥4 and so on. Sooner or later the sequence will stop, either because it reaches the King, or because the card required is in the widow. The ♦7 is always a stopper, because the ♦8 has been removed from the pack. A player can lay two or more cards on one turn, for example if he holds ♥2, 3, 4 he can play them all at once. A player holding a card eligible for play must play it – in other words, it is illegal to hold up a card which might lead to another player collecting the chips in any category.

When a run is brought to a stop, the player who played the last card begins a new sequence. It can be in the same suit or another, but the card led must be the lowest he holds in the suit.

If a player lays the Ace, King, Queen or Jack of the trump suit, he collects the chips from the appropriate place. If he lays the Pope (♦9) he collects those chips. If he plays both Queen and King of the trump suit he collects as a bonus the chips from the Matrimony space, and if he plays the Jack and Queen of the trump suit he collects the chips from the Intrigue space.

Finally, the first player to get rid of all his cards collects the chip from the Game space, and the game ends. He also collects one chip from each of the other players for each card they still hold in their hands, although an unlucky player caught with the ♦9 in his hand – and who has therefore missed his opportunity to win the large number of chips for Pope – is excused the additional annoyance of having to cough up any chips for his failure to go out.

Any chips not collected from the board at the end of the hand remain there for the next one, in addition to the new chips added by the next dealer when he dresses the board.

Variants
Some players prefer not to bother ensuring that all players start with the same number of cards. Instead they deal an extra hand (the hand after the dealer's) which becomes the widow. It means there are more cards in the widow and fewer in the hands when compared to the table above. With eight players, for example, some players will get only five cards.

Some players prefer that rather than the dealer dress the board, each player distributes chips on the board before each deal. For example, one method is for each player to put three chips in Pope, two each in matrimony and intrigue and one each in the other categories. Another method is for players to stake one chip in all categories.

Some players require a player beginning a new sequence to change the suit colour from the previous sequence. Others allow a player to begin a new sequence with whatever card he likes, not restricting him to the lowest he holds in a suit, but this can be seen to destroy the whole point of the game.

Preference

Preference is a gambling game popular in Central and Eastern Europe and Russia. It is a trick-taking game which includes an auction in which the suits are ranked in an unusual manner. The game described here is a Westernized version published in Germany in 1975.

Type	Trick-taking
Alternative names	None
Players	Three
Special requirements	Chips or coins for staking

Aim

To win chips by making enough tricks as declarer to land your contract, or, if a defender, to defeat the declarer.

Cards

The standard pack of 52 cards is used, from which are removed the 6s, 5s, 4s, 3s and 2s, leaving a pack of 32 cards. The cards rank from Ace (high) to 7 (low). The suits are also ranked with hearts (known as the suit of 'preference') the highest, followed by diamonds, clubs and spades in that order.

Preparation

Players each draw a card from a spread pack to determine the first dealer. Cards rank for this purpose from ♥A to ♠7, so there cannot be a tie.

It is customary to establish a pot from which winning declarers take their winnings and to which losing declarers add their losses. The winnings and losses will be the value of the trump suit (hearts 4, diamonds 3, clubs 2, hearts 1) multiplied by a figure which must be agreed. Five is a reasonable figure. Since this means a winning declarer in hearts will take out 20 chips, a pot of 45 chips (15 per player) would allow at least two successful hearts declarations before the pot needs to be replenished.

The dealer deals three cards face down to each player clockwise, then one card to a 'talon', followed by four cards to each player and another to the talon, followed by three more to each player. Each player therefore has ten cards and the talon two, all face down.

Bidding A bid is a promise to make the majority of the tricks, ie six or more, with the suit named as trumps. The 'eldest hand' (the player to the dealer's left) begins the bidding, which continues in a clockwise direction. The first player may pass or bid one of the four suits, as may subsequent players, provided that once a bid has been made, subsequent bids must be of a higher ranked suit than the last. If two players pass consecutively, then the player who bid last wins the contract and becomes the declarer.

If all three players pass, a second round of bidding begins. In this round of bidding, a bidder may again pass or may add a chip or chips to the pot for the privilege of taking the two cards of the talon into his hand in exchange for discarding. If a player adds chips to the pot, a subsequent player may add more. The player who adds most to the pot wins the right to be declarer and to name the trump suit as before, but this time he is allowed to exchange any cards in the talon (none, one or two, according to their value to him) for the same number from his hand. The talon is only used if the bidding goes to a second round. If all players pass on both rounds, the deal is abandoned and passes.

Incidentally, this second round of bidding is the reason the multiplier is necessary in calculating winnings. If a declarer in spades or clubs, say, took out only one or two chips from the pot if successful, he would certainly not pay a chip into the pot merely on the possibility of improving his hand with the talon.

Play

The eldest hand leads to the first trick; see p383 for an explanation of tricks and trick-taking. The play is clockwise. Players must follow suit if possible, and if unable to may trump or discard. A trick is won by the highest trump it contains, otherwise by the highest card in the suit led. The winner of a trick leads to the next.

Play ends when all ten tricks have been played, although once the declarer has made six tricks, or the defenders five, it is not necessary to play out any tricks remaining.

A successful declarer takes from the pot the number of chips corresponding to the value of the trump suit (hearts four, diamonds three, spades two and clubs one), multiplied by the agreed multiplier, for example five, as suggested. An unsuccessful declarer adds to the pot the number of chips he would have won; for example, had the contract been in hearts, he would add 20.

Example hand

The hands are dealt as shown, using the Bridge convention of calling the players North, East and West (South not being used as this is a three-player game).

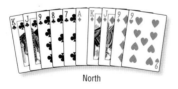

North

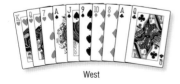

West

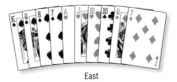

East

East is the dealer. West passes, having no long suit. North has a good hand with two long suits, clubs and diamonds. With clubs as trumps, he thinks he should make three tricks in the suit, as there are only three trumps against him. He will probably lose to ♣A and ♣Q, but unless all three missing trumps are in the same hand, he will make three trumps. Unless diamonds are led and trumped, he will almost certainly make three diamonds, too – if each of his opponents holds two diamonds, he will make all four. He knows that East cannot overbid him in spades, as spades is a lower ranking suit than clubs, but he fears that East might overbid in hearts. He is confident enough to bid clubs on the first round, which means he cannot look at the talon, but which also deprives East of the chance of bidding on a second round when he might have use of the talon. As it happens, East has no suit he can bid on any round, so North becomes declarer in clubs.

West has the lead. West knows that he will make two trump tricks when North leads trumps, and he wants to keep a double guard in hearts, in case that is North's second suit. He decides to lead a 'neutral' diamond. The play proceeds:

	West	North	East
1	♦8	<u>♦A</u>	♦7
2	<u>♣A</u>	♣K	♣10
3	♦10	<u>♦K</u>	♦Q
4	<u>♣Q</u>	♣J	♠7
5	♠A	<u>♣7</u>	♠8
6	♠9	<u>♣9</u>	♥10

At this point North will probably show his remaining trump card and his two master diamonds to show that he cannot be stopped from making seven tricks in all. He therefore makes his contract, and as the value of his trump suit was two, and the multiplier is five, he collects ten chips from the pot.

President

President is a Western game based on the Chinese game of Zheng Zhangyou, and has been gaining in popularity since the 1970s. It is a game with very relaxed rules, and players tend to add or subtract rules as they wish. Its purpose is to rank the players in a hierarchy, and during the game players move up and down the social scale as they win or lose. These games have come to be called climbing games. During play there is always one at the top of the order, who sits in the best chair, and another at the bottom, who has to deal and do any other chore his betters may impose upon him. Players change position according to their status during the game.

Type	Climbing
Alternative names	Arsehole, Bum, Scumbag and many similar others
Players	Four to seven
Special requirements	Ideally, an assortment of seating, so that President may have an armchair and Scumbag perhaps a beer crate, with grades in between; pen and paper for scoring

Aim
To be the first to reach eleven points; more immediately in each hand, to get rid of your cards as quickly as possible and thus become President, or at least to avoid being last and thus becoming Scumbag.

Cards
The standard pack of 52 cards is used, the cards ranking 2 (high), A, K, Q, J, 10, 9, 8, 7, 6, 5, 4, 3 (low).

Preparation
The first task is to determine the names for the ranks of the players. There must be one rank for each player. Since the game, under US influence, is often called President, President would suffice for the top rank, but it could be Monarch, Boss or whatever else the players prefer. Lower ranks could follow a company hierarchy, for example Vice President, Director, Manager, Foreman, Worker, Scumbag, or again whatever else might be preferred. The lowest rank usually carries a very demeaning name, of the Scum, Bum, Ratbag or Arsehole variety.

The player occupying the lowest position has to collect the cards after each hand, to shuffle and deal them for the next hand, and must perform any menial chores that might become necessary during the game. The seats should be arranged so that the best, most comfortable chair (reserved for the President) has the next most comfortable (say, the Vice President's) to its left, with each succeeding chair to the left being the standard lower than the previous one. Thus the worst chair (reserved for the Scumbag) is to the right of the President's chair.

For the first round of the game, players draw from a spread pack to determine their seats, with the highest (2 high, 3 low, as in the ranking above) taking the President's chair, and the others taking their seats in the order of the cards drawn, so the player drawing the lowest card will have the Scumbag's seat. Players who draw equal cards draw a second to determine precedence between them.

The player occupying the Scumbag's seat shuffles and deals the cards face down, one at a time clockwise, to all players until the whole pack is dealt. It does not matter that some players might receive a card more than other players. On subsequent deals it is always the player who is the Scumbag who deals.

Play

The player to left of the dealer (ie he in the President's chair on the first round, the President himself thereafter) begins the play by leading any card, or set of cards of the same rank, face up to the table. Each player in turn to the left must then either play a card or cards to beat the previous card or pass. To beat a single card one must play a card of a higher rank. To beat a triple or four of a kind one must play a similar set of a higher rank. It is always necessary to play the same number of cards as was led. For example, if a pair of 5s is to be beaten, and a player holds three 8s, he can play two 8s and keep the third in hand, or he may pass. Passing is always allowed, and to pass does not prevent a player from playing on his next turn.

The play continues round the table as many times as necessary until a player lays a card or cards and every other player passes so the turn comes round to him again. All the cards played are then turned face down and put to one side and the player who played last begins a new round (for convenience often called a trick) by playing any card or matching cards to the table.

The first player to get rid of all his cards becomes President for the next deal. The next player becomes Vice President, and so on. If a player gets rid of his cards and all other players pass, of course that player cannot lead to a new trick as he has no more cards left. In this case, the first active player to his left leads to the new trick.

Play ends when all but one player have got rid of their cards and established their place in the hierarchy for the next deal. The player still with cards becomes the Scumbag. Players move to their new seats if necessary and the Scumbag shuffles and deals the next hands. When the deal is complete, the Scumbag then gives the President the highest card in his hand, and the President gives the Scumbag any card he likes in exchange. The President then leads to the first trick of the new deal.

Scoring A system of scoring over a number of deals is to award the President two points on every deal and the Vice President one point. Others score nothing. The first to eleven points is the overall winner.

Strategy It is important to get rid of low cards as quickly as possible. A player with a 3 can only play it by getting the lead, and to get the lead a player must play a card or set of cards which the others players cannot beat. Therefore cards which are likely to win the lead, such as a pair of 2s or Aces, should be played with this purpose.

Example hand

Four hands are dealt as shown, using the Bridge convention of calling the players North, South, East and West.

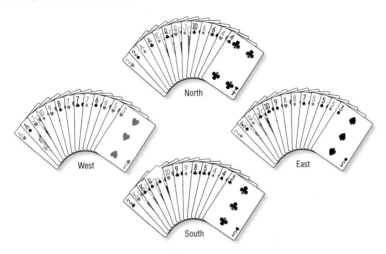

North

West

East

South

North is the President, and therefore is to lead. Play proceeds, with the underlining indicating the end of a trick, ie when three players have passed consecutively. The player who last played leads to a new trick.

North	East	South	West
4–4	5–5	9–9	Pass
Q–Q	Pass	Pass	<u>Pass</u>
6–6	8–8	Pass	Pass
<u>Pass</u>	3–3	4–4	6–6
A–A	Pass	Pass	<u>Pass</u>
10	J	Q	Pass
K	2	Pass	Pass
<u>Pass</u>	7	8	9
J	Q	2	Pass
Pass	<u>Pass</u>	3	5
2	Pass	Pass	<u>Pass</u>
2 (out)	Pass	Pass	<u>Pass</u>
	9	10	J
	K	Pass	A
	Pass	<u>Pass</u>	3

North	East	South	West
	10 (out)	J	A
		Pass	7–7–7
		Pass	8
		K	Pass
		K	Pass
		5 (out)	

So North is President, East is Vice President, South is Worker and West is Scumbag. North retains the comfy chair as President, while West as Scumbag must collect the cards, shuffle and deal the next hand. North has two points towards overall victory and East one point.

In the example hand, West held up his pair of Aces because it was more or less his only chance of getting the lead. Had he played them earlier, and been beaten by North's pair of 2s, he might never have got the lead at all and was certain to become the Scumbag. Timing is all.

Variants

President is a game which lends itself to idiosyncratic rules and variations. Some of the more commonly found are listed:

Jokers   Some players include one or two Jokers in the pack. When included, Jokers rank above the 2s. If Jokers are used, the Scumbag, if dealt one, need not hand it over to the President, but must hand over his next highest card. Some players prefer the Jokers to be wild cards, thus 9–9–Joker can be played as three 9s.

Sequences   Another combination which can be played is a sequence of three or more cards. In this case a four-card sequence of, say, J–10–9–8, can only be beaten by a four-card sequence of higher rank such as K–Q–J–10. A four-card sequence doesn't beat a three-card sequence. The number of cards in the sequence cannot change during the course of the trick. If sequences are allowed, sometimes multiple sequences are as well, for example two or more sequences of equal length and rank, such as 3–4–5, 3–4–5, or put another way, 33–44–55. This particular multiple sequence can be beaten only by another pair of identical sequences of a higher rank, for example 7–8–9, 7–8–9. Sequences are a regular feature of the Chinese game Zheng Zhangyou.

Opening lead   Rather than the President always leading to the first 'trick', the player who holds the ♣3 makes the initial lead, either with a single card or a combination including ♣3.

Single round   Some players prefer that after a lead, players get one opportunity
play   to beat the lead. Once the play reaches the leader, he does not get a second chance to play to the trick, which ends. The last player to play to the trick leads to the next one. Some players stay with

the multi-round play as described, but do not allow a player who passes to play at a subsequent turn in the same trick. Others prefer a rule which states that a player cannot pass if he can beat the previous play.

Equal play Some players allow a card or a combination to 'beat' a card or combination of equal rank. By this means a player can play 5–5, for example, on a previous 5–5.

Card exchange Some players prefer that after the deal the Scumbag must give the President his two best cards, rather than one, and the second-to-last player must give the Vice President his best card in exchange for whatever the Vice President wishes to give him.

Scoring Some players give the winner of a hand three points, the second two and the third one. In this case, a target for game might be 21.

Pyramid

Pyramid is a single-pack patience with a very pleasing tableau. But beware – it can be infuriating. The chances of getting it out are only about 1 in 50. The game takes only five minutes or so, but one can play for the same number of hours without reward if unlucky.

Type	Patience
Alternative names	Pile of Twenty-eight
Players	One
Special requirements	None

Aim
To finish with all the cards in a discard pile.

Cards
The standard pack of 52 cards is used.

Preparation
The cards are dealt face up in the form of a pyramid of seven rows, increasing from one card at the apex to seven at the base, with each card except those on the bottom row being overlapped by two other cards. The pyramid forms the 'tableau'.

Play
The cards on the bottom row are available for play. As play proceeds, the removal of two adjacent cards in a row uncovers a card in the row above which becomes available for play.

From the initial tableau, pairs of available cards whose pip total equals thirteen, irrespective of suit, are removed. For this purpose Aces equal one, Jacks equal eleven and Queens equal twelve; Kings equal 13 and so are removed singly. Cards removed are placed to one side in a discard pile.

The remaining cards form the 'stock'. When all possible cards have been paired and removed from the initial tableau, the stock is turned over one card at a time. If the card turned can be paired with an available card from the tableau, it is paired and discarded; if it is a King, it is discarded immediately on its own. If it cannot be paired, it is played face up to a 'talon'. The top card of the talon is always available and may be paired with the next card turned from the stock or with any available card in the pyramid.

The game is won if all the cards end in the discard pile, or lost if no further moves can be made. Once the stock is turned over, there is no redeal.

From the tableau illustrated, ♦K is removed to the discard pile. Other cards to be paired and played to the discard pile are ♦Q and ♦A, which releases ♣K to the discard pile. The ♠3 and ♠10 are also discarded, thus releasing ♦5 which can in turn be paired with ♥8 and discarded.

No more moves in the initial tableau can now be made and so the first card is turned from the stock. Suppose it is ♥9. This is paired with ♦4 and discarded, releasing ♣6 and ♦7 to be paired and discarded. Again no more moves can be made in the tableau and the next card is now turned from the stock. It is ♠8. This pairs with nothing, so begins the talon. The next card is turned from the stock... and so on.

Quinto

Quinto is a trick-taking game which deserves to be better known. It was invented around 1900 by one 'Professor Hoffman', a prolific writer on card games, whose real name was Angelo Lewis. It has the unusual characteristic of all the cards being ranked, which allows three suits to be used as trumps.

Type	Trick-taking
Alternative names	None
Players	Four, playing in partnerships of two
Special requirements	Pen and paper for scoring

Aim
To win tricks, particularly those containing cards or combinations called 'quints'.

Cards
The standard pack of 52 cards is used, plus a Joker. The cards rank from Ace (high) to 2 (low). The suits also rank, in the order hearts, diamonds, clubs, spades. The Joker has no rank, as it has no trick-taking value, but it has value when won in a trick.

Preparation
Players each draw a card from a spread pack, the two lowest playing against the two highest, with the lowest being the first dealer (there cannot be a tie, as all cards have a rank from ♥A to ♠2). Partners sit opposite each other. The deal subsequently passes to the left.

The dealer shuffles and the player to his right cuts. The dealer deals the first five cards to the table. These five cards are the 'cachette', and they are put to one side for the time being. The remaining 48 cards are dealt face down, one at a time, clockwise to each player, beginning with the 'eldest hand' (the player to the dealer's left).

Play
Each trick won during play is worth five points, but after examining their hands each player in turn, beginning with the eldest hand, has the opportunity to double the value of each trick to ten points. If the trick value is doubled, a succeeding player on the opposite side may redouble, thus making the value of each trick 20 points. A player may not redouble a double made by his partner.

The eldest hand leads to the first trick; see p383 for an explanation of tricks and trick-taking. A player must follow suit if he can. If he cannot, he may trump with any card from a suit ranking higher than the suit led, or he may discard. Notice that it is impossible to discard when a spade is led, as all the other suits are trumps on a spade lead.

A trick is won by the highest value card it contains. (It can be seen that this is true no matter which suit was led, or how many discards or trumps it might contain.)

The Joker has no trick-taking value, but is a 'quint' (see Scoring, below) and can be played by its holder whenever he likes, whether he can follow the suit led or not. If the Joker is led (which would not normally happen but might be forced on the last trick), there is no need to specify a suit to follow, since the trick is won in any case by its highest-ranking card.

The winner of a trick leads to the next. The winner of the last trick takes the cachette, which counts as a thirteenth trick, and scores as a trick won.

Scoring There are 13 possible quints to win during play, although only five are certain to be scored.

The highest scoring quint is the Joker, which is known as the 'quint royal'. To take it in a trick is worth 25 points. The 5 of each suit is a quint, as are any two cards of a suit whose pip value is five (ie A, 4 and 2, 3). To score points for a quint consisting of a pair, the pair has to be taken in the same trick. The scores for these quints vary from 20 points each in hearts to five points each in spades, as shown below.

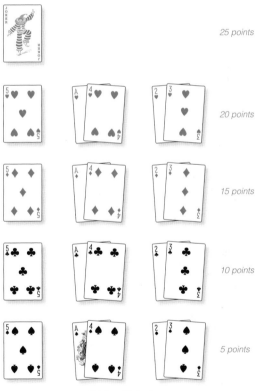

Quints and their values

The scores for quint royal and other quints are entered on the score-sheet as they are won during play. At the end of the deal are added the scores for tricks won, either five, ten or 20 per trick, depending upon whether the value of the tricks remained at five or was doubled or redoubled. The winner of cachette scores for it as a trick, and also scores for any quints it might contain.

The first partnership to reach 250 points wins, so because quints are scored as they are won during play, the game might be won without the need to complete the hand. If the hand is completed, and both pass 250 on the same deal, the higher score wins. In the unlikely event of a tie, a new hand is dealt and whoever gets the first score for a quint wins the game. Usually a 'rubber' of the best of three games is played, so a rubber might last two or three games. If played for stakes, each side's score for each game is totalled, with the winners of the rubber adding a bonus of 100 points to their total.

Example hand

The hands are dealt as shown, using the Bridge convention of calling the players North, South, East and West.

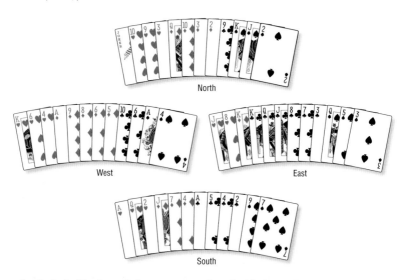

South dealt. No player feels strong enough to double (normally strong hearts and diamonds would suggest a double, but no player has more than three hearts). West decides to lead ♠A, expecting to win the trick, and giving his partner the opportunity to play the quint royal to it if he holds it. The play proceeds as follows, which also shows the running score for quints scored:

	West	North	East	South	W/E	N/S
					Running score	
1	♠A	♠J	♠5	♠7	5	

East does not have quint royal, but can play ♠5 (quint) to the trick, scoring five points for his side.

2	♠4	♠K	♠3	♠9		
3	♣6	♣9	♣K	♣A		
4	♣10	♦10	♣3	♣4		
5	♦5	♠2	♠Q	♣5	25 (30)	

South hoped to make ten points by trumping with ♣5, but West was also out of spades and won with ♦5, thus picking up 25 points for two quints.

6	♦6	♦2	♦K	♦7		
7	♦8	♦Q	♣Q	♣2		
8	♦A	♦3	♣7	♦J		
9	♦9	♥3	♣8	♦4		
10	♥K	♥9	♥J	♥Q		
11	♥4	♥10	♥8	♥2		

South is holding up his ♥A in order to win the last trick and cachette. North is now forced to lead quint royal. Everything depends on this last trick, as the winner will get cachette as well as quint royal.

| 12 | ♥6 | Joker | ♣J | ♥A | 25 | |

So North/South win 25 points for quints to West/East's 30. North/South also take cachette as an extra trick, and since it contains ♥5, score another 20 for quints. They took eight tricks, including cachette, for another 40 points to West/East's five tricks for 25. Final score: North/South 85, West/East 55.

Strategy The holder of quint royal will play it as soon as he is certain his partner can win the trick. In the example hand, North was never certain enough to play it. The player with the opening lead, if he does not hold quint royal, will usually lead an Ace so that if his partner holds quint royal he can play it. After the first trick in the example hand, each player would have a suspicion that North/South held quint royal (unless it was in the cachette). Had South been able to obtain the lead with any other card but ♣A, he could have led ♣A on the grounds that North could probably play quint royal to it. As the only other card he could get the lead with was ♥A, he was forced to trust North not to play quint royal prematurely. The holder of ♥A, which is certain to win a trick, will usually try to hold it up until the last trick, in order to win cachette and an extra trick, especially if the trick value is doubled.

Ranter Go Round

Ranter Go Round is a children's game said to have been invented in Cornwall, where it is also called Cuckoo. However, Cuckoo is a game which is played in many countries in Europe, sometimes with special cards, such as the Italian *Cuccu* pack, which dates from the 17th century.

Type	Children's
Alternative names	Chase the Ace, Cuckoo
Players	Any reasonable number; five to 20 is best, ideally between the ages of seven and twelve
Special requirements	Counters; a saucer or similar receptacle

Aim

To be the last player left in, by not holding the lowest card when the cards are revealed at the end of each deal.

Cards

The standard pack of 52 cards is used, the cards ranking from King (high) to Ace (low).

Preparation

A saucer or similar should be placed in the centre of the table. Each player is given three counters, which represent three 'lives'.

Any player may become the first dealer by agreement, but if there is a dispute any player may pick up the cards, shuffle and begin to deal cards one at a time to each player round the table until a Jack appears. The player dealt the Jack becomes the first dealer. The deal subsequently passes to the left.

The dealer shuffles the cards. Each player is then dealt one card, face down. The remainder of the cards are put into a pile to one side.

Play

Each player looks at his card. Play begins with the 'eldest hand' (the player to the dealer's left), who has the choice of keeping his card (which he will do if he considers it unlikely to be the lowest dealt) or of exchanging it with the card of the player to his left. This he does by offering it face down to him and saying 'change'. The player asked to change must do so unless he holds a King, when he can reply 'King', forcing the player who wished to change to keep his card.

Each player in turn has the opportunity to keep his card or pass it on. Obviously, a player who has to pass on a card to the preceding player and who receives a higher card than that he passed on in exchange will not wish to pass on his new card on his go, as he knows it is not the lowest.

A player who is asked to change and who returns to the player on his right an Ace, 2 or 3 must announce the rank of the card passed on. Each succeeding player then knows whether or not his own card is safe, and on his own turn will ask to change only if the card he holds is equal to or lower than the card whose value was announced.

The dealer is the last to play, and if he wishes to exchange his card he must do so by cutting the part of the pack not dealt and taking the top card of the lower part of the pack. He must show the card he draws, and if it is a King he is the loser and puts one of his counters into the saucer. Otherwise, all players show their cards and the player with the lowest loses a 'life' and puts a counter into the saucer. If there are equal lowest, they all put in a counter.

The deal passes clockwise, and a player who loses his three counters must drop out of the game. The winner is the last person left in. Children generally do not mind dropping out, as a new game comes round quite quickly.

Red Dog

Red Dog is a simple gambling game best played among families for pennies rather than taken seriously. The reason is that a serious gambler, prepared to work out his chances on every hand (which can be done quickly), will certainly win in the long run. It is therefore not a game found in casinos. The game is similar to Slippery Sam.

Type	Gambling
Alternative names	High-card Pool
Players	Three to eight
Special requirements	Chips or coins for staking; a bowl, saucer or similar receptacle

Aim
To win stakes by betting on your hand to beat the turn-up card.

Cards
The standard pack of 52 cards is used, the cards ranking from Ace (high) to 2 (low).

Preparation
A bowl or saucer is placed in the centre of the table, and a pool is made by all players contributing chips or coins to it. The amount per player will depend upon the number of players: three or four might contribute ten chips each, and seven or eight players might contribute six chips each. It is advised that a maximum stake should be agreed before play begins.

Red Dog

Any player may pick up the cards, shuffle and deal a card to each player. The player dealt the highest card becomes the first dealer. The deal subsequently passes to the left. The dealer may have a hand himself and partake in the game, or, if there are more than four players, it might be preferable for him to deal and collect the cards only.

The dealer shuffles and the player to his right cuts. The dealer deals five cards face down, one at a time clockwise, to each player beginning with the 'eldest hand' (the player to the dealer's left). The remaining cards are placed face down to form a 'stock'.

Play

The eldest hand examines his cards, and bets that he has a card in his hand of the same suit and of a higher rank than the card on top of the stock. To make a bet, he places the chips he wishes to bet to the side of the bowl containing the pool and announces the amount. Each bet must be of a minimum of one chip. Traditionally, the maximum bet is the total value of the pool, but it seems sensible that if the game is played among friends or family there should be a maximum of, say, five chips. Otherwise, since good play – play intended to win – suggests that the maximum bet should be made whenever the chances of winning are odds-on, which is often, the pool would be won almost every deal, and as much time could be spent replenishing the pool as in actual play (see Strategy, below).

The dealer then turns over the top card of the stock. If the eldest hand has a card to beat the turn-up, he shows it and takes back his stake from the side of the bowl plus an equal amount from the pool. If he hasn't a card to beat the turn-up, he instead places his chips into the pool. His hand and the turn-up are then placed face down to a waste heap.

The player to the eldest hand's left then makes a bet, similarly placing his chips and announcing the amount, the dealer turns over the next card, and so on.

If the whole pool is won, the players must replenish it by the same amounts as at the beginning.

Strategy The advantage is entirely with the player, since he can bet as little or as much as he wishes. The optimum play would be to bet the maximum whenever there is an odds-on chance of winning and the minimum whenever the chance is odds-against. It is easy to calculate the chances. The player holds five cards and there are 47 unknown (unless some players have played and cards have been exposed, when there will be fewer). So far as the eldest hand is concerned, there are 47 unknown. If he subtracts the rank of the top card he holds in each suit from 14 (counting Aces as 14, Kings as 13, Queens as 12 and Jacks as 11 and a 'void' – not holding any cards in a particular suit – as one) and adds the four figures together, he will know how many cards of the 47 can beat him, and by subtracting that number from 47 how many will not beat him.

Hand A

Hand B

Suppose he holds hand A in the illustration above. Using the method outlined above, his cards count (showing the highest card he holds in each in brackets):

♣ (J)	3
♥ (7)	7
♠ (6)	8
♦ (2)	12
Total	30

There are therefore 30 cards which will beat him and 17 which will not. The odds are against him and, if playing solely to win, he will bet the minimum.

If he held hand B, the cards count:

♣ (Q)	2
♥ (−)	13
♠ (K)	1
♦ (Q)	2
Total	18

There are therefore 18 cards to beat him and 29 which will not. The odds are in his favour, and he should bet the maximum. But this makes for a very boring game and, as stated, it is advised that there is a modest maximum stake.

Variants

Some players give the player a choice of bet: whether he has a card to beat the turn-up, as described, or whether he hasn't. If he bets that he hasn't, he must show his whole hand after the turn-up whether he wins or not. This variant tilts the prospect of winning even more in the player's favour, since he can bet on odds-on chances in every hand he gets.

Rockaway

Rockaway is a children's version of the various games of the Switch family.

Type	Children's
Alternative names	Go Boom
Players	Two to eight; four to six is best, ideally aged about eight to thirteen
Special requirements	Pen and paper for scoring

Aim
To get rid of all the cards in your hand.

Cards
The standard pack of 52 cards is used, the cards ranking from Ace (high) to 2 (low). If five or more play, then two packs shuffled together can be used.

Preparation
Any player may pick up the cards, shuffle and begin to deal cards one at a time to each player round the table until a Jack appears. The player dealt the Jack becomes the first dealer. If a series of deals is played, and a running score kept, the deal subsequently passes to the left.

The dealer deals the cards clockwise, face down, one at a time to each player beginning with the 'eldest hand' (the player to the dealer's left) until each player, including himself, has seven cards. He then turns over the next card, which is called the 'widow', and places it face up in the centre of the table. The remaining cards are placed face down beside it to form the 'stock'.

Play
The eldest hand begins play by placing on the widow a card of the same suit or rank as the widow, or an Ace. If he cannot, he must draw a card from the top of the stock, and must continue to draw cards from the stock until he draws one which allows him to cover the widow. The next player to the left must then play a card of the same suit or rank as the new card at the top of the widow, or an Ace, and if he is unable to he must draw until he can, and so on.

When the stock is exhausted, a player unable to lay a legitimate card on the widow at his turn merely passes. If the game becomes blocked, and nobody can go, the player who last played a card to the widow lays any card he wishes, and the game proceeds as usual.

The first player to get rid of all his cards is the winner.

Scoring If a series of deals is required, the game can last until each player has dealt once. At the end of each hand a running score is kept for each player, with each player debited with a score against them according to the cards they hold. Each Ace counts 15, court cards ten, and other cards their pip value. When all players have dealt, the player with the lowest minus score is the winner.

Strategy A player should try to keep in his hand cards in as many suits and rank as possible, to ensure that he has the maximum chance of being able to play a card on his turn. If he holds a card in each suit he is certain to be able to play a card on his next turn.

Example hand

Suppose hands are dealt to five players, as shown.

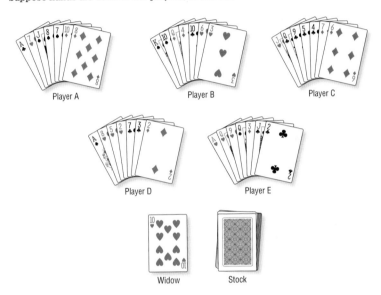

Player A   Player B   Player C

Player D   Player E

Widow   Stock

The ♥10 is the widow, and Player A is to play first. The play might proceed:

	Player A	Player B	Player C	Player D	Player E
1	♥7	♥6	♦6	♦2	♣2
2	♣A	♣10	♣Q	♣7	♣J
3	♠J	♠10			

Player C becomes the first player who cannot play and must draw cards from the top of the stock until he can, when play will proceed.

It was good play of Player E to play his ♣2 on the ♦2 on the first round, as this meant he kept a card of each suit in his hand. Had he played ♦3 instead, he would have been 'void' (without a card) in diamonds. Player A should perhaps have played his ♦10 to lead, as playing ♥7 left him void in hearts.

It was also good play, though less obvious, of Player B to play ♠10 rather than ♠K on his third round. This is because he had already played one 10, and another was the widow, leaving only one more to come. As there are three Kings to come, it is more likely that he will be able to play a King rather than a 10 in future play.

Obviously, Aces are valuable because they can be played on any card, and so should not be played if there is another option. In the example hand, Player A had no alternative to playing his ♣A on the second round.

Variants

Go Boom Go Boom is the US name for Rockaway, but is also the name by which this variant of the basic game is known. It is played slightly differently. It is limited to six players, and is a good game for introducing children to the principles of trick-taking. There is no widow and the Ace has no special properties.

The eldest hand has the first lead and all players must play a card of the same suit or rank as the card led (not of the previous card played). If unable to play such a card, a player draws cards from the stock until he can go, as in the basic game.

When all players have played to the card led, the cards form a trick, and are collected up. The trick itself is worthless and put to one side, but the player who 'won' it, ie who played the highest card of the suit led, has the advantage of leading to the next, and can lead whichever card he likes.

As in the basic game, when the stock is exhausted a player who cannot go misses his turn. The player who gets rid of all his cards first is said to 'go boom' and is the winner. Unlike Rockaway, the game cannot be blocked, as each trick is separate and there is always a winner to lead to the next.

A series of games can be played with players debited with points at the end of each deal as described above, and a running score kept.

Rolling Stone

Rolling Stone is unrelated to the pop group, though it has the similar quality of being something that goes on nearly forever… Its alternative names are French and German words which mean 'swollen' or 'to swell', and the game's characteristic is that as soon as a player thinks he is about to get rid of his cards and win the game, his hand suddenly swells in number and he is back where he started.

Type	Children's
Alternative names	Énflé, Schwellen
Players	Four to six
Special requirements	None

Aim
To get rid of all your cards by playing them to the table.

Cards
The standard pack of 52 cards is used, from which cards are removed depending on the number of players; each player must have eight cards. For four players, therefore, the 6s, 5s, 4s, 3s and 2s are removed, leaving a pack of 32 cards. For five players, the 4s, 3s and 2s are removed, leaving a pack of 40 cards. For six players, the 2s are removed, leaving a pack of 48 cards.

The cards rank from Ace (high) down to the 7s, 5s or 3s (low) according to the size of the pack.

Preparation
The cards are shuffled and each player draws a card from the spread pack; the player who draws the highest becomes the dealer.

The dealer deals the cards one at a time, face down, in a clockwise direction to all players until the pack is exhausted. Each player will have eight cards.

Play
The 'eldest hand' (the player to the dealer's left) leads to the first 'trick', although it is not a trick in the usual sense as we shall see; see p383 for an explanation of tricks and trick-taking. All other players must follow suit if they can. If all follow suit, the player who played the highest card 'wins' the trick. He collects up the cards and puts them to one side face down. They play no further part in the game. The trick itself is of no value, but it allows the winner to lead to the next trick.

If a player cannot follow suit to the card led, he must pick up all the cards that have been played to the trick and add them to his hand. He then leads to the next trick by playing any card he likes, except a card of the suit he has just picked up.

Play continues until one player has got rid of all his cards, and is the winner.

A deal is almost always a game in itself (ie cumulative scores aren't kept over a series of deals) because with good players a deal can last a long time. By watching which suits other players have to pick up, all players can get a reasonable idea of the suits other players hold. A player down to one card will almost certainly not find his suit led and will be forced to pick up cards of another suit; he must then lead what was his singleton card, since he is not allowed to lead the suit he picked up, so all other players then know exactly what cards he holds. When each player's cards are more or less known by all the others the game could be everlasting...

Variants

The game is often played for stakes, with each player placing a chip into a pool which is taken by the winner. Alternatively, the winner can collect a chip for every card each loser holds in his hand at the finish. Some players allow a player picking up the incomplete trick to lead the same suit to the following trick.

Rummy

Rummy is the family name of that popular group of games in which players take cards from a stock or a discard pile and try to meld them in sets or sequences. Yet the name was unknown before 1900. The game is descended from Coon Can and spread rapidly in South and North America where it acquired the name Rum, probably from the alcoholic drink. It is one of the best-known and most-played of all card games, and there are countless variants. What might be called the basic game is described first.

Type	Melding
Alternative names	Rum
Players	Two to six
Special requirements	Pen and paper for scoring

Aim

To play all your cards to the table by melding them into groups and sequences.

Cards

The standard pack of 52 cards is used, the cards ranking from King (high) to Ace (low).

Preparation

Each player draws a card from a spread pack; the player who draws the lowest card becomes the first dealer. The deal subsequently passes to the left.

The dealer shuffles and the player to his right cuts. The dealer deals one card at a time clockwise, face down, until each has the following number of cards: with two players, ten each; with three or four players, seven each; with five or six players, six cards each.

The dealer places the remainder of the pack face down in the centre to form the 'stock'. The top card of the stock is turned over and placed beside it to become the first card of a discard pile.

Play

Each player in turn, beginning with the 'eldest hand' (the player to the dealer's left) and proceeding clockwise, has the opportunity to take into his hand the top card of the discard pile, or if he doesn't want it, the top card from the stock. He then discards a card from his hand to the discard pile, which becomes available to the next player to play.

On his turn, between drawing a card and discarding, a player may 'meld', which is to lay down before him on the table sets of cards, which can be groups of three or four cards of the same rank, or sequences of three or more cards of the same suit (Ace being low). These sets are called melds. In this interval between drawing and discarding, a player may also add a card or cards to any melds he has on the table, or 'lay off' cards onto melds of other players. He can do any or all of these things on the same turn. When a player goes out, the hand ends and opponents cannot lay off cards onto his (or other players') melds.

The first player to get rid of all his cards, called 'going out', wins the hand. On his last turn he can discard as normal but is not obliged to – he may meld all the cards in his hand.

Should the stock become exhausted before any player has managed to go out, the player who took the last card turns over the discard pile which becomes the stock, and his discard begins a new discard pile. Play then proceeds as normal.

Scoring When a player goes out, other players are debited with the cards held in their hands. For this purpose court cards count as ten points and all other cards with their pip value (Ace counting one). If a running score is kept, the winner is the player with the lowest debit score when another player passes 100. If the game is played for stakes, it is usual for the losers to pay the winner after each hand.

Strategy A player's task is to assess which cards in his hand give him the best chance of melding, and he should try to build his hand to improve those chances.

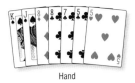
Hand

Discard pile

Stock

The holder of the hand in the illustration should certainly take the ♥4 from the discard pile and discard ♠K. The ♥4 doubles the player's chances of melding, as ♥3 or ♥6 will provide a sequence, whereas only one card, ♠Q, will complete the sequence with ♠K and ♠J. Moreover the exchange reduces the count of the hand by six points should an opponent go out. The ♠J should be discarded at the earliest opportunity afterwards.

Players should note which cards have already been discarded. For example, in the hand illustrated on the previous page, if the ♥3 and ♥6 have already been discarded or taken from the discard pile by another player, it would be pointless to take the ♥4. It would be better to take the top card of the stock. However, two cards counting ten points each, such as ♠K, J, with only one card available to meld with them, should not be held for more than a round or two.

On the other hand, a collection of court cards providing an opportunity to meld should not be broken up too quickly just for the sake of reducing the adverse point count. Suppose a player holds the hand illustrated below, for example, and draws from the stock ♥J. Adding ♥J to the two Queens and ♦10 that he holds increases the number of cards which would allow him to meld from these cards to five from the current three. To retain the ♥J and discard the ♠7, which is useless to him, would be a sound move, despite increasing his liabilities if another player goes out. Of course, the state of the game and the proximity to going out of another player will also affect the decision. In particular, if the player suspects his left-hand opponent is able to use the ♠7 he might decide not to discard it. In this case, his best discard would be ♦10, which needs one specific card, the ♦J, to be drawn to be of any use. In any case, to reject the card drawn, the ♥J, as many players might without thinking, would be a mistake.

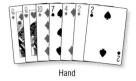

Hand   Draw

Two cards in sequence need the addition of one of two cards to make a meld (unless they include the King or Ace), as do two cards of the same rank. But the two in sequence is better to hold since, if a card is acquired to make a meld of three, there still remain two more cards which will increase the meld to four, whereas a meld of a group of three cards of equal rank leaves only one other card which will improve it to a group of four.

Melds do not have to be played to the table as soon as they are acquired and sometimes if a player holds a combination of cards which can be melded in different ways it might pay to keep the melds in hand for a round or two to see what other cards might be obtained. Holding melds in hand also prevents opponents laying off to them. However, melds in hand become debits if another player surprisingly goes out, so delaying declaring them is taking a chance.

Variants

There are many variants of Rummy. Some have their own names, and are described below. Other common variations to the basic game described above include:

Laying off   Laying off on opponents' melds is not permitted, except when a player goes out. In that case other players can lay off cards to the winner's melds only.

Going out   A player must make a discard on going out. This means that a player holding two cards cannot go out except by laying off.

Deadwood   Players do not declare their melds but keep them in their hands. When a player goes out, the other players then lay down their melds, lay off if possible on the winner's melds, and are debited with the unmelded cards remaining in their hands, called 'deadwood'.

Going rummy   A player who melds all his cards and goes out in one turn, without having previously melded, is said to have 'gone rummy', and his opponents' debits are doubled.

Stock exhaustion   Play ends if the stock is exhausted. The winner is the player with the lowest count of unmelded cards.

Knock Rummy Knock Rummy, also known as Poker Rum, is best for three to five players. Each receives seven cards. Players do not meld during the game. A player goes out by 'knocking', ie he knocks on the table after making his draw. He then lays down his melds and may discard.

The main difference from the basic game is that the player going out is allowed to have an unmatched card or cards, with which he is debited. It is possible for the player, picking up a hand of all low-count cards, to knock immediately, even without a meld at all.

When a player knocks, other players lay down their melds and are debited with their deadwood (unmatched cards). There is no laying off. If the game is for stakes, players pay the winner according to the differences in their scores (if a cumulative score is being kept, the losers are debited with the difference).

It is possible that the knocker will not have the lowest count. If so, the player with the lowest count is the winner, and the others settle accordingly, with the knocker paying an additional ten units (or, if scoring, being debited with an additional ten points). If the knocker and another player tie, the other player is the winner, but the knocker does not have to pay the ten points penalty. If two or more players other than the knocker tie, they share the winnings if playing for stakes.

If a player knocks and 'goes rum' (ie does not have any unmatched cards) the other players pay him a bonus of 25 units (or 25 points) in addition to the difference in their counts. A 'rum hand' cannot be tied, so if another player also has a hand with no unmatched cards, he must pay the knocker the 25-point bonus too (apart from an accident, this could also happen because the unfortunate player so caught has not yet had a turn).

There are also some variations to Knock Rummy. Some players impose a maximum count on the unmatched cards with which a player is allowed to knock. A popular figure is 15.

A version of the game often played in the UK restricts the knocker's options further. The knocker may not knock with more then one unmatched card. This requires him to have two three-card melds. Moreover, the unmatched card's rank cannot be above 3, so the knocker can go out only with a count of three, two or one. He is said to 'come up' for three, two or one (unless he goes rum, when he comes up for none). In this version, other players lay down their melds and can lay off onto the knocker's melds. The knocker has to pay the penalties given above if it turns out that another player has a lower count.

Boathouse Rummy Boathouse Rummy is best for three to five players. The number of cards dealt to each player is nine minus the number of players.

A player on his turn has the option, as in the main game described above, of taking the top card of the discard pile or the top card of the stock, but if he takes the top card of the discard pile he must also take either the next card in the discard pile or the top card of the stock. He discards only one card, so by following this course he increases his hand by one card.

The Ace is either high or low, so can be in sequences of A, K, Q, or A, 2, 3. 'Round-the-corner' sequences are also allowed, making K, A, 2 a legitimate sequence.

Melds are not made during play, so a player goes out in one turn, and must discard when going out. The other players then lay down their melds and are debited with the values of their unmatched cards. In this version the Ace counts eleven rather than one. Cards cannot be laid off on other players melds, including the winner's.

Continental Rummy Continental Rummy is a game which had a vogue in the 1940s and is played with more than one pack. It is suitable for up to twelve players. If two to five play, two packs are used. If six to eight play, three packs are required. If nine to twelve play, four packs are necessary. Each pack must contain a Joker. All packs are shuffled together to form one pack.

Each player is dealt 15 cards, the remainder forming the stock. The procedure is as in the basic game, with players drawing either from the discard pile or the stock.

All melds are sequences – groups of cards of the same rank are not recognized. Jokers are wild cards and can represent whatever card their holders require. Players do not declare melds but keep them in their hands to go out on one turn. To go out, a player must have all his 15 cards melded, and his melds must conform to one of these patterns: five three-card sequences; three four-card sequences plus one of three cards; one five-card sequence, one four-card sequence and two three-card sequences. Since sequences of six or more can be split, this in effect covers all possible combinations.

The winner collects one unit from each player, plus two units for each Joker a losing player holds in his hand. A cumulative score can be kept by listing each player's debits, the winner being the player with the lowest total of debits when another player reaches, say, eleven.

Kalookie This game, also spelt Kaluki, is a two-pack rummy with some similarities to Canasta. It is for two to six players, and is played with two Canasta packs, ie two standard packs plus four Jokers (108 cards in all).

The number of cards dealt depends on the number of players. Two to four players receive 15 cards each; five players receive 13 cards; and six players receive eleven cards. Jokers count as wild cards.

The cards are valued thus: Joker 25 points, Ace eleven points, court cards ten points, other cards their pip value.

The play is as for the main game described, with the following differences:

i) Ace counts high or low in sequences, ie A, K, Q and A, 2, 3 are sequences, but 'round-the-corner' sequences (K, A, 2) are not allowed.

ii) A group of three or four cards of the same rank may not contain duplicates, ie two cards of the same suit, two Jokers, or a Joker and a card of the suit it represents. In effect, this limits the number of cards in a group to four, with or without a Joker, since the Joker must represent one of the suits.

iii) Until he has melded, a player can take the top card of the discard pile only if he uses it in a meld, and then only if the meld, plus any other melds he might make at the same time, has a card value of 51. Until he can do this, therefore, a player on his turn may only draw from the stock. Once he has melded he can draw from the discard pile or the stock.

iv) Until a player has melded, he cannot lay off cards to other players' melds.

v) Whether he has melded or not, a player on his turn may replace a Joker in another player's meld with a card which the Joker might be said to represent, taking the Joker into his own hand. For example in a meld of Joker, ♠4, ♣4, the Joker may legitimately be said to represent either ♦4 or ♥4, and a player holding either of these cards could, on his turn, exchange it for the Joker.

Play is otherwise as in the basic game, with players being debited for the unmatched cards held in their hands according to the values above.

Russian Bank

Russian Bank is one of a small family of games which might be called competitive patiences, double patiences or, in the USA, double solitaire. It has been popular under a variety of names since the 19th century and seems to have acquired the name Russian Bank only when it became fashionable in the USA in the 1920s.

Type	Patience
Alternative names	Crapette, Robuse, Stop!
Players	Two
Special requirements	Two packs of cards

Aim
To be first to play all your cards to the foundations.

Cards
Two standard packs of 52 cards are used, one for each player, the cards ranking from King (high) to Ace (low). It is convenient to have cards with different patterns on the back, for ease of sorting after the game, in which they get mixed.

Preparation
Players each draw a card from one of the packs. The drawer of the lower card has the choice of packs and plays first. The players sit opposite each other. Each player shuffles his opponent's pack.

The first player plays twelve cards face down in a pile to his right. This is his 'reserve'. Above the reserve pile he deals four cards in a line towards his opponent. These are his 'files'. He places the remaining cards face down in a pile to his left, forming his 'stock'.

The second player now does the same. Between the two columns of files must be spaces for two more columns of cards; these rows will be the 'foundation' columns.

The two outside columns (the files) are known collectively as the 'tableau'. The two inside columns (the foundations) are known collectively as the 'centre'.

Play
During the game every Ace, as it becomes available for play, must be moved to the centre, from where it is built on in suit sequence up to the King. Cards in the tableau may be packed on in descending sequence of alternate colours. Available for this exercise are the cards on the top of any other tableau pile, the top card of the reserve (which during the game will be turned face up) and a card turned up from stock. Only one card at a time may be moved from a tableau pile to elsewhere. A space created in the tableau may be filled from the tableau or from the reserve, or, when the reserve is exhausted, from the stock.

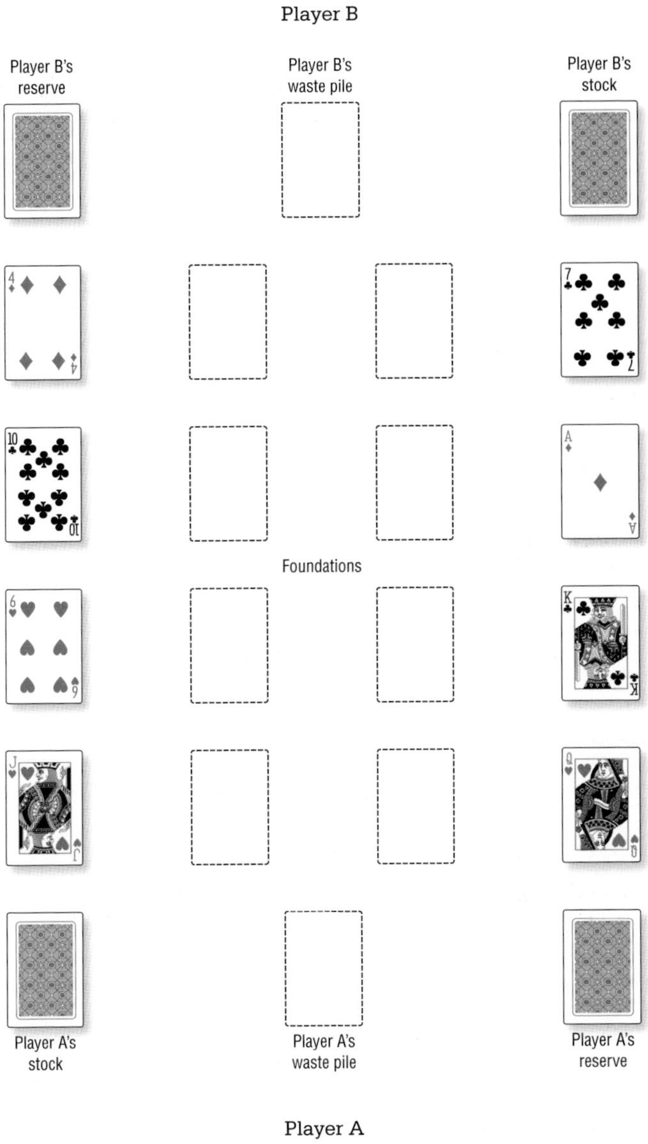

Player B

Player B's reserve

Player B's waste pile

Player B's stock

Foundations

Player A's stock

Player A's waste pile

Player A's reserve

Player A

However, these different plays must be made in a set order. When the preparation stage is complete and the tableau is in position, the first player begins play. First of all, he must make all possible plays from the tableau to the centre.

Then he turns the top card of his reserve over. (At all turns after the first, the player may turn over the top card of his reserve, should it be face down, before making any plays.) When the top card of the reserve is played, the next card is turned face up.

The top card of the reserve must be played to the centre, if eligible, before any available card in the tableau. However, when packing on the tableau, or filling blank spaces in the tableau, tableau cards and the reserve card can be used in any order. Generally, players will wish to get rid of their reserve cards as quickly as possible.

When a player has completed all possible plays to the centre, and his reserve card cannot be packed to the tableau, the player turns up the top card of his stock. Before turning the first card of his stock, all tableau spaces must be filled, but the player is not obliged to manipulate the tableau in order to create a tableau space.

The turned stock card is available for play to the foundations or to the tableau. When played, the next stock card is turned over, and may be played under the same rule, that all possible cards have been built to the centre and the reserve card cannot be packed to the tableau (it may be that the play of the preceding stock card has made these further plays possible).

The player continues turning the stock cards while he can continue to play each one and the provisos are maintained. Eventually, he may turn up a card which cannot be played, and this he must play to a waste pile which is situated between his stock pile and reserve pile. His turn ends as soon as he lays the card to the waste pile, and he cannot retract it if he later sees a possible play.

Cards in the waste pile are not available for play at any time. But when a player has exhausted his stock, he turns over the waste pile (without shuffling) and moves it to form a new face-down stock.

When the first player has completed his turn, the second player must first satisfy himself that the first player has not missed any possible plays to the centre, and if he has he must make them. He then turns face up the top card of his reserve, and begins his turn.

From now on there are further plays which may be possible. A player may 'load' cards onto his opponent's reserve or waste pile by packing on them cards in suit sequence in either ascending or descending order. The order may change; for example, on ◆6 he may load ◆7, ◆8, ◆9, ◆8, ◆7 and so on.

It is worth repeating here rules of play, because if any are violated, the opponent of the player breaking the rule is allowed to call 'stop!' and bring the player's turn to an end. They are:

i) A play to the centre takes precedence over all else, except the act, on a turn other than the first, of turning face up the top card of the reserve. The top card of a tableau pile must be played to the centre if available.

ii) In playing to the centre, the reserve takes precedence over playing from tableau and stock.

iii) A stock card may not be turned if the reserve card is playable. The reserve card is always playable if a space exists in the tableau, but it is not obligatory for a player to manipulate the tableau in order to create a space to play the reserve card.

iv) Except for the above rules, there is no precedence among plays involving playing the reserve card to the tableau, packing in the tableau, creating a space in the tableau, or loading the opponent's reserve or waste pile.

v) A card turned from stock is playable only to the centre or to the tableau or to the opponent's reserve or waste pile in the loading procedure. Further manipulation of the tableau to make a place for it in the tableau or centre is prohibited. If it cannot be played when it is turned it must be played to the waste pile which makes it unplayable until the stock is exhausted and the waste pile is turned to form a new stock.

Any error made by violating any of the above rules of procedure can be punished by the opponent calling 'stop!'. Play stops on such a call while the error is verified. If an error has indeed been made, then the perpetrator's turn immediately ends. A wrongly moved card must be put back and a wrongly turned over card in reserve or stock turned face down again. Some players penalize a false call of 'stop!' by transferring a face-down reserve card from the falsely accused's reserve to the caller's reserve. In the strictest rules (following the game of chess) a player touching a card signals his intention to play it, and if it is an illegal play his opponent may successfully call 'stop!'. Again like chess, a player can prevent this by saying 'I arrange' before touching a card he does not intend to play. Players must decide how strict they wish to be in this regard. In any case, a player who completes a further play after an unchallenged illegal one cannot be 'stopped' in retrospect.

The first player to get rid of his reserve and stock is the winner (the waste pile automatically disappears as it becomes the stock).

Scoring If one wishes to score for a succession of games, the winner scores 30 points for winning, plus one point for each card left in his opponent's stock and waste pile and two points for each card left in his reserve.

St Helena

Although Napoleon played cards while in exile on St Helena, the idea that he played numerous patience games seems to have been based on a misunderstanding. This has not prevented a whole range of patience games being invented which carry either his name or the name of the island. This particular one is an easy two-pack patience which should nearly always be got out.

Type	Patience
Alternative names	Napoleon's Favourite, Washington's Favourite
Players	One
Special requirements	Two packs of cards

Aim
To finish with the four Kings built on in descending suit sequence to the Aces, and the four Aces built on in ascending suit sequence to the Kings.

Cards
Two standard packs of 52 cards, shuffled together, are used, making a pack of 104 cards. Cards rank from King (high) to Ace (low).

Preparation
The four Kings and the four Aces are removed from one pack and arranged in two rows as 'foundations'. The remaining cards are shuffled and dealt one at a time, face up, around the rows clockwise in twelve packs, beginning with the top left corner. There will be eight cards in each pile. These form the 'tableau'.

Play
The top cards of the piles in the tableau are available for play to the foundations, with these restrictions: the cards in piles 1 to 4 (at the top of the tableau) may be built only on to the Kings, and the cards in piles 7 to 10 (at the foot of the tableau) only to the Aces. The cards in the piles at the side of the tableau – piles 5, 6, 11 and 12 – may be played to any foundation.

In addition, available cards can be packed from one tableau pile to another in descending or ascending sequence irrespective of suit or colour. The sequence may go up or down at will, ie the direction can be reversed in the same pile; for example, 3, 4, 5, 4, 3 and so on. However, the sequence is not 'round-the-corner'; only a 2 can be packed on an Ace, and only a Queen on a King. Only one card at a time may be moved, not sequences (ie only the top card is available). A space caused by the whole pile being played is not refilled (except by a redeal, as described below).

Redeals All possible moves are made. When no further play is possible, the cards in the tableau are collected up in reverse order to that in which they were dealt; for example, pile 12 is picked up first (face up), pile 11 added on top of it, and so on. When all the piles are picked up and the combined pile is turned face down, the top cards will be those that were originally in pile 12. The cards are now redealt without shuffling, face up, one at a time clockwise to the twelve spaces as at the beginning of play. Play continues as before, except that restrictions which prevent cards from certain tableau piles being built on certain foundations are lifted, and the top card of any pile is available to be played to any foundation.

A second redeal is allowed, but if all cards are not on the foundations at the end of that redeal the game is lost.

Example game

With the cards as dealt in the illustration, ♥2 can be built on ♥A, but ♦2 cannot be built on ♦A. Similarly, ♣Q can be built on ♣K but ♦Q cannot be built on ♦K. However, ♦Q can be packed on ♥J in pile 4, and thus becomes eligible for building on ♦K. It will be noticed that once ♥2 is built to its foundation, ♥3 can follow, but it would be better to pack ♦2 on ♥3 because from there it can be built on ♦A, after which ♥3 and ♥4 can be built to the foundation. The moving of these cards will expose others which become available for play.

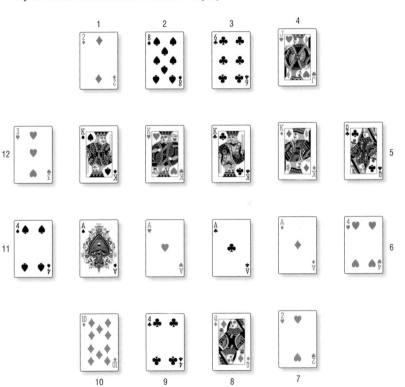

Salic Law

This double-pack patience game requires the eight Queens to be discarded and take no part in the action at all. This is why it is called Salic Law, after the code which excluded women from succession to the throne in certain European countries like Spain and France. However, in these more enlightened times some players like to place the eight Queens in a row across the top of the tableau so that if the game succeeds they end by looking down in haughty fashion at a row of Jacks and a row of Kings. It is a game in which success should occur roughly once every three games.

Type	Patience
Alternative names	None
Players	One
Special requirements	Two packs of cards; playing surface large enough for potentially lengthy columns of cards

Aim

To end with eight piles of cards, irrespective of colour or suit, each in sequence from Ace up to Jack.

Cards

Two standard packs of 52 cards, shuffled together, are used, from which are removed the eight Queens, leaving a pack of 96 cards.

Preparation

The eight Queens are placed in a row across the top of the tableau.

Play

One King (of any suit) is taken from the pack and placed below the left-hand Queen, with enough space between them to place another card; between the two will eventually be placed an Ace, which will begin a foundation row.

The cards are shuffled, and onto the first King is dealt a column of overlapping cards, face up, until another King appears, which is placed beside the first one to head a new column. The Aces, as soon as they appear, are played immediately to a foundation row between the Kings and the row of Queens.

Once an Ace has been built to the foundation row, a 2 of any suit can be built on it as soon as one appears in the deal, followed by a 3 when one appears, and so on, so the building is actually in progress while the deal continues.

When the cards being added to the second King to form a column arrive at a third King, then a third column is begun, and so on.

When the deal is complete, there will be a row of eight Queens at the top of the tableau, a row of eight Aces below, many of them already built on to varying levels, and a row of eight Kings below that, most or all of them with columns of overlapping cards descending from them.

The play then continues with the top cards (ie those at the foot of the columns) available for play to the foundations. When a bare King appears (ie all the cards in its column have been played to foundations) the column is deemed to be vacant, and any available card may be moved there to fill the vacancy (this privilege is open only when the deal is complete, and vacancies are not filled while the deal is in progress).

Vacancies can prove vital as the game progresses, and it is an advantage if at least one can be created during the dealing. This can be done by trying to vary the speed at which the foundations are built during the deal. A good tip is not to build the foundations too high during the deal – not beyond five, say.

Example hand

The hand in the illustration shows the situation of a game immediately after the deal. The ♥6 and ♣6 can be built on the first two foundations, the ♣5 can be built on ♥4, releasing ♥4 to be built on ♥3. The ♣3 can be built to ♦2 and so on. It will be possible to make vacancies on the last two Kings, giving a prospect of getting the game out.

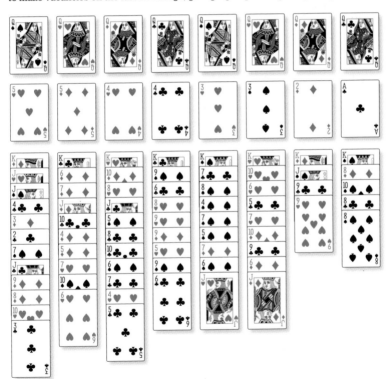

Schafkopf

Schafkopf, which means 'sheepshead', is the ancestor of the national German game of Skat. The game is over 200 years old, being first mentioned in print in 1811. It has spread around the world, and there are many distinct versions of it in different countries. The description here is a basic version for four players still popular in Germany.

Type	Trick-taking
Alternative names	None
Players	Four
Special requirements	Chips or coins for staking; a bowl or similar receptacle

Aim

If playing solo, or on the side holding the 'old women', to win in tricks sufficient point-scoring cards to win the majority of the points (61 or more). If on the other side, to score 60 points.

Cards

The standard pack of 52 cards is used, from which are removed the 6s, 5s, 4s, 3s, and 2s, leaving a pack of 32 cards.

All Queens and Jacks are trumps, as are diamonds, although in some circumstances the trump suit of diamonds can be changed for another. The trump suit ranks ♣Q, ♠Q, ♥Q, ♦Q, ♣J, ♠J, ♥J, ♦J, A, 10, K, 9, 8, 7. The two black Queens, as the top trumps, are known as the 'old women' (*die Alten*).

In the plain suits the cards rank A, 10, K, 9, 8, 7.

Preparation

The dealer is decided by any acceptable method, such as any player picking up the cards, shuffling and beginning to deal cards one at a time to each player round the table until a Jack appears. The player dealt the Jack becomes the first dealer.

The dealer shuffles, the player to his right cuts, and the dealer deals eight cards to each player in two bundles of four, clockwise beginning with the 'eldest hand' (the player to his left).

The game is usually played for stakes, and a pool is formed. A convenient number of chips or counters for each player to contribute to a pool is 50, making a pool of 200.

Play

Each player plays for himself, but in each hand there are likely to be temporary partners, as the two players dealt the old women (♣Q and ♠Q) play as partners against the other two. They do not identify themselves, so no player knows who his partner is until it becomes clear during the play.

A player dealt both old women has the choice of playing solo or calling for a partner. His options are:

i) To call for a partner by naming any card he does not hold. The player who holds the card becomes the partner but does not identify himself.

ii) To play solo in secret. His opponents will not know he is playing solo.

iii) To declare before play starts that he is playing solo. This gives him the opportunity to change the trump suit from diamonds to whatever he wishes. He must, of course, announce the trump suit when making his declaration. The Queens and Jacks remain trumps in their usual order, but are followed as trumps by A, 10, K, 9, 8, 7 of the named suit.

A player dealt only one of the old women also has the chance of playing solo. He has two options if he wants to play solo:

i) To play solo in secret. As soon as the other black Queen is played, he must declare he is playing solo, so that the holder of the other black Queen knows he is an opponent of the declarer and not his partner.

i) To declare he is playing solo before play starts, which gives him the opportunity to change the trump suit as described above.

It is necessary to hold a black Queen to play solo. A player playing solo against the other three players must still score 61 or more points to win.

Players examine their hands, during which time a player wishing to declare solo must do so. The 'eldest hand' (the player to the dealer's left) then leads to the first trick; see p383 for an explanation of tricks and trick-taking. Normal trick-taking rules apply, ie players must follow suit to the card led if they can (bearing in mind that all Queens and Jacks are trumps and not therefore part of a plain suit), and if they cannot they may trump or discard. When a trump is led, all players must follow with a trump if they can. A trick is won by the highest trump it contains if any, and if not by the highest card in the suit led. The winner of a trick leads to the next.

Scoring Some cards have a value when captured in tricks, as follows:

Ace	11 points	King	4 points
10	10 points	Queen	3 points
	Jack	2 points	

The other cards have no scoring value. Hence, there are 120 points in the whole pack to be won.

If the players holding the old women win (ie score 61 or more points), they each take chips from the pool as follows:

61–89 points	5 chips
90–120 points (known as *schneider*)	10 chips
winning all ten tricks (known as *schwarz*)	15 chips

If the players holding the old women lose (ie fail to score 61 or more points), their opponents take from the pool as follows:

60–89 points	10 chips
90+ points (*schneider*)	20 chips

When players go solo, they settle individually without recourse to the pool. A soloist who wins receives five chips from each opponent for 61–89 points, ten chips from each for schneider and 15 for schwarz. If he loses, he pays double these amounts.

Example hand

The hands are dealt as shown, using the Bridge convention of calling players North, South, East and West. West is the dealer.

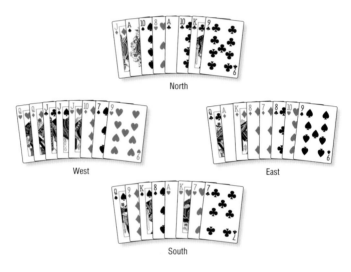

North

West

East

South

Neither East nor South, the holders of the old women, have a hand with which they could possibly go solo. North, who has the opening lead, decides that as he is strong in the black plain suits, he will lead a trump in the hope of clearing enough trumps to make some plain suit winners, a policy which could go wrong. Play proceeds:

	North	East	South	West
1	♦ J	♦ A	<u>♠ Q</u>	♥ J

East, presuming North did not hold ♠ Q, played ♦ A to allow his partner, whoever it might be, to win it with ♠ Q. He would prefer the holder of the ♠ Q to be West, because West could win the trick, containing 13 points already, with as small a trump as necessary. However, it is South who holds ♠ Q, and he can see little choice but to win the trick. West played his lowest valued trump on it. South is now stuck for a lead. He tries ♥A, hoping all will follow suit and so collect eleven points for it. It does well as East puts ♥10 on it. All now know that East and South are partners, and already have 39 points, but things go wrong for East and South from trick 3, when South, rather than lead his only trump, leads his bare club:

2	♥8	♥10	♥A	♥9
3	♣A	♣8	♣7	♠7
4	♠A	♠9	♠8	♦10

From trick 4, West holds nothing but trumps. He knows the only trick he can now lose is to East's ♣Q. East does as well as possible by taking North's ♠10, and hopes that South can play ♣10 upon the same trick, which would win the game for East and South, but unfortunately North holds ♣10.

5	♣9	♦7	♦9	♠J
6	♣K	♦8	♥7	♥Q
7	♠10	♣Q	♥K	♣J
8	♣10	♦K	♠K	♦Q

So East/South scored 58 points, despite holding the old women, and North/West made 62. North and West each take ten chips from the pool.

Scotch Whist

Scotch Whist is a strange game in that it is not Whist, and seems to have nothing to do with Scotland. It was first mentioned in a book published in New York in 1887, and its antecedents are unclear. It is a simple but not unskilful game.

Type	Trick-taking
Alternative names	Catch the Ten
Players	Four, playing in partnerships of two; two to eight for variants
Special requirements	Pen and paper for scoring

Aim

To win tricks containing scoring cards.

Cards

The standard pack of 52 cards is used, from which are removed the 5s, 4s, 3s, and 2s, leaving a short pack of 36 cards.

The cards rank in plain suits in the usual order, from Ace (high) to 6 (low), but in the trump suit the Jack is promoted above the Ace, so that the trump suit ranking is J, A, K, Q, 10, 9, 8, 7, 6.

Preparation

Players draw from a spread pack to determine partners, the drawers of the two highest cards (Ace high) playing as partners against the other two. The highest card drawn indicates the first dealer. Partners sit opposite each other. The deal subsequently passes to the left.

The dealer deals the cards clockwise one at a time, face down, to each player, beginning with the 'eldest hand' (the player to the dealer's left) and continuing until all the cards have been dealt. The last card (the dealer's) is turned face up to indicate the trump card before being taken into the dealer's hand.

Play

The eldest hand leads to the first trick; see p383 for an explanation of tricks and trick-taking. The normal rules of trick-taking apply: players must follow suit to the card led, and if they cannot may trump or discard as they wish. A trick is won by the highest trump it contains, or if there are no trumps by the highest card of the suit led. The winner of a trick leads to the next.

Scoring The scoring cards are the top five trumps and their values are:

Jack	11 points
10	10 points
Ace	4 points
King	3 points
Queen	2 points

The holder of the Jack must win with it, as it is the highest trump, so the main object is to capture the 10, hence the alternative name for this game: Catch the Ten.

The side which captures the scoring cards in the trump suit scores their values as stated. In addition, the side which takes the majority of the tricks scores one point for every card captured over 18 (the number of cards in play being 36).

A running score is kept, and the first side to reach 41 points is the winner.

Example hand

The cards are dealt as shown, using the Bridge convention of calling the players North, South, East and West.

West dealt, so North leads. The last card dealt to the dealer was ♥6, so hearts are trumps. The play proceeds, with North leading his singleton:

	North	East	South	West
1	♣6	♣8	♣A	♣7
2	♥A	♣J	♣9	♣K

	North	East	South	West
3	♦A	♦10	♦6	♦7
4	♠6	♠A	♥J	♠10
5	♠8	♣Q	♣10	♦8
6	♠9	♠7	♦9	♠K
7	♠Q	♥7	♥9	♠J
8	♦K	♥Q	♦J	♥10
9	♥K	♥8	♦Q	♥6

As the cards lay, East/West did very well to make ten points for the ♥10, as North/South held the three top trumps. As it happened, East holding three trumps was crucial.

So North/South won 18 points for Jack, Ace, King of trumps, and East/West twelve for 10, Queen. North/South won the tricks six to three, so scored an extra six points (24 cards minus 18 = six points). After the first hand, North/South lead by 24 points to twelve.

Variants

Two, three, five or seven people may play, with each player playing for himself. Six or eight may play with each playing for himself, or in partnerships of two, with partners sitting opposite each other.

The number of cards in the pack must be adjusted according to the number of players. If five or seven play the ♠6 is removed from the pack, and players receive seven cards each (five players) or five cards each (seven players). If eight play, the four 5s are added to the pack, making a pack of 40 cards, with each player receiving five.

With two, three or six players, the 36-card pack is used as in the basic game. With six players, each player receives six cards. If two or three play, the arrangement is slightly different. With two players, each player is dealt six cards face down one at a time, to form one hand, then six more one at a time to form a separate hand, then six more to form a third hand. The last card of all is turned up to indicate the trump suit for all three hands. The three hands are played separately. With three players, each is dealt two separate hands of six cards each.

No matter how many play, or how many hands the players have, the scores for taking the top five trumps in tricks are the same. The points scored for the majority of tricks are calculated by counting one point for each card won in tricks above the number the player (or the partnership) was dealt.

French Whist French Whist (again with no connection to either Whist or France) is played in the same manner as Scotch Whist, with the addition of another value card. Ten points are awarded for winning the ♦10 (if diamonds are trumps the usual rules apply, ie there is not an extra ten points for winning the ♦10, which carries ten points for winning it anyway).

Shithead

The unfortunate name of this game appears to be the one which is most popular in Britain, where it is a favourite among students. Similar games are thought to be common in other parts of the world, possibly with equally pejorative names, since like Old Maid, Pig and President it is a game in which the main object is to find a loser rather than a winner. Typically, the loser has to perform some menial task, like fetching the beer.

Type	Discarding
Alternative names	Karma, Palace
Players	Two to six; four or more is best
Special requirements	None

Aim
To get rid of all your cards, and thus avoid being the 'shithead'.

Cards
The standard pack of 52 cards is used. If six play, two Jokers are also required, since all players start with nine cards.

The cards rank with 2s as high or low, as… 2, A, K, Q, J, 10, 9, 8, 7, 6, 5, 4, 3, 2… Jokers, if used, have special properties which do not involve a rank.

Preparation
Any player may pick up the cards, shuffle and begin to deal cards one at a time to each player round the table until a Jack appears. The player dealt the Jack becomes the first dealer. The deal subsequently passes to the left.

The dealer deals clockwise a row of three cards, face down, to each player. (For convenience, he can deal the cards face down and the players themselves can arrange them in a row of three. They must not look at them.) The dealer then deals three cards to each player face up to cover each of the three face-down cards. These rows of cards remain undisturbed until later in the game (although the face-up cards can be exchanged, as will be seen).

Finally, the dealer deals a further three cards one at a time, face down, to each player. Players pick up this new three-card hand; the row of cards each player has before him on the table is not taken into the hand.

The undealt cards are placed face down in the centre of the table to form a 'stock'.

Play
Before play, any player may exchange any number of the three cards in his hand with the face-up cards in the row before him. Generally speaking, most players exchange cards in their hands with lower cards in the rows, since high cards in the

rows become valuable in the later stages of the game.

If any player was dealt a 3 among his face-up cards, that person becomes the first player to lead a card. If more than one 3 is exposed, the player nearest to the dealer's left who holds a 3 plays the first card. If no 3s are exposed, a player who can claim a 3 in his hand leads first (again, precedence is given to the player nearest the dealer's left). Failing that, a player who can claim a 4 leads, and so on. It is not obligatory for a player to lead the card which earned the lead.

The first player may play a single card or any number of cards of the same rank to the table to begin a discard pile. Having done so, he must draw the same number of cards from the stock to bring his hand back to three cards. The next player must play a card or cards of equal or higher rank then the previous player, and so on.

The game continues until a player cannot (or chooses not to) play a card equal or higher than the previous card or cards. Then he must take all the cards from the discard pile into his hand. The player to his left then plays a card or cards to the table to begin a new discard pile.

Some cards or groups of cards have special properties, as follows:

i)   The 2, being high or low, can be played on any card or cards (being high) and can also have any card or cards played on it (being low). While 2s are played, sequences can therefore be continuous and can build up to quite a number of cards.

ii)   The Jokers, if used (as they have to be with six players), may be played at will, singly or together, and have the effect of reversing the direction of play. Thus the first Joker played makes the play anti-clockwise, and the player who laid the card previous to the Joker has to play again. He must therefore equal or beat his own card or pick up the pile. Note that Jokers are not wild, and cannot be played together with any other cards.

iii)   If a 10 is played (it must be higher in rank than the previous card), the whole discard pile is removed from play. The player of the 10 then plays another card to start a new discard pile. The 10 can be played to an empty discard pile, whereupon, of course, it is removed from play and its player plays a new card to the discard pile.

iv)   A set of four cards of the same rank on top of the discard pile also causes the whole pile to be removed from the game. The player who played the card or cards which completed the four of a kind (or the player who laid all four) then plays another card or cards to begin a new discard pile.

If a player, having played, has fewer than three cards in his hand, he must draw from the stock sufficient cards to make his hand up to three cards. If the stock does not contain enough cards to enable this, the player takes as many cards as there are.

When the stock has been exhausted, play continues as before except that players cannot replenish their hands. This leads to the end-game.

End-game A player with no cards in his hand, and with none in the stock, may now play from his face-up cards.

A player who begins playing his face-up cards and finds he cannot go (or does not wish to) must take the discard pile into his hand, but before doing so he adds one of his face-up cards to the pile. The next player then begins a new discard pile. A player who begins playing his face-up cards and then picks up the discard pile acquires a hand, of course, and must then play from this hand in the usual manner and can only return to playing his face-up cards when he has played all the cards in his hand again.

A player cannot play from the table while he has cards in his hand.

When the face-up cards have been played, and a player has no cards in his hand, he begins to play his three face-down cards. These are played blindly. When the player's turn comes, he picks up his first face-down card and plays it to the discard pile. If it is a legitimate card (ie equal or higher in rank than the top card of the pile) it remains there and play continues. If, however, it is not a playable card, the player takes the whole discard pile in his hand, including the card he played. The player to his left then plays to begin a new discard pile. The player who picked up the discard pile now has to play from his hand again.

Players will almost certainly find, having got rid of their original hands, that they acquire new hands as they play their table cards, so that the table cards usually disappear in stages, with the player acquiring hands in between.

A player who gets rid of all his table cards as well as all the cards in his hand drops out of the game. The last person who remains in, ie the last person left with any cards, is the loser and, sad to say, is the shithead (or whatever more polite name players may agree beforehand to call him). The pleasure of the game is improved if it is agreed in advance that some task can be given to him, adding more significance to being the shithead than being called rude names. Among his penalties is to deal the next hand.

Example hand
Suppose four players have three-card hands, as shown below, using the Bridge convention of calling players North, South, East and West.

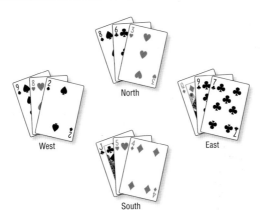

Players have already swapped cards with their face-up table cards. North, who swapped one of his hand cards for the ♥3, is the player who begins. The play proceeds as follows, with the cards in brackets showing the cards drawn from the stock at each play:

North	East	South	West
♥3 (♣K)	♣7 (♥Q)	♣J (♠Q)	♠2 (♥7)
♣6 (♥6)	♣9 (♣2)	♠Q (♦10)	

West now does not have a card in his hand to play, so must pick up the discard pile. North now leads:

♥6 (♠4)	♥Q, ♦Q	
	(♦K, ♦7)	

East plays two Queens together, and draws two cards. Now South must pick up the discard pile and West leads to the next round.

Variants

Dealing   Some players prefer that after the first deal of three face-down cards, the dealer deals each player six cards face down one at a time. The players take these six cards into hand, and choose the three cards which they wish to place face up onto their three face-down cards. This causes no difference to the hand of an individual player because, in the deal as described above, he could choose his three face-up cards and the three in his hand anyway. But it makes the difference that no cards of any player's hand are known to any other players, as they might be in the other method of dealing.

Special cards   Some players allow a 10 to be played at any time, and not only when it can be played legitimately (ie by being equal or higher in rank than the card at the top of the discard pile). A 10 has the same quality of removing the discard pile from play. When this convention is played, an 8 also has a special quality. It, like a 10, can also be played on any card at any time, and it has the effect of reversing the order of play. The next player (who with the reversal is the player who played the card below the 8) must now beat that card. In other words the 8 is disregarded and the discard pile is deemed to be headed by the card below it. If the 8 is played to an empty discard pile, it reverses the direction of play as usual, and any card can be played, as the discard pile is regarded as empty (ie the 8 is disregarded as usual).

When the 8 has this special quality, the 7 also becomes a special card. When a 7 is played, the next card played must be equal to or lower than 7. But once that card is played, the normal course of having to play equal to or higher than the previous card is resumed. An 8 or a 10 can be played on a 7, as these cards can be played at any time. If an 8 is played on a 7, then the player who played the 7 becomes the next player and must play a card equal to or lower than a 7.

Sir Tommy

One of Sir Tommy's alternative names is Old Patience, and this game has certainly been around for a long time. It is the simplest of games, and requires no elaborate preparations: one just picks up the cards and starts.

Type	Patience
Alternative names	Old Patience, Try Again
Players	One
Special requirements	None

Aim
To end with four piles of cards in ascending sequence from Ace to King, irrespective of suit or colour.

Cards
The standard pack of 52 cards is used, the cards ranking from King (high) to Ace (low).

Preparation
The cards are shuffled and taken face down into the hand.

Play
Cards are turned over one at a time and played to the table.

The cards are played face up to four waste piles until an Ace appears, when it is played to a foundation row above the waste piles. The cards at the top of each waste pile are available for play. Once an Ace is played to a foundation, any available 2, of any colour or suit, can be played to it, and then any available 3 and so on up to King. Each Ace, as it appears, is played to a foundation and built upon.

Once played to a waste pile a card cannot be moved until it is built on a foundation. The cards in the waste piles can be overlapping, so that the player can see what cards each pile contains. There is no packing from one waste pile to another.

The game is won when all four foundations are built up to Kings. It is unsuccessful if all the cards have been played to the four waste piles and none of the cards available at the top of the waste piles can be built to foundations.

Strategy It is a good idea, if possible, to keep one waste pile for high-ranking cards like Kings. It is best if cards played to a waste pile can be placed on a higher-ranking card rather than a lower-ranking card, but this, of course, is not always possible. Cards of the same rank should be kept in different waste piles, if possible.

This patience succeeds once in about every five attempts, and needs the Aces to appear fairly early on. It can be very infuriating when waste piles get large and unmanageable while the Aces refuse to appear. However, if the game fails it takes only seconds to collect the cards, shuffle them, and, as one of its alternative names suggests, Try Again.

Example game

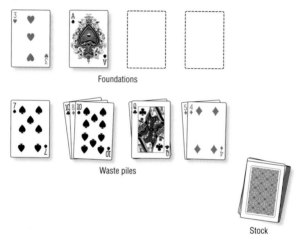

Foundations

Waste piles

Stock

The illustration shows a game in progress.

Skat

Skat developed from the ancient game of Schafkopf, to which players at the Tarock club in Altenburg between 1810 and 1820 added elements of other games to invent Skat. It became immensely popular throughout Germany and its neighbours and, although played differently, has big followings in the USA and Australia. It is a very complex game and is difficult to learn, but there are few more skilful. It has no social barriers (unlike, perhaps, Bridge), and is Germany's national card game. It is mentioned frequently in the novel *The Tin Drum* by Nobel prize-winner Günter Grass. The game described here is a modern German version.

Type	Trick-taking
Alternative names	None
Players	Three; four for variants
Special requirements	Pen and paper for scoring

Aim
The object of the 'declarer' is to win 61 card points (the majority of the points available) by capturing cards in tricks. The declarer's opponents, the 'defenders', need 60 to beat him.

Cards
The standard pack of 52 cards is used, from which are removed the 6s, 5s, 4s, 3s and 2s to leave a short pack of 32 cards.

The four Jacks are always part of the trump suit, and in fact are the four top trumps, ranking in the order clubs (high), spades, hearts, diamonds (low). Among the other ranks, 10 ranks between Ace and King. This means the ranking of the trump suit is ♣ J, ♠ J, ♥ J, ♦ J, A, 10, K, Q, 9, 8, 7. The trump suit therefore contains eleven cards.

In the other three suits the ranking is A, 10, K, Q, 9, 8, 7. Plain suits therefore contain seven cards each.

There is a 'contract' (see Bidding, below) called 'grand' in which the four Jacks are the only trumps. In effect this means they form a suit of their own (four cards) while there are four plain suits, each with seven cards.

Each Ace, 10, King, Queen and Jack have point values when won in tricks. These 'card points' are set out below under Scoring.

Preparation
Any player may pick up the cards, shuffle and begin to deal cards one at a time to each player round the table until a Jack appears. The player dealt the Jack becomes the first dealer. The deal subsequently passes to the left.

The dealer shuffles, the player to his right cuts, and the dealer deals three cards face down in a bundle to each player clockwise, then two cards face down to the centre to form the 'skat' (which in other games might be called a 'widow'), then further bundles of four and three to each player. Players therefore receive ten cards each.

The player to the dealer's left is called 'forehand' and the player to the dealer's right is 'middlehand'. The dealer can be called 'rearhand', but we will continue to call him the dealer.

Bidding The players examine their cards. There then follows an 'auction', in which players bid by offering to make a stated number of points. The player who bids the highest becomes the 'declarer', and plays against the other two players combined. He has the advantage of the use of the skat, and of naming the trump suit.

There are two kinds of points in Skat. The 'card points' relate to the values of cards captured in tricks (see Scoring, below); the declarer needs to make at least 61 card points to win. Then there are the points used in bidding, which relate to the value of the game. These determine how much the declarer actually wins or loses for the purposes of settlement or keeping a running score. Hence, the declarer makes 61 card points to win, and the value of the game he wins must be at least equal to the value of the game he contracted to make.

The bids are numbers representing the value of the game the bidder contracts to score if he becomes 'declarer'. If he makes a higher value game he scores what he makes. The contract is always dependent on making 61 card points (or 90 if '*schneider*' is declared, or all ten tricks if 'schwartz' is declared, or none if 'null' is declared; see below).

Before knowing how the bidding is conducted, therefore, it is necessary to know how the value of the game is worked out.

Game value The value of the game is worked out by multiplying two numbers, the 'base value' and the 'multiplier'.

The base value depends upon the trump suit as follows:

Diamonds	nine		Spades	eleven
Hearts	ten		Clubs	twelve
	Grand	twenty		

Grand is the contract in which the four Jacks are the only trumps.

The multiplier depends mostly on the number of top trumps the declarer holds, with several additional factors as follows:

i) If the declarer holds the top trump (♣J), the multiplier is the number of top trumps he holds in sequence from the ♣J down. For example if he held the top three Jacks (♣J, ♠J, ♥J) the multiplier is three. This is called 'with' three.

ii) If the declarer does not hold the top trump, the multiplier is the number of top trumps he is missing. For example, if his top trump is ♥J, he is missing ♣J and ♠J, so the multiplier is two. This is called 'without' two.

Notice that the multiplier for trumps is the same whether the hand is with the top three trumps, say, or without the top three trumps. To this multiplier are added other factors:

i) One is always added to the multiplier for 'game'. This denotes the undertaking made by the bidder to win 61 of the card points.

ii) One is added to the multiplier if the declarer plays 'in hand'. This means he does not look at the skat or take it into his hand (although it still belongs to him and cards in it will count to his card point score).

iii) One is added to the multiplier if the declarer makes schneider, ie 90 or more card points in tricks.

iv) One is added to the multiplier if the declarer announces his intention to make schneider at the beginning of the hand. This is in addition to the one added just for making schneider. The declarer cannot announce his intention to make schneider unless he is playing in hand. If he declares schneider but fails to make the 90 card points, then the multipliers for schneider and schneider declared remain, but the declarer loses.

v) One is added to the multiplier if the declarer makes '*schwartz*', ie makes all the tricks in the trick-taking phase. This is in addition to those added for schneider, and schneider declared.

vi) One is added to the multiplier if the declarer announces his intention to make schwartz. This is in addition to all the others added for schneider and schwartz. As with schneider declared, the declarer can announce the intention to make schwartz only when playing from hand. If he fails to take all the tricks, the multipliers remain but he loses.

If the declarer succeeds in winning 61 points (or 90 if he declarers schneider, or in taking all the tricks if he declares schwartz) he wins the value of the game. If not, he loses what he would have won (if he played in hand) or double what he would have won if he looked at the skat (but see Scoring, below).

Null 'Null' is an additional contract to the normal trump ones. It is a contract to lose all the tricks. Card points do not count with this contract, and if the declarer makes a trick, the play ends. There are no trumps, and the Jacks return to their suits. The 10 loses its ranking below Ace, and the ranking in each suit is as usual: A, K, Q, J, 10, 9, 8, 7.

Null can also be played 'open', ie the declarer lays his cards face up on the table and plays them from there. There are four null contracts, which depend upon whether the declarer plays in hand or with the skat. Their values are:

Null	23 points
Null hand	35 points
Null open	46 points
Null hand open	59 points

If the declarer loses he loses what he would have won if playing in hand, and double if he looked at skat.

Bidding continued Bidding is conducted between two players at a time. Middlehand begins by announcing a figure or passing. Forehand responds by saying 'yes' after each bid if he proposes to bid higher, thus forcing middlehand to raise his bid. Eventually, either forehand or middlehand will say pass, whereupon the dealer, if he wishes, can begin bidding with the survivor of forehand and middlehand saying 'yes', if he wishes. When a second player passes, the player left is the declarer and he must make a game of a value not lower than the last bid.

Each bid made must be higher than the one preceding it and one may bid only numbers which it is possible to score. The lowest possible bid is 18 with diamonds as trumps and holding one of ♣J or ♠J. With ♣J but not ♠J, the game value is 'with one, game two, times nine'. With ♠J but not ♣J, the game value is 'without one, game two, times nine'. In both cases the bid is 18.

Possible game values up to 100 are shown in the table. There are possible bids of 200 or more, but rarely does the bidding exceed 60.

Possible bids up to 100 at Skat

18 ♦2	44 ♠4	70 ♥7
20 ♥2	45 ♦5	72 ♦8; ♣6
22 ♠2	46 null open	77 ♠7
23 null	48 ♣4	80 grand 4; ♥8
24 ♣2	50 ♥5	81 ♦9
27 ♦3	54 ♦6	84 ♣7
30 ♥3	55 ♠5	88 ♠8
33 ♠3	59 null open (hand)	90 ♦10 ♥9
35 null (hand)	60 grand 3; ♥6; ♣5	96 ♣8
36 ♦4; ♣3	63 ♦7	99 ♦11 ♠9
40 grand 2; ♥4	66 ♠6	100 grand 5; ♥10

Each value shows the suit (or grand or null) plus the number of multipliers.

If all the players pass, the hand is abandoned and the deal passes to the next player.

An auction might proceed as follows, where M is middlehand, F is forehand, and D is dealer:

M: 18	F: yes	M: 27	F: pass
M: 20	F: yes	D: 30	M: yes
M: 22	F: yes	D: 33	M: pass

Dealer becomes the declarer and must make a game of 33 points or more.

Play

The declarer plays against the other two players. The skat belongs to the declarer. Usually he takes it into his hand and discards two cards before the play begins, but he may not. He may discard any card he picked up. He then announces the trump suit (or grand, or null).

If he doesn't wish to use the skat, he puts it to one side (without looking at it) and announces trump, grand or null, in hand and, if applicable, 'schneider declared', 'schwartz declared', or 'null open'.

Forehand always leads to the first trick; see p383 for an explanation of tricks and trick-taking. The normal trick-taking rules apply: players must follow suit to the card led if able, and otherwise may trump or discard. A trick is won by the highest trump it contains or, lacking a trump, by the highest card of the suit led. It must be remembered that all Jacks are part of the trump suit, and not of the suit to which they would normally belong, for example if a spade is led, the holder of ♠J cannot play it if he holds another spade, because to do so would be to trump illegally. The winner of the trick leads to the next. Players keep their cards won in tricks face down before them, with the defenders keeping theirs together.

Scoring At the end of the trick-taking, the declarer takes the two cards of the skat (or if he took the skat into his hand, the discards) and adds those to his hand, adding the count of any counting cards to his total (sometimes a declarer will deliberately discard a 10, say, to make sure it counts for him and that he cannot lose it in a trick).

The 9s, 8s and 7s have no value. The other cards, when taken in tricks, have a point value as follows:

Each Ace	11 points
Each 10	10 points
Each King	4 points
Each Queen	3 points
Each Jack	2 points

This makes a total of 120 points in the pack to be won on each hand.

At the end of the hand, the declarer announces the score, and what he claims to have won or lost. For example:

i) Suppose the declarer plays with spades as trumps (base value eleven), holding the two top trumps (♣J, ♠J) and makes 67 card points. He announces 'with two, game three, times eleven, makes 33'.

ii) Suppose the declarer, in the same contract, had made only 57 card points (and lost). He announces, 'with two, game three, off six, times eleven, loses 66'. He has added 'off six'. 'Off' means he failed to get the necessary 61 points, which requires the multiplier of three to be doubled to six before it is multiplied with the base value of eleven (for spades being trumps).

iii) Suppose the declarer plays in hand with hearts as trumps and holding the top three trumps (♣J, ♠J, ♥J) and declares schneider. He gets only 87 card points (and loses). He announces, 'with three, game four, in hand five, schneider six, declared seven, times ten, loses 70'. Because he played in hand, the multiplier wasn't doubled.

For the declarer to win, he must not only get 61 in the card count (or 90 if he declared schneider) or all ten tricks if he declared schwartz or none at all if he declared null, but the value of the game he made must not be lower than his successful bid. It can happen, that either by accident or bad luck, a player can overbid.

Suppose a declarer bids 48. Spades are trumps, he is without three, plus game four, plus hand five, times eleven equals 55. He scores 72 card points. However, when he looks at skat after playing the hand, he finds it contains ♠J. So the game he won is not without three, but without one. The value of the game is reduced to 33. He has not made the value of his bid so loses. He loses the next multiple of his trump suit's base value above the value of his bid. Spades base value is eleven, the next multiple of which above his bid of 48 is 55, so he loses 55 points. Sometimes a declarer may look at skat, which perhaps he hoped to find useful, but finds that it is actually harmful, and that he has no chance of making his contract. In this case, he is entitled to concede. He must name a contract of the value or above of his bid, so that his loss can be worked out by using the method above, it costing him, if he named a trump suit, the nearest multiple of the base value of that suit above his bid.

In the majority of places where skat is played, it is played for small stakes, and settlement is made at the end of each hand. The declarer collects the value of the game from each opponent if he wins, and pays to each opponent if he loses according to the principles stated above.

If the game is played over a series of hands for recreation only, then the game can be scored on a piece of paper, merely by crediting each player with the number of points they won on each hand. It is not necessary to bother with debit totals. If Player A, for instance, wins a game valued at 48, he scores 48. If he loses a game value 48, and has to pay each opponent 96, they score 96 each.

Strategy

Bidding a suit
Jacks and Aces are the important cards, and they constitute one quarter of the pack, so the average hand will contain 1.3 each of them. So to hold three such is to hold only just more than the average. Aces and 10s are the important cards for scoring card points, but plain suits contain only seven cards each, so while the chances are that an Ace led will win a trick, a 10 on the second trick is quite likely to be trumped. A bid in a suit should ideally be backed by at least five trumps and an Ace or Ace, 10 bare in a plain suit. If a declarer's Ace is backed by three or four smaller cards in the suit, it is quite likely that his Ace will be trumped.

Bidding grand
Normally five Jacks and Aces are needed to bid grand, although four might be sufficient for forehand, who has the lead.

Bidding null
Plenty of 7s, voids, or runs of low cards to protect high cards are necessary to bid null. A singleton above the rank of 9 is dangerous, as is a suit of two or three high cards not backed by low ones, or a long suit of four cards or so missing the 7, since one round of the suit might find one defender void and the other just waiting to get the lead so as to lead the 7 and force one to lose.

Going in hand

One should be pretty confident when playing in hand, since sacrificing the extra multiplier can sometimes ward off disaster or lead to a better contract anyway. If the skat supplies a card which makes the difference between scoring schneider or not, then the multiplier for schneider will cancel out the one lost for not playing in hand. Also the skat might contain a Jack or Ace which might make a contract of Grand feasible, which with its base value of 20 will wipe out several times the loss of the multiplier for playing in hand. Also, taking the skat avoids the shock of discovering a Jack in it which devalues the game value of the contract as has been seen above. Taking the skat also allows the placing in it of a bare 10, say, for which the declarer will get ten card points he might have lost otherwise. The skat could make a likely game into a certain one.

Discarding

When taking the skat and discarding, the declarer should try to create a void suit. By this means he could pick up with a trump an Ace or 10 or both. One low card in a suit will make it unlikely that he will capture the Ace and 10 in that suit by trumping.

Choosing trumps

If, after looking at skat, the declarer finds that he has two long suits, it is better to choose the longer as trumps, even if it is the weaker. By forcing out trumps, he can make scoring cards in his plain suits.

Counting

As in all trick-taking games, keeping a check on the number of trumps played can be vital. The declarer, particularly if he has looked at skat, should know at every stage how many trumps his opponents hold between them.

Example hand

Suppose the cards are dealt as shown.

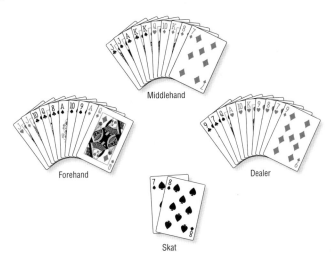

Middlehand

Forehand

Dealer

Skat

With two Jacks and two Aces, and the lead, forehand can see prospects in bidding spades and would be happy to bid 33 (spades without two) with the hope of being able to improve with the skat. Middlehand could play diamonds as trumps (with two), but this is worth only 27 points. The dealer has a hand suitable for null if it were not for the bare ♠Q. Could he swap that for a low card in any suit he could bid up to 35 (his hearts are safe) and even 46 for null.

The bidding goes:

M: 18	F: yes
M: 20	F: yes
M: 22	F: yes
M: 23	F: yes
M: 27	F: yes
M: 33	F: yes
M: 35	F: pass
D: pass	

Middlehand has bid to 35, which was his limit, as it is equivalent to diamonds with three, which looks reckless. Forehand was not going to go past 33, which was his maximum (spades without two). A bid of 35 being equal to the game value for null, the dealer did not go beyond, although could he have known what was in the skat, he would have done so (and even made null open). Thus middlehand is declarer, and needing the extra multiplier to make a game of 35 points, declares 'diamonds, hand'.

Forehand leads, and the play progresses:

	Forehand	Middlehand	Dealer	Running score
1	♠A	♠K	♠Q	M: 0 F/D: 18
2	♠10	♦K	♦9	M: 14 F/D: 18

Middlehand did not risk ♦10 on this trick, as he could guess from forehand's bidding that the dealer could be void in spades, and feared his ♦10 could be overtrumped. The dealer decided to undertrump since it frees him to play his valuable ♥A, 10 on trump tricks to be won by his partner.

3	♦Q	♦7	♥A	M: 14 F/D: 32

Middlehand led ♦7 to see what would happen, and the dealer's play worked perfectly as he was able to give ♥A to his partner, who played ♦Q rather than ♦A (scoring three points for it instead of eleven if he'd played Ace, as he expects to win a later trick with ♦A). Forehand, however, lacks a good lead at this point and leads ♠9 in the hope that middlehand will waste a trump on it. But middlehand discards ♥Q instead, which at least allows the dealer to give his partner ♥10.

4	♠9	♥Q	♥10	M: 14 F/D: 45
5	♣8	♣K	♣7	M: 18 F/D: 45

Middlehand played ♣K instead of Ace on trick 5 because, if the Dealer had won with 10, it would give his opponents 59 points and Middlehand could still win if there were a trump in skat.

He can still win if there is a trump in skat, because he could draw the two still out against him and make the remaining tricks. His other hope is that if he has to lose a trump trick, then the dealer will be able to park upon it nothing higher than a Queen, which would leave the defenders on a very satisfactory total (for middlehand) of 59 card points. So he leads ♣J.

6	♦ J	♣J	♣9	M: 22 F/D: 45
7	♥ J	♠J	♥7	M: 26 F/D: 45
8	♦ A	♦8	♥K	M: 26 F/D: 60

Unluckily for middlehand, the dealer not only has ♥K but the realization that playing it is his side's best chance of defeating declarer and middlehand has to suffer the pain of his opponents' celebratory whoops of joy. He lays down his final two cards claiming 60.

As is customary in Skat, the players recount to confirm that middlehand has lost by the narrowest margin. Middlehand has to recount: 'with two, game three, hand four, times nine, loses 36'. He pays 36 to each opponent.

Variants

Although rules for Skat have been formalized and revised (the earliest date back to 1886), it is a game more like Rummy than Bridge in that it is played in bars, clubs, trains and anywhere else where enthusiasts might gather, and there will be variants to the rules everywhere.

It is worth mentioning that, although strictly a three-handed game, it is a game popular for four players. One player sits out in turn, but deals the hand. The other three players are then forehand, middlehand and rearhand. It is a good social arrangement as befits the nature of the game, as with four it is continuous, with there being always regular intervals for a player to attend to other things.

Slap-Jack

Slap-Jack is a hurly-burly party game for children, which is best played when there is a firm adult overseeing to prevent violence and tears. It is a game which should be played with one of those old packs consisting of 51 dog-eared cards, the other one having mysteriously disappeared many years ago, and which its owners cling onto in case the card should mysteriously appear again from under the settee: the sort of pack to be found in half the homes in the land.

Type	Children's
Alternative names	None
Players	Any reasonable number
Special requirements	A table around which the players can gather and be in reach of the centre

Aim
To collect all the cards by touching the Jacks every time they appear.

Cards
The standard pack of 52 cards is used.

Preparation
Any player can pick up the cards and start dealing them, face down, one at a time to all players. Some will get more than others but it doesn't matter. All players arrange their cards in a face-down pile in front of them. They must not look at their cards.

Play
Beginning with the 'eldest hand' (the player to the dealer's left), each player picks up the top card of his pile and plays it face up to a discard pile in the centre of the table. The player must not show the value of the card as he is playing it, but just turn it over as it is placed on top of the pile.

The other players must watch out for a Jack to be played. When a Jack is played, the first player to slap his hand on the pile wins all the cards in the pile. The player who lays the Jack can win the pile, but must take his hand away before he slaps the Jack. He cannot lay the Jack and slap it all in one movement.

This is where the adult referee comes in, because there will be disputes to sort out. It is a good idea to tell the players that when they slap the Jack they should leave their hand there. It makes it easier to decide whose hand is at the bottom.

If a player slaps a card which is not a Jack, that player must give the top card from his pile to the player who laid the card.

When a player wins the pile, he turns it over and adds it to his current pile, then shuffles the pile and sets it down before him ready to continue to play. The player to his left begins a new pile by turning over his top card and laying it on the table.

A player who loses all his cards has one more chance. He is out of the game unless he can slap the next Jack which appears after he lost his cards. If he manages to do this he picks up the pile and is in the game again, but if not he is out.

Eventually the players will be reduced to two, and the one who still has cards when the other player has laid all his is the winner.

Slippery Sam

Slippery Sam is a very simple gambling game which is almost the same game as Red Dog. It favours the players against the bank, so to be fair all players must hold the bank an equal number of times.

Type	Gambling
Alternative names	Shoot
Players	Three to ten; five or six is best
Special requirements	Chips or coins for staking

Aim
To hold a card of the same suit but higher rank than the banker's card, and to win by betting accordingly.

Cards
The standard pack of 52 cards is used, the cards ranking from Ace (high) to 2 (low).

Preparation
Any player may pick up the cards, shuffle and begin to deal cards one at a time to each player round the table until a Jack appears. The player dealt the Jack becomes the first dealer, and consequently the banker. The deal subsequently passes to the left.

The banker must put chips into a pool to a fixed amount, to be agreed beforehand. He shuffles the cards and the player to his right cuts. Starting with the player to his left, he then deals the cards face down, one at a time, clockwise to all players, until each player has three cards. He then places the remainder of the pack face down in front of him to form the 'stock'.

Since Slippery Sam is a banking game, it must be agreed beforehand that each player will hold the bank for an agreed number of hands (three is suggested), after which time he may withdraw any chips remaining in the bank. A minimum stake should also be agreed.

Play

The banker deals with each player in turn, beginning with the player to his left. After studying his cards, this player must bet an amount, between the minimum agreed stake and the whole of the bank, that he has a card in his hand of the same suit but a higher rank than the card on top of the stock. He advances his stake halfway towards the bank in the centre and announces its amount.

The banker then exposes the top card of the stock. If the player has in his hand a higher card in that suit, he shows it and withdraws his stake plus an equal amount from the bank. If the player cannot beat the exposed card, he puts his stake into the bank. In either case, the banker takes the four cards (the hand and the exposed card from stock), and keeps them in a face-down waste pile beside him. No player may look at the cards in this pile.

If anything in the bank remains, the banker deals with the next player in turn in the same manner. No player may look at his cards until it is his turn to bet.

It is customary for a player who wishes to bet the whole amount of the bank on his hand to say 'shoot'. If he wins he takes the whole bank, and the player to the banker's left becomes the new banker and must put up the agreed amount to the new bank.

A banker holds the bank for the agreed number of rounds, but because the odds are stacked in favour of the player, it is unlikely that the bank will survive for the full number of rounds (for example, three). If it does, the banker withdraws any chips or currency remaining and the next player becomes banker.

Between each round the cards, including the discards, are shuffled and cut again.

Strategy As with Red Dog, it is easy to calculate the chances of any hand winning. The highest card in each suit is deducted from 14 (Aces count 14, Kings 13, Queens 12 and Jacks 11, and other cards at their face value). The totals are added and 13 is added for each void suit. The overall total is the number of cards in the stock (or dealt elsewhere) that will beat the hand. As there are 49 unknown cards, the number subtracted from 49 will give the number of cards that will not beat the hand. The illustration shows how it works.

Hand A

Hand B

Hand A has no cards that will beat it in spades, one in diamonds, four in clubs and thirteen in hearts. This makes 18 cards to beat it and 31 which will lose, or odds on winning of approximately 5–3. Hand B's figures are 43–6 or approximately 7–1 against winning. As a player with a better than even chance of beating the up-turned card from the stock will usually shoot (and win), the banker's best policy is to regard the money he puts into the bank as lost (or to regard it as a bonus if he takes some of his bank back) and to rely on winning when it is his turn to be a player.

Snap

Snap is possibly the best-known of all children's card games. Commercial manufacturers have frequently dressed it up and published special cards for it, but it can be played as well, if not better, with ordinary playing cards. It is a simple children's game testing awareness and speed of reaction.

Type	Children's
Alternative names	None
Players	Any reasonable number; two to six is best
Special requirements	None

Aim
To win all the cards in the pack.

Cards
The standard pack of 52 cards is used, but as it is likely to get some hard treatment, it is best played with an old pack, and it doesn't matter if a card or two is missing.

Preparation
Anybody may deal, as there is no advantage in it. The cards are dealt round face down in a clockwise direction, one at a time, to all players until the pack is exhausted. It does not matter that some players have more cards than others.

Play
Players do not look at their cards, but square them up into a pile which each places face down on the table before him. The player to the left of the dealer begins the play by turning over the top card of his pile and placing it face up on the table beside his pile. The next player does the same and so on. As the play goes round and round the table, players on their turn take the top card from their face-down pack and turn it over onto what builds up into a face-up pile. Note that a player cannot win his own face-up pile by turning over a card which matches the top card of his own pile, since the turned-over card must go on top of the face-up pile and thus cover up the previous top card. Piles can only be won in pairs.

Every so often a player will turn a card onto his face-up pile which matches in rank the card on another player's face-up pile. When this happens any player may shout 'snap'. The first to do so wins all the cards in both piles and puts them face-down underneath his own face-down pile.

After a successful call of 'snap', the player sitting to the left of the last player to turn over a card starts the game again by turning his next face-down card over to his face-up pile, and so on.

A player who has turned over all his face-down pile is not quite out of the game.

While he has his face-up pile in front of him he can still call 'snap' and win himself another face-down pile. But if he loses his face-up pile, having already lost the face-down one, he must leave the game and await the next one.

If a player calls 'snap' when there are no cards on top of the face-up piles which match, that player must give a face-down card from his pile to each of the other players, beginning with the player to his left (in case there are not enough cards to go all the way round).

A game is hardly ever completed without a dispute about who called 'snap' first, so it is a good idea if there is an adult referee around to settle matters. Also, the referee should not allow players to turn over their cards in such a way that they get a good look at the card being turned over before the other players do.

The last player to have any cards left, and who therefore holds all the cards, is the winner.

Variants

Some players play that all players turn their cards over onto a single central pile and 'snap' is called only when the two top cards are equal in rank. This is fine if there are only two or three players, but otherwise it gets a bit unruly.

Another variant is to allow a player whose face-down pile gets exhausted to turn his face-up pile over and resume, but this gets a little silly when there are only a few cards in the face-up pile and at every few turns the pile gets turned over.

Snip-Snap-Snorem

Snip-Snap-Snorem, like other games now regarded as children's games, possibly arose from a simple gambling game. It can still be played for counters, if one wishes. It is a very old game with a possible reference to it dating back to the 18th century.

Type	Children's
Alternative names	Earl of Coventry
Players	Three or more
Special requirements	None

Aim
To get rid of all your cards.

Cards
The standard pack of 52 cards is used.

Preparation
Any player may pick up the cards, shuffle and begin to deal cards one at a time to each player round the table until a Jack appears. The player dealt the Jack becomes the first dealer. The deal subsequently passes to the left.

The dealer deals the cards clockwise one at a time, face down, until the pack is exhausted. It does not matter if some players receive a card more than others.

Play
Players pick up their cards and examine their hands. The 'eldest hand' (the player to the dealer's left) begins play by leading any card he wishes face up to the table and announcing its rank. The player to his left must play to the table a card of equal rank, if able; if he cannot, he must pass. He cannot hold back a card if able to play.

The turn goes round the table clockwise until a player can play a second card of the rank led. As he plays it to the table, he says 'snip'. The turn passes until a third card of the rank is played, the player of it saying 'snap'. The turn passes until the fourth card of the rank is played with the announcement 'snorem'.

The player of 'snorem' picks up the four cards and discards them to one side face down. He then leads the first card of a new round by laying any card he likes and announcing its rank, and so on.

The player who first gets rid of all his cards is the winner.

Variants
In the game described above, a player with two or more cards of the same rank plays them separately. Some players prefer that they are played at once, so that a

player might, for example, play 'snip' and 'snap' together. This seems, however, to detract from the ceremonial nature of the game.

Earl of Coventry Earl of Coventry is exactly the same game as that described above, except for the announcements with the playing of the cards. Suppose the first card led is a 10. Its player says 'There's as good as 10 can be'. The player of the second card says 'There's a 10 as good as he'. The third player says 'There's the best of all the three' and the fourth says 'and there's the Earl of Coventry'.

Playing for counters When playing for counters (or coins), each player starts with a certain number of counters, say 20. A player who cannot go on his turn passes a counter to the last player who played a card. At the end of the game the player with most counters is the winner.

Alternatively, each player who announces 'snorem' collects a counter from each other player. Of course, players who can play a card must do so – it is illegal to pass while holding up a card for 'snorem'.

Solo Whist

Solo Whist came to Britain in the 19th century, and seems to have more roots in Ombre than Whist itself, with which it developed a rivalry in the late 19th century until Bridge submerged both. Solo, as it is usually called, still flourishes as a game in pubs, canteens, railway carriages and family social evenings, being one of those widely played games where local rules apply. It is usually played for small stakes.

Type	Trick-taking
Alternative names	None
Players	Four
Special requirements	Chips or coins for staking, or pen and paper for scoring

Aim

To win the contract through bidding and thereafter to make the number of tricks required by the contract. Otherwise, as a defender, to defeat the soloist's contract.

Cards

The standard pack of 52 cards is used, the cards ranking from Ace (high) to 2 (low).

Preparation

Players draw cards from a spread pack to determine the first dealer. The drawer of the highest card deals. The deal subsequently passes to the left.

The cards are shuffled by the dealer before the first deal and cut by the player to his right. After the first deal, however, the cards are not shuffled, merely collected up and the pack cut. The dealer deals the cards in four bundles of three cards to each player, the last four cards being dealt singly. The last one of all (the dealer's) is turned face up to indicate the trump suit (it might be changed later).

Bidding Beginning with the 'eldest hand' (the player to the dealer's left), each player may make a bid or pass. Each bid must be higher than a previous bid, except when accepting a proposal (see below). A player may not bid after he has passed, with the exception of the eldest hand, who may accept a proposal. The bidding ends after three consecutive passes, with the last bidder becoming the soloist. The possible bids, in ascending order, are:

Proposal   A player who states 'I propose' is asking for a partner with whom he can make eight tricks playing against the other two players, with the turn-up as trumps. Unless there is an intervening bid, any player can accept the proposal by saying 'I accept'. In practice, the popular terms usually used for 'I propose' and 'I accept' are 'prop' and 'cop'. If no other player makes a bid, the two players become 'joint soloists'. They do not change seats to sit opposite each other. If the eldest hand has passed, and another player proposes, the eldest hand is not barred, because he passed, from accepting the proposal. The eldest hand has another privilege. If he proposes, and all others pass, he may upgrade his bid to one of solo, if he wishes.

Solo   An undertaking to make five tricks with the turn-up suit as trumps.

Misère   An undertaking to lose all the tricks. This contract is played without a trump suit. The popular term is 'mis'.

Abundance   An undertaking to win nine tricks with the declarer naming the trump suit.

Royal   An undertaking to win nine tricks with the turn-up suit as trumps.
abundance   This bid is not necessary (just abundance would suffice) unless a previous bidder has bid abundance. A bid of royal abundance takes precedence, although the rewards are the same.

Misère ouvert   An undertaking not to win any tricks, with the hand exposed on the
(open misère)   table for opponents to see after the first trick has been played. The contract is played with no trumps. Opponents see the exposed hand but are not allowed to discuss ways of defeating it.

Abundance   An undertaking to win all 13 tricks, the declarer naming the trump
declared   suit.

If all players pass, the sorted hands are collected up without them being shuffled. The combined pack is then cut and the next player deals. This is called a 'goulash' deal and leads to freak hands.

Play
If the contract is abundance or abundance declared, the soloist names the trump suit. The eldest hand leads to the first trick, unless the contract is abundance

declared, when the soloist leads. If the contract is misère ouvert, the soloist lays his cards on the table after the first trick has been played.

The usual rules of trick-taking apply; see p383 for an explanation of tricks and trick-taking. Players must follow suit to the card led if able, and if they cannot may trump or discard. A trick is won by the highest trump it contains, or if it contains none by the highest card in the suit led. The winner of a trick leads to the next.

Settlement is made after each hand, with the soloist, if successful, winning from each opponent according to the following scale:

Proposal and acceptance	2 units	Abundance	4 units
Solo	2 units	Misère ouvert	6 units
Misère	3 units	Abundance declared	8 units

If he fails he pays each player on the same scale.

Note that in proposal and acceptance, each winning partner receives two units from one of the two defenders, so the profit is two units per player. In solo, which apparently has the same tariff, the winner receives six units (two from each opponent) or loses six, so solo has a higher tariff than proposal and acceptance.

Strategy Solo and abundance contracts normally rely on the distribution of the cards – it is difficult to squeeze extra tricks by skill. The most interesting bid is misère, and skill can play a part here. One thing to be avoided is to bid misère with a long suit lacking the 2. Opponents can discover the weakness and discard in that suit until they hold the 2 only, which can defeat the contract.

Example hand

The hands are dealt as shown, using the Bridge convention of calling the players North, South, East and West.

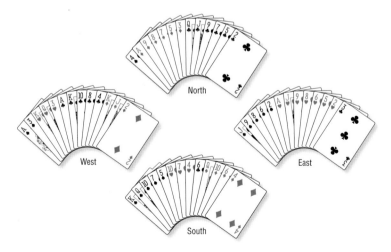

Both North and East's hands would be considered freakish in Bridge, but they are typical of Solo, where the cards are not shuffled between hands. South dealt and the last card he was dealt was ♣6, which makes clubs trumps.

West bids first and bids solo, expecting to make two or three trumps, a spade and one or two tricks in the red suits. North bids misère, which somewhat surprises East, who was going to bid misère himself. East decides not to bid misère ouvert, fearing his spade suit might be vulnerable if his cards were laid down. East and South pass, and North becomes soloist in misère. West decides to lead ♠A, then ♠3 (a ploy which would have sunk East on the third trick had East been allowed to play misère). However, when North played ♠4 (presumably his highest spade) on the Ace, West decided there was no future in spades and decided to repeat his tactics in diamonds. The play went as follows:

	West	North	East	South
1	♠A	♠4	♠J	♠K
2	♦K	♦9	♥J	♦Q
3	♦J	♦8	♥9	♦10
4	♦2	♦3	♥8	♦6
5	♥K			♦4

North was sunk. West and East were out of diamonds, and North was unable to get below South's lead of ♦4. It was excellent play by West. Most Solo players would have called misère with the North or East hands, and would have failed.

Variants

Common variants are:

i) Many players prefer the cards to be dealt in four bundles, of four, three, three and three cards.

ii) Many players ignore the 'prop and cop' bid, on the grounds that it rarely fails and is boring.

iii) Exposing the dealer's last card to indicate the trump suit is not liked by many and should it be an Ace, say, it affects the game too much. The most popular method of avoiding it is to choose trumps by rote: for example hearts, clubs, diamonds, spades. Each player deals the same trumps every deal, so it is an easy system to operate.

iv) When the contract is abundance, many players prefer that the first trick is played with the original suit as trumps, with the soloist naming his trump suit before the second trick. Many soloists in abundance have so many trumps that another player is void. If the player who leads can guess the trump suit and lead it, and another player can trump it with the original trump suit, then the soloist is deprived of a trick. It adds an extra angle to the call of abundance and is recommended.

v) Some players do not like the artificially created freak hands which often result from goulash deals, and prefer a light shuffle.

Auction Solo Auction Solo is played like Solo, but there is a greater variety of bids. This makes the game more interesting, as a drawback of Solo is that there are no positive bids between solo, which is often a laydown, and abundance. Many hands fall between a certain solo and one trick short of abundance.

Auction solo drops the proposal and acceptance bid. Bidders can bid to make any number of tricks over five. Bids to make five to eight tricks are all called solos (solo of five, solo of six etc). In each a player can choose his trump suit, but a bid of a certain number in the designated trump suit ranks higher than a bid of the same number in the bidder's own suit (as royal abundance overcalls abundance in the game described). A player bidding solo of seven in the trump suit of his choice will bid merely 'solo of seven', which could be overcalled by 'solo of seven in trump suit'.

Misère ranks above solo of eight in trump suit and below an abundance of nine.

Contracts of nine to twelve are called abundances, and again abundance in the trump suit overcalls an abundance of the same number in the bidder's own suit.

After abundance of twelve in the trump suit is ranked misère ouvert, and after that comes abundance declared and abundance declared in the trump suit. Only in abundance declared in his own suit does the soloist have the advantage of the lead. In all other contracts the eldest hand leads.

Settlement to be received from each opponent if successful, and to be paid to each if unsuccessful, is as follows:

Solo	2 units, plus one for each overtrick or undertrick
Misère	4 units
Abundance	6 units, plus one for each overtrick or undertrick
Misère ouvert	8 units
Abundance declared	12 units, plus one for each undertrick

The rewards or penalties for solo and abundance contracts do not change with the number of tricks contracted for. Overtricks and undertricks are based on the number of tricks contracted.

A soloist would be advised to get the contract at as low a level as possible, to maximize overtricks or minimize undertricks, but of course bidding six, say, and getting overbid, means then bidding eight to get the contract when it might have been had for seven.

Spade the Gardener

Spade the Gardener is of the family of children's games of which Go Fish is probably the best-known. Happy Families is a commercial game of the same type, with special cards. In fact, Spade the Gardener is almost the same game, but the fun comes with the names the children have to remember for each card. It is best if the children playing are of roughly the same age.

Type	Children's
Alternative names	None
Players	Three to eight; age eight to ten is best
Special requirements	None

Aim
To collect a 'family' of cards, a family being all the cards of a single suit.

Cards
The standard pack of 52 cards is used. For up to five players, the 9s, 8s, 7s, 6s, 5s, 4s, 3s and 2s are removed, leaving a pack of 20 cards. For six players, the 9s are reinstated, while for seven or eight players the 8s are reinstated too. The cards rank from Ace (high) downwards.

Preparation
Any player may pick up the cards, shuffle and begin to deal cards one at a time to each player round the table until a Jack appears. The player dealt the Jack becomes the first dealer. The deal subsequently passes to the left.

Play
The first player to play is the one to the dealer's left, and he may ask any other player by name for a particular card. The only drawback is that he does not ask, for example, for the Queen of Spades, he asks for the family name, which in this case is Samuel Spade the Gardener's Wife. To get the card he must ask for it by the correct name. All the cards have a family name, as set out overleaf.

The Spade Family

| Samuel | His wife | His son | His servant | His dog | His cat | His canary |

The Spade Family

♠ K is Samuel Spade the Gardener

♠ Q is Samuel Spade the Gardener's Wife

♠ J is Samuel Spade the Gardener's Son

♠ A is Samuel Spade the Gardener's Servant

♠ 10 is Samuel Spade the Gardener's Dog

♠ 9 is Samuel Spade the Gardener's Cat

♠ 8 is Samuel Spade the Gardener's Canary

The Heart Family

♥ K is Henry Heart the Butcher

♥ Q is Henry Heart the Butcher's Wife

♥ J is Henry Heart the Butcher's Son

♥ A is Henry Heart the Butcher's Servant

♥ 10 is Henry Heart the Butcher's Dog

♥ 9 is Henry Heart the Butcher's Cat

♥ 8 is Henry Heart the Butcher's Canary

The Diamond Family

♦ K is Dominic Diamond the Jeweller

♦ Q is Dominic Diamond the Jeweller's Wife

♦ J is Dominic Diamond the Jeweller's Son

♦ A is Dominic Diamond the Jeweller's Servant

♦ 10 is Dominic Diamond the Jeweller's Dog

♦ 9 is Dominic Diamond the Jeweller's Cat

♦ 8 is Dominic Diamond the Jeweller's Canary

The Club Family

♣ K is Clarence Club the Policeman

♣ Q is Clarence Club the Policeman's Wife

♣ J is Clarence Club the Policeman's Son

♣ A is Clarence Club the Policeman's Servant

♣ 10 is Clarence Club the Policeman's Dog

♣ 9 is Clarence Club the Policeman's Cat

♣ 8 is Clarence Club the Policeman's Canary

If a player uses the wrong name, for example instead of asking for 'Clarence Club the Policeman's Dog' he says by accident 'Have you got Clarence Club the Butcher's Dog?' or 'Samuel Club the Policeman's Dog', or even 'the ten of clubs', he gets nothing except, perhaps, laughed at. The turn passes to the next player. On the other hand, if he asks correctly for a card, and the player in question has it, then it must be handed to him. A player who receives a card thus may ask the same player, or another player, for a different card and may keep on asking for cards for as long as he gets them. He must name the player he is asking, to avoid confusion. When he meets with a refusal, his turn ends and the next player takes over.

A player can ask for any card, and need not have one of the family in his hand to ask for it. It follows that if a player asks for Samuel Spade the Gardener, and gets it, the next player on his turn can ask him for Samuel Spade the Gardener and he must hand it over again. Therefore it could take a long time for a player to get a whole family together. When he does, he lays them down on the table and continues in the game.

A player who runs out of cards, either because he has laid them down, or has had to give them to other players, or both, drops out of the game (but if he has laid down a family might still be a joint winner, because there are only four families in the whole game). The player who collects most families is the winner.

It can be a very frustrating game for young temperaments, especially when every time a child collects a few cards together towards a family, he is asked for them one by one and must give them up, so it is as well for a sympathetic adult to be on hand to preserve the peace, and also to prevent any infringements of the rules or spirit of the game.

Spider

Spider is a patience game which, according to *Redbook Magazine*, was the favourite of Franklin D Roosevelt, the four-times president of the USA, and the president during World War II. It is a game which is played in different ways, but the following description is that most commonly found in US books of the time, and likely to be the version played by Roosevelt.

Type	Patience
Alternative names	None
Players	One
Special requirements	Two packs of cards

Aim
To end with eight piles of cards, in descending suit sequence from King down to Ace.

Cards
Two standard packs of 52 cards, shuffled together, are used, making a pack of 104 cards. The cards rank from King (high) to Ace (low).

Preparation
A row of ten face-down cards is dealt to the table from the pack. Three further face-down rows are dealt to them, each card overlapping the card below, making ten columns. Then another face-down card is dealt to each of the first four columns. Finally, a face-up card is dealt to each column. The 'tableau' therefore contains 54 cards, as illustrated overleaf. The remaining 50 are placed to one side, face down, as the 'stock'.

Play
The ten piles serve as both 'tableau' and 'foundations'. The top card of each column (ie the face-up card at its foot) is always available for play. Available cards may be built upon in descending order, regardless of suit, from King to Ace. An Ace cannot be built upon at all.

Cards can be played from one column to another singly, unless there is a sequence of the same suit in correct descending order at the foot of a column, when it can be moved as a whole to any card at the foot of another column, provided the correct descending sequence is maintained, ie ♥7, 6, 5 can be built upon any 8.

A face-down card at the foot of a column, exposed because the face-up cards which overlapped it have been moved elsewhere, is turned face up and becomes available for play.

A space created by the removal of a whole column may be filled by any available card or suit sequence from another column. Since a King cannot be played to an

Ace, it may be moved only to a space created when all the cards in a column have been played elsewhere.

The object is to build a whole suit of 13 cards, in correct sequence from King down to Ace, within the tableau. When this is achieved the pile is removed, and discarded to one side. It is not obligatory to do this immediately – it may be used to help in further operations in the tableau. The game is won if all the cards can be removed from the tableau in eight separate piles of suit sequences from King down to Ace.

When all the moves have been made in the initial tableau (and any spaces which might be created are filled), the stock is taken in hand and ten cards are dealt face up to the foot of each column, overlapping the card previously at the foot. These cards immediately become available, and the remainder of the stock is set aside while further building takes place in the tableau. While dealing a row of ten cards to an existing tableau, no moves are allowed. The whole row has to be dealt before any manipulation of the tableau can take place.

Whenever play comes to a standstill thereafter, and provided all spaces are filled, a further ten cards are dealt face up to the foot of each column. After the initial tableau has been laid out, there will be five such further deals to the tableau (because there are initially 50 cards in the stock). If at the end of the final deal there is a card short or a card over, there has been a misdeal somewhere during the game.

This is a game of 20 minutes or so, which will come out about once in three or four efforts. It is a game which can move slowly at first, but if it gets into a rhythm, and spaces occur, can come with a run at the end. A priority is to try to create spaces by transferring elsewhere all the cards in a column. This gives the opportunity to move cards or suit sequences which might be blocking progress elsewhere to the spaces. When building from one column to another, try to build in suit sequences, since these can be moved wholesale. Sometimes spaces can be used to shuffle cards around into suit sequences.

Example game

The initial tableau is shown opposite. The ♥3 can be built on ♥4. The ♦9 can be built on ♦10, and ♦8 built on that. The ♠8 can be built on ♣9, and ♠5 on ♥6 with ♣4 on that. This leaves six cards at the foot of columns to be exposed and become available for play. Furthermore, when this is done the three right-hand columns will have only three face-down cards in each. When the cards exposed have been built and others exposed it may be that the extreme right-hand columns are on the way to being cleared. When no further moves can be made in the initial tableau, the stock is picked up and one face-up card is played to the foot of each of the ten columns, and the manipulation begins again. And so on…

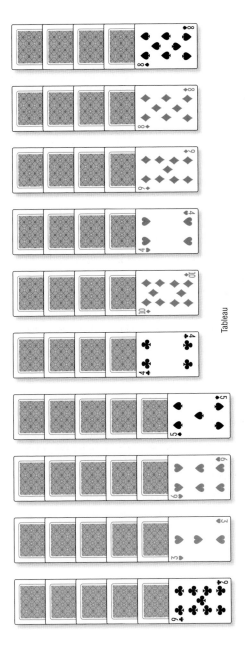

Tableau

Spinado

Spinado, or Spin, is a simplified form of the old game Pope Joan, but the name
is frequently applied to any of the games of the family, such as Newmarket.
Spinado retains the Pope Joan features of 'matrimony' and 'intrigue'.

Type	Gambling
Alternative names	Spin
Players	Two to seven; four or five is best
Special requirements	Chips or coins for staking; three saucers or similar receptacles

Aim

To win stakes by getting rid of all your cards first, and by playing certain bonus
cards.

Cards

The standard pack of 52 cards is used, from which are removed the ♦8 and all the
2s, leaving a pack of 47 cards. Cards rank from King (high) to Ace (low).

Preparation

Three saucers need to be labelled with the words 'matrimony', 'intrigue' and 'game',
and placed in the centre of the table.

Any player may pick up the cards, shuffle and begin to deal cards one at a time to
each player round the table until a Jack appears. The player dealt the Jack becomes
the first dealer. The deal subsequently passes to the left.

It should be agreed that the game will not end until all players have dealt an equal
number of times. On each deal, the dealer contributes twelve chips to the matrimony
pool, and six to each of the other two pools. The other players each contribute three
chips to the game pool.

The dealer shuffles and the player to his right cuts. The dealer deals the cards one at
a time clockwise, face down, to each player including himself and also to a 'widow'
which is the first hand to his left. The widow is placed to one side face down and
not used. Players are dealt an equal number of cards, with any remainder being
added to the widow. Players and widow therefore receive cards as follows:

Number of players	Cards received	Widow	Number of players	Cards received	Widow
2	15	17	5	7	12
3	11	14	6	6	11
4	9	11	7	5	12

Spinado

Play

The 'eldest hand' (the player to the dealer's left) begins by playing any card he likes to the table before him, announcing its rank and suit. The player with the next highest card in the suit then plays it, announcing its rank (the suit needs to be announced only at the beginning of the sequence). The player with the next highest card in the suit then plays that, and so on. Players may play two or more cards at once if they hold a sequence.

Eventually the run will come to a stop, because the sequence reaches a King, or because the next card required is not available. A card is unavailable either because it has been withdrawn (ie the ♦8 and the four 2s), or because it is in the widow. The player who played the last card before a stop then begins a new sequence by playing any card from his hand.

During the game, stakes are won from other players by playing certain cards. One of them is ♦A, known as 'spinado' or 'spin'. A player who plays it collects three chips from each of the other players. A player can play spinado at any time that he is playing a legitimate card, for example if the sequence reaches ♠8 and the holder of spinado holds ♠9, he can play ♠9 and add ♦A, announcing 'nine and spin'. Spinado is a stop so, after collecting from the opponents, the player of spinado begins a new sequence by playing a card of his choice.

Spinado   Marriage   Intrigue

The special cards in Spinado

During the game, a player who plays both ♦J and ♦Q claims 'intrigue', and picks up the chips in the saucer so marked. A player who plays both ♦Q and ♦K picks up the chips in the 'matrimony' saucer. If a player is lucky enough to hold and play ♦J, Q, K he picks up the chips in both saucers.

A player who plays ♦K, whether he also collects for matrimony or not, receives two chips from each of the other players. The players of any of the other three kings collect one chip from the others.

A player who gets rid of all his cards takes the stakes in the 'game' saucer. He also collects one chip from the other players for each card remaining in their hands, and two chips per card from a player unlucky enough to be caught with spinado in his hand. The winner of the game is also exempt from putting a stake into the game pool for the next deal, unless he happens to be the dealer, who must always put the requisite amounts into the three saucers.

More often than not, the matrimony and intrigue pools are not collected during the hand. The stakes in them remain for the next deal, and since their saucers are added to with each deal, the stakes contained in them can rise to large amounts.

Strategy Players should be aware of the stop cards, which are the Kings, the

353

Aces, ♦7 and any card immediately below a card which has already been used to begin a sequence. For example, if ♣J has been played, the holder of ♣10 knows it is a stop card and that he can play it with impunity. Players with cards which carry a bonus, such as spinado, Kings, matrimony or intrigue will usually play them at the first opportunity in case the chance never comes again. This is not always best play, but is sound if there are many players holding small hands; for example, with seven players holding five cards each (and twelve in the widow) a player may not get a chance to play a card, let alone two chances, so holding up a bonus card could be fatal.

Spoil Five

Spoil Five is one of those ancient trick-taking games of the Euchre, Écarté and Napoleon family, all included in this book, in which the hand consists of five cards and the ranking of the cards is eccentric. Spoil Five is the version which gained popularity in Ireland, and is, or was, frequently referred to as the national card game of Ireland. It borrows from the Spanish game of Ombre, and under an old name, Maw, was the favourite of James VI of Scotland (James I of England).

Type	Trick-taking
Alternative names	Forty-five, Maw, Twenty-five
Players	Two to ten; five or six is best
Special requirements	Chips or coins for staking; a saucer or similar receptacle

Aim

To win three of the five tricks in each deal, or to win all five; if neither is possible, to prevent another player from doing so.

Cards

The standard pack of 52 cards is used. The ranking of the cards differs according to which suit is trumps. The highest trump is always the 5, followed by the Jack. The third trump is always ♥A, no matter which suit is trumps. The rank of the cards in a trump suit is as follows:

hearts	5 (high), J, A, K, Q, 10, 9, 8, 7, 6, 4, 3, 2
diamonds	5 (high), J, ♥A, A, K, Q, 10, 9, 8, 7, 6, 4, 3, 2
clubs	5 (high), J, ♥A, A, K, Q, 2, 3, 4, 6, 7, 8, 9, 10
spades	5 (high), J, ♥A, A, K, Q, 2, 3, 4, 6, 7, 8, 9, 10

The rank of the cards in a plain suit is as follows:

hearts	K (high), Q, J, 10, 9, 8, 7, 6, 5, 4, 3, 2
diamonds	K (high), Q, J, 10, 9, 8, 7, 6, 5, 4, 3, 2, A
clubs	K (high), Q, J, A, 2, 3, 4, 5, 6, 7, 8, 9, 10
spades	K (high), Q, J, A, 2, 3, 4, 5, 6, 7, 8, 9, 10

Notice that the rank of the cards below the court cards is reversed in the black suits, expressed by 'highest in red, lowest in black'. Aces rank above the court cards when trumps, and below when in plain suits.

Preparation
Each player puts one chip into a saucer placed in the middle of the table, forming the pool.

Any player may pick up the cards, shuffle and begin to deal cards one at a time to each player round the table until a Jack appears. The player dealt the Jack becomes the first dealer.

Beginning with the 'eldest hand' (the player to the dealer's left), and dealing clockwise, the dealer deals five cards to each player, in bundles of three and two, or two and three, whichever he prefers. The dealer places the remainder of the cards face down on the table and turns up the top card to indicate the trump suit.

Robbing the trump Unless the turn-up is an Ace, any player who holds the Ace of trumps must announce it before he plays to the first trick. If he fails to do this, the Ace is demoted to be the lowest trump in that deal. Announcing the Ace allows him to take the up-card into his hand by passing a discard face down to the dealer, who places it unseen under the pack and hands the player the turn-up. The player receiving the turn-up does not have to play it, or the Ace, on that trick. If the holder of the Ace does not want the turn-up, he announces his Ace but tells the dealer to 'turn it down', whereupon the dealer turns the card over.

If the turn-up is an Ace, the dealer is allowed to exchange a card for it. To do so, he must discard any card face down before a card is led, although it is customary that he leaves the Ace on the pack until it is his turn to play, when he takes it into his hand. If the dealer has not discarded when the eldest hand wants to lead to the first trick, the eldest hand must call upon the dealer to do so. In the unlikely event that the dealer does not wish to take the card, the dealer says 'I play with these', and play begins.

Play
The eldest hand makes the first lead; see p383 for an explanation of tricks and trick-taking. Trick-taking rules are unusual. A player who can follow suit must do so or trump, ie he may trump even though he can follow suit. A player who cannot follow suit may play any card. Players must follow suit if able when a trump is led, except when 'reneging' (see below)

A trick is won by the highest trump it contains, otherwise by the highest card in the suit led. The winner of a trick leads to the next.

Reneging A privilege attaches to the three highest trumps, ie to the 5, J and ♥A. They cannot be forced out by the lead of a smaller trump. If a small trump is led, a player is not forced to follow with one of these trumps, and if he has no smaller trumps he may discard. This is called 'reneging'. The lead of a superior trump, however, calls for the play of an inferior trump, ie if the trump 5 is led, a player must follow with J or ♥A if he holds no other trump.

Each player plays for himself, with his main object to win three tricks, which entitles him to the pool. If a player cannot win three tricks, he tries to prevent any other player doing so. If nobody wins three tricks, the hand is 'spoiled', hence the name of the game, and the pool is carried forward to the next deal. Once a player takes three tricks, the rest of the hand is not played, unless the tricks won are the first three.

The winner of them may throw in his remaining cards and take the pool, or he may 'jink it'. This is an announcement that he proposes to take the last two tricks as well, for which he not only takes the pool, but is paid a bonus of one chip from each of the other players. If he jinks it and fails, however, he loses his entitlement to the pool and the hand is spoiled.

Strategy Most Spoil Five hands are won by a player being dealt a strong hand in trumps (either high ones or length) and leading them out. The majority of hands, with five or more players, are spoiled. Frequently, players see they cannot make three tricks as soon as they see their hands, and concentrate on spoiling other players.

If a player leads three high trumps to win the first three tricks it sometimes pays for a player holding a big trump to renege and allow the winner of the three tricks (who may well hold a fourth) to jink it and attempt to win all five. The hand can then be spoiled.

Example hand
Suppose five hands are dealt by Player A, as illustrated.

Player A   Player B   Player C

Player D   Player E

The turn up was ♦10, which Player E, on his turn, took into his hand, discarding another card, by announcing that he held ♦A before playing to the first trick. The illustration, for convenience, shows Player E with ♦10 already in his hand.

Player B leads to the first trick with prospects of taking three tricks. He bases his hopes on the fact that there are 27 cards not in play. If they include two of ♦5, ♦J and ♦A, Player B hopes that by leading trumps he may win ♥A or ♦K, and later a second trump (which by the third trick might be the only trump left) then he has ♣K to make a third trick. He accordingly leads ♥A and play proceeds:

	Player A	Player B	Player C	Player D	Player E
1	♣6	♥A	♦4	♦2	♦10
2	♠5	♦K	♠9	♠6	♦A

Player D held up ♦5 on the first trick, hoping to make it on the third trick, with the possibility that if ♣K is not in play he could then make ♣Q and ♣7. On the second lead, therefore, he reneged, knowing that Player E held ♦A and that Player B's ♦K would not win the trick.

3	♥5	♦7	♥10	♦5	♥K
4	♠3	♣K	♠8	♣Q	♥8

Having been disappointed that Player D held ♦5 and foiled his plan, Player B now has a second chance by virtue of Player D leading ♣Q. Player B is now very optimistic that ♣3 will win him the game, since only by Player D holding ♣J or ♣A will he be beaten.

5	♥J	♣3	♠J	♣7	♠7

So Player B won his three tricks and collected the pool.

In the example hand, Player B's tactics were correct, but he succeeded only because Player D saw the chance of winning himself. Player D could have prevented Player B from getting his third trick by reneging again when ♦7 was led at trick 3. He could have used ♦5 on Player B's ♣K on trick 4, and then led ♣Q to foil Player B on the last trick. On the other hand, Player B could have given himself a better chance by discarding ♣3 on trick 3 rather than trumping. If another player had reneged by holding up ♦5 or ♦J, hoping to make these tricks himself (as Player D had) that player would have had to have played it on trick 3. Player B would then have held the last trump and the master club for the last two tricks.

Variants
Forty-five Forty-five is a way of playing Spoil Five without the spoiled hands. It is played in two teams, so is suitable for two, four or six players. A team which wins three tricks scores five points, a team that wins all five tricks scores ten. No hand can be spoiled because one side or other must make three tricks. The first side to reach 45 points is the winner, hence the name.

Switch

Switch is a general name for a game which goes by many others, including Swedish Rummy, a misleading name which probably originated in the USA. The game is not Swedish and nothing like Rummy. In the version described, Jacks are wild cards, and the game is also called Crazy Jacks. In some versions other cards are wild, leading to names like Crazy Aces or Crazy Eights for what is virtually the same game. Rules vary everywhere.

Type	Stops
Alternative names	Black Jack, Crazy Jacks, Swedish Rummy
Players	Two to six, with four or five best
Special requirements	Pen and paper for scoring

Aim
To get rid of all your cards.

Cards
The standard pack of 52 cards is used, the cards ranking from Ace (high) to 2 (low).

Preparation
Any player may pick up the cards, shuffle and begin to deal cards one at a time to each player round the table until a Jack appears. The player dealt the Jack becomes the first dealer.

The dealer deals the cards one at a time to each player, face down. If two to four people play each player is dealt seven cards; if five or six play each receives five cards. The remainder of the cards are placed in the centre of the table face down to provide a 'stock'.

Play
The 'eldest hand' (the player to the dealer's left) plays any card he wishes to a discard pile in the centre, and the player to his left must play a card of the same suit or rank upon it. If he cannot, he must draw the top card of the stock, and continue to do so until he draws a card which will enable him to discard it to the centre. Play proceeds in this way, but some ranks of cards have special properties as follows:

Jacks   A Jack is a wild card and can be played at any time. Furthermore, the player of a Jack can change the suit to the suit of his choice.

Deuces   When a player plays a 2, which also can be played at any time, the following player, unless he can play a 2, must take two cards from the stock and forego his opportunity to discard. However, if he can play a 2, the following player, facing two consecutive 2s, must either play a 2 himself or draw four cards from the stock without discarding any. A third consecutive 2 forces the following player to draw six cards, and four consecutive 2s forces the next player to draw eight.

Treys   The play of a 3, which also can be played at any time, operates like the 2. The following player, unless he can play a 3, must take three cards from stock without discarding, and successive 3s force a player to take six, nine or twelve cards from the stock.

Kings   The play of a King, which must be of the correct prevailing suit, reverses the order of play from clockwise to anti-clockwise. Of course, the play of a second King reverses it back to normal again.

Eights   The play of an 8, which must be of the correct suit, forces the following player to miss a turn.

When the stock is exhausted, play continues with a player unable to play a legitimate card merely missing a turn.

The player to get rid of his cards first and go out is the winner of the deal.

The ranks of special significance in Switch

Scoring When a player goes out, each of the others is debited with the cards held in his hand. Jacks count as 15, Aces eleven, court cards as ten and other cards at their pip value. Scores are kept, and when one player's debit score reaches 100, the player with the lowest debit score is the winner.

Tablanette

Tablanette is a game of the Casino type, said to have originated in Russia, although it has also been suggested that its name might come from the French *table nette*, meaning clean table, a term used in the game when the table has been cleared of cards.

Type	Fishing
Alternative names	None
Players	Two
Special requirements	Pen and paper for scoring

Aim

To collect points by capturing cards from the table by matching them with cards in the hand.

Cards

The standard pack of 52 cards is used. Cards have their pip values during play, with Aces counting as eleven or one, at the player's discretion, Kings as 14 and Queens as 13. Jacks do not have a value, but play a special part in the game.

Preparation

The players draw from a spread pack to decide first dealer, the player with the higher card (Ace high, 2 low) dealing. The deal alternates thereafter. It is best if players sit opposite each other.

The dealer deals six cards face down, one at a time, to each player alternately, beginning with his opponent. He then deals a row of four cards face up to the table between the players. Should any Jacks be dealt to the table, they are removed and buried in the pack, being replaced by a card dealt from the top. The remaining cards are placed face down in a pile to one side for later use.

Play

The non-dealer plays first. If he can play a card of the same rank as one or more cards on the table, he claims the card or cards. The card played and those he claims are kept in a face-down pile beside him as they will later contribute to his score. If he can play a card whose value equals the value of two or more cards on the table when their values are added together, he can claim those as well. For example, if there is a 9, 5 and 4 on the table, a player can play a 9 and claim all three cards, the 9 for being the same rank as the card he played, and the 5 and 4 because the sum of the two cards also equals his 9.

If, however, a player does not have a card in his hand which will allow him to capture any cards on the table, he must play one of the cards from his hand to the table, and the dealer has his turn.

Each player plays one card in turn from his hand until both hands have been played. During the course of the hand the number of cards on the table will vary as players capture them and as they are forced to play cards to the table because they are unable to make a capture.

If at any time a player clears the table by taking all the available cards (there might be only one or there might be more than four) he claims 'tablanette' and scores the value of all the cards he took plus the card he played to capture them. These scores are added to the score-sheet as they are made. The illustration below shows an example. If there are five cards on the table as shown, and the player plays ♥Q, he can clear all the cards (Q = 13 and A, 2, 4, 6 = 13). He scores 13 × 3 = 39 points for tablanette, and puts all the cards into his pile as captures.

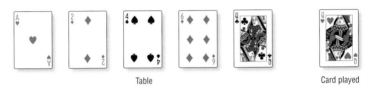

Table   Card played

A tablanette worth 39 points

Playing a Jack enables a player to clear all the cards from the table and add them to his pile. He does not score for tablanette, but this is obviously a valuable play, because all the cards go to his pile, which will help his score later, and it also forces his opponent to play one of his cards to the table on his turn, as there are none on the table he can claim.

Players play their cards alternately until all are played, whereupon the dealer deals six more cards to each, and the play is repeated. After each deal, the non-dealer plays first.

In each deal there will be four such hands of six cards each, all dealt by the same dealer. When the players have played their final hands of six cards, any cards which remain on the table are taken by the player who last took a card from the table.

Scoring When all cards have been played, and the table emptied, the only scores on the score-sheet will be those scored for tablanettes (which are likely to be the significant ones).

Players then add scores according to the cards they have collected as follows:

♦ 10	two points
♣ 2	one point
Ace	one point
King	one point
Queen	one point
Jack	one point
10 (except ♦ 10)	one point

In addition, the player who has the majority of cards, ie 27 or more, scores three points.

That concludes the deal, and the player who was non-dealer takes the cards, shuffles well, and deals.

The game is won by the first player to score 251 points.

Example hand

Suppose the cards are dealt as illustrated.

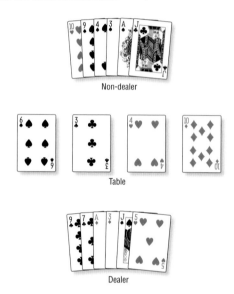

Non-dealer

Table

Dealer

The non-dealer plays first. He can play ♥10 and take ♦10, ♠6 and ♥4, assuring himself of two points for ♦10 at the end of the hand and another for ♥10, and leaving only ♣3 on the table. The dealer has ♦3, so can play it and claim ♣3 and tablanette, scoring six points immediately. The non-dealer must now play a card to the table and plays ♠3, on the grounds that dealer is unlikely to have another 3 to score for tablanette again. The dealer plays ♣9 to the table, since it prevents the non-dealer clearing the table for tablanette, as there is not a card of value 12. The non-dealer plays ♠9 and claims the ♣9. The dealer now plays ♣7, on the grounds that as two 10s have been played, the non-dealer will be unlikely to have another to score tablanette. The non-dealer decides that to play Ace or 4 would be dangerous (he was right), so plays Jack to clear the table. It earns him three cards for the count at the end and leaves the table bare for his opponent.

The dealer, with an empty table before him, plays ♥5 to it. As two 9s have already been played, the non-dealer plays ♠4 to the table. The dealer decides now to play ♦A to the table on the grounds that he knows the non-dealer does not have a 10 to score tablanette, and that he himself can clear the table on his turn with his Jack, thus presenting non-dealer with a clear table when he comes to play first to the next hand. As it happens, he was somewhat unlucky, because the non-dealer had ♠A, and captured the ♦A. The dealer played ♠J and took the two cards remaining on the table, leaving it blank. He then dealt the next six cards, with the non-dealer having to start by playing a card to the blank table.

So far the dealer has six points for tablanette, but the non-dealer has eleven cards towards the count at the end, including six points in counting cards, to the dealer's five cards, only one of which is a counting card. Perhaps the odds are slightly in the dealer's favour, but there is little in it.

Thirty-One

The number 31 has featured in many card games, usually of a gambling nature, some of them used as vehicles to relieve the innocent of their cash. The gambling game Trente et Quarante is one such and is still to be found in casinos, although it is a comparatively fair game. The game described here is a simple game which can be enjoyed by young players.

Type	Gambling
Alternative names	Trente-et-Un
Players	Three or more (the more the better)
Special requirements	Pen and paper for scoring

Aim
To acquire a hand, the count of which is nearer to 31 than that of any other player.

Cards
The standard pack of 52 cards is used. Aces count as eleven, court cards ten and other cards by their pip values.

Preparation
Any player may pick up the cards, shuffle and begin to deal cards one at a time to each player round the table until a Jack appears. The player dealt the Jack becomes the first dealer. The deal subsequently passes to the left.

The dealer shuffles and the player to his right cuts. The dealer then deals cards face down, one at a time, to each player clockwise from his left until all players have three cards. He then deals a row of three cards face up in the centre of the table.

Play
Each player in turn, beginning with the 'eldest hand' (the player to the dealer's left),

has the opportunity to take one of the face-up cards into his hand, replacing it with one from his hand.

Each player is attempting to collect three cards whose pip count is nearer to 31 than those of the other players. Thirty-one can be achieved only by holding an Ace and two ten-point cards (court cards and 10s). If there are two such hands, one consisting of cards of the same suit beats one of mixed suits. A secondary hand is one of three cards of the same rank. This counts as thirty-and-a-half points. Among similar hands, three Aces are best, then three Kings, down to three 2s.

Players continue to exchange cards with the centre until one player thinks his hand might have a higher count than anybody else's. Instead of exchanging a card on his turn, he knocks on the table. Play does not end immediately, but continues round the table, giving each player one more chance to change his hand, until the turn reaches the player who knocked, when it ends. Players show their hands, and the player whose count is nearest to thirty-one wins.

A simple way to score over a number of games is as follows. The player with the best hand scores three points. If there is a tie, each player who ties scores three points. If the knocker wins, or ties, he scores an extra two points in addition to the three for winning. If however, the player who knocked does not win, a point is deducted from his score. The winner is the first to score 15 points.

Towie

Bridge in the 1920s and 1930s became such a giant among card games that devotees who 'couldn't find a fourth for Bridge' were like drug addicts looking for a fix. Numerous attempts were made, therefore, to adapt Bridge for three-handed play. The game which has survived longest is Towie, invented around 1931. The description here assumes that the reader can play Bridge.

Type	A version of Bridge for three players
Alternative names	None
Players	Three
Special requirements	A score sheet, as in Bridge

Aim
Each player attempts to win two games and thus the rubber.

Cards
The standard pack of 52 cards is used, the cards ranking from Ace (high) to 2 (low). The suits rank as in Bridge: spades, hearts, diamonds, clubs.

Towie

Preparation

The players draw from a spread pack to determine the first dealer, the highest drawer becoming the first dealer. The deal subsequently passes to the left.

The dealer deals all the cards one at a time face down to each player, beginning with the player to his left, and including, in the space opposite him, a dummy hand. The dealer then exposes six of the dummy hand's cards at random and arranges them in suit order, as in Bridge.

Bidding The bidding is as in Bridge, each player imagining that he will be declarer facing dummy, basing his bidding on the strength of knowing six of dummy's cards. Part scores are not considered in Towie, so bids must be worth game (100 points or more).

If no player makes a bid at the level of game, there is a 'goulash' deal. In a goulash deal, the players sort their cards into suits (the dealer sorting the dummy's cards) and the hands are collected into one pack. Without being shuffled, the pack is cut, and the same dealer redeals the cards in bundles of five, five and three. This encourages freak hands and the likelihood of a game bid from one of the players. If none is forthcoming, a further goulash deal takes place, and the same dealer continues to deal goulash deals until a player makes a game bid.

The highest bidder becomes the declarer. The dummy, of course, since it belongs to declarer, will need to be opposite him. If the dealer is declarer, it can stay where it is, but if another player is declarer then the dummy must switch places with the third player. The point to remember is that the three players, ignoring dummy, retain their relative positions to each other.

Play

The player to the declarer's left makes the opening lead, whereupon the seven face-down cards in dummy are turned over and the hand is arranged as it would be in Bridge. The play of the cards is now identical to that in Bridge, with the declarer attempting to make his contract and the defenders trying to prevent him.

Scoring There are a few differences to the scoring of Bridge. These are:

i) In no-trump contacts, each trick is worth 35 points.

ii) For winning a first game, a declarer scores 500 points and becomes vulnerable. For winning a second game, and thus the rubber, a player scores 1,000 points.

iii) A declarer who makes a doubled or redoubled contract scores a bonus of 50 points if not vulnerable and 100 points if vulnerable.

iv) For undoubled overtricks, the declarer scores 50 points each. If doubled or redoubled, he scores them as in Bridge.

v) Penalties for undertricks are:

Not vulnerable Undoubled: 50 points per trick. Doubled: 100 points for each of the first and second tricks, 200 points for each of the third and fourth tricks, 400 points each for the fifth and subsequent tricks.

Vulnerable Undoubled: 100 points for the first trick, 200 points for the second and each subsequent trick. Doubled: 200 points for the first trick, 400 points for the second and each subsequent trick.

If the contract is redoubled, the penalties are twice those for doubled contracts.

The first player to win two games wins the rubber.

Example hand

The hands are dealt (after four goulashes) as shown, with the six cards of the dummy exposed and with the bidding to start.

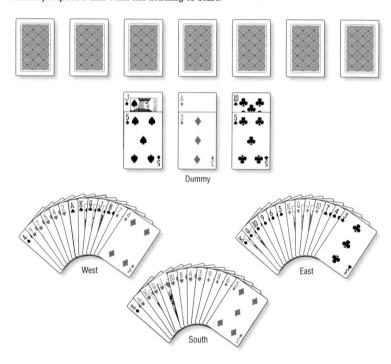

Dummy

West

East

South

South has a certain eight tricks in hearts, and with ♦A in dummy decides to bid four hearts. West can bid nothing. East, with spades as trumps, will certainly make five trump tricks, and should make four diamond tricks, so bids four spades, as one more spade in dummy should make his contract safe. East becomes declarer and West and dummy change positions.

South thinks East's second suit might be clubs, and would lead a club if he had one, in the hope that West might be able to trump it. He leads ♥A instead, hoping East might have a couple of small hearts which South could take, with perhaps West trumping a third, say.

The rest of the dummy is exposed, and is shown in the illustration.

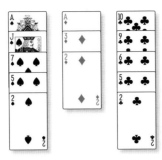

The Ace of trumps plus two more small ones make East's contract a laydown, with his three small clubs the only losers.

Trente et Quarante

Trente et Quarante is a very old game, possibly well over 300 years old. It was a popular casino game of the heyday of the plush European casinos of the late 19th and early 20th centuries, but began to decline as the glamorous, privileged lifestyle of that time faded; it never crossed the Atlantic to the more vulgar casinos of Las Vegas.

It is a gambling game of no skill whatever.

Type	Gambling, played in casinos
Alternative names	Rouge et Noir
Players	Any number
Special requirements	Played in a casino, which provides the venue, table, cards and chips

Aim
To place winning bets on certain outcomes of chance, ie the relative pip counts of two rows of cards and the colour of a certain card.

Cards
Normally six standard packs of 52 cards are used, shuffled together. Cards have their pip value, with court cards counting ten and Aces one.

Preparation

Players bet by placing their stakes upon the table. The table is double-ended: only half is illustrated.

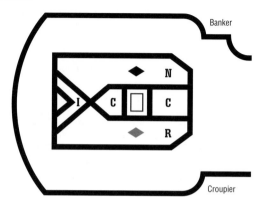

Banker

Croupier

Play

A dealer deals, one at a time face up, a row of cards from the pack and stops when the total value of the cards exceeds 30 (ie when it reaches 31–40). He announces the total. This row represents *noir*, or black. He then deals a second row below it until this row also exceeds 30. He announces this total. This row represents *rouge*, or red. An example of the two rows is shown below. The winning row is that nearer to 31, ie the lower count of the two. In the illustration below, rouge wins. Gamblers who bet on rouge, by placing their stakes on the part of the table marked with R and the red diamond, win the amount of their stake. The bettors on noir (N and the black diamond) lose.

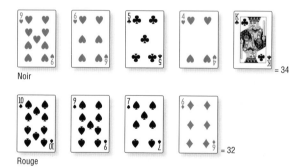

Noir

= 34

Rouge

= 32

There is another bet the gamblers can make. They can bet that the first card turned up (in the illustration ♥9) will be the same colour as the winning row. This is a bet on *couleur*, and a gambler wishing to bet on couleur places his stakes in the spaces marked C on the table. A bet is also possible on 'inverse', which is a bet that the colour of the first card turned will be the opposite colour to that of the winning row. These bets are placed on the small space on the table marked I.

When the banker completes the second row of cards, and has announced the total, he announces the two winning bets. If he dealt the cards in the illustration, he would announce 'rouge, couleur'.

If the two rows of numbers are equal, the bets are void and gamblers retain their stakes. They can either ask the croupier for their return or leave them for the next rows of cards to be dealt.

All bets are settled at odds of 1–1, or evens. However, since the casino is there to make a profit, there is one occasion when it does so. This is when both rows of cards tie at 31. This is known as a *refait*. When it occurs, the casino claims half of all the stakes. The croupier will return half the stake to each player, or if the player prefers, he may leave the whole stake 'in prison' on the table for the next coup, getting it back if his bet wins or losing the whole stake if it doesn't.

The refait represents the house edge. A tie at 31–31 is estimated to happen roughly once in 40 coups, and it gives the casino an edge of 1.28%. This is one of the smallest of advantages in casino games. A player can reduce it to 1% by insuring against a refait. By purchase of a special chip of 1% of his stake, he does not lose half his stake when refait occurs.

Vacancies

Vacancies is a good patience game because it repays skill. It is nevertheless difficult, and around 19 times in 20 the player will be frustrated after about ten minutes.

Type	Patience
Alternative names	Gaps, Spaces
Players	One
Special requirements	Playing surface large enough to lay out four rows of 13 cards

Aim
To arrange the pack so that each row is made up of cards of the same suit, ranging in sequence from 2 on the left to King on the right.

Cards
The standard pack of 52 cards is used, the cards ranking from 2 (low) to King (high). Aces play no significant part in the game.

Preparation

The cards are shuffled and the whole pack is dealt face up in four rows, each of 13 cards, forming the 'tableau'.

Play

From the tableau the four Aces are removed and set to one side. They play no part in the game.

Removing the Aces creates four spaces in the tableau. A space can be filled by one card only: the card of the same suit as that on the left of the space but of one rank higher. Thus, if ♦4 has a space to its right, the space can be filled only by ♦5.

The transfer of each card creates another space to be filled. By this means, cards are moved around the tableau one by one, and the object is to so manoeuvre the cards so that each row comprises 2 to King in a single suit sequence. It does not matter which suit fills which row, but once a row is started with 2 at the left it cannot be moved elsewhere.

However, there is a limit to what one can achieve, because if a space occurs to the right of a King, nothing can be moved there, there being no card one rank higher than a King. At the beginning, if none of the Aces to be removed is to the right of a King, there are four spaces to fill and four cards which might fill them. The skill lies in trying to avoid for as long as possible creating a space to the right of a King, which reduces the number of spaces operable to three.

Even the cleverest player will not be able to avoid this for long, and only with exceptional luck will it be possible to avoid eventually all four spaces being to the right of Kings, and thus useless.

However, the game does not end there. When this situation arises, all the cards which are not in their correct places are picked up, shuffled and redealt. The four spaces left on the redeal are the spaces in each row to the right of the cards which are in their proper places. If one or more of the rows does not yet have even the 2 in its final position (and this is not uncommon), then the space in that row is left at the end of the row, in the space reserved for the 2. This means that after the redeal there will be four spaces vacant and each is ready to accept the card which should be there if the game is to be got out. If at the time of the redeal one row has been completed from 2 to King, obviously no cards from that row are picked up and when the cards are redealt there will be only three spaces to leave (this is because in the completed row, the space is actually there, to the right of the King).

When the game is once more stopped by all the spaces being to the right of Kings, one more redeal is allowed, following the principles of the first. After that, if all the cards aren't in their correct places, defeat must be conceded.

Example game

In the tableau at the start of the game as illustrated opposite (which has two Kings together, which can be a help), ♣6 can be played to ♣5; then ♥5 to ♥4; ♠2 to the space left by moving the ♥5, followed by ♠3; ♦2 to the space at the left of the bottom row; ♥Q to ♥J; ♥6 to ♥5, allowing another 2 to be played to the space, and so on.

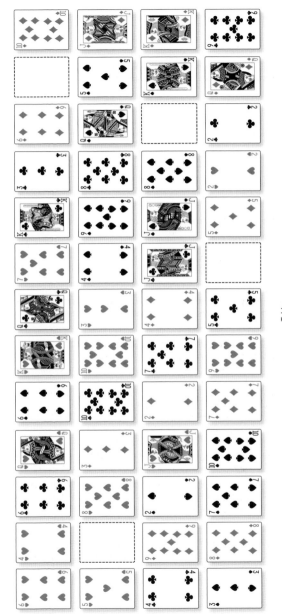

Tableau

Vanishing Cross

Vanishing Cross is a one-pack patience game with an attractive tableau. It should succeed on about one in ten tries.

Type	Patience
Alternative names	Corner Card, Czarina, Four Seasons
Players	One
Special requirements	None

Aim
To end with four piles of cards in ascending suit sequence upon their foundations.

Cards
The standard pack of 52 cards is used.

Preparation
The cards are shuffled and five are dealt in the form of a cross to form a 'tableau'. The next card is dealt to the top left corner of the cross. This card is the first 'foundation'. The remaining cards are taken in hand, face down, as the 'stock'.

Play
The rank of the foundation card determines the rank of the other three foundations. As they become available, they are played to the other corners of the tableau. They are built on in ascending suit sequence 'round-the-corner', meaning that when the King is the top card of the pile it will be followed by Ace.

Cards in the tableau (ie the cross) can be packed on in downward sequence irrespective of suit and colour. These sequences are also round-the-corner, so in this case King is packed on Ace. All the exposed cards in the tableau are available for play. They can be moved only one at a time; sequences cannot be transferred.

When all possible moves have been made in the initial tableau, cards are turned over one by one from the stock and played to a foundation or the tableau if possible. If not, they are played to a single waste heap. The card on top of the waste heap is always available for play. The stock is dealt only once. A space in the tableau can be filled by a card from the tableau, the waste heap or the stock.

Example game
In the illustration that follows, the tableau cross has been dealt and ♣9 is the first foundation.

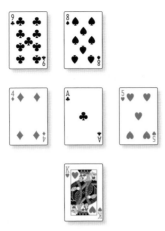

The ♦4 can be packed on the ♥5 and the ♥K on the ♣A. The first card is then turned from the stock and played to a foundation, a card in the tableau or to one of the spaces, then the next and so on.

The main thing to remember is that foundations are built up and tableau cards are packed down.

Whist

Whist is a venerable English game arising out of a 16th-century game called Triumph, whence came the word 'trump'. It has moved up and down the social ladder ever since. Regarded for a century or so as a plain game for common men, it was catapulted into high society in 1718 when the gentry who gathered at the Crown Coffee House in London, led by Lord Folkestone, took it up in earnest and analysed its play.

In those days it was called Whisk, for reasons which can only be guessed at, which also goes for the change to Whist. There is no doubt, however, that the game was soon known to a wide public thanks to its promotion by Edmond Hoyle, whose book *A Short Treatise on the Game of Whist* in 1742 is perhaps the most famous of all card books and established him as the ultimate authority on the rules of games and the principles of fair play. Since then 'Hoyles' have appeared regularly, and one modern dictionary defines Hoyle as 'an authoritative book of rules for card games'.

For more than 150 years Whist remained the most popular card game in Britain. Then Bridge arrived, was taken up by society, and Whist returned to the middle classes, being played in Whist 'drives' in village halls, where everybody played everyone else, money was raised for charity, and many went home with various categories of prizes. Whist drives seem now to have been supplanted by quiz nights, and Whist has probably become best known for the many games which have taken its name, some of which are in this book. It remains, however, one of the best partnership games in its original version.

Type	Trick-taking
Alternative names	None
Players	Four, playing in partnerships of two
Special requirements	Pen and paper for scoring

Aim
To win more tricks than your opponents.

Cards
The standard pack of 52 cards is used, the cards ranking from Ace (high) to 2 (low).

Preparation
Players draw cards from the pack to determine partners, the two highest playing the two lowest (Ace counting low for this purpose only), and the lowest of all being the first dealer. The deal subsequently passes to the left. Of course, many players will prefer to make their own partnership arrangements.

The dealer deals the cards one at a time, face down, clockwise to all players, and exposes the last card (his own) to denote the trump suit. It is customary to leave this card exposed on the table until the dealer has played to the first trick, unless he wants to play it straightaway.

Play

The 'eldest hand' (the player to the dealer's left) leads to the first trick; see p383 for an explanation of tricks and trick-taking. The usual rules of trick-taking apply: players who can must follow suit, otherwise they may trump or discard. A trick is won by the highest trump it contains or if it contains none by the highest card in the suit led. The winner of the trick leads to the next. One player collects the tricks for his side.

Scoring The winning side scores points according to the number of tricks it makes in excess of six (the first six tricks being known as the 'book').

Points are also scored for 'honours', which are the Ace, King, Queen and Jack of the trump suit. A side dealt all four scores four points, a side dealt three of them two points.

A game is to five points. The points for honours are taken after the points for tricks, so a side which passes five points by taking tricks cannot be overtaken by the opponents scoring for honours. A 'rubber' consists of three games, so the first side to win two games wins the rubber.

Alternatively, instead of playing rubbers, a game can be played to as many points as one wishes. Some players ignore the points for honours, which seem to be out of proportion to those for actually winning tricks.

Strategy The best weapon is to remember which cards have been played, and in particular how many cards have been played in each suit, particularly trumps. It is possible to form a picture of each player's hand.

Some ideas have been handed down over the years and are particularly useful when playing with new partners. Probably the best-known is 'second player plays low, third player plays high', which is based on the idea that when a player leads a suit he is trying to establish it and wants his partner to help drive out high cards. The principle of returning partner's suit is based on the same idea.

Not 'finessing' against your partner is another good principle. A 'finesse' is when a player holds, for example, Ace and Queen in the suit led, and is third to play. If the fourth player holds King and another, then the holder of Ace, Queen cannot make them both. But if another player holds the King, the third player can play Queen, which wins, and he still has Ace to win later. This is called finessing the Queen, and is a useful tactic in Bridge. But in Whist, if your partner leads, to play the Queen is called 'finessing against partner' and is considered bad play. 'Trust partner' is the motto. Play the Ace and return the suit, and your partner will probably hold the King.

A table of advised leads has been drawn up by experienced players for certain holdings. These are:

In the trump suit

Holding	First lead	Second lead
A, K, Q, J	J	Q
A, K, Q	Q	K
A, K, xxxxx and more	K	A
A, K, xxxx	fourth best	

In plain suits

Holding	First lead	Second lead
A, K, Q, J	K	J
A, K, Q	K	Q
A, K x and more	K	A
A, K	A	K
K, Q, J, x	K	J
K, Q, J, xx	J	K
K, Q, J xxx and more	J	Q
A xxx and more	A	fourth best of remainder
K, Q, x and more	K	fourth best of remainder
A, Q, J	A	Q
A, Q, J x	A	Q
A, Q, J, xx and more	A	J
K, J, 10, 9	9	K (if A or Q falls)
Q, J, x	Q	
Q, J, xx and more	fourth best	

Without any of these holdings, you should lead your fourth highest card in your longest suit.

Example hand

The hands are dealt as in the illustration, using the Bridge convention of calling players North, South, East and West.

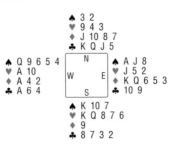

West dealt and his last card, which he turned up as trumps, was ♦4. North decides to lead ♣K, and the play proceeds:

	North	East	South	West
1	♣K	♣10	♣2	♣A
2	♥3	♥2	♥6	♥A
3	♥4	♥5	♥Q	♥10
4	♣Q	♣9	♣3	♣4
5	♣J	♦3	♣7	♣6
6	♥9	♥J	♥K	♦2
7	♠2	♠A	♠7	♠4
8	♠3	♠8	♠K	♠5
9	♦7	♠J	♠10	♠Q
10	♣5	♦5	♣8	♠6
11	♦8	♦6	♦9	♦A
12	♦10	♦K	♥7	♠9
13	♦J	♦Q	♥8	♦4

So East/West won nine tricks to North/South's four and score three points towards game. They also score two points for honours, so win the first game by 5–0.

Yukon

Yukon was once reported as having been played by the miners during the Klondike gold rush at the end of the 19th century, and the claim has been repeated since by later writers, but with scepticism. So here is the story repeated again, which doesn't make it any more likely to be true.

Type	Trick-taking
Alternative names	None
Players	Two to four
Special requirements	Pen and paper for scoring

Aim

To be the first player to reach 250 points, by winning tricks containing scoring cards.

Cards

The standard pack of 52 cards is used. If there are three players, the ♣2 must be removed from the pack.

The four Jacks are trumps, the ♠J being known as the 'Grand Yukon', and the other Jacks are 'Yukons'. The Grand Yukon is the highest ranking card, and the other Yukons are of equal value. They form a suit of their own, and all rank higher than the other cards, which rank A (high), K, Q, 10, 9, 8, 7, 6, 5, 4, 3, 2 (low).

Preparation

The first dealer is decided by each player drawing a card from the pack, the drawer of the highest card (Ace high, 2 low) being first dealer. The deal subsequently passes to the left.

The dealer shuffles, and the player to his right cuts. The dealer deals the cards one at a time, face down, to each player clockwise until each player has five cards. The rest of the pack forms the 'stock', and is placed down in the centre of the table.

Play

Players take up their hands and the 'eldest hand' (the player on the dealer's left) leads to the first trick; see p383 for an explanation of tricks and trick-taking. Players must follow suit to the card led, and if they cannot must play a Yukon if they have one. Only if a player cannot follow suit, and does not have a Yukon, may he discard. A trick is won by the Grand Yukon if it has been played, it not by a Yukon, and if no Yukons have been played by the highest card in the suit led. If two ordinary Yukons have been played in the same trick, the first Yukon played wins the trick.

The winner of a trick takes the cards in the trick and keeps them face down by his side until the end of the deal, when the points are totalled. The winner of each trick takes the top card of the stock and adds it to his hand. The other players in turn, clockwise from the trick winner, each take the new top card of the stock so that all player's hands are restored to five cards. When the stock is exhausted, the players play out the last five cards.

Scoring Each player adds up the points contained in his tricks. Points are won by capturing the scoring cards, of which there are 20:

Grand Yukon	15 points	each Ace	5 points
each other Yukon	10 points	each King	3 points
each 10	10 points	each Queen	2 points

The total points won in each round is therefore 125.

The winner is the first player to reach 250 points. Scores are entered on a score-sheet until a player passes 250. If two or more pass 250 on the same round, the player with the most points wins.

Strategy It is usually best to lead a low card, rather than a points-scoring card. This is because, should an opponent be dealt a Yukon, he must play it and take the trick, including the points-scoring card. If no Yukon is played on the first trick, the only way an opponent can hold one on the second trick is to have drawn it from the stock. A high card is more likely to win a later trick than the first.

Example hand
Three hands are dealt as shown, using the Bridge convention of calling the three players South, East and West.

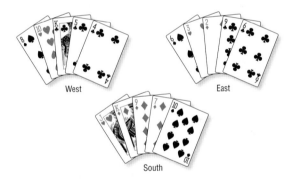

West leads, and chooses ♣4. East plays ♣6. South, without a club, must play ♥J, his Yukon. South takes the first trick, and restores his hand to five cards by taking the top card from the stock. West takes the second card from the stock, and East the third. South then leads to the next trick.

Variants
Yukon can also be played by four players in partnerships of two, the partners sitting opposite each other and adding their points together.

More About Playing Cards

Card Games Basics

There are certain basic facts, rules and customs which apply to all card games.

The pack

The standard pack consists of 52 cards containing four suits, each identified by a symbol: spades (♠), hearts (♥), diamonds (♦) and clubs (♣). Hearts and diamonds are printed in red, spades and clubs in black. There are 13 cards in each suit, each having a rank: Ace (A), King (K), Queen (Q), Jack (J), 10, 9, 8, 7, 6, 5, 4, 3, 2. When buying a pack, it is usual to find two additional cards called Jokers, often illustrated with a figure dressed as a court jester, with cap and bells. The Jokers are rarely used but have been added to the pack specially for a few games.

Some games require two or more packs, and some, particularly games which originate from Spain, Italy, Germany or Switzerland, require a 'short pack', which is formed from the standard pack by removing the lower ranking cards: for a 40-card pack, the 4s, 3s and 2s are removed; for a 36-card pack, the 5s are also removed; for a 32-card pack, the 6s are also removed. For more about foreign packs, see Playing Cards History, p397.

The suits in most games are of equal value, but some games, as explained in the main text, grade the suits in order of importance. So far as the ranks of individual cards are concerned, in most games the cards are ranked in importance as set out in the list above, with the Ace the highest ranked. Originally, the Ace was the one and ranked lowest, but early in the history of card games (ie before 1500) the Ace began to take precedence over all others. In some games, however, the old order stands, and Ace counts as the lowest card. Some games, especially those which originate in continental Europe, have eccentric rankings of the cards, particularly regarding 10s and 2s. Rankings are given, where appropriate, in the descriptions of all the games in the main text.

Deciding partnerships

In games of four players requiring partnerships, respective partners can be decided by mutual agreement or by chance. If by chance is preferred, the usual method is for any player to shuffle the cards and another to cut (see Shuffling and Cutting, below). Each player then cuts the pack, with the two players cutting the lowest cards forming a partnership against the two highest. The lowest of all is the dealer and he chooses his seat with his partner sitting opposite. Any variations from this practice are mentioned in the individual descriptions of games.

Rotation of play

In most games the right to deal, the order of bidding (if any) and the turn to play rotate to the left, ie clockwise. However, in some games originating in continental Europe the converse is true, and play rotates to the right, ie anti-clockwise.

Shuffling

A safe way to shuffle the pack is to place it on the table, and divide it roughly into two by taking the top half and placing it end to end with the lower half. Then, holding the two halves

abutting each other, riffle them together by running the thumbs up the sides of each half while holding the two packs firm with the fingers on the opposite edge, as shown in the second illustration. With the two halves interleaved, slide them together as in the third illustration. Then, take about a third of the cards from the top and place the bottom two-thirds on top of them. Repeat the whole process twice more, not forgetting the final cut, and the pack should be well shuffled.

Cutting

There are two types of cut. In the cut whereby each player cuts the pack to determine partners or who deals, the player merely takes a packet of cards from the top of the pack, which should be face down on the table, and turns it over to expose the bottom card.

The cut made before another player deals has another purpose. It is the final insurance that the pack has not been arranged. In this cut, the player takes a packet from the top of the face-down pack (the packet should be of at least five cards), places it on the table face down and places what was previously the lower part of the pack on top of it.

Dealing

It is customary before the deal for the pack to be shuffled by the dealer. Although any player may ask to shuffle prior to the dealer, the dealer has the right to shuffle last. He then places the pack face down before his right-hand neighbour, who cuts it as described above. It is in order for this player merely to take a packet from the top of the pack and place it on the table, leaving the dealer to complete the cut by placing the lower portion on top. It is open for a player to refuse to cut, in which case any other player may volunteer. If none wishes to, the dealer must cut the cards himself. This description is for games where the play rotates to the left; in games where play rotates anti-clockwise, the left-hand neighbour of the dealer cuts.

The dealer deals the cards, in nearly all games face down, to each player in turn, either one at a time or in packets as the game requires, until all players have the required number. It is customary and courteous for players to wait until the deal is complete before touching their cards (see also Customs, Practices and Etiquette, p401).

Misdealing

If there is a misdeal, which can occur for various reasons, such as a card being turned face up, or being already face up in the pack, or there being cards missing, the cards must be gathered up and the dealer must begin again. However, if there is an advantage in being the dealer, then the misdealer loses the deal, which passes to the next player.

Trumps and tricks

Many games involve taking 'tricks'. A trick is a round of play to which each player contributes a card. The usual rule (and one must emphasize the *usual* rule) is that all players must follow suit to the card led, eg if the leader (the player who contributes the first card to the trick) leads a heart, all other players must contribute a heart if they are able to, ie if they hold a heart in their hand. If a player does not hold a card of the suit led, he must play any other card. The card which wins the trick is the highest card that it contains of the suit led.

However, in most trick-taking games, there is a 'trump' suit, which is decided by various different methods according to the rules of the game being played. The word 'trump' is a corruption of 'triumph', and a card from the trump suit triumphs over one from any other suit. Thus, where there is a trump suit, a player who does not hold a card of the suit led, but who does hold a card of the trump suit, may play the trump, which will win the trick, unless a subsequent player who is also devoid of a card in the suit led plays a higher trump. Thus, a trick is won by the highest trump it contains, or if it does not contain a trump, by the highest card in the suit led.

A player's first obligation is to play a card in the suit led. If he is unable to, he may play a trump, thus beating all cards of the suit led. He is not allowed to play a trump if he holds a card of the suit led. On the other hand, if he does not hold a card of the suit led, he is not obliged to play a trump – he may play any other card (called a 'discard'). A discard, of course, can never win a trick. A player is not obliged to try to win a trick.

To sum up: the leader plays a card of a certain suit (which may or may not be a trump). Subsequent players must follow suit if they can, and if they cannot may play a trump or discard as they wish. The highest trump wins the trick – if none is played the highest card of the suit led wins.

This is what is meant by the phrase often used in this book: 'the normal rules of trick-taking apply'.

Of course, inevitably there are games where the normal rules do not apply. In these games it might be compulsory to trump, or it might be that you can trump even if holding a card of the suit led, or it might even be that it is not obligatory to follow suit to the card led. In all games where these deviations from the normal rules apply they are carefully explained in the individual descriptions of play.

Duration of play
It is advisable, and important in games where money is changing hands, to agree a time when play will stop, or at least a time when any player who wishes to leave the game may do so. This saves a lot of hard feeling in games where players who are winning feel obliged to play for longer than they wish because losing players insist on nobody leaving while they themselves are losing.

Card Games Glossary

The glossary does not include game names or variants, for which the index can be consulted.

à cheval in Hoggenheimer, a bet laid on two adjacent cards

above the line in Bridge, where a bonus score which does not count towards the winning of a game is placed

abundance in Solo Whist, an undertaking to win nine tricks

> **abundance declared** in Solo Whist, an undertaking to win all thirteen tricks

> **royal abundance** in Solo Whist, an undertaking to win nine tricks with the turn-up suit as trumps

Acol in Bridge, a system of bidding

all in in Texas Hold 'Em, to have all your chips in the pot

ante (*a*) in Brag and Poker, a compulsory stake put down by a player before the deal (*b*) a contribution to a pot before the deal which belongs to all players

auction the period in which bidding takes place

avec la table in Chemin de Fer, a call which allows a player to bet half the value of the amount in the bank

banco (*a*) in Chemin de Fer, a call which allows a player to bet the whole of the amount in the bank (*b*) in Punto Banco, a bet on the bank rather than the players

banco suivi in Chemin de Fer, a call which allows a player to bet the whole of the amount in the bank, having already made and lost a bet of banco

bank an amount of chips or coins put up by a banker for players to bet against

banker a person who keeps or acts as the bank (sometimes representing the casino)

basto in Ombre, ♣A, which is always a trump

baulking in Cribbage, the practice by the non-dealer of laying away cards to the crib from which it is difficult to score points

bed in Flower Garden, one of the six rows of six cards that form part of the tableau

beg in All Fours, as the non-dealer, to decline the turn-up card as trumps

bella in Klaberjass, the 20 points scored by

the player who holds and plays the King and Queen of trumps

below the line in Bridge, where scores which count towards the winning of a game are placed

bête in Klaberjass, applied to the maker if he has the lower total points

> **double bête** in Pinochle, the defeat of the bidder if he has scored fewer points than his contract

> **single bête** in Pinochle, the concession of defeat by the bidder without leading to a trick

bezique in Bezique, the scoring combination of ♠Q and ♦J

> **double bezique** in Bezique, the scoring combination of two ♠Q and two ♦J

> **quadruple bezique** in Bezique for four players, the scoring combination of four ♠Q and four ♦J

> **quintuple bezique** in Rubicon Bezique, the scoring combination of five ♠Q and five♦J

> **sextuple bezique** in Rubicon Bezique, the scoring combination of six ♠Q and six ♦J

> **single bezique** *same as* bezique

> **triple bezique** in Bezique for three players, the scoring combination of three ♠Q and three ♦J

bid an offer to make a certain number of tricks or points in play

> **artificial bid** *same as* conventional bid

> **bidding** the act or process of making bids, or the bids made

> **conventional bid** in Bridge, a bid which conveys a special meaning to a player's partner

> **cue bid** in Bridge, a bid in a suit other than the intended trump suit, to indicate control of the suit bid

> **limit bid** in Bridge, a bid that conveys to a partner limited strength

> **open the bidding** in Bridge, to be the first player to make a bid

> **pre-emptive bid** in Bridge, an unusually

high bid intended to deter others from bidding

psychic bid in Bridge, the bid of a suit in which a player is not strong in order to deceive the opponents or hinder their bidding

rebid in Bridge, the opener's second bid after his partner's response

rescue bid in Bridge, a bid to rescue a partner whose bid suit has been doubled

shut-out bid *same as* pre-emptive bid

signing-off bid in Bridge, a bid intended by the bidder to close the auction

Stayman bid in Bridge, a response of 2♣ to a bid of 1NT, asking the opener to bid a four-card major suit

underbid in Bridge, a bid less than the value of the hand warrants

big casino in Casino, two points won for capturing ♦10

Black Maria in Black Maria, ♠Q

blackjack in Blackjack, a two-card combination of an Ace and a ten-point card, giving a value of 21 points

Blackwood convention in Bridge, a way of enquiring how many Aces a player's partner holds by bidding 4NT

blind bets in Texas Hold 'Em, small compulsory stakes put in by the first two players to the left of the dealer

big blind in Texas Hold 'Em, a small compulsory stake put in by the second player to the left of the dealer, larger than that put in by the first player to the left of the dealer

small blind in Texas Hold 'Em, a small compulsory stake put in by the first player to the left of the dealer

blind betting making a bet without seeing the cards held

blitzed in Gin Rummy, applied to a losing player who did not score a point

blücher in Napoleon, an optional extra bid to win all five tricks, bid only after a previous player has bid wellington

bluff usually in Poker, to seek to deceive by betting as if you have a stronger or weaker hand than you really hold

book (*a*) in Pelmanism and Pig, a set of all four cards of the same rank (*b*) in Whist, the first six tricks

bouquet in Flower Garden, a crescent of 16 cards that forms part of the tableau

bower in Euchre, the Jack of trumps or the Jack of the same colour

left bower the Jack of the same colour as the Jack of the trump suit

right bower the Jack of the trump suit

box (*a*) in Cribbage, *same as* crib (*b*) in Gin Rummy, one deal or the score for winning one deal

bragger in Classical Brag, one of three wild cards: ♦A, ♣J or ♦9

brisque in Bezique, an Ace or a 10 won in a trick, each scoring ten points

build (*a*) in patience games, to transfer cards to foundations or to other cards in the tableau (*b*) in Casino, to play a card to the layout which will allow a card or cards to be captured on a future turn

multiple build in Casino, an attempt to capture several cards in a future turn by making more than one build at a time

single build in Casino, an attempt to capture two or more cards in a future turn by building

burn to discard a card without its value being shown, usually prior to a deal

burying in Pinochle, the laying away face down by the bidder, after taking the widow, of any three cards not used in a meld

bust in Pontoon, to exceed the score of 21 when drawing cards

button in Texas Hold 'Em, a disc moved round the table on each deal to indicate which player is the 'dealer' and thus which players must put in the blinds

buy in Pontoon, to receive a card face down, for a stake not exceeding the original stake

cachette in Quinto, the first five cards dealt to the table as a widow to be taken by the winner of the last trick

call (*a*) in Bridge, to declare, bid or pass; any pass, double, redouble or bid (*b*) in Poker, to make a bet exactly equal to the previous bet (*c*) in Calabresella and Euchre, to make a legal demand for a card held by another player

overall in Bridge, the bid of a suit, or no trumps, over the opponents' bid

calypso in Calypso, a complete set of a player's trump suit

canasta in Canasta, a meld of seven cards of the same rank, with or without wild cards

mixed canasta in Canasta, a meld of seven cards of the same rank, including wild cards

natural canasta in Canasta, a meld of seven cards of the same rank, without wild cards

capot (a) in Piquet, the winning of all twelve tricks and the 40 points scored thereby (b) in Polignac, a declaration that a player intends to win all the tricks

captain in Le Truc, played by four in partnerships, the dealer and the eldest hand, who each lead their side

capture to win possession of a card during play, thus taking it into the hand or scoring points from it

card one of a pack, usually of 52 cards, divided into four suits used in playing games

bare card a card which is the only one held in that particular suit

boodle card a card on which coins or chips are placed which can be won by players

card sharp, card sharper a person who cheats at cards

community card in Poker, a card that can be used by any player to help form a hand

court card the King, Queen or Jack of each suit

face card *same as* court card

grace card in Limited, one of the four cards from the waste pile that become available for play when all other options have been exhausted

guarded card a card in a suit in which lower-ranking cards are also held, eg a King which becomes master card when a lower card has been played on the Ace

high card in Brag and Poker, a hand lacking any combinations and thus ranked by the highest ranked card it contains

hole card in versions of Poker, eg Stud, a card dealt face down to a player

honour card (a) a high card, especially one with a scoring value, eg in Bridge, each of the five highest trumps, or in a no-trump contract, each Ace (b) in Whist, the four highest trumps

master card the highest card not yet played

in a suit, and therefore the card that controls that suit

natural card a card that is not a Joker or a wild card

non-valle card in Panguingue, any card except the 7s, 5s and 3s

penalty card a card which brings a scoring or other disadvantage to the player who holds or wins it

picture card *same as* court card

plain card a card other than a court card

trump card a card turned up to determine the trump suit; any card of that suit, or a card otherwise designated a trump by the rules of the game

unmatched card in Gin Rummy, a card which does not belong to a meld

upcard the top card of a pile, turned face up

valle card in Panguingue, the 7s, 5s and 3s

wild card a card which can represent any card its holder wishes and which can be used in place of any other card

cards (a) in Casino, three points won for capturing the majority of the cards (b) in Piquet, the ten points scored by the player who makes the majority of the tricks

carte blanche a hand containing no court cards

double carte blanche in Rubicon Bezique, the situation in which neither partner's hand contains court cards

casino a gambling house

casino edge the percentage advantage that a casino has on the bets it offers and therefore the percentage it would expect to win over the long run

check in Poker, the option to stay in the deal without staking

chip a token of wood, plastic or similar, used to represent money

clubs (♣) one of the four customary suits of playing cards, comprising 13 cards with black trefoil pips

codille in Ombre, the situation in which one opponent wins more tricks than ombre

colour the colour of the pips and characters on a card: red for diamonds and hearts, black for spades and clubs

combination in Bezique, a number of cards

which form beziques, sequences and quartets for scoring purposes

combining in Casino, a way of capturing two or more cards by playing a card the pip total of which equals the sum of the pip totals of the cards

comet in Comet, the wildcards: ♦9 in the black pack and ♣9 in the red pack

condition in Panguingue, certain melds which allow a player to immediately collect chips from the other active players

contract an undertaking by a player or partnership to win a certain number of tricks

cop in Solo Whist, a call that signifies acceptance of a proposal bid

couleur in Trente et Quarante, a bet that the first card turned up will be the same colour as the winning row

counting out in All Fours, the scoring of enough points to win the game before the deal is played out

crib in Cribbage, the extra hand formed by the players' discards

crossing it in Euchre, the choice of a trump suit of a different colour to the rejected turn-up

croupier a person who officiates at a gaming table, collecting the stakes and paying the winners, and sometimes dealing

curse of Scotland ♦9

cut to divide a pack of cards by lifting the upper portion at random, either to expose a card or suit, or in order to replace the parts of the pack in a different order before dealing

dead hand an extra hand which plays no part in a game

deadwood in Rummy, the unmelded cards remaining in players' hands after a player has gone out and other cards have been laid off where possible

deal (a) to distribute cards to each player, or the act of distributing cards (b) the period between one deal and the next, including bidding, playing, scoring etc

dealer a person who deals cards, or whose turn it is to deal, or who has dealt the hand in play

dealing shoe same as shoe

goulash deal a re-deal of cards without shuffling

deck same as pack

declaration (a) a call or bid (b) in Bezique, a point-scoring combination of cards placed on the table

declare (a) to show cards in order to score (b) in Bridge, to announce the chosen trump suit or no trumps

declarer (a) in Bridge, the player on the contracting side who first named the trump suit (b) in Napoleon and Skat, the highest bidder

defenders in Bridge, the partnership attempting to prevent the contracting side from making the number of tricks promised in the contract

denial pass in Bridge, a pass showing lack of support for a partner's opening bid

deuce the 2 of each suit

diamonds (♦) one of the four customary suits of playing cards, comprising 13 cards with red diamond-shaped pips

die Alten same as old women

discard to throw away a card or cards, as not needed or not allowed by the game; to throw down a (useless) card of another suit when you cannot follow suit and cannot or will not trump; the act of discarding; the card or cards thrown out of the hand

distribution in Bridge, how the hand is divided into suits in respect of the number of cards of each suit held

dix (a) in Bezique and Klaberjass, the 7 of trumps (b) in Pinochle, the 9 of trumps

dog's chance, dog's life in Knockout Whist, a last turn offered to a player who would otherwise be knocked out of the game

double in Bridge, a bid that increases the trick values and penalties should the bid which is doubled become the contract

double down in Blackjack, an option for a player to double his stake and receive a third card face down

doubleton in Bridge and Whist, a holding of two cards in a particular suit

draw (a) to take a card from a face-down pack to determine seats, dealer etc (b) to take a card or cards from the stock, either to replace discards or to increase the number of cards held

draw trumps to repeatedly lead trumps in order to exhaust opponents' hands of trumps

dressing the board in Pope Joan, the placing of chips or coins by the dealer onto the board

drop out to cease to play any part in a game, either by choice or necessity

dummy in Bridge, the declarer's partner; the hand laid down by him which the declarer plays

eighty Kings (a) in Bezique, the scoring combination of any four Kings (b) in Pinochle, the scoring combination of one King of each suit

elder, eldest hand the player on the dealer's left (or, in games of Spanish derivation, the player on the dealer's right)

endplay in Bridge, to place an opponent in a situation near the end of a game whereby he cannot prevent the declarer making a vital trick

entry a card with which to win a trick in order to take the lead

euchred in Euchre, applied to the side which chose the trump suit if it fails to win at least three tricks

exit to lose the lead deliberately

expose to show the cards in a hand to other players or the banker

face the printed side of a playing card that shows its pip value, as opposed to the back

face down with the side of the card that displays the pip value hidden

face up with the side of the card that displays the pip value visible

false draws in Chemin de Fer, a practice in which both player and banker are allowed to draw or stand at their discretion

fan cards arranged in a crescent shape, usually with each card slightly overlapping another

faux tirages *same as* false draws

fifth street in Poker, a final fifth card dealt to the row of community cards on the table in Texas Hold 'Em and Omaha

file in Russian Bank, one of four cards dealt in a line towards a player's opponent

finesse an attempt by a player holding a higher card to take a trick with a lower card, risking loss

flop in Poker, the first three community cards dealt face up to the table in Texas Hold 'Em and Omaha

flush (a) a hand in which all the cards are of the same suit (b) in Pinochle, a meld of the Ace, 10, King, Queen and Jack of trumps

royal flush in Poker, a sequence of Ace, King, Queen, Jack and 10 of the same suit (the highest hand of all)

running flush in Brag, three cards in sequence of the same suit

straight flush in Poker, a sequence of five cards of the same suit

fold in Poker, to drop out

foot in Panguingue, the lower part of the stock

force (a) to force an opponent to play a particular card, usually a trump (b) in Bridge, to make a bid that forces a partner to bid in order to comply with the bidding system being used

forehand in Skat, the player to the dealer's left

forty Jacks (a) in Bezique, the scoring combination of any four Jacks (b) in Pinochle, the scoring combination of one Jack of each suit

foundation in patience games, a card which is separated from the pack or tableau and upon which a whole suit or sequence must be built

four of a kind in Poker, four cards of the same rank with an unmatched card

fourth street in Poker, a fourth card dealt to the row of community cards on the table in Texas Hold 'Em and Omaha

freeze-out a game which cannot end until only two players are left in or a limit is reached

frozen in Canasta, applied to the discard pile when a player may only draw the top card from it when he can make a new meld by adding the top card to two natural cards from his hand

full house in Poker, three cards of one rank with two of another

game (a) in All Fours, California Jack and Pitch a point for winning the highest value of scoring cards in tricks (b) in Cinch, the 10 of trumps

game call in Bridge, a bid which, if successful, will win a game

gate in Monte Bank, the bottom card of the pack when exposed

general in Polignac, a declaration that a player intends to win all the tricks

get out to win a patience game by achieving the aim of the game

gift in All Fours, a point given to the non-dealer if the dealer wishes to accept the turn-up as trumps

go in Cribbage, an announcement that a player cannot play without exceeding 31; the score for an opponent's failure to play

go boom in Go Boom, to win by being the first to get rid of all the cards held

go bust *same as* bust

go down in Bridge, to fail to fulfil a contract

go gin in Gin Rummy, to go out with all ten cards melded and no unmatched cards

go on top in Panguingue, a declaration made out by a player to indicate he is dropping out by placing a forfeit on top of the foot of the stock

go out to win by getting rid of all the cards in a hand

go rummy in Rummy, to meld all the cards held and go out in one turn, without having previously melded

grand in Skat, a contract in which the four Jacks are the only trumps

group in Panguingue, a type of meld

guard a card or cards that protect a high card so that an opponent cannot win several instant tricks with a long suit

hand the set of cards held by a player at one deal; the play of a single deal of cards

balanced hand *same as* even hand

concealed hand in Canasta, a hand with which a player goes out without having previously melded

even hand in Bridge, a hand in which the suits are evenly split, eg 4–4–3–2

unbalanced hand in Bridge, a hand with at least six cards in one suit, or two suits of five cards

hard in Blackjack, a hand which does not contain an Ace or which counts an Ace as one

head in Panguingue, the upper part of the stock

hearts (♥) one of the four customary suits of playing cards, comprising 13 cards with red heart-shaped pips

heel *same as* talon

high (*a*) in All Fours and Pitch, a point for winning the highest trump in play (*b*) in California Jack, a point for winning the Ace of trumps

high-card point in Bridge, one of 40 points allocated to cards in a hand using the Work count method

his nob in Cribbage, a point scored for holding the Jack of the same suit as the start

hit in Blackjack, a request for an additional free card (*cf* twist in Pontoon)

hitting the moon (*a*) in Black Maria variants, to take all the penalty cards to reduce your total score to zero (*b*) in Omnibus Hearts, the scoring of 26 points by a player who takes all fifteen counting cards

honours a score for holding honour cards in Bridge or Whist

huitième in Piquet, a sequence of eight

hundred Aces (*a*) in Bezique, the scoring combination of any four Aces (*b*) in Pinochle, the scoring combination of one Ace of each suit

in hand in Skat, playing without looking at the skat or taking it into your hand

in prison in Trente et Quarante, a stake left on the table after a refait

insurance in Blackjack, an optional bet offered to players by the banker when he has an Ace, showing that he will get a natural (thus saving the player his stake)

in the hole in Five Hundred and Pitch, having a minus score

inverse in Trente et Quarante, a bet that the colour of the first card turned will be the opposite colour to that of the winning row

invitation to game in Bridge, a bid inviting a partner to continue bidding to the level required for game

jack in All Fours, California Jack and Pitch, a point for winning the Jack of trumps

jambone in Railroad Euchre, a bid to play alone in which the player lays his cards face up on the table and an opponent directs which card he must play

jamboree in Railroad Euchre, a hand of the five highest cards which is shown and scored without play

jasz in Klaberjass, the Jack of trumps

jeux de règles in Écarté, a list of hands with which a player is advised to play

jinking it in Spoil Five, an undertaking by a player who has won three tricks to take the last two tricks as well

joint soloist in Solo Whist, one of the players in temporary partnership in a proposal and acceptance bid

Joker a 53rd or 54th card in the pack, used in some games

kicker in Poker, an unpaired card that determines which of two otherwise equivalent hands wins the pot

kitty *same as* pool

knave a Jack

knock in Rummy, to signify the end of the deal by laying down your hand, sometimes accompanied by knocking on the table

lay off in Rummy, to add cards to a meld already on the table

layout the arrangement of cards upon the table, especially in patience games

le grand in Baccarat, a two-card hand with a point of 9

le petit in Baccarat, a two-card hand with a point of 8

lead to play the first card of a round or trick; the first card laid

light in Bridge, falling short of the number of tricks contracted

line in Gin Rummy, the score for winning a deal

little casino in Casino, a point won for capturing ♠2

looed in Loo, applied to a player who played but failed to win a trick

low (*a*) in All Fours and Pitch, a point for winning the lowest trump in play (*b*) in California Jack, a point for winning the 2 of trumps

majeur in Piquet, the non-dealer

make to declare as trumps; to win a trick

maker (*a*) in Cinch and Euchre, the player who named the trump suit (*b*) in Klaberjass, the player who accepts the proposed suit as trumps

making it next in Euchre, the choice of a trump suit of the same colour as the rejected turn-up

manille in Ombre, the 7 of trumps when a red suit is trumps or the 2 of trumps when a black suit is trumps

march in Euchre, the winning of all five tricks by one side; the score for doing so

marking the King in Écarté, the scoring of a point by the dealer if a King is dealt as the trump indicator

marriage in Bezique and Pinochle, a scoring combination of King and Queen

   common marriage in Bezique and Pinochle, the scoring combination of the King and Queen of a plain suit

   royal marriage in Bezique and Pinochle, the scoring combination of the King and Queen of trumps

matador in Ombre, one of the three top trumps: spadille, manille and basto

meld a combination or group of scoring cards, usually three or more of the same rank, or of the same suit and in sequence; to show or announce such a group

menel in Klaberjass, the 9 of trumps

middlehand in Skat, the player to the dealer's right

mineur in Piquet, the dealer

mis *same as* misère

misdeal any departure from the correct procedure in dealing

misère an undertaking to lose all the tricks

   misère ouvert in Solo Whist, an undertaking to lose all the tricks, with the hand exposed on the table for opponents to see after the first trick has been played

   open misère same as misère ouvert

miss in Loo, an extra hand

muggins in Cribbage, a call by which, if a player overlooks points when scoring, his opponent can claim the points for himself

nap same as napoleon

napoleon in Napoleon, a bid to win all five possible tricks

natural (*a*) a set or sequence of cards containing no wild cards (*b*) in Blackjack, *same as* blackjack (*c*) in Baccarat, Chemin de Fer and Punto Banco, a two-card hand with a point of 9 or 8 (*d*) in Classical Brag, a scoring combination without a bragger (*e*) in Pontoon, *same as* pontoon

   natural 8 same as le petit

natural 9 *same as* le grand

noir in Trente et Quarante, black, or the row representing it

non-dealer in a two-handed game, the player who is not currently acting as the dealer

NT no trumps

null in Skat, a contract to lose all the tricks

old maid in Old Maid, the losing player who holds the odd Queen at the end of the game

old women in Schafkopf, the two black Queens

ombre in Ombre, the player who has the right to name the trump suit and to exchange cards by discarding and drawing from the stock

one-eyed Jack ♥J or ♠J

opening lead in Bridge, the first lead of the trick-taking phase

pack a complete set of playing cards, usually comprising 52 cards

Italian pack a pack of cards traditionally used in Italy, comprising 40 cards

pack on in patience games, to overlay one card on another, either partially or completely overlapping

Spanish pack a pack of cards traditionally used in Spain, comprising 40 cards

packet a small stack of cards

pair two cards of the same rank

no pair in Poker, *same as* high card

one pair in Poker, a hand of two cards of one rank plus three unmatched cards

open pair in Stud Poker, a pair among a player's cards face up on the table

pairing in Casino, a way of capturing a card by matching it to a card of the same rank already held

pair-royal three cards of the same rank

double pair-royal four cards of the same rank

pam in Five-Card Loo, ♣J

partie in Piquet, a game consisting of six deals, three by each player

partnership a team of two, or occasionally more, players

pass (*a*) to abstain from making a bid, declaration or other play (*b*) in Klaberjass, to reject the proposed suit as trumps

pat hand in Poker, a hand whose holder does not wish to try to improve by drawing

patience a card game for one (called 'solitaire' in North America)

pedro in Cinch, the 5 of the trump suit and the 5 of the same colour

left pedro in Cinch, the 5 of the same colour as the trump suit

right pedro in Cinch, the 5 of the trump suit

pegging in Cribbage, the scoring during the first part of the game, and the keeping of the score by moving pegs round the Cribbage board

peter in Bridge and Whist, to play a card higher than necessary to a lead by a partner to encourage the partner to lead the suit again

Pink Lady in Black Maria variants, ♥Q

pinochle in Pinochle, ♠Q and ♦J

double pinochle in Pinochle, two ♠Q and two ♦J

pip a suit symbol spot on a card

pip value the total of the pips on a playing card, for example a 3 card has a pip value of 3

pique in Piquet, an extra 30 points scored if a player reaches 30 points on the deal during the trick-taking phase before his opponent has scored

pitch in Pitch, the opening lead, which fixes the trump suit

pitcher in Pitch, the player who plays against the other players and makes the opening lead

player in Calabresella, the player who plays alone against the other players

playing over in Pinochle, the requirement that each player must, if able, play a higher trump than any previously played if a trump is led

playing the board in Texas Hold 'Em, choosing to use neither of the two hole cards held in a hand

point in Piquet, a scoring combination, scored by holding a suit containing a greater number of pips than any held by the opponent; the points scored thereby

point count *same as* Work count

polignac in Polignac, ♠J

pone (*a*) in games where the deal rotates clockwise, the player to the right of the dealer, who cuts the cards (*b*) in two-handed games, the non-dealer

pontoon in Pontoon, a two-card hand of 21, consisting of an Ace and a 10-count card

pool the collective stakes of a number of players, which can be won during the game

scoop the pool to win the total amount of money in the pool

pot *same as* pool

pre-empt in Bridge, to make a pre-emptive bid (*see* bid)

preferential bet in Baccarat, a bet of banco, banco suivi or avec la table

prial (*a*) in Brag, three cards of the same rank (*b*) in Pontoon, a hand of three 7s

prop in Solo Whist, a proposal bid

proposal in Solo Whist, a bid that asks for a partner with whom to make eight tricks with the turn-up as trumps

puesta in Ombre, the situation in which one or both opponents wins the same number of tricks as ombre, with ombre doubling the amount in the pool and the doubled pool being carried forward to the next deal

punt to stake against the bank

punto (*a*) in Punto Banco, a bet on the players rather than the bank (*b*) in Ombre, the Ace of trumps when a red suit is trumps

quart in Piquet, a sequence of four cards

quartet in Bezique, a scoring combination comprising any four Aces, Kings, Queens or Jacks

quatorze in Piquet, four cards of the same rank

quint (*a*) in Piquet, a sequence of five cards (*b*) in Quinto, a point-scoring combination of cards

quint major in Piquet, a sequence of five cards from Ace to ten

quint minor in Piquet, a sequence of five cards from Jack to seven

quint royal in Quinto, the Joker

raise (*a*) in Bridge to make a higher bid (*b*) in Poker, to put in an amount equal to the previous stake plus a further amount to raise the stake higher

double raise in Bridge, a raise which misses out one level by raising the previous bid higher than necessary

jump raise same as double raise

triple raise in Bridge, a raise which misses out two levels by raising the previous bid of, say, one to four

rank the grade or position of a particular card in its suit, for example 3, 10 and Jack are ranks

rearhand in Skat, the dealer

redouble in Bridge, to double again the trick values and penalties after the opponents have already doubled a previous bid

refait in Trente et Quarante, an occasion in which both rows of cards tie at 31

refusal (*a*) in Écarté, the rejection by the dealer of the proposal that cards may be exhanged for others from the stock (*b*) in All Fours, the rejection by the dealer of a beg (ie the refusal to allow the eldest hand to score for gift)

release in patience games, to make a card available for play (usually by playing the cards blocking it)

renege *same as* revoke

renounce *same as* revoke

repique in Piquet, a bonus of 60 points scored for scoring 30 points in the combination categories alone, before the opponent scores a point

reserve in patience games, cards that are available for play which are not part of the foundations, stock, tableau or discard piles

respond in Bridge, a bid made in reply to a bid made by a partner

revoke (*a*) to fail to follow suit when able (*b*) to play a card which contravenes the rules of the game

robbing the pack in Cinch, the entitlement of the dealer to look through the stock and take any cards he wishes into his hand

rouge in Trente et Quarante, red, or the row representing it

round-the-corner applied to a continuous sequence of cards in which the Ace counts both high and low, ie one running highest to lowest as in Queen, King, Ace, 2, 3 and so on

rubber in Bridge and Whist, the winning of, or play for, the best of usually three games

rubicon in Bezique and Piquet, a minimum score which the loser must attain to avoid further penalty

ruff *same as* trump

rule of eleven in Bridge, the fact that when a player plays his fourth best card in a suit on the opening lead, the difference between its pip value and 11 is the number of cards of higher rank the other players hold, from which the leader's partner can calculate how many of those cards are held by the declarer

run (a) in Brag, three cards in sequence (b) in Cribbage any number of cards in sequence

run the cards in All Fours, to discard the initial turn-up, deal three extra cards to each player and turn up a new card as the trump indicator

sabot *same as* shoe

sacardo in Ombre, a situation in which ombre takes more tricks than either of his opponents and hence takes the pool

schmeiss in Klaberjass, to offer to accept the turn-up card for trumps or to abandon the deal

schneider in Schafkopf and Skat, to take more than 90 points in tricks

schneidered (a) in Schafkopf and Skat, applied to a losing side which failed to score 31 points in tricks (b) in Gin Rummy, applied to a loser who did not score a point

schwartz, schwarz in Schafkopf and Skat, winning all the tricks

septième in Piquet, a sequence of seven cards of the same suit

sequence (a) a set of three or more cards consecutive in value (b) in Bezique, the scoring combination of the Ace, 10, King, Queen and Jack of trumps

ascending sequence a sequence in which cards run up, for example from 2 to King

descending sequence a sequence in which cards run down, for example from King to 2

set in Bridge, to defeat an opponent's contract

set back in Five Hundred, the deduction of the value of his bid from his score if the bidder fails to make his contract

sharper *same as* card sharp

shoe a box-like device for dispensing cards singly

short pack, shortened pack a pack which has been reduced from 52 cards to some other number by the removal of all cards of a certain rank or ranks

show in Cribbage, the second part of play

showdown in Poker, the exposure of players' cards face up on the table at the end of a game

shuffle to mix cards at random

shutout in Gin Rummy, a game in which the loser did not score a point

signal any convention of play intended to give information legally to a partner

sign off in Bridge, to make a bid that is intended to be the final bid in the auction

singleton in Bridge and Whist, a holding of one card only in a particular suit

sinking in Piquet, the omission of announcing a scoring combination in order to deceive an opponent as to the cards held

sixième in Piquet, a sequence of six cards of the same suit

sixty Queens (a) in Bezique, the scoring combination of any four Queens (b) in Pinochle, the scoring combination of one Queen of each suit

skat in Skat, the widow

skunked in Gin Rummy, applied to a loser who did not score a point

slam (a) in Whist, the winning of every trick (b) in Omnibus Hearts, the same as hitting the moon

grand slam in Bridge, a contract to win every trick, and the achieving of such

little slam *same as* small slam

small slam in Bridge, a contract to win all but one trick, and its achievement

sleeping applied to a card or cards not in play

smudge in Pitch, a bid to win all four points

soft in Blackjack, a hand which counts an Ace as eleven

solitaire the North American term for games of patience

solo (a) in Solo Whist, an undertaking to make five tricks with the turn-up suit as trumps (b) a bid to play without using a widow or without help of a partner

spades (♠) (a) one of the four customary suits of playing cards, comprising 13 cards with black shovel-like pips (b) in Casino, a point won for capturing the majority of the spades

spadille in Ombre, ♠A, the highest trump

spin, spinado in Spinado, ♦A

split in Blackjack, to divide a hand of two

cards of the same rank into two separate hands

spoiled in Spoil Five, applied to a hand in which nobody wins three tricks

spread in Panguingue, a meld of three cards

squeeze in Bridge, an endplay used by the declarer to force the opponents to make discards which will help the declarer make his contract

stack to shuffle or arrange the order of cards for cheating

stake money or chips staked on an outcome not yet known; to deposit as a wager

maximum stake the highest amount of coins and chips which players may contribute in a gambling game

minimum stake the lowest amount of coins and chips which players are obliged to contribute in a gambling game

stand (*a*) in Blackjack, to keep a hand unchanged, rather than drawing another card in the hope of improving it (*b*) in All Fours, as the non-dealer, to accept the turn-up card as trumps

stand pat in Poker, to play a hand as it was dealt, without drawing any cards

start in Cribbage, the top card of the lower half of the cut pack, which is revealed by the dealer and placed face up on the top of the reunited pack

stay in Poker, to remain in the game without raising

stick in Pontoon, a declaration that a player is happy with his count and will not take any more cards

stock the undealt part of a pack of cards, which may be used later in the deal

stop in Newmarket and Pope Joan, an interruption of play caused by the required next card in the sequence not being in play

straight in Poker, a hand of five cards in sequence, but not of the same suit

straight flush in Poker, a hand of five cards in sequence and of the same suit

stringer in Panguingue, three cards of the same suit in sequence

suit one of the sets of cards of the same denomination: clubs, diamonds, hearts or spades

bare suit a suit of which no cards are held in a hand

cross suit in Euchre, the two suits not of the same colour as the trump suit

follow suit to play a card of the same suit as the one which was led

long suit the suit with most cards in a hand, or a suit with a large number of cards held in a hand

major suit in Bridge, spades or hearts, valued more highly than diamonds or clubs

minor suit in Bridge, diamonds or clubs, valued less highly than spades or hearts

next suit in Euchre, the suit of the same colour as the trump suit

plain suit a suit other than the trump suit

side suit *same as* plain suit

suited in Poker, hole cards of the same suit

suit of preference in Preference, the hearts suit

trump suit a suit that ranks higher than any other suit

sweep in Casino, the taking of all the cards in the layout at once; the score for this

sweep the board to take all the cards

switch change from one suit to another in leading or bidding

tab in Coon Can, *same as* tableau

tablanette in Tablanette, the clearing of the table by taking all the available cards

tableau (*a*) in patience games, the main part of the layout of cards on the table (*b*) in Baccarat, the cards on the table upon which players may bet (*c*) in Coon Can, a tied game in which neither player goes out before the stock is exhausted

Table of Play in Baccarat and its variants, a chart which sets out the best option for play in any given situation

take-all in Omnibus Hearts, *same as* hitting the moon

take it in Klaberjass, to accept the proposed suit as trumps

take-out in Bridge, to bid a different suit from a partner, as distinguished from a raise

take-out double in Bridge, a call not meant to double the points at stake but to request a partner to bid an unbid suit

talon (*a*) in patience games, a waste pile;

cards laid aside as unplayable when turned up from stock, but which are available for play later (*b*) in Piquet, cards laid aside after the deal for later use

tenace in Bridge and Whist, a holding of two cards in a suit, one two ranks below the other, eg A, Q

imperfect tenace a holding of two cards in a suit with two or more intervening cards, eg A, 10

major tenace the highest and the third highest cards remaining in a suit, eg A, Q

minor tenace the second highest and the fourth highest cards remaining in a suit, eg K, J

the river *same as* fifth street

three of a kind in Poker, a hand of three cards of the same rank with two unmatching cards

tierce in Piquet, a sequence of three cards of the same suit

trailing in Casino, the adding of a card from a player's hand to the layout when unable to build or take in

trap pass in Bridge, a pass made by a player with a good hand in the hope that the opponents will bid themselves into a contract they cannot make

trey the three of each suit

trick a round of play at cards, in which each player contributes one card; the cards so played and taken by the winner

overtrick a trick in excess of the number specified in a contract

quick trick in Bridge, a holding that should win a trick in the first or second round of the suit

undertrick a trick short of the number specified in a contract

trio in Piquet, three cards of the same rank

trump, trumps a suit that ranks higher than any other suit, so that any card of this suit ranks higher than any card of the other three suits; a card of this suit; to play a trump card instead of following suit

no-trump, no-trumps in Bridge, a bid to make a contract without a trump suit

trump indicator the card turned up to determine the trump suit

turn *same as* fourth street

twist in Pontoon, the option for a player to receive a further card face up, for which he does not pay

two for his heels in Cribbage, two points scored by the dealer when a Jack is turned up as the start

two pairs in Poker, two cards of one rank, two of another and an unmatched card

undercut in Gin Rummy, to show a hand, after laying off, that counts the same or fewer than that of an opponent who has knocked

unlimited in Loo, a version of the game which obliges a player looed to put chips into the pool for the following deal equivalent to the amount of the pool at the beginning of the deal

void the total absence of cards of a particular suit in a hand

vole in Écarté, the making of all five tricks by one player

vulnerable in Contract Bridge, the position of a side that has won a game towards the rubber, and is therefore liable to increased penalties (or bonuses)

waiving in Miss Milligan, the option, after all cards in the stock have run out, to take into the hand temporarily an exposed card which is blocking play

wellington in Napoleon, a bid to win all five tricks called only after a previous player has bid nap

widow an extra hand

Work count in Bridge, a basic method for evaluating a hand

younger in Piquet, the dealer

Yukon in Yukon, a Jack

Grand Yukon in Yukon, ♠J

Playing Cards History

The well-known Western pack, or deck, of playing cards seemed to have suddenly appeared, ready-made in a form recognizable today, over 600 years ago in Spain or Italy. Many theories were elaborated about likely origins in the mysterious East: that the pack was based on Chinese money cards, or Indian cards. However, there were always serious objections to each, such as Chinese cards being long strips of paper and Indian cards being circular. There appeared no route by which cards could have been brought from the East at relevant times to be the basis of the modern pack.

All this speculation ended with the discovery in 1939 in a museum in Istanbul of a large proportion of a pack of playing cards from Egypt, which had an undeniable claim to be the forerunner of the current pack. A piece of card from a similar pack, discovered some years later in a private collection, has been dated as earlier than the 14th century, which makes the card older than the first definite reference to the current European pack in 1377. The pack in the Istanbul museum is from the Mameluke era, the Mamelukes being a military class, originally of Turkish slaves, who ruled in Egypt from 1250 to 1517 and remained influential for many more years.

The Mameluke pack consisted of 52 cards with four suits: swords, polo sticks, cups and coins. This relates closely to the traditional Italian pack, of which the suits are the same, with the exception that the polo sticks in the Italian pack are batons (polo being unknown in Italy). As well as the cards being numbered one to ten in each suit, there are three superior cards – a King, an over-deputy and an under-deputy – which also corresponds well to the Italian cards: King, Cavalier, Footsoldier. Furthermore, the Arabic *na'ib*, meaning 'deputy', the name of the game played with the Egyptian cards, could explain the Italian *naibbe* and Spanish *naipes*, meaning playing cards. From this it seems certain that the first European playing cards were manufactured in either Italy or Spain, and were based on the Mameluke cards.

The first unarguable reference to European playing cards comes in a copy of a manuscript written in Latin by a German monk living in a Swiss monastery, dated 1377. The copy was made in 1472, and is in the British Museum, with a duplicate in the Imperial Library in Vienna.

The monk, John of Rheinfelden, described how 'a certain game, called the game of cards, has come to us in this year, viz the year of the Lord 1377'. He goes on to describe the pack, which has four Kings, each of which has two marshals, one holding the King's sign (suit) upwards and the other downwards (the over- and under-deputies), after which are ten other cards each holding the King's sign, the first once, the second twice and so on up to the tenth.

The monk goes on to describe other packs, in which two of the Kings are replaced by two Queens, the pack remaining at 52 cards, and yet others in which, as well as the four Kings with their marshals, there are also four corresponding Queens, each with an attendant, making a pack of 60 cards. Unfortunately, the monk, whose manuscript is in six parts outlining the virtues and advantages of playing cards, does not describe any actual games or even the signs or suits. It is likely that the references to the Queens were not in the original manuscript but added by the copier of 1472, by which time the packs had been improved.

Once Europe had discovered playing cards, mass production with the aid of wood engraving was soon in place in Germany, and a little later in Switzerland. The Germans introduced their own suit marks: hearts, bells, leaves and acorns, with the court cards being the King and the over- and under-deputies. In the Swiss packs the leaves became shields or escutcheons. Both packs were short, of 36 cards with no cards numbered below the 6 except the 2 (*der Daus*), which became the highest card, ranked above the King (some games still played and described in this book rank the 2 higher than King). Sometimes the German pack omitted the 6s to make a 32-card pack.

The Italian pack, meanwhile, retained batons, swords, cups and coins as suits, and the King, Cavalier and Footsoldier as the court cards, but omitted the 10, 9 and 8 to make a pack of 40 cards. The Spanish, with a clearer design than the Italian cards, also cut the pack to 40 by omitting 10, 9 and 8, but sometimes reinstated 9 and 8 to make a 48-card pack.

It was the French who became the chief card-manufacturing nation, perfected playing card design and produced the standard suit signs and court cards as we know them today. A famous knight, Étienne de Vignoles, known as La Hire and a supporter of Joan of Arc, is said to be partly responsible for developing the suit symbols, although the influence of German symbols is clear. The French suit symbols were *pique*, a pike-head said to represent the aristocracy (spades); *carreau*, a paving tile representing the military or citizenry (diamonds); *tréfle*, a clover leaf representing fodder or the peasantry (clubs); and *coeur*, a heart representing the church (hearts).

The French established the custom of making the hearts and diamonds suits red, and the spades and clubs suits black, and also preferred a Queen (although they called her *dame* rather than Queen) and a *valet* (Jack) as the court cards below the King. The Jack was originally known in English (and sometimes still is), as the Knave, an early meaning of knave being a menial male servant. In the 17th century the Knave began to be called the Jack, as the Knave of trumps was called in the game All Fours. Jack meant a saucy or vulgar fellow, and Shakespeare uses the term 'Jack-slave' to mean a low servant.

There are no references to cards in Britain before about 1460, and when packs were printed in England they were based on the French designs. The suit names are a mystery, since 'spades' and 'clubs' are based on the Italian/Spanish names (*spade/espadas* for swords and *bastoni/bastos* for clubs), while the symbol for clubs is the French clover leaf. 'Diamonds' is also a strange name for the rhombus or lozenge shape of the French tiles, but it satisfyingly echoes the rich Italian/Spanish suit of coins.

The last major development in card design came in the mid-19th century, when the index marks in the top-left and bottom-right corners appeared (nowadays often on all four corners). They were originally called 'squeezers', as they allowed a hand of cards to be squeezed up into a fan with the denomination of each card visible. The 'J' for Jack makes impossible a revival of the term Knave (which would have the same index as King). The index marks of rank and suit are not universal, and current Spanish packs, for example, carry only the rank in the corner, the suit being indicated by the number of breaks in a line running around the card to frame the main image.

It was US card makers, whose designs were based on British cards, who around 1850 introduced the Joker, specifically for the game of Euchre in which it was the highest trump. Gradually, most packs came to contain a Joker, which was incorporated into some games as a wild card. The invention of Canasta in the 1950s required a second Joker, and now most packs include two Jokers, although the vast majority of card games do not require one.

Court Cards

' "Off with her head!" the Queen shouted at the top of her voice. Nobody moved.

"Who cares for *you*?" said Alice… "You're nothing but a pack of cards!" '

Lewis Carroll, *Alice's Adventures in Wonderland*

Since the days of Alice, the home computer has added millions to the number of people who play cards. That is if manipulating images on a screen by means of a mouse can be called 'playing cards'.

Playing with real people and handling real cards is surely more satisfying. Alice found in Wonderland that the cards themselves for a time became real people. And in a sense they are.

Court cards manufactured in France carried the names of real kings, queens and knights from as early as the 1500s. The names occasionally changed, or switched suits, but not by much. The generally accepted identities of those monarchs and their courts who are dealt to us whenever we play cards were well established by the time a representative pack was issued in Paris in 1760.

In this pack, the Queen of hearts, famous in *Alice* for chopping off the heads of all who crossed her, is named as Judith, the heroine of one of the apocryphal books of the Bible. She was the widow of the Jew Manasseh, and she seduced the conquering Assyrian general, Holofernes, taking the opportunity to chop off his head in his own tent, thus saving Israel from destruction. Clearly the Reverend Charles Dodgson, who used the pen name Lewis Carroll, knew all about Judith's reincarnation as the Queen of hearts when he invented the playing card story for his young friend Alice.

Judith's card consort, the King of hearts, was Charles, known as Charlemagne, the great Charles, King of the Franks and Holy Roman Emperor. For centuries he has been left-handed, holding his sword (which for a time was a battle axe) in his left hand, while grasping his ermine with his right. He might be considered the leader of the pack. The Jack of hearts is La Hire (1390–1443), a real knight (see Playing Cards History, p397). A friend of Joan of Arc, he was notorious as a bandit and pillager, some of his exploits being so terrible that mothers would threaten their naughty children that La Hire would get them. The current Jack of hearts in English packs is shown holding a foppish leaf or feather in his right hand, but La Hire was originally holding a truncheon. The lower part of the truncheon got lost from the card design around 1800 and the handle of it, which was slightly curved, became a leaf, no doubt by an artist's error, so La Hire now is quite out of character. He has always been moustached, and in profile, being one of the 'one-eyed Jacks', the other being the Jack of spades.

The King of spades in the 1760 Paris pack is King David, who is famous as the young slayer of the giant Goliath. He felled Goliath with stones from his sling and then cut off his head using the giant's sword. He still holds the sword, and is King of swords (*spade* in Italian). In early cards he also held a harp, which is now lost. His Queen is a Greek goddess, Pallas or Pallas Athene, the goddess of wisdom. The Jack of spades is Hogier or Ogier, sometimes called Hogier the Dane, although this is a misunderstanding, since he seems to have come from the Ardennes rather than Denmark. He was a cousin of Charlemagne, and married an English princess.

The King of diamonds who, as Alexander Pope noted in his 1712 poem, 'shows but half his face', is Julius Caesar, and he still shows half his face, having always been in profile. He was marked Caesar on playing cards as long ago as 1490. His Queen is a Biblical character, Rachel, wife of Jacob and mother of Benjamin. The Jack of diamonds is Hector, but this is a mystery. The French like to think he is Hector of Troy, but that mighty Hector would not be a mere Jack or valet. In early packs the Jack was Roland, another of Charlemagne's court. When Roland became Hector on the pack, it is most likely that he represented Hector de Maris, a noble knight who was a half-brother of Sir Lancelot, friend of the Lady of the Lake (Lancelot also belongs to the pack of playing cards as the Jack of clubs).

The King of clubs is Alexander the Great. He is the only king who has an orb, which has remained unchanged for centuries, and above which is the French *fleur-de-lis*. In early playing cards this orb was held in his right hand, which some time in the 18th century disappeared, so that on current cards the orb is unsupported and merely decorative. The Queen of clubs is labelled Argine, which is but an anagram of *regina*, the Latin for queen. She is the only genuine queen in the pack, therefore. The Jack of clubs, as mentioned, is Lancelot, the son of a French king and the chief knight of King Arthur's Round Table. Having been accidentally wounded in his rear by an arrow shot by a huntress, which he removed himself, he is depicted on early cards holding an arrow. Sadly, on modern designs, the flights have disappeared from the arrow and he holds what looks more like a pointed staff.

These, then, are the heroes and heroines who battle for us over the card table.

Customs, Practices and Etiquette

Apart from the actual rules of individual card games, described in the main text in this book under each game, and the common elements of card games, such as the cards themselves, choosing partners, shuffling, dealing and so on, which are dealt with in the section Card Games Basics on p382, there is another aspect surrounding games which is not much discussed or written about. This concerns the customs and etiquette of playing at cards, which if observed make the enjoyment of them greater.

Some games are played for money, some for the love of the game only and some for a mixture of the two, ie where players enjoy the game for itself, but enjoy it more if an element of seasoning is added by the prospect of a small monetary gain or loss (but not so much that a loser might be encouraged to jump into the sea, as used to happen at Monte Carlo to the distress of the police, who had somehow to explain away the unusual number of 'accidents' near the casino).

Clearly, if money is involved, the utmost care must be taken to ensure that all players obey the rules scrupulously, and there must be no doubt that everything is above board. On the other hand, it should be recognized that games which are played for enjoyment only should also be taken seriously. Thus certain rules of etiquette have been established which should be observed if all players are to find the game enjoyable. Informality is fine, but players who are too interested in gossip to remember the rules, or whose lead it is, or which suit is trumps, should perhaps be occupied in some other amusement. A brief list of things to be avoided follows.

Playing or bidding out of turn
Nothing is more annoying than a player in a trick-taking game who leads out of turn. If it is a partnership game the lead out of turn conveys sometimes valuable – and always illegal – information to the partner of the offender.

When another player has led to a trick, a player might know immediately which card he will play (he might have no option), but absent-mindedly playing it before it is his turn is more than irritating – it can influence a player who should have played previously to change the card he would have played. In games where there is an auction, players should take care not to bid out of turn, as this illegally conveys information to a partner.

Picking up the cards as they are dealt
The dealer should be allowed to finish dealing before any players pick up their cards. Picking up the cards prematurely is not only considered bad manners, but the removal of cards mid-deal could lead the dealer to miss out the hand next round, causing a misdeal. Also, if all players pick up their hands together they have a similar time to consider them before play begins.

Chatting during play
This leads to a general lack of concentration all round and causes mistakes and annoyance. Between deals is fine for a little chatting, but the game should not be merely a background to gossip, and real scandal should be aired before the game (after all, nobody wants to wait until afterwards).

Playing a card and then asking for it back

Players should consider which card to play and play it smoothly. Do not ask for it back, as (in the words of notices in shops warning customers not to ask for credit) 'a refusal may offend'.

Commenting on the play

This falls into many categories. Comments which convey information to a partner are obviously unacceptable, but some players do not realize that innocent remarks can convey information. Picking up a hand and saying 'this looks promising' could be enough to affect how other players play their hands. 'Don't rely on me, partner!' certainly will. Under this heading could come the fault of making statements which are necessary (as in bidding) in such a manner as to convey information, eg appearing to bid reluctantly. It is also irritating when players comment on another player's play, particularly if the comment is critical. And knowing remarks, such as 'I know who's got the Ace', are very annoying, not least to players who do not know who's got the Ace.

Gesturing

If passing information to other players by saying things out of turn or in a certain manner is not acceptable, it follows that doing the same thing with gestures is also to be discouraged. Frowning, shrugging, winking and sighing are not part of the game.

Playing too slowly

There is a line to be drawn between taking a game seriously and agonizing over every card played, to the extent that other players get impatient. Of course, playing too quickly, without any thought at all (and therefore probably playing badly) is just as annoying.

When sitting down to play cards, each player should appreciate that this is what they have decided to do, in preference to watching television, say. They owe it to the other players to concentrate on the game and play their part. Playing cards is not like knitting, which can be performed while thinking of something else. These rules of etiquette are all based on common sense and do not preclude conviviality, gossip between hands, glasses of wine or whatever else you want to do among family and friends. Win gracefully and lose sportingly.

Card Sharp's Guide

Cheating at cards is a fascinating subject, but not one that many people take seriously. Paintings of card games that show players slipping Aces under the table for use later, or sticking them in their belts or up their sleeves, are usually viewed with amusement. After all, this is not something that happens in your own household while playing with family and friends. And if you do sometimes get irritated with the friend who casually takes a peek at the bottom card while shuffling or cutting – well, he's probably doing it unconsciously and not meaning to cheat.

The average card player would be surprised at some of the apparatus that can be bought specially to aid cheating. How about a little reflector, with a hinge that opens and shuts like a ladies' compact, which can be easily attached to the underside of a table so that when opened the projecting reflector allows a dealer to see each card he deals? Or, if this seems cumbersome, a pipe with a tiny mirror in the bowl, which left casually on the table with the bowl facing the dealer gives him the same advantage (of course, the pipe's no good for smoking)? A ring for the finger which has a tiny point projecting from the underside will enable its owner to prick a tiny hole in any card or cards he wishes to recognize each time they appear in a deal. And a tiny dye box, like a button, to be sewn to clothing will, if touched with the finger which then touches the back of a card, leave a smudge of dye on the card just sufficient to allow it to be spotted easily from then on.

These are ways of marking cards during a game, but it is better to play with cards already marked. Card manufacturers do not make marked cards, but there are gambling supply houses which will mark packs made by standard manufacturers and reseal them. However, it is easy enough to mark cards yourself. Even cards which have complicated designs on the back (or, perhaps, especially these cards) can easily be marked with spots or lines added in carefully selected places, using ink which more or less matches the colour of the design. It is not necessary to be too subtle about it, since how often do other players examine the backs of cards to check if there are marks? On the other hand, cards can be marked so skilfully that the marks will stand out to the marker who put them there but will be difficult to find by another player even if he were told they were there.

Rather than adding marks to cards it is possible, with a razor blade, to scrape off minute areas of the pattern to make them instantly recognizable. Of course, a card marker needs to mark both ends of the card in identical fashion, so that he can recognize the mark no matter from which end he is viewing it.

The poor card marker finding himself in a game with honest cards and no apparatus or dye to mark them as he goes along need not despair. Digging his thumbnail halfway up each side edge of an Ace will enable him to spot it whenever it is dealt. A thumbnail dig three-quarters of the way up will help him spot the Kings. Imagine the advantage to a player of Texas Hold 'Em or Stud Poker if he knows how many Aces or Kings are among the hole cards of his opponents.

More sophisticated cheating involves false shuffles, palming or dealing from the bottom of the pack. A swindle many will have seen is the Three-Card Trick, or Find the Lady. This was often practised by gangs at race tracks, and can employ both sleight of hand and marking. Three cards are shown to the 'punters', one of which is a Queen. They are laid on a portable table and the audience invited to bet on which is the Queen (ie they are invited to 'find the lady'). It looks so obvious which card is the Queen, but anyone foolish enough to put his money down will certainly lose it, as a neat bit of sleight of hand has switched the positions of the cards (if somebody does get it right, it will be an accomplice of the operator). Occasionally the Queen will be seen to have a corner of the card creased. How can you then go wrong? Down goes the money on the creased card, only for the punter to find that somehow it has become a completely different card, with an identical crease in the corner. A reference to a version of this swindle has been discovered in court records in France dated 1408. By the way, the Find the Lady trick is operated by gangs. Do not become too interested, even academically, without keeping your hand on your wallet, since picking pockets is a well-known secondary source of income for the operators.

For the cards used at home, little guillotines can be bought to trim playing cards. The backs of playing cards are often printed with patterns centred on the card, leaving a white margin at the edges of around 4 mm. Trimming one millimetre from one side of all the Aces will make the pattern on the back so off-centre as to make them immediately recognizable to one who knows what to look for. Of course, to disguise the trimming you have to trim half a millimetre off each side of all the other cards to make all the cards the same width, but this is no problem to a dedicated cheat.

Of course, you can cheat with perfectly legitimate cards and no sleight of hand by having an accomplice. When casinos were introduced into Britain, the Gaming Board restricted the options offered to players and the dealer at Blackjack, partly to reduce the house edge against poor players, but also to prevent the possibility of the dealer cheating in collusion with a player by indicating to him the value of his face-down card, which is a scam casinos have always had to look out for. In private games, of course, it is the 'kibitzer', or casual onlooker, who can easily pass information about one player's hand to another who might be his friend.

In card games where players have partners, it is not difficult or unknown for players to pass information secretly to one another, and indeed in the 1965 World Bridge championships, two of the world's leading players were convicted by the World Bridge Federation of signalling to each other the number of cards each held in the heart suit by means of how they held the cards in their hands. This would be very valuable information for experts. After a later special inquiry, both players were acquitted of any wrongdoing.

One of the most famous instances of cheating occurred in 1890 when, at a private house party during the St Leger race meeting, the Prince of Wales – later Edward VII – decided to play Baccarat. Although the Prince possessed his own cloth and counters with which he travelled, the game was then illegal. Some of the players suspected the Prince's friend, Sir William Gordon-Cumming, of cheating by manipulating his betting counters after the result was known. In a subsequent session he was watched carefully, the suspicions confirmed, and the information passed to the Prince, who forbade him to play. Later, when the story began to circulate in society, Sir William sued for slander, and the Prince was forced to give evidence in the witness box, and admit to illegal gambling, which did not amuse Queen Victoria.

Cheating at cards is clearly something that can happen in the highest circles, but is not advocated, and this section is provided, like card games themselves, for amusement only.

Index

Games by Alternative Names

Games by Number of Players

Games for One Player

Games that can be played by a single player against a banker in a casino are marked*.

Games for Two Players

Games for Three Players

Games by Type

Games by Player Type